# MY LIFE WITH LITERACY: THE CONTINUING EDUCATION OF A HISTORIAN

## The Intersections of the Personal, the Political, the Academic, and Place

## Practices & Possibilities

Series Editors: Aimee McClure, Kelly Ritter, Aleashia Walton, and Jagadish Paudel

Consulting Editor: Mike Palmquist

The Practices & Possibilities Series addresses the full range of practices within the field of Writing Studies, including teaching, learning, research, and theory. From Richard E. Young's taxonomy of "small genres" to Patricia Freitag Ericsson's edited collection on sexual harassment in the academy to Jessie Borgman and Casey McArdle's considerations of teaching online, the books in this series explore issues and ideas of interest to writers, teachers, researchers, and theorists who share an interest in improving existing practices and exploring new possibilities. The series includes both original and republished books. Works in the series are organized topically.

The WAC Clearinghouse and University Press of Colorado are collaborating so that these books will be widely available through free digital distribution and low-cost print editions. The publishers and the series editors are committed to the principle that knowledge should freely circulate and have embraced the use of technology to support open access to scholarly work.

### Other Books in the Series

Linda Flower, *Outcomes of Engaged Education: From Transfer to Transformation* (2024)

Charles Bazerman, *Unfinished Business: Thoughts on the Past, Present, Future, and Nurturing of Homo Scribens* (2024)

E. Shelley Reid, *Rethinking Your Writing: Rhetoric for Reflective Writers* (2024)

Asao B. Inoue and Kristin DeMint Bailey (Eds.), *Narratives of Joy and Failure in Antiracist Assessment: Exploring Collaborative Writing Assessments* (2024)

Asao B. Inoue, *Cripping Labor-Based Grading for More Equity in Literacy Courses* (2023)

Jessie Borgman and Casey McArdle (Eds.), *PARS in Charge: Resources and Strategies for Online Writing Program Leaders* (2023)

Douglas Hesse and Laura Julier (Eds.), *Nonfiction, the Teaching of Writing, and the Influence of Richard Lloyd-Jones* (2023)

Linda Adler-Kassner and Elizabeth Wardle, *Writing Expertise: A Research-Based Approach to Writing and Learning Across Disciplines* (2022)

Michael J. Faris, Courtney S. Danforth, and Kyle D. Stedman (Eds.), *Amplifying Soundwriting Pedagogies: Integrating Sound into Rhetoric and Writing* (2022)

Crystal VanKooten and Victor Del Hierro (Eds.), *Methods and Methodologies for Research in Digital Writing and Rhetoric: Centering Positionality in Computers and Writing Scholarship, Volumes 1 and 2* (2022)

# MY LIFE WITH LITERACY: THE CONTINUING EDUCATION OF A HISTORIAN

## The Intersections of the Personal, the Political, the Academic, and Place

By Harvey J. Graff

The WAC Clearinghouse
wac.colostate.edu
Fort Collins, Colorado

University Press of Colorado
upcolorado.com
Denver, Colorado

The WAC Clearinghouse, Fort Collins, Colorado 80523

University Press of Colorado, Denver, Colorado 80203

© 2024 by Harvey J. Graff. This work is released under a Creative Commons Attribution-NonCommercial-NoDerivatives 4.0 International license.

ISBN 978-1-64215-131-2 (PDF) | 978-1-64215-242-5 (ePub) | 978-1-64642-704-8 (pbk.)

DOI 10.37514/PRA-B.2024.1312

Library of Congress Cataloging-in-Publication Data

Names: Graff, Harvey J., author.
Title: My life with literacy : the continuing education of a historian : the intersections of the personal, the political, the academic, and place / by Harvey J. Graff.
Description: Fort Collins, Colorado ; Denver, Colorado : The WAC Clearinghouse ; University Press of Colorado, [2024] | Series: Practices & possibilities | Includes bibliographical references.
Identifiers: LCCN 2024053389 (print) | LCCN 2024053390 (ebook) | ISBN 9781646427048 (paperback) | ISBN 9781642151312 (adobe pdf) | ISBN 9781642152425 (epub)
Subjects: LCSH: Graff, Harvey J. | College teachers—United States—Biography. | Historians—United States—Biography. | Literacy—United States—History. | Interdisciplinary approach in education—United States—History.
Classification: LCC LA2317.G626 A3 2024 (print) | LCC LA2317.G626 (ebook) | DDC 378.1/2092 [B]—dc23/eng/20241214
LC record available at https://lccn.loc.gov/2024053389
LC ebook record available at https://lccn.loc.gov/2024053390

Copyeditor: Karen Peirce
Designer: Mike Palmquist
Cover Image: Harvey Graff, professor of humanities at The University of Texas at Dallas, poses with some of his then more than 13,000 books at home. Photo by Ariane Kadoch. © Dallas Morning News, 1995. © 2024 Harvey J. Graff. Used with permission.
Series Editors: Aimee McClure, Kelly Ritter, Aleashia Walton, and Jagadish Paudel
Consulting Editor: Mike Palmquist

The WAC Clearinghouse supports teachers of writing across the disciplines. Hosted by Colorado State University, it brings together scholarly journals and book series as well as resources for teachers who use writing in their courses. This book is available in digital formats for free download at wac.colostate.edu.

Founded in 1965, the University Press of Colorado is a nonprofit cooperative publishing enterprise supported, in part, by Adams State University, Colorado School of Mines, Colorado State University, Fort Lewis College, Metropolitan State University of Denver, University of Alaska Fairbanks, University of Colorado, University of Denver, University of Northern Colorado, University of Wyoming, Utah State University, and Western Colorado University. For more information, visit upcolorado.com.

**Citation Information:** Graff, Harvey J. (2024). *My Life With Literacy: The Continuing Education of a Historian*. The WAC Clearinghouse; University Press of Colorado. https://doi.org/1010.37514/PRA-B.2024.1312

**Land Acknowledgment.** The Colorado State University Land Acknowledgment can be found at landacknowledgment.colostate.edu.

# Contents

Acknowledgments . . . . . . . . . . . . . . . . . . . . . . . . . . . . . . . . . . . . . . . . . . . . . . . .vii

Introduction. The Intersections of the Personal, the Political, the Academic, and Place . . . . . . . . . . . . . . . . . . . . . . . . . . . . . . . . . . . . . . . . . . 3

Chapter 1. Endings from Beginnings: A Culmination of Learning and Practice . . . . . . . . . . . . . . . . . . . . . . . . . . . . . . . . . . . . . . . . . . . . . . . . 15

Chapter 2. First Formations: Early Years in Pittsburgh, 1949–1963 . . . . . . . .49

Chapter 3. Coming of Age in Pittsburgh, Squirrel Hill, and Taylor Allderdice High School, 1963–1967 . . . . . . . . . . . . . . . . . . . . . . . . . . . .65

Chapter 4. Northwestern University and Chicago: Higher and Wider Learning, Inside and Outside Classrooms, 1967–1970 . . . . . . . . . .79

Chapter 5. The Great Canadian Adventure, the New Social History, and Beginning to Study Literacy, 1970–1975. . . . . . . . . . . . . . . . . . . . . . 101

Chapter 6. A Not-So-Great Migration to Big D, Dallas, Texas: New Frontiers, New University, New City, 1975–1979 . . . . . . . . . . . . . . . . . . 127

Chapter 7. Interlude: In Exile at the Newberry Library and Chicago, 1979–1981. . . . . . . . . . . . . . . . . . . . . . . . . . . . . . . . . . . . . . . . . . . . . . . . . 151

Chapter 8. Dallas and UTD: Negotiating a Return and Beginning Again, 1981–1998 . . . . . . . . . . . . . . . . . . . . . . . . . . . . . . . . . . . . . . . . . . 159

Chapter 9. San Antonio: Flirting With and Separating From Administration, 1998–2004 . . . . . . . . . . . . . . . . . . . . . . . . . . . . . . . . . . . 181

Chapter 10. Transitions and Challenges in Mid-Career: The Ohio State University and Columbus, 2004–2017 . . . . . . . . . . . . . . . . . . . . . . . . . . 199

Epilogue. Intersecting Endings and Beginnings . . . . . . . . . . . . . . . . . . . . . 231

Afterword. Near Final Reflections on Literacy and Literacy Studies, 2022: Excerpts From *Searching for Literacy: The Social and Intellectual Origins of Literacy Studies* . . . . . . . . . . . . . . . . . . . . . . . . . . . . . . . . . . . . . 235

Epilogue. Many Paths, Many Futures . . . . . . . . . . . . . . . . . . . . . . . . . . . . 255

References . . . . . . . . . . . . . . . . . . . . . . . . . . . . . . . . . . . . . . . . . . . . . . . . . 259

Appendix. Harvey J. Graff Curriculum Vitae. . . . . . . . . . . . . . . . . . . . . . . 281

# Dedication

For my life partner, Vicki L. W. Graff; my three advisors, J. Bruce Forry of Taylor Allderdice High School in Pittsburgh, Lacy Baldwin Smith of Northwestern University, and Michael B. Katz then of the University of Toronto; our many cats and dogs, especially Harrison (1981–1997), McDonald (1998–2013), and Vincent (2023-); and my colleagues and students, 1969 to tomorrow.

# Acknowledgments

This is not a book I expected to write in my 73rd and 74th years. It reflects my personal, professional, engaged, and activist life in six cities and five universities over almost three-quarters of a century. The impetus to draft it and to publish it is multidimensional and complex. It reflects not only what sociologists term my life course but also my transition to retirement; my ongoing efforts to understand myself and the full, complicated nature of my historical contexts including the present moment; the challenges of human memory; and the pandemic of 2020 and beyond.

I have 75 years of family, friends, colleagues, students, neighbors, and acquaintances to acknowledge. Most but not all (for reasons of privacy and authorial responsibility) are named in the text.

Special, impossible-to-calculate thanks go to my life partner since 1969 and spouse since 1971, Vicki L. W. Graff, who has shared the joys and weathered the storms of so many decades, far more than either of us anticipated. As I wrote in the acknowledgments to my first book, she is one "for whom there are no appropriate words of gratitude." Because of her retired status, she was able to edit this book just as she did my first book, The Literacy Myth, in 1978. She prepared that book's index with me on 3x5-inch cards sorted on the living room floor.

Although two of the three advisors, models, and examples to whom this book is dedicated are no longer with us, I am certain that J. Bruce Forry (with whom I have spoken about this book), Lacey Baldwin Smith, and Michael B. Katz each knew both how much they contributed to me and how appreciative I am. I did my best to express that to them. I add my gratitude to longtime colleagues and friends who recently passed away: in 2021, Jan Reiff, Allison Prentice, Jerry Zaslove, and Mike Rose; and in 2023, Natalie Zemon Davis.

Other friends, colleagues, students, and neighbors whose personal and professional contributions merit acknowledgment include Patrick Berry, Mike Bevis, Michael Bezbatchenko, Bobby Gene Black, Bob Bradley, Cathy Civello, Marvin Cohen, Elizabeth Dillenburg, Ava and Art Doppelt, Michael Doucet, Johanna Drucker, John Duffy, Bob Eckhart, Ed and Dianne Efsic, Alan Farmer, Tony Fracchia, Mike Frisch, Chad Gaffield, Gary Graff, the late Bob Holub, the late Rebecca Jackson, Jerry Jacobs, Soledad Jasin, Brian Joseph, Edda Katz, Bradley Kayser, Cynthia Kreger, Rebecca Kuennen, Cindy Maciel-Reyes, Ellen Manovich, Dianne Martinez, Paul Mattingly, Tom Mauger, M. J. Maynes, Brian McHale, Leslie Moch, the late Paul Monaco, Sarah Neville, Wing Chung Ng, Dan Orlovsky, Grey Osterud, Jake Risinger, Steve Rissing, Randy Roth, Gail Rudenstein, Andrea Sawchyn, Marie Scatena, Matthew Snyder, Bill Stehle, Andy Toth, Steve Weissman, Michael Wilson, Jeanelle Wu, Peter Zafaridis, and Gretchen Zody. To those I unwittingly am not remembering, I do not slight you.

Along the way, Patrick Berry, John Duffy, and Rachael Levay, editor at University of Colorado Press, all suggested that I contact Mike Palmquist, professor of English at Colorado State University and founder/publisher of the WAC Clearinghouse. This quickly became a fruitful collaboration. In 2023, the Clearinghouse published new editions of my earlier books, *The Literacy Myth* and *Literacy Myths, Legacies, and Lessons: New Studies on Literacy* in its Landmark Publications in Writing Studies series. Under contract with them, I am currently editing a collection of original first-person essays titled *Scholarly Lives in Transition, 1960s to 2020s and Beyond: Misunderstood and Untold Paths in Shaping the American University*.

After thorough conversation, review, and agreement on selected revisions, Mike and his series editor colleagues agreed to publish *My Life With Literacy*. I thank Aimee McClure, Jagadish Paudel, Kelly Ritter, Aleashia Walton, as well as Mike. They provide a fine home for *My Life*.

# MY LIFE WITH LITERACY: THE CONTINUING EDUCATION OF A HISTORIAN

The Intersections of the Personal, the Political, the Academic, and Place

# Introduction. The Intersections of the Personal, the Political, the Academic, and Place

My life partner for 55 years titles this endeavor, "collecting, re-collecting, and recollecting." She is not wrong. For me and for the two of us together, preparing this account is a focused and ordered interdisciplinary "trip down memory lane" that includes sharing and comparing memories, mementos, old photos, and the contents of files and drawers unopened for years, many before hard disks or the cloud.

Until summer 2021, I did not expect drafting a historical, contextual, and intellectual memoir to occupy a place in my time or among my books. My previous personal writing addressed specific works and occasions. For example, my major books on the history of literacy, children and youth, Dallas, and interdisciplinarity led to some short, first-person essays and interviews in which I mentioned personal experiences as they were relevant. I had opportunities to publish retrospective reflections on all my major subjects but seldom on the personal, social, political, and institutional contexts of their production. My career-long public history and public humanities contributions seldom involved the personal dimensions. Little of those particular uses of my literacy appeared, by choice and by occasion.

The circumstances of my retirement and several years of adjustment to a new niche role for myself in what I call "public education" and "teaching outside the box" prepared the way (for details, see my 2021–2024 reflective essays in the Appendix). Recovery from a series of illnesses from late 2016 through 2019 left me with a fuller, more active memory reaching back to early childhood and a new search to understand critical, life-shaping relationships and influences. The almost two years of isolation during the first waves of the Covid-19 pandemic also laid the foundation.

During this period of three to four years, I achieved a clearer focus on both overarching and underlying patterns that connected my development and lived experience from childhood to my early- to mid-70s. I call this a *new intersectionality*. Put simply—as this book explores—these are the inextricable interconnections of *personal* experiences and relationships; the *political*, broadly defined to include life-shaping contexts and historical events, influences, values, commitments, and experiences; the social, intellectual, and political dimensions of *academics and scholarship*—a life of learning (to borrow the American Council of Learned Society's phrase used for its Charles Homer Haskins Prize Lecture—see https://www.acls.org/resources/occasional-papers/) and using literacy and literacies; and the circumstances of *living in six major cities* from age one to the present and *studying and then teaching in five universities* (for more details, see citations to my 2021–2024 essays under Retirement as "Public Education,"

Universities, Disciplines and Interdisciplines, Literacy and Communications, Media and Communications, Book Banning, Critical Race Theory and Education, Ohio State University, Columbus Past and Present, Ohio Issues, National Issues, and Personal).

The *political* embraces my experiences from childhood through the 1960 John F. Kennedy presidential campaign; the 1965–1970 grape boycott led by Cesar Chavez for the United Farm Workers; the civil rights movements from the early to mid-1960s; the anti-Vietnam War movement; student movements from the mid-1960s; women's rights, feminism, and movements for equality, equity, affirmative action, and choice for underrepresented people; Eugene McCarthy's 1968 presidential campaign; and much more (among an ungainly and uneven literature on the time period involved, see Kevin Boyle, 2021, and the literature cited therein).

These experiences include five years in Canada in graduate school during the Vietnam War at a time of political awakening in the northern nation. They encompass entering the academic job market at one of its lowest ebbs and at the time that affirmative action and equal opportunity were first raised. This prompted reaffirming my lifelong commitments to equity, equality, mutuality, and respect. At each major intersection, I reconfirmed my role as an egalitarian and a connector of people, learning, and issues past, present, and future in teaching, scholarship, and living. My lived experience and my active learning are inseparable from my formal education and professional historical and pedagogical practice.

The years from the mid-1960s through the 1970s were also a formative transitional period in *cross- and interdisciplinary scholarship*, especially in the humanities and social sciences but also in the natural sciences. Several "new histories" developed when I was an undergraduate and graduate student. Some of my most influential professors were innovators and leaders. The fields that laid the ground for my nearly 50 years of scholarly research and writing are the "new" social history, quantitative history, history of social structure, history of education and culture and especially literacy, history of children and families, history of women and gender, urban history, historical demography, theory and method in the humanities and social sciences, and interdisciplinarity itself.

Over decades, often resisting institutional as well as disciplinary pressures and divides, I strove to interrelate these fields, methods and approaches, and theoretical perspectives. I straddled departments, colleges, and other boundaries, more and less comfortably. For far too many, then and more recently, both inside and outside universities, this critical history is forgotten (for one introduction to the literature, see my *Undisciplining Knowledge,* 2015a; see also my *Looking Backward and Looking Forward* with Leslie Page Moch and Philip McMichael, 2005, and essays and books on new histories and literacy studies in the Appendix and References).

These four factors are collectively determinative. They do not stand alone. They are instructive not only for me but also for understanding the historical times from the 1950s into the 2020s, conditions of life, educational institutions, and geographical places. Together they bear examination and narration to others who may be interested in the history, individual factors including agency and relationships, academic institutions and professional life, and physical and institutional places. No one factor is independently powerful. Their intersections are complex and dynamic, sometimes contradictory and conflictual. That is among the lessons this book unveils. Together, they ground a "life course" perspective in regularly shifting times and spaces (for more on life course, see Glen H. Elder, Jr., 1974/1999; see also Elder, Monica Kirkpatrick Johnson, and Robert Crosnoe, 2003).

The surrounding, shaping context is the critical history of this era that spans the early Cold War and Eisenhower presidency through the tumultuous—and for me, life-orienting—1960s; the rise and fall of the Cold War; civil rights and voting struggles especially for Black people and members of other underrepresented racial groups, women, and LBGTQ people; the semi-normality of the 1980s and 1990s; and the startling ups and downs of the first decades of the 21st century. The period is encapsulated by the distance between Ike and the 45th president, on the one hand, and, on the other hand, between the 1960s social movements and the right-wing counterrevolution of the 2010s and 2020s, as well as popular movements including the new progressivism, Black Lives Matter, and environmentalism. These are, were, and will continue to be shaping currents.

For me, the key intersections begin with the post-World War II romance of my parents, who were born and grew up primarily as children of immigrant parents in working-class mill towns on opposite sides of the then steel capital, Pittsburgh, Pennsylvania. The first college graduate in his small business-class family, my father served in noncombatant roles in World War II's South Pacific theatre. My mother attended college for one year.

Upon marriage in 1947, they settled in the small town of Greensburg, Pennsylvania, near Pittsburgh, where they purchased a house, and where my father opened a jewelry store. I was born in a Pittsburgh hospital less than two years later, on Father's Day, in 1949, Juneteenth before Juneteenth was generally recognized. After my first birthday, my father was diagnosed with tuberculosis and committed to a Veterans' Administration hospital in Pittsburgh. My parents sold their house and business, and my mother and I moved into my grandmother's small apartment near Highland Park in the East Liberty neighborhood of Pittsburgh. My earliest memories are etched in that apartment and occasional visits to see my father in the visitors' room at the hospital.

Following my father's recovery, we moved into a two-bedroom apartment in the Squirrel Hill section of Pittsburgh. My father joined his brother-in-law's Braddock, Pennsylvania, jewelry business, working effectively as the manager of the Main Street store for almost the next four decades before joining a nephew's delicatessen and catering company as manager. For the next four years, we lived in a medium-sized apartment complex on the Homestead side of the city. I began nursery school at age three and kindergarten at five, rebelling against my early classroom immersion. At that time, I was a subject in both the Salk and

Sabin polio vaccine trials that originated in the University of Pittsburgh's medical school. I was and remain resolutely pro-vaccine.

When I turned six and entered first grade in 1955, we moved into a larger two-bedroom unit in a four-plex on the other side of Squirrel Hill, one block from Linden Elementary School, which housed kindergarten through eighth grade. I spent the next eight years there, changing schools when I entered high school. Adlai Stevenson's 1956 and JFK's 1960 presidential campaigns influenced me, as did my parents' moderate Democratic liberalism. Our Conservative Jewish synagogue, the now famous Tree of Life, site of an antisemitic mass murder in 2018, was nearby. In 1963, my parents purchased a small house not far from the public high school I attended.

I graduated from Taylor Allderdice High School in 1967 with honors, National Merit and advanced mathematics commendations, and a full year's worth of Advanced Placement college credits. J. Bruce Forry, who taught me advanced-track world history in 10th grade and AP European history in 12th grade, was a fundamental influence, as was my experience on the debate team. So, too, were the campaign of Cesar Chavez for the rights of the National Farm Workers Association with its grape boycott, the civil rights movement, the student free speech movement, and the beginning of the anti-Vietnam War and the women's movement actions.

After working for the summer in a steel mill in Homestead across the river from Pittsburgh, I entered Northwestern University on scholarships and loans with second-year standing. Chicago was a special attraction. With the presidency of my first-year dormitory, my high school political activism expanded in the turbulent second half of the 1960s. The civil rights and anti-war movements were most prominent, but student-stimulated curriculum reforms and Eugene McCarthy's 1968 presidential campaign also galvanized me.

I majored in history with a minor in sociology. Meeting my future wife in 1968–1969, I decided to enter graduate studies in history rather than law school as my parents long urged. I had a cloudy vision of a future academic career. I drove a taxicab in Evanston and Chicago the summer following graduation and before beginning graduate school.

Vicki Wells and I moved to Toronto and the University of Toronto in August 1970. I began a master's degree in British and European history while Vicki pursued her remaining two years of university, shifting from anthropology to a major in geography, a popular option in Canada. We first lived in a tenement apartment in the center of the city above a convenience store not far from the university.

We fell in love with our new city. Not only was Toronto a beautiful, affordable, and inviting place, it welcomed anti-Vietnam War Americans with left-liberal politics. Ontario's Progressive Conservative Party instituted universal health care, and we became landed immigrants, not resident aliens as we would have been known had we moved to the United States from another country.

As I will discuss in Chapter Five, at the end of my first semester I shifted from studying modern British history to studying United States, Canadian, and comparative social history after I met a young, field-transforming professor, Michael B. Katz. That association changed my life and set the course for my professional career. It laid the seeds for my future book projects and course offerings on the history of literacy and education, children and families, cities, theory and method, and interdisciplinarity. Vicki followed her Bachelor of Arts degree with a one-year Bachelor of Education degree and taught geography in a private girls' school for two years.

When I completed my dissertation in 1975, I confronted one of the worst academic job markets in American history—now forgotten. Although we wished to remain in Canada, a wave of Canadian nationalism (as well as the overhiring of too often mediocre American professors during the rapid expansion of universities in the 1960s) effectively prevented universities from hiring U.S. citizens. There was also ignorant opposition to the new quantitative social history among many Canadian historians. The most attractive job offer came from the new, avowedly interdisciplinary campus of the University of Texas at Dallas (UTD).

Hired following a Toronto airport interview, our shocking first sight of the infamous JFK assassination site city and the suburban university under construction came upon our arrival in August 1975. We rented a townhouse facing an expressway and the largest Texas Instruments facility not far from the campus that is "near"—not "at"—Dallas. Thus began a difficult transition to a professional career for me and a comfortable life for both of us.

Neither Big D, as Dallas is known, nor UTD were welcoming personally, socially, culturally, or intellectually. I encountered face-to-face antisemitism for the first time in Texas, Dallas, and UTD. These experiences have contemporary parallels but are dramatically different than 21st century currents.

UTD was interdisciplinary only in promotional rhetoric and nonessentials. In many ways, the absence of disciplinary departments had more to do with cutting expenses, including staff and administrators, than with serious intellectual activities. The extraordinary quality of the junior members of the largely novice faculty, especially those of us with multiple homes in the Schools of Arts and Humanities, Social Sciences, and General Studies, far exceeded that of the small number of tenured faculty and administrators. The majority of faculty, in other words, far outshone the minority who held superior, tenured positions. Almost none of the faculty came from Texas, the South, or the Southwest, another challenge and miscalculation.

After four years, completion and printing of my first book *The Literacy Myth* (1979c), and denial of early tenure, a National Endowment for the Humanities fellowship year at Chicago's Newberry Library provided a necessary respite, indeed an escape from what had proven to be a negative human and intellectual environment for many of the founding younger faculty. With that move came a return to a more satisfying and stable intellectual, social, cultural, and political environment. Chicago was always our "second city."

A Spencer Fellowship, employment at the Newberry in the then pioneering Family and Community History Center for Vicki, and a one-course visiting appointment at Loyola University allowed a second year away from UTD. Our mental, intellectual, and social life all renewed with a roster of old and new friends, marches in downtown Chicago, ethnic cuisine and deep-dish pizza, jazz and classical music, and parks and lake shore. Unfortunately, the sudden bankruptcy of the state of Massachusetts canceled the offer of an attractive alternative position at the University of Massachusetts-Boston and propelled us back to Dallas.

Returning to Dallas in August 1981, we renegotiated our relationships with the university and the city. We relocated to Old East Dallas, an older, more landscaped historic neighborhood. In defiance of Texas custom, I formed a carpool with other faculty and graduate students and went to UTD only on teaching and meeting days. We acquired a wonderful cairn terrier who we named Harrison who was part of our family for the next 16 years.

I secured tenure despite jealousies and ethnic prejudice, published several edited books, and completed *The Legacies of Literacy* (1987b) in the next few years. We purchased our first house in Old East Dallas. Combined with enlarging our social circle across and beyond the university, life became more comfortable. I created the Dallas (area) Social History Group and also worked with several local institutions and organizations, expanding the public dimensions of my scholarly and intellectual life.

My group of graduate students and close colleagues grew. Vicki developed several careers in education, public relations, architectural marketing, and communications, culminating in a long stint as manager of editorial and media production at the American Heart Association.

We wisely chose to have a family of about a dozen cats and three dogs, two of them for more than 15 years each. Although we love young children, we decided not to raise our own. We have had many loving relationships with young relatives and the children of friends and students. In retirement, we spend time with our growing body of "surrogate" grandchildren who give us some hope for the future.

Although I faced numerous challenges at UTD, I managed my relationship with it until a different intellectual and professional challenge presented itself in 1998. An offer to become director—like a deanship—of the Division of Behavioral and Cultural Studies (BCS) at the University of Texas at San Antonio (UTSA) emerged. This was another supposedly interdisciplinary grouping of programs embracing American studies, anthropology and archeology, history, and psychology in a new, suburban branch campus of a large state university. I replaced a long-serving psychologist. What I failed to anticipate was the immediate opposition and obstructionism of the numerically preponderant experimental psychologists and the purported needs of their labs—needs that seemed to trump other options for developing the division.

Happily settled in a century-old Victorian house in a central-city historic district called Monte Vista far from the suburban campus, with a new West Highland white terrier who was born in Norway with the name McDonald, with both personal difficulty and tremendous support, I weathered the storm and resigned the directorship after less than one year. My flirtation with administration was brief.

Unlike Dallas, we thoroughly enjoyed the history, beauty, and charm of the Alamo City. We quickly built our network of friends in fair measure outside UTSA and on campus outside BCS. I supervised doctoral students in Literacy, Language, and Linguistics in the College of Education and in the English department as well as master's students in history. I also taught in the Urban Studies department where my graduate courses were cross-listed. I also developed relationships with historians at Trinity University. We continue friendships with my former physician, neighbors, and a few colleagues.

We were comfortable with our lives in the city. Vicki worked remotely for the American Heart Association, supported by a computer and telephone connected with Dallas. During our six-year tenure, I had the distinction of being elected president of the Social Science History Association (SSHA) for its 25th anniversary year in 2000 and the next year was awarded an honorary Doctor of Philosophy degree from Sweden's Linköping University for my "contributions to knowledge." It was a surprise when, late in 2003, Ohio State University's (OSU) English department asked if I were interested in their new, endowed, Ohio Eminent Scholar in Literacy Studies position.

We were not actively looking to relocate and had never considered Columbus or Ohio. But I knew that UTSA had not turned out to be an ideal intellectual home for me. OSU's all-but-certain offer was attractive professionally and a new challenge. A joint appointment in history as well as English was proposed immediately, with history voting even more quickly than English on my appointment. The intellectual opportunity for developing a university-wide literacy studies program with genuine support was simply too attractive.

I agreed to visit OSU early in 2004, present a public lecture, meet prospective colleagues, and briefly tour the city. As an old friend from both the Newberry Library and the SSHA in the department of history emailed me, "the position is yours to lose." The visit was mutually satisfying, and I accepted the position after routine negotiations.

Another August, another major relocation, this time with two moving vans for our furniture and my books and the transition of McDonald, our Westie. He adapted quickly to his new historic house in the attractive University District, a 10-minute walk to my English department office, and the more temperate climate. By September, I began a new and final institutional adventure.

The 13 years spent at OSU before my unexpected retirement were challenging. The history department was outwardly welcoming but practically distant, except for a modest number of old friends, some new colleagues, and graduate students. Some of the latter were quite interested in literacy's history. My courses were cross-listed—some with the education department—and I developed a graduate student population from English, history, education, dance, and the arts, among other areas.

The English department as a whole never really accepted a card-carrying interdisciplinary historian into its ranks. For the most part, the rhetoric and composition group, to which literacy and I were added as the new "L" to "RC," did not warm to my scholarship and my positioning outside of "rhet/comp." As with other large English departments, the lines between literature, criticism, rhetoric and composition, and creative writing were rough. With a few important exceptions, most of my closest intellectual relationships and friendships came from the literature faculty and, outside the department, from literacy studies or university-wide, senior scholar committees and campus reform efforts.

Beyond maintaining my scholarly production and supervising a new generation of graduate students across disciplines, my greatest achievement in that period was the creation and direction of LiteracyStudies@OSU, a university-wide—and sometimes external—interdisciplinary initiative. With the irreplaceable contribution of my assistant for 13 years, Susan Hanson, I managed to do what colleagues and administrators deemed impossible. Between successes amid different and variable structures, it was the intellectual and institutional culmination of a lengthy career and my life with literacy.

We involved hundreds of faculty, graduate students, staff, some undergraduates, and others from the community in a variety of working groups, workshops, forums, presentations, lectures, and conferences including a landmark international conference for graduate students organized by graduate students. We brought dozens of guest lecturers from North and South America and Europe to OSU. We engaged individuals from almost every college and most departments in the massive university—from the arts, humanities, and social sciences to engineering, veterinary science, agriculture, and many from medicine, health sciences, and the natural sciences.

Among our most successful programs were the GradSem, a graduate student monthly seminar, and multiple-year topical working groups on literacy in translation, literacy in science and medicine, literacy in dance, and history of the book. I am proud of the number of students who came together from across the university, led by but not limited to English, education, history, and the arts. I worked with doctoral students broadly across campus not restricted to those in my primary areas. I learned from all of them. I remain in close contact with many of them. LiteracyStudies@OSU gained national and international attention.

LiteracyStudies@OSU ended in 2016–2017 when the university reneged on promised funding for our program's indispensable associate director and our basic activities. That was the final stone in a crumbling wall that willfully contradicted OSU's slogans about advancing interdisciplinarity and cross-campus initiatives. This reversal led to my retiring several years earlier than I had anticipated doing. Not surprisingly, a few years later, there is no active element of literacy studies within the English department. Even the name of my endowed chair was changed (without the permission of the state funding agency).

In retirement, after a transitional period, I now occupy a new niche in what I call "public" rather than university-based education. In ways that will become clear, this book is an outgrowth of that niche and my surprising memory recall in the face of aging.

As I discuss in the first chapter, my retirement activities focus on writing for larger publics in general through targeted letters to editors and opinion essays on a variety of topics including but not limited to my scholarly areas; speaking (virtually) on NPR and in-person in public forums locally, nationally, and internationally; advising newspaper reporters and NPR stations on key issues; counseling elected representatives in Columbus, Ohio, and Washington, DC; consulting with Columbus city councilors; assisting members of the state board of education and various advocacy groups; and continuing to work with other scholars and students. I delight in cross-generational relationships with high school and undergraduate students without classroom or gradebook involvement.

I continue to publish scholarly books and articles but reach out to a larger audience in part through open-access publishing. Drawing directly on my expertise in literacy, children and youth, cities, education, and interdisciplinarity, I have developed special foci on the nondebate over critical race theory, opposition to book bans, and urban issues, as well as a range of university-related topics. I am using my skills and knowledge without dealing with universities directly. My life with literacy continues apace but in new spaces.

~~~

This book is a self-conscious experiment in critical memory and its related literacy(ies) and their historical contextualization. Intersectionality and interdisciplinarity stand out among its watch words (for more on these terms, see Jaume Aurell, 2015, and the literature cited there—Aurell's comments are relevant, but his notion of "interventional" differs from my constructions and applications, and I do not see "paradox," "refashioning," or "iconoclastic" where he does; see also Carolyn Steedman, 1992; Mary Jo Maynes, Jennifer L. Pierce, and Barbara Laslett, 2008; and Sigurdur Gylfi Magnusson, 2021, with an excellent bibliography).

*My Life With Literacy* differs from other recent academic autobiographies. I think, for example, of two noted 1960s-centered accounts, one by Mickey Flacks and Dick Flacks (2018), *Making History/Making Blintzes: How Two Red Diaper Babies Found Each Other and Discovered America*, and one by Paul Lauter (2020), *Our Sixties: An Activist's History*. Both of those important accounts pivot closely around their authors' experience as 1960s activists and the lasting impact of those engagements.

I intend no slight in contrasting my book with these works or with others that center lives around one complex set of experiences as a single pivot point. The Flacks' (2018) passionate book—told alternatively by each of them in each chapter—is a family history: it's about their families of origin and their own romance and marriage set in a dynamic political context. It is a political romance. Lauter

(2020) focused more closely on his 1960s experiences and the ways in which they shaped his future as a professor and a citizen. The Flacks and Lauter are my seniors by a decade.

Lewis H. Siegelbaum's (2019) *Stuck on Communism: Memoir of a Russian Historian* takes an instructively different approach. *Stuck on Communism* is an impressive intellectual biography of a scholarly journey into and through Russian communist history, not a full autobiography. Siegelbaum and I are the same age, with similar adolescent and university experiences but not similar families of origin or fields of study.

In Siegelbaum's (2019) words, *Stuck on Communism* is a biography of Soviet history written by Anglophones. Equally importantly, it is an illustration that "no matter what historians take as their subject, they are always writing about themselves." That realization is only occasionally recognized by scholars in memoirs or other writings. It is even less often fully assimilated. These autobiographies take that acknowledgment as their point of orientation. So do I (for other relevant examples of academic autobiography, see Linda Mercadante, 2006, and David Martin, 2013; see also Bruce F. Pauley, 2016, who combined two centuries of family and personal history with the history of Volga Germans).

*My Life With Literacy: The Continuing Education of a Historian* is different. It spans 75 years and encompasses five universities and six cities. The 1960s are part of my story, along with earlier and later, continuously shaping and reshaping periods. So are my scholarly periods of being "stuck" on the histories of literacy, children and youth, cities, theory and method, interdisciplinarity, and now "public education" and "teaching outside the box."

This book searches for and explicates intersections and their consequences in multiple, complex, connective relationships across my full life span. A life course perspective, learned during my research, teaching, and writing about "growing up," guides my understanding (see my *Conflicting Paths*, 1995a). So does my understanding of how literacy changes over time and across individuals and cultures. From age 22 to the present, I have been a pioneering scholar in the history of literacy and literacy studies as a field (see later chapters for references to my writings in these areas).

My years as an urbanist also shape my understandings. They begin with growing up in a city, Pittsburgh, a place in dramatic transition from "steel town" to a never fully realized "new city"; then living in the Chicago suburb of Evanston but frequenting the city while studying at Northwestern University; living in Toronto while in graduate school at the central-city University of Toronto; and then teaching at three public universities in Dallas and San Antonio, Texas, and Columbus, Ohio.

This book's explorations derive from and reflect retrospectively on my first book *The Literacy Myth: Literacy and Social Structure in the Nineteenth-Century City* (1979c), then *Undisciplining Knowledge: Interdisciplinarity in the Twentieth Century* (2015a), and finally *Searching for Literacy: The Social and Intellectual Origins of Literacy Studies* (2022e). My own paths connect them.

*My Life With Literacy* explicates and interrelates the simple and the complex, the straightforward and the contradictory in the shaping of a life over more than 70 years. The principal factors, which become clearer to me almost every passing day, are the *personal* from my family of origin to friendships and collegial relationships and my 55 years with Vicki Graff; the *political* broadly defined to include experience, practice, ideology, and theory; the *academic*, including the institutional, pedagogical, and scholarly; and the crucial roles of *places* in which I have lived and worked.

The book begins with its final phase. My retirement thus far is an outcome of the following chapters and the forces discussed there. From an ending still in composition, I follow chronologically from early childhood through my six cities, two universities as a student, and three universities where I long served in a variety of capacities. I end with reflections from my final book on literacy, *Searching for Literacy: The Social and Intellectual Origins of Literacy Studies* (2022e).

# Chapter 1. Endings from Beginnings: A Culmination of Learning and Practice

## Retiring My Way

Retirement in 2016–2017 came earlier than we anticipated. We did little of the specific, detailed, advance planning that is recommended. Prepared financially, we were not ready intellectually and personally. In retrospect, I can state without hesitation that this is the not-unexpected culmination of 42 years of professorial service and success at three poorly managed, public universities, two of them new, suburban campuses of the University of Texas System and one the 150-year-old, 65,000-student, main campus of *The* Ohio State University (for details on these experiences, see my essays under Universities and Ohio State University in the Appendix).

When I transitioned into retirement first with medical leave in winter 2017, I had completed 13 years as the inaugural Ohio Eminent Scholar in Literacy Studies, professor of English and history, and founding director of LiteracyStudies@OSU, a university-wide, interdisciplinary initiative. At OSU I published seven single-author or edited books and drafted one more, and received honors and international recognition and frequent invitations to speak, write, and advise.

I taught courses cross-listed in several departments and supervised graduate students from various disciplines, departments, and colleges. I served on departmental and university committees and worked actively on general education reform and university support of the arts, humanities, social sciences, and natural sciences. My unusually wide circle of colleagues and students spanned the entire large and divided campus, including suburban branches and senior administrators. Our personal social network built on those relationships.

I retired in spring 2017. I could no longer work actively in a department, college, and university that refused to acknowledge my accomplishments—some of which I had been told were impossible—*and* that increasingly violated its commitments to me, my program, and my program associate director. Many of these promises were in writing.

Chairs, deans, and provosts acknowledged the promises but refused to honor the obligations. Successive department chairs showed no interest in defending my contributions to their programs and to the university. These problems were not unique to me. By 2016–2017, I had had enough.

For the next three years, I battled a series of illnesses beginning with depression. Collectively they were severely limiting. Four years of Trumpism, social isolation, and the 2020–2022 Covid-19 pandemic did not help. With extraordinary personal support at home and excellent physicians, I completely recovered. My internist continues to exclaim, "Harvey's back!" Other doctors echo that sentiment. Friends and colleagues concur. In their own ways, I now understand in retrospect, they all contributed toward my "new normal" of 2020 and beyond. Among the lessons that I share with colleagues and friends now retiring is you need a transitional period, a break; no one goes from one role to another immediately.

## Transition and Translation

By 2020, my life shifted toward normal and then new normal rhythms. I first became a dedicated consumer of news in print, audio, and television. By 2021, I completed my transformation to what I call my retirement niche of public education and teaching outside the box combined with selective continuing scholarship. In ways that become clearer to me daily and weekly at age 75 and counting, the intersecting forces of the *personal, political, scholarly/academic,* and *place* broadly, intimately, and interactively shape these outcomes and pave my paths. In other words, the themes of this exposition reveal themselves most starkly at this relatively late date. I now understand that is to be expected. The transition to retirement is real and complicated.

Some days I think I'm changing the world. On others, I feel that I'm "tilting at windmills." A former Texas doctoral student and longtime friend, Soledad Jasin, insists on updating my quip: I'm "tilting at wind turbines." In fulfilling ways, I'm using my skills and knowledge without dealing with universities and free of often false notions of objectivity, nonpartisanship, and nonactivism (for examples, see my 2021h, 2022n, 2022q, and 2022aa essays under Retirement as Public Education in the Appendix.)

We retain close friendships and good relationships with OSU faculty, students, and neighbors. Some parts of the university call for my help. Others seek to ban me for my fact-based, published, constructive commentaries about higher education with OSU as a major example. These include, among others, "Slogans Are No Substitute for Concrete University Policies and Programmes" (2022h) and "Collegiality Needs a Reboot" (2022o). We are connected with colleagues and friends, old and new, including many former students throughout the country and the world. I discuss them in later sections of this chapter.

I am also making new contacts and friends among scholars, including a journalist-historian of literacy in Spain named Diego Moldes Gonzalez; the faculty of Zayed University in the United Arab Emirates, especially applied linguist Wafa Zoghbor; and James Chapman, professor emeritus of education in Wellington, New Zealand.

## Public Education and Teaching Outside the Box

I began the draft of my essay, "A Post-Retirement Career as a Public Academic Meets the Moment's Need" (2021h), as follows: "I am a 72-year-old retired professor. . . . As a scholar and teacher from graduate school forward, I also engaged in a variety of extramural activities that are known as 'public history' and less frequently as 'public humanities.'" These activities I referred to included co-authoring *Children and Schools in Nineteenth-Century Canada* (1979) with Alison Prentice for the pioneering Canada's Visual History of the National Museum of Civilization (then the National Museum of Man); assisting historical societies and museums with exhibits and programming (for example as advisor for the Museum of Chicago History's multi-year Teen Chicago initiative); writing brochures for public historical landmarks in Dallas; assisting newspaper, NPR, and television reporters with background and sources (in Dallas, San Antonio, and Columbus as well as other locations nationally and internationally); and serving as advisor, panelist, and speaker for public radio and television (in Dallas, San Antonio, and other locations nationally).

In my specialty areas, I advised public American and international agencies about literacy, children, and interdisciplinarity. In retirement, I am more engaged publicly across my research specialties. In particular, in my retirement my social and historical knowledge about literacy and young people led to both outreach and demand for commentary on issues from critical race theory to book banning and the question of the putative "unprecedentedness" of our times (see my "The Dilemmas of Disciplines Going Public," 2022g).

This work during my professorial years was rarely time-consuming, but it was a stimulating and fulfilling extension of my teaching and research. It facilitated the application of my skills and knowledge, and it reached a larger, nonacademic audience. It also facilitated making new contacts, collegial relationships, and friendships. At least as significant, it spoke to the social, political, and cultural imperatives that shaped my personal and academic life from my early teen years forward. On occasion, I taught exciting and mutually enriching graduate seminars on public history and humanities.

The circumstances that led to my retirement left me unwilling to continue an active, institutional relationship or a traditionally defined role. My goals as a scholar and a classroom teacher are largely fulfilled. My books on the history of literacy and the contemporary relevance of that history; the history of children, youth, and families; the history of cities; and interdisciplinarity—including their interrelationships—are foundational to their fields. A final, scholarly book on literacy, *Searching for Literacy: The Social and Intellectual Origins of Literacy Studies*, has been published (2022e). Since retirement, I have conducted only three reviews of scholarly book proposals; written one book manuscript review; and completed no grant, fellowship, article, or book reviews.

I do not wish to continue research and writing principally for academics. I have done more than my fair share. I continue to advise scholars and students around the world at all levels, publishers, and institutions. I call this "teaching outside the box." I often meet with undergraduate students in my university neighborhood. Sometimes we jokingly call this "Harvey U" (see my essay "I'm Retired but I'm Still Running My Own Unofficial University," 2022aa).

I attempt to balance my general audiences, broadly academic, and more focused scholarly publications and related activities. Learning from our pasts—variously defined—and communicating with targeted but broad audiences results from my education and career. For example, I publish regularly in *Times Higher Education, Against the Current,* and *Columbus Free Press,* among many outlets.

At the same time, I am drafting *Reconstructing the "Uni-versity" From the Ashes of the "Mega- and Multi-versity"* and editing a collection of original first-person essays, *Scholarly Lives in Transition, 1960s to 2020s and Beyond: Misunderstood and Untold Paths in Shaping the American University.* These projects continue my professional practices of reorienting understanding by asking new questions, reinterpreting historical understanding, correcting myths typically uncritically repeated over decades and centuries, and challenging my audiences through multiple media.

Prompted in part by the political and social climate, in the place of more traditional academic roles I developed a new focus on "public education." That orientation lies in public history and humanities, active engagement with contemporary issues, and presenting uncommon perspectives and alternative contexts for understanding today's pressing issues, especially by challenging those who ignore or misunderstand history in a variety of ways.

My specific actions, in writing and forging connections, draw directly on the political and the academic and seek to ground the connections in the personal. Given my history, I no longer need an institutional base from which to operate.

As a "public educator" or public intellectual teaching outside the box, I build on established paths. Public history dates from the 19th-century founding of historical societies, museums, and other institutions as well as popular historical writing. It is not new to the activism of the 1960s or job crises since the 1970s (see my essays under Disciplines and Interdisciplines in the Appendix; in contrast, see, for example, Feisal G. Mohamed, 2021.) Almost all discussions of "knowledge in the public" or "applied knowledge" across disciplines are too constrained chronologically, conceptually, and institutionally. The precedents and opportunities are much longer and wider.

## Writing Familiarly but Differently

By early winter 2021, the pieces of my retirement niche fell into place. It was a process of redefinition, redirection, and translation, analogous literally and figuratively with the uses of literacy as I came to understand them during decades of study and teaching. It depended on my new flexibility with time. I began by writing opinion essays and letters to editors for metropolitan daily newspapers in increasing quantity. This form of writing remains a regular activity and shapes other elements of my public education campaigns. My target publication sites and audiences, however, changed over time.

After several years away from regular writing and time spent online, I started writing by hand on yellow legal pads with MSNBC, CNN, or NPR playing in the background. I dictated the text to my wife Vicki (Vic-tated, we say) as she sat at the computer. We then Vic-edited and revised. After a few months, I returned to my former practice of composing at the keyboard and doing first revisions myself. As former manager of editorial services for the American Heart Association, Vicki edits as much of my writing as she can before it leaves the computer and the house.

In retirement, I am more intentionally personally engaged in my writing than I was as a full-time professor and public university employee. That adaptation intertwines with my advising of office holders, candidates, and advocacy groups especially on matters of public education, anti-illegal censorship and free speech violations, gun safety, and voting rights, among others I describe later in this chapter.

Some of the circles I am completing stretch over decades. That is part of the dynamic, ever-changing intersectionality of the personal, the political, the academic, and place in practice.

None of my subjects are new to me, and I draw unhesitatingly on my background and experience. Writing for a more general audience than I used to requires refined communication skills, aided by my wife's sharp editing. She commits "adverbicide" and "adjectivectomy," among other clinical treatments. Our editorial practices delight my editor at *Times Higher Education*, who occasionally on Fridays wishes me "an adverb-free weekend." After more than 50 years together, editing is *almost* always fun amid a swamp of bad puns, writing jokes, hilarious typos, and occasional pokes in the ribs.

At first, my submissions to newspapers and magazines depended on trial and error, sometimes provoking frustration. Although I previously published letters and what we used to call OpEds, or opinion—now guest—essays, in local dailies in Dallas, San Antonio, and Columbus; in the *Wall Street Journal*; and in education outlets like *The Chronicle of Higher Education* and *Inside Higher Ed*, I was introduced to a new world where recipients almost never acknowledge submissions, seldom communicate decisions, and almost never copyedit or fact-check. I discovered some of my letters had been published in print or on websites when reading the daily paper or checking online. I was not informed.

My learning curve improved with the advice of Steve Weissman, a longtime friend and former colleague who moved from a faculty position to positions in government service and nonprofit advocacy organizations. He shared his experiences in writing for and locating nonacademic publishers. This was far more helpful than standard guides to opinion writing.

As with scholarship, practice helped. I had to learn the unwritten rules of the road. For example, few newspapers or news/opinion sites provide guidance. What advice they do give is general and simplistic to a fault. Issues central to scholarly publishing, from single vs. multiple submissions, making pitches in advance of submitting textual material, expecting confirmation of receipt among other forms of professional courtesies, and anticipation of a decision in a predictable amount of time are almost nonexistent. The waiting time for publication after acceptance is also erratic.

I spent several frustrating months learning, with few stated exceptions, that multiple, simultaneous submissions are permitted. Of the outlets I have submitted to, only the *The New York Times*, *The Washington Post*, and Cleveland's *The Plain Dealer* require exclusivity; the *Times* and *Post* usually provide decisions within two to five days. Otherwise, copyrights, ownership rights, and exclusivity are seldom mentioned. Keeping records of which essays are with which outlets for how long is challenging. In addition, most but not all newspapers have a policy of publishing an individual once every 30 days, a small number every 60 days, and many have no policy at all.

All this has to be learned. In my experiences with outlets across the US and in the UK, only *The Plain Dealer* and occasionally *The Washington Post* fact-check letters and opinion essays. In contrast to others, it shows on their pages. Neither standard editorial practices nor journalistic ethics are the norm today.

In part this reflects the general shift from news reporting to opinion writing in both national and metropolitan dailies. This is one of the responses to financial strains (for more on this topic, see my "Busting Myths: The Disappearance of Journalistic Standards As Opinion Essays Replace the News," 2022k). It also limits opportunities for guest essayists in favor of regular members of editorial boards and established opinion writers. Many of the unaffiliated writers are promoting new books or lobbying for one or another interest group, from political office holders and candidates to corporate representatives selling products—often fraudulently. The lobbying and payments from agents, publishers, and authors are never discussed publicly or in print.

Opinion writing is largely a random and unprofessional world. My experiences include being banned from the opinion page of *The Columbus Dispatch* because I accurately referred to its operations as "muddled" and "uninformed" on its readers' comments site. This banning took place despite the fact that I was a frequent contributor, provided advice to the new opinion editor, and had praised the editor in print. Another Gannett-owned outlet, *The Cincinnati Enquirer*, banned me because I dared to ask after about six weeks when an accepted essay would be printed.

Earlier, I withdrew an essay from *The Cincinnati Enquirer* after it failed to print my article three weeks after its acceptance and more than two weeks after its promised date. The opinion editor responded, "Do what you need to do," without a word of explanation or apology. Another Ohio newspaper, the *Dayton Daily News*, accepted the same essay immediately and gave me a near-immediate publication date. Four days later, it rescinded that written agreement without a relevant or coherent explanation. Another editor claimed that it had only accepted the essay for review, a nonexistent category contradicted by the stated publication date.

In a third case, on a local news site called *Columbus Underground*, I published an essay that criticized the city's media for their complicity in Columbus, Ohio's, lack of identity (see my "Columbus' Identity Crisis and Its Media," 2021a). I was soon viciously attacked by another local, pseudo-news (actually an entertainment) magazine (see Downing & Oliphint, 2021). Calling my essay "trash," the "response" mainly agreed with my arguments but ridiculed my publisher and dishonestly defended its fellow Gannett affiliates against my criticism. No local outlet would publish my rejoinder, including the original publisher, because they did not want to "risk further" or "escalate" conflict (See Graff, ""Response to *Columbus Alive*," 2021m). Journalistic standards and ethics, including the First Amendment, are missing in action.

After four to five months, matters changed. Almost simultaneously, I began to engage highly professional editors at the following national and international higher education publishing sites and national monthly magazines with regularly updated websites:

- *Times Higher Education*
- *Inside Higher Ed* (this relationship ended in fall 2023)
- *Washington Monthly* (this relationship ended in late 2022)
- *Academe Blog* (this relationship ended in early 2023)
- *Publishers Weekly* (this relationship ended in fall 2023 with the abolition of the "Soapbox" feature)
- *Against the Current*

In summer 2021, another news site editor (Suzanna Patzer) led me to the independent, progressive *Columbus Free Press*. Oddly, no one at OSU or in my neighborhood ever mentioned the *Free Press*, which had been in operation since 1970. After I published a stream of essays with the *Free Press*, we decided that my contributions should become a regular column titled "Busting Myths," a reference to my books *The Literacy Myth* (1979c) and *The Dallas Myth* (2008a).

These editors acknowledge receipt of my essays. They promptly accept submissions as written or return them with reasonable requests for revision and their reasons why, typically related to their publication's goals.

I revise within a day or two, refocusing, reorganizing, or clarifying arguments. Within another day or two, I receive an acceptance, soon followed by professional copyediting with occasional queries or requests for documenting URL links. I also receive rejections, often but not always stating the reasons why. I typically resubmit those essays to another publication, sometimes revising them.

Each of these editors expresses concern that they may not be able to publish my writings as quickly as I might wish. I assure them that my essays are almost never breaking news. I would rather wait a few weeks for professionalism and competence. As it happens, these publications have high reputations and broad circulation, unlike the newspapers and sites that do not conduct themselves professionally.

## Writing for Publics

For me, while only a few of my letters are published, writing a letter to the editor often becomes a first step toward an opinion or guest essay or sometimes a scholarly article—a recognized literacy practice. At other times, it is an act of "intellectual therapy." Letter writing, especially to *The New Yorker*, *The Atlantic*, *Harper's Magazine*, *The New York Times*, *The Washington Post*, and *The New York Times Magazine*, is sometimes the beginning of larger projects.

At first, I concentrated on the contradictions of state and national policies and political parties with a focus on the increasingly radical, right-wing emphasis among elected Republicans in the Ohio state legislature and the U.S. Congress. Speaking to the moment, I wrote letters and essays critical of state and national responses to the Covid-19 pandemic. I placed essays and letters in metropolitan dailies across Ohio and co-authored a letter with Vicki on federal Covid-19 pandemic policies in *The New York Times* (for lists of essays and letters, see the Appendix). These efforts led to limited collaborations with Common Cause Ohio and the Ohio chapters of the American Civil Liberties Union and the League of Women Voters.

I write as a professional historian and long-published author. I add historical and comparative perspective and understanding of American institutions and the U.S. Constitution. I continue to practice the craft of historical knowledge as an applied and critical act that I was taught in graduate school at the University of Toronto by my model and example—social, educational, and urban historian and social critic Michael B. Katz.

No longer a university professor on the payroll, I see no grounds for complaints about my compromising objectivity or abusing my office. I speak only for myself, no other person or institution.

One thread of my new efforts focused on Ohio's public Covid-19 pandemic actions. I wrote a series of essays and letters to editors in state and national newspapers and magazines on Governor Mike DeWine's large-scale surrender to the pandemic. My attention centered on the shift from early activism under former Ohio Department of Health Director Dr. Amy Acton to combined inaction, sloganeering, and publicity stunts like the ineffective Vax-a-Million lottery (for details about the Vax-a-Million lottery program, see https://odh.ohio.gov/media-center/odh-news-releases/odh-news-release-05-17-21). The Ohio Department of Health never recovered from its loss of a capable, qualified director. Poor politics and almost no policy initiatives replaced responsible, public health action.

A second series of essays and letters I wrote shed critical light on Ohio's dominant Republicans and their seemingly limitless failures. I evaluated the state attorney general's unfamiliarity with the U.S. Constitution; various means of voter suppression; attacks on honest, responsible education including the ignorant campaign against critical race theory, which is not taught in Ohio K-12 schools; the state legislature's and U.S. Congressional representatives' refusal to respect and serve their public; and their regular practice of imitating other red, or Republican, states (for details about these topics, see essays under Ohio Issues in the Appendix).

Severe political gerrymandering is the usual reason given for the Republican domination of Ohio in recent years. But I took critical aim at the silence, disorganization, and internal hierarchy of the state Democratic Party. I also called attention to the undemocratic Democratic majority among Columbus mayors and city councilors (see essays under Ohio Issues and Columbus Past and Present in the Appendix).

On the national level, I published an original excavation of the agenda of Donald Trump and his Trumpists, their policies, and a platform within which there were no coherent statements of organized points or policies. I also wrote an exposé on the most right-wing, Republican state governments, Texas' and Florida's, rhetorical flirtations with secession and Ohio's ignorant imitation of their governments' actions.

I criticized the Centers for Disease Control and Prevention's Covid-19 pandemic policies, actions, and reactions, including the dominance of politics over science, from the Trump to the Biden administrations. The rapid and radical decline of the United States Postal Service (USPS) under corrupt Postmaster General Louis DeJoy attracted my attention in conjunction with my filing a formal complaint through my U.S. senator, Sherrod Brown, about the inability to provide daily mail delivery as required by law. That connected me with a USPS regional coordinator, who forwarded my documented complaint to the federal inspector general's office. Not surprisingly, that led to no action. (See essays under National Issues in the Appendix.)

From those early topics I expanded my writing into other arenas surrounding the changing news and broadcast media combined with contemporary political and cultural issues. I addressed the biases of conservative columnists at *The New York Times* and *The Washington Post*, the shift in newspapers from reporting news to publishing opinion essays, and the decline in both national and local print and broadcast journalism. As 2021 turned into 2022 and 2023, I wrote factually and historically about critical race theory, book banning, and higher education, all in historical and critical contexts.

## Civics in Theory and Practice: From Education to the State of Democracy

Drawing on my expertise in the history of education and literacy, I also write about the lack of civic knowledge and the startling ignorance of current elected officials with respect to history, including the U.S. Constitution. In my opinion piece "Testing Can Save Democracy" (2021j), I semi-seriously proposed a civics test as a requirement for running for public office. Responses to that proposal—from nonpoliticians—are quite positive. The politicians, if they can read it, are silent.

In other essays I explored civics, knowledge, and ethical declines that connect politics to the mass media (see titles listed under Media and Communications, Critical Race Theory and Education, and National Issues in the Appendix).

## From Urban History to Contemporary Urbanism

Central to my concerns as an urban historian and lifelong large-city resident, I often write about the exceptional shortcomings of Columbus, Ohio's, major print, audio, and video media and their responsibility for the city's combined failures to develop a distinctive identity; absence of a written history; lack of a tradition of constructive public criticism and independent professional institutions; inability to protect neighborhoods and residents; and incompetent, leaderless, unrepresentative government. The facts on the ground belie the city's current ranking as 14th largest in population in the United States.

I began to do this kind of writing in conjunction with constructive conversations with local reporters, city of Columbus departmental and city council aides, city attorneys, and police officers. As my research advanced and I more deeply penetrated the city's fictitious veneers, many of those interactions ceased without notice or explanation. Interestingly, those with police on their beat remain the most mutually interactive and instructive.

Essays I've written on these topics have stimulated local comment and controversy. Some reporters and a number of citizens have responded more sympathetically to my arguments than senior editors, management, and city boosters. I often write about *The Columbus Dispatch*'s and NPR WOSU station's flailings and failings. Both are in desperate need of new management and reform.

I learned far more about Columbus city government in 2021 than in the preceding 17 years. I remain astonished. The city council of the United States' 14th largest city is undemocratic and unrepresentative. All seats are elected at large, as if it is an unreformed, mid-19th-century city. Against all reasonable odds and expectations, the city government is disorganized and disconnected, with no city manager or realistic vision of the entire city. It is a city lacking in leadership and knowledge, and it is in physical disrepair.

I learned to navigate city government partially and personally with determination and the guidance of two excellent, young, soon-to-be-former legislative aides and neighborhood engagement staff. In the aftermath of my urgently calling on the city attorney in September 2021 to mobilize city departments to confront the disorder and law-breaking behavior on OSU football weekends in my University District neighborhood, heads of adjacent departments spoke to each other for the first time. Of course, that quickly ended. Neither responding to facts nor sustaining interest or action are part of what I dubbed "The Columbus Way."

Overall, in my writing on these topics I demonstrate the city's lack of urban identity, vision, and planning, and its subservience to major private developers and corporations. I call for a democratic "revolution" in Columbus city government along with a sustained search for an appropriate identity and all that accompanies that complex endeavor (see my essays under Columbus Past and Present in the Appendix). This follows more or less directly from teaching urban history for decades, including the first course on the history of Dallas, Texas, and the critical conceptualization that led to my writing *The Dallas Myth: The Making and Unmaking of an American City* (2008a).

## From Cities to Their Universities

Reflecting my time served within universities from 1967–1975 as a student and 1975–2017 as a professor, I developed a historically based critique and proposed rethinking of relationships of people and their fields of study.

My post-retirement series of essays and books in progress follow the personal and the academic more directly with respect to place in general terms but often with a focus on Ohio State University as a major example. My most personal example of this sort of writing is "Colleges Must Learn From Sports Figures About Mental Health (2021e). Decades of reflection and my experiences with depression and anxiety came together with the immediate stimulus of women's tennis champion Naomi Osaka, gymnast Simone Biles, and other athletes revealing their mental health struggles in the spring and summer of 2021.

I wrote in part about how my own experiences with anxiety and depression helped me become a better teacher and a much better graduate supervisor. But my larger focus was how inadequately universities deal with the consequences of our often poorly conducted guidance and development of younger and especially female and minority scholars—both as faculty members and as graduate students.

The response to the essay, particularly from strangers, is powerful. Both old friends and new correspondents tell me how "brave and courageous" I am. I don't see it that way. I'm being self-aware *and* responsible and learning from my own and others' experiences. The institutional response, as expected, lags despite endless rhetoric and self-promotion to the contrary.

A continuing cluster of essays focuses on *The* Ohio State University, sometimes as the sole subject and at other times as a touchstone for larger academic issues. These are on topics I addressed in earlier writings. For example, I wrote an opinion essay in *The Wall Street Journal* titled "An Education in Sloganeering" (2015b) concentrating on OSU's two-time president, E. Gordon Gee. That publication stimulated a considerable response•. Around the same time or even earlier, I published "Not a Popularity Contest" (2015c), "Early-College Programs Lack Many Benefits of The Real Thing" with my colleague biologist Steve Rissing (2015), "Throwing the Baby Out With the Interdisciplinary Bath Water" (2014c), and "The Troubled Discourse of Interdisciplinarity" (2010c; on the latter, see my *Undisciplining Knowledge: Interdisciplinarity in the Twentieth Century*, 2015a).

I updated and broadened those views in my continuing essays, including "The Banality of University Slogans" (2022f), "Slogans are No Substitute for Concrete University Policies and Programmes" (2022h), and "Sloganeering and the Limits of Leadership" (2022i).

Together with my revisioning of the history and "crisis" of the humanities and universities more generally and the "myth of collegiality," these writings constitute an overarching critique and reinterpretation of typical "leadership" that failingly substitutes slogans for responsible executive actions in the form of programs, policies, budgets, and timetables as well as broad involvement at all levels. Writing about the uses and abuses of "collegiality" is stimulated by conversations with younger especially female colleagues.

Some essays have focused more pointedly on OSU (see, for example, "For Ohio State, bigger is not better," 2021g), an ongoing investigation of what I consider to be among the worst managed, large public universities in the United States, the equivalent of a modern tragedy. This singular failure contradicts the efforts of many outstanding faculty, staff, and students and a lovely central campus oval. This investigative and interpretive work integrated more than one half century in higher education as student, teacher, and researcher with historical understanding.

## Columbus, Ohio, and Ohio State University

As an urban historian and 20-year homeowner in Columbus' central historic University District adjacent to sprawling Ohio State University, I struggle to understand this 200-year-old city's lack of an identity—and especially an urban identity—and its "bromance" with private property developers as a substitute for urbanism and a useful sense of itself (for background and comparison, see my book *The Dallas Myth*, 2008a).

Drawing on informed and challenging conversations with my colleague Kevin R. Cox, geographer and author of *Boomtown Columbus* (2021), and my friend and former student Ellen L. Manovich, urban historian and researcher of the University District (see, for example, her article "'Time and Change Will Surely Show': Contested Urban Development in Ohio State's University District, 1920–2015," 2018), I developed a continuing series of critiques of city government and Ohio State University, sometimes in relationship with each other. This writing advanced hand-in-hand with my at-once critical and constructive engagement with city government and to a lesser extent with a diminishing number of OSU senior administrators. In April 2022, all OSU administrators stopped communicating with me, without explanation, on order of the former president. No criticism, however documented *and* constructive, is acceptable it seems.

Reflecting my unique vantage point as an Ohio Eminent Scholar; a member of two departments and affiliate in others; and founding director of the university-wide, interdisciplinary initiative LiteracyStudies@OSU, I long worked at university reform and responsible, constructive criticism (see, for example, my *Undisciplining Knowledge*, 2015a, and *Searching for Literacy: The Social and Intellectual Origins of Literacy Studies*, 2022e).

In retirement, I further developed my criticism of OSU and higher education more generally. This writing is inseparable from my research and writing on the city of Columbus; OSU colleagues, students, and administrators; and interdisciplinarity in historical context. I actively seek to stimulate more informed discussion and provoke further study—and consideration of possible actions.

My expanding critique progresses step by step, in part putting OSU in a larger comparative context. I began with: "For Ohio State, Bigger Is Not Better" (2021g), "Ohio State's VAX-A-NICKEL Giveaway" (2021c), "The Decline of a Once Vital Neighborhood: Columbus' University District" (2021f), "Columbus' University District: Students and the Institutions That Fail Them" (2021i), "Ohio State Isn't Having a Crime Crisis; It's Having a Leadership Crisis" (2021l), and "Busting Myths: The Ohio State University Promotes Public Health Crises" (2021o), and then continued my series on the University District with "Busting Myths: Ohio State Versus 'Campus Safety'" (2022p) and also wrote the two-part "Busting Myths: The United States' Worst Managed Large Public University? Ohio State's 5½ 'D's': Disorganization, Dysfunction, Disengagement, Depression, Dishonesty, and Undisciplined" (2022w, 2022x).

In my article currently under review, "Disconnecting Gown and Town: Campus Partners for Urban Community Development, Ohio State University," I explore universities as agents of urban development and their contradictory relationships with their urban locations. As I explain, the "the public university's 'private development arm'" overpays for properties adjacent to campus and then sells them at a financial loss to unregulated developers, who in turn overbuild and literally wall off the "campus in the city" from its city.

Simultaneous to all this writing, I advise OSU graduate and undergraduate students as well as local reporters on their research on either or both Columbus and OSU. Increasingly, I have discussed the same issues with Columbus city attorneys, neighborhood engagement groups, the zoning department, and city council legislative aides. Not, however, with OSU itself, city councilors, or the mayor. They waver between declared ignorance and denial. Despite its rhetoric, OSU seems to have little connection with, and even less regard for, the community.

## Universities, Missing Histories, Disciplines, Interdisciplines

My expertise in the development and current practices of literacy studies and interdisciplinarity constitutes a major area of direct scholarly translation across disciplines and disciplinary clusters. How could it not after more than 50 years?

Along with addressing critical race theory and book banning, my essays on literacy studies and interdisciplinarity aim at a more targeted audience than those that focus on political interventions. They are among the most attractive to editors and have the most influence. This writing grows from decades of research and teaching, culminating in the publication of *Undisciplining Knowledge* (2015a), my critical study of interdisciplinary efforts over time and across disciplines. *Searching for Literacy* (2022e) extended those intersecting paths.

In a continuing series of essays in *Times Higher Education* (with editor Paul Jump), *Inside Higher Ed,* and *Against the Current,* I criticize recent unknowledgeable and ahistorical approaches to interdisciplinarity, the humanities, and universities past, present, and future; the misrepresentations of the relationships between the arts and humanities on the one hand and the sciences on the other; the lack of historical memory *and* historical understanding among disciplines; and the challenge of scholars and knowledge in the public spheres.

I explore these topics in depth and historical context in my forthcoming book , *Reconstructing the "Uni-versity" From the Ashes of the "Mega- and Multi-versity."* It is another example of how the personal, the politics of universities and scholarship including issues of theory and commitment, my relationships to changing disciplines and interdisciplines, and the institutions where I studied and taught come together in the final stages of my lifelong pursuits.

Of special concern to me now, and in my crystalizing conversations with colleagues, is what I call the "myth of collegiality." I strive to promote a wide-ranging conversation about collegiality's replacement and/or reconceptualization among all human components of contemporary universities. Relatedly, I continue my decades-long quest to respond to the many proclaimed "crises" of higher education—especially in the humanities—and the dramatically misconstrued conceptions of interdisciplinarity.

An enriching episode of this conjunction took place with my invitation to address the faculty of Zayed University in the United Arab Emirates in January 2022 about conceptions and examples of interdisciplinarity. Despite my long-distance appearance online via Webex in the wee hours of the morning Eastern Standard Time, 10:00 a.m. in Dubai, an excellent, meaningful exchange transpired. We have plans to continue. Neither employment status nor distance need be obstacles.

## Literacy, Myths, Old, and New

Provoked by an ignorant and offensive, full-page advertisement in *The New York Times* in August 2021 for a corporate-promoted program called "FL4ALL"—that is, "financial literacy for all"—I responded strongly. No one with any understanding of literacy uses the abbreviation FL. Only a third-rate advertising copywriter would construct "FL4ALL."

This is a major clue to the incoherence of an effort to promote a concept rather than to make a responsible or constructive statement about or develop a program to encourage literacy. A quick online search after seeing this advertisement led me to several hundred proclaimed distinct and independent "literacies." That is not only nonsense but also a radical obstacle to both understanding and teaching literacy. I detailed these arguments in "Busting Myths: The Misrepresentation and Marketing of 'Financial Literacy'—The Fallacies and Dangers of FL4ALL" (2022j; for more on this line of thinking about the multitude of literacies, see *Searching for Literacy*, 2022e, and *Literacy Myths, Legacies, and Lessons*, 2011/2023c).

That effort to investigate contemporary, popular uses of the term "literacy" reconnected me with literacy studies in general and the need to reevaluate the complicated and contradictory field of study and its place in universities and beyond. Updating my knowledge of recent developments, I wrote "The New Literacy Studies and the Resurgent Literacy Myth" (2022c). In it I reviewed the development of the then "new literacy studies" in the 1970s and 1980s to which my first book *The Literacy Myth* (1979c) was a major contribution, followed by *The Legacies of Literacy: Continuities and Contradictions in Western Culture and Society* (1987b) and several collections of my essays, widely reprinted and translated into various languages.

The then new New Literacy Studies emphasized the critical role of historical, social, and cultural contexts in the definition and understanding of literacy both in theory and equally importantly in practice. Disconnected especially with the institutionalization, disciplinarization, and professionalization of knowledge from the 14th through the 20th centuries but especially from the *18th* and 19th, those perspectives were largely replaced by what I named in 1979 "the literacy myth," the undefined, uncritical, and exaggerated acceptance of the nearly universal power of literacy acting alone, that is, as an independent variable irrespective of human social, cultural, economic, or political differences and special social and cultural contexts.

The accepted view neglected specific abilities in actual use by real people in specific contexts and in association with others. To the contrary, the literacy myth emphasized often mythical notions of literacy by itself. By my use of the term "myth," I followed cultural anthropologists and historical literary critics: a myth is not necessarily a falsehood. To the contrary, a degree of familiarity, however unrepresentative, is required for circulation and acceptance.

Many of my critics and those of other new literacy studies scholars (such as Shirley Brice Heath, Brian Street, Sylvia Scribner, and Michael Cole) have not understood that distinction. Not surprisingly, they clustered in social psychology and within basic splits among the fields of rhetoric and composition, now mainly styled writing studies. In response to the often-illuminating work of Deborah Brant in particular, I named her emphases in her interpretation "the writing myth" (see my "Epilogue: Literacy Studies and Interdisciplinary Studies With Notes on the Place of Deborah Brandt," 2014a).

Historically, the writing myth simultaneously prevented understanding, obstructed efforts at transmission and instruction, and led to negative judgements of those people deemed to be lacking literacy, with or without evidence or contextual understanding. In the rhetoric of the 1970s, this was "blaming the victims."

In my "The New Literacy Studies and the Resurgent Literacy Myth" (2022c) and at much greater length in the later publication *Searching for Literacy: The Social and Intellectual Origins of Literacy Studies* (2022e), I took stock of not only the major reorientation of the field in the last one-third of the 20th century but also the lessening of its influence in recent years with the flow of an endless stream of "many literacies."

At one time or another, almost every field and activity has proclaimed its own "literacy" with little or no discussion of what literacy actually may be. A significant number are promotional and sales efforts by self-defined "specialists" inside and outside of universities and private marketers. Multi- and cross-disciplinarity and both commercial and rhetoric promotion compete, often contradictorily, with interdisciplinarity as I, for one, define it (see my *Undisciplining Knowledge*, 2015a.) Of course, I feel a personal as well as professional stake in renewing the debates of the 1970s–1990s at all levels inside and outside universities.

In autumn 2021, I revisited my 2015–2016 critical review of and set of proposals for literacy studies, *Searching for Literacy: The Social and Intellectual Origins of Literacy Studies* (2022e). Originally written under contract for a major publisher, the acquisitions editor broke the contract, telling me to keep my advance on royalties, with no discussion or request for review. The academic series editor objected to two paragraphs critical of his writing. The publisher refused to discuss the issues. The incident was among the factors that led to the timing of my depression and my retirement.

By mid-summer 2021, I was ready to resume its publication. My review of the complete, professionally edited manuscript and the principal literature revealed no need for further revision. I wrote to about a dozen relevant, scholarly presses. Half of them asked to see at least part of the book. In short order, three offered contracts to publish.

After discussion with acquisitions and executive editors, I signed a contract with Palgrave Macmillan. My editor and I decided to add several new chapters with recent essays. Palgrave published the delayed book in print and e-editions in late summer 2022.

Another retrospective, stock-taking literacy contribution was the publication of the assessments of my contributions from a special session, "Literacy Studies and Composition Through the Work of Harvey J. Graff," at the 2017 annual meeting of the Conference on College Composition and Communication. I am moved and humbled by these tributes. It appears as "Harvey J. Graff: A Tribute" in *Across the Disciplines*, Spring 2024 (Duffy et. al, 2024 https://wac.colostate.edu/docs/atd/volume21/duffyetal.pdf ).

## From Literacy Studies, the History of Children and Youth, and Social and Cultural History to the Crises of Education Today

### The "New Illiteracy": Critical Race Theory, Book Banners, and the Right-Wing Assault on Children

#### The Second Big Lie: Critical Race Theory

Both unpredictably and predictably, the period beginning in 2021–2022 demanded the action of a knowledgeable social and cultural historian of literacy, children and youth, and education. An organized, well-funded, national *disinformation* campaign largely on social media culminated two-thirds of a century's right-wing fears and grievances. Its perpetrators are racist, sexist, segregationist, anti-diversity, intolerant, and lack mutual respect. They mounted a historically unprecedented, unconstitutional, and inhumane attack on the free speech and maturity of the young—especially those from nondominant racial and ethnic groups, disabled people, and gender non-conforming people, their teachers and schools, honest and inclusive history and learning, and the fundamental bases of "We the People" and the public.

The first major issue—a fake issue built on lies and a nondebate—broke over what was misrepresented as critical race theory (too often shortened to CRT because of laziness; CRT stands for cathode ray tube or cardiac resynchronization therapy). A well-organized, dark-money, national campaign propagated via websites and right-wing media turned a highly specialized theoretical framework used primarily in legal studies and schools of law into a demon threatening all that members of these nondominant groups feared. The three words—*critical, race, theory*—aided by ignorant media sucked almost all the oxygen out of the air waves, school board meetings, and state legislatures.

In too many ways, it really did not matter that there was *no* actual debate or *two* sides to any difference of views or that critical race theory is nowhere taught in K-12 schools and only rarely outside of laws schools anywhere in the nation. The nondebate is the result of active mis- and disinformation, fearful and gullible people, unconscionable politicians and influence-grubbers, and a massive failure in both public and private education.

Thanks to them, the right-wing campaigns of distortion and fear against critical race theory expanded to embrace criticisms of teaching about the history of race, racial relations, slavery, civics, and other aspects of American history. Right-wing radicals call this "divisive," "contentious," or "uncomfortable" education despite the fact that the great majority of people—right, center, and left, including the young—value the challenge of its learning. I call this nondebate "the Second Big Lie" (second to the Big Lie about the 2020 election and its resulting January 6, 2021, insurrection).

Given these events and conflicts, in response I published a continuing series of essays in newspapers, magazines, higher education periodicals and sites, and scholarly journals (see my essays under Media and Communications and Critical Race Theory and Education in the Appendix.). My essays present an original, historical contextualization and interpretation of today's ongoing crisis, which has origins both in the three quarters of a century since the 1954 Brown v. Board of Education Supreme Court ruling that "separate but equal" is not equal (National Archives, 1954) and over the four centuries that made America. Today's divisions can only be understood in those contexts.

The essays that I write about the nondebate over critical race theory, and 18 months later book banning, attract the most attention. They circulate widely, and my phrases such as "the Second Big Lie" and "white fright and flight" have joined the larger public and academic conversation (see, for example, my "Fiction and Fact About Critical Race Theory," Forum, Kirwan Institute for the Study of Race and Ethnicity, Ohio State University, Sept. 9, 2021). They lead to NPR radio appearances (such as various NPR talk shows and interviews available online); presentations at university forums; advising reporters locally and nationally; counseling elected state and federal officials; assisting state board of education members; and advising local, state, and national advocacy and professional groups, faculty, and both college and high school students.

~~~

### Book Banning, the "New Illiteracy," Moms Against Liberty, and the Assault on the Rights of the Young

Literally on the heels of the nondebate about critical race theory, another overflowed it: a historically unprecedented wave of book bannings, especially for younger readers from school and local libraries, beginning in Republican-led states like Texas, Utah, and Florida. Falsely presented as "protecting the vulnerable young" or "parental rights," the blatantly dishonest intimidation of local boards of education and school district superintendents through unconstitutional and unenforceable state legislation, are neither. They represent an outright attack on the free speech rights of students and teachers and an inhumane, anti-child challenge to growing up, education, development, and maturity. "Parental rights" is no more than a rhetorical pitch rooted in fear and grievance.

Ironically, the books challenged since 2021 sat comfortably on library shelves for years, often when the youngsters of the shrillest book banners were actually in school—not at the time of the campaigns to remove them. Not in the least ironic is the dramatic fact that young adult and other books containing at least a scattering of obscenity or profanity are almost never targeted. Studies by the American Library Association, PEN, and Book Riot demonstrate conclusively that it is books authored by persons of color, women, gender non-conforming people, and disabled people—and with comparable protagonists—that are challenged.

Unlike previous campaigns to ban and sometimes to burn books, going back at least a thousand years—and memorably during the Protestant Reformation, Anthony Comstock's late 19th century efforts to keep obscenity (actually birth control information) out of the U.S. mail, and now laughably the 1920s "Banned in Boston" movement —today's right-wing aggressors are unfamiliar with the contents of the literature they strive to remove and suppress. They either do not or cannot read it, or both. I label them the "new illiterates."

Contrary to ignorant, partisan rhetoric, they are the purveyors of identity politics or "cancel culture" in their unconstitutional movements rooted in bullying and other forms of political assault. Tragically, the most vulnerable, the young, are the great losers. Instead of "protecting them," the banners attack them (see my responses to such efforts in essays on Book Banning and Critical Race Theory and Education in the Appendix.).

*Figure 1.1. Harvey in Read Banned Books shirt, made into a coffee mug after Zayed University online lecture, January 2022.*

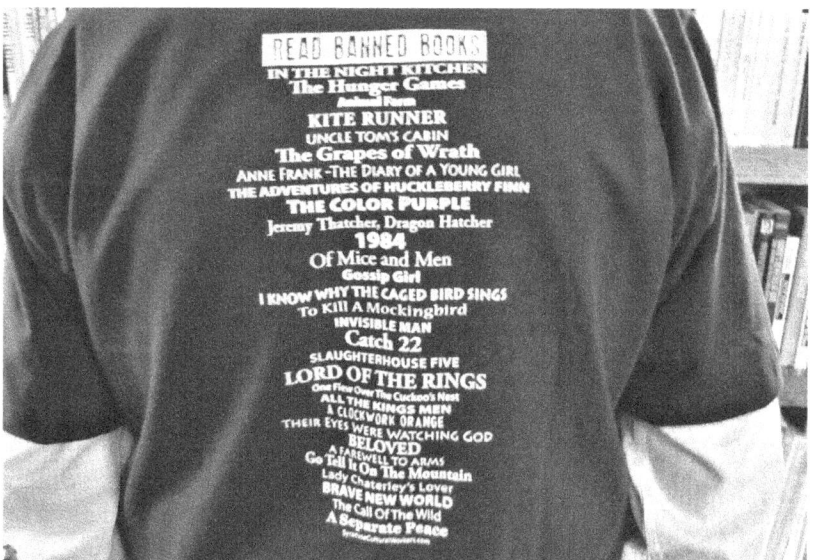

*Figure 1.2. Back of Read Banned Books shirt, SyracuseCulturalWorkers.com.*

My essays on this topic lead to a continuing wave of contacts, requests for assistance, new contributions and challenges, and collegiality and friendships. These efforts range widely from informing and assisting reporters and NPR affiliates across the country and in London and Dublin, to taking part in various activities with state ACLU chapters including preparing courtroom testimony, the American Library Association, and PEN America. The contacts, mutual exchanges and learning, and new friends and acquaintances are indeed rewarding.

## The Brighter Side

I often remind myself that the young are among the brightest sources of hope in our dark times. For Thanksgiving 2021, my writing shifted focus dramatically to celebrate "My Young Heroes" (2021n). For some time, I collected accounts of amazing young people aged 2 to 22 across the nation and the world of many races and genders who stimulate positive thoughts. I compiled my notes into an organized roster at the request of friends so they could share the stories with their children and grandchildren. I published it in a *Columbus Free Press* column. I later commemorated "The Young Heroes of the Writing World" in *Publishers Weekly* (2023i).

I wrote another column, this one with Ameer Abdul, called "Busting Myths: The Other Immigrants and Diverse American Dreams" (2022) to celebrate his story. I met Ameer, a 26-year-old Palestinian American social and political activist, through Morgan Harper. Morgan is a young, progressive, Black attorney who I advised on her Ohio political campaign. Ameer's and his family's stories are testaments to the potential of the American dream.

## A Shift from Writing to Personal Engagement: Connecting, Reconnecting, Renewing

In retirement, I have the time, experience, knowledge, and stature to reach out to elected officials, news media, and advocacy groups. Sometimes I respond to opinion essays and letters in the press by contacting the authors directly.

With respect to the attacks on education and the young more generally, this led quickly to working relationships and then friendships with the following people:

- Michelle Newman, member of the Ohio State Board of Education, who shared my input with like-minded colleagues
- Jeanne Melvin, member of the board of directors of the Ohio chapter of Public Education Partners, an advocacy group for public education
- John McNay, University of Cincinnati, and Lisa Voight, then OSU and now Yale University, of the Ohio Conference of the American Association of University Professors (AAUP)

- Ariel Hakim, founder of Banned Books Box
- Crystall Lett, formerly Ohio Program Director of RedWine.Blue, an organization that sponsors the program Book Ban Busters
- Ameer Abdul, political activist and former national policy coordinator and national campaigns manager for PERIOD
- Matt Ides, organizer with the Ohio Education Association
- Jonathan Friedman, director of U.S. free expression and education programs at PEN America
- Joyce McIntosh, program officer with the Freedom to Read Foundation, an affiliate of the American Library Association
- The statewide coalition of almost 40 advocacy groups and individuals in Honesty for Ohio Education
- Leila Green Little, library and freedom to read advocate from Llano County, Texas
- Joe Motil, Columbus political activist and 2023 candidate for mayor of the city
- Bill Lyons, environmental activist and math teacher
- Jerry Nuovo, Richard Fishel, and Kristine Yoder, all biomedical scientific researchers at OSU College of Medicine and OSU Wexner Medical Center
- Lisa Voight, anti-gun violence volunteer with Ohio Moms Demand Action
- Others, whose positions and activities I wish to protect

Most of these inspiring, talented people are now my friends as well as comrades.

I joined forces with executive director (Jim Grossman) and immediate past president (Jacqueline Jones) of the American Historical Association and the editors of the AAUP Academe journal (Mike Ferguson) and blog (Kelly Hand).

My expertise led the American Civil Liberties Union in Missouri (Molly Carney, Anthony Rothert, Tom Bastian) and Ohio (Collin Marozzi) to work with me. I advised Molly on history, context, and current issues; contributed expert written testimony in one lawsuit; and wrote opinion essays for Missouri newspapers.

With Honesty for Ohio Education and affiliate groups, I served in leadership and communications roles and helped to link this coalition to others in Ohio and across the country. I provided them with intellectual and media resources and advice on strategies. They placed my relevant writings on their *News Resources* page of their website in a section titled "From the Desk of Harvey Graff" (see https://www.honestyforohioeducation.org/news--updates.html).

An example of another partnership occurred when a mutual friend led the Llano, Texas, Friends of the Llano Public Library and their dedicated and inspiring leader Leila Green Little to me in winter 2022. The right-wing takeover of the public schools of the county and the firing of a librarian are among the most egregious actions I saw in this difficult year. I advised them and through my ACLU

Missouri contacts was able to stir the ACLU Texas into action. I connected Leila with NPR in Dallas and faculty at the University of Texas at Austin. I also wrote an opinion essay to publicize the unconstitutional actions of the county judge and commissions and their right-wing activities.

Through my relationship with Jeanne Melvin, member of the board of directors of Public Education Partners (PEP), an advocacy group for public education in Ohio, I contributed historical knowledge to the lawyers suing the state of Ohio to change its policies on "open" vouchers for school-age children, and I connected PEP with other scholars.

These groups and individuals circulate my essays widely across various media. As a result, the essays have been shared with local school boards and given to school principals in support of inclusive history teaching, public education, teachers' rights, and free speech in several states. I testify (in writing) before the Ohio Legislature and the State Board of Education by request and by choice.

National radio interviews and online public forums that allow for Q&A sessions and other interactions with audiences are stimulating and fulfilling after almost 50 years in classrooms and lecture halls. Although many of today's audiences are virtual, it is exciting and stimulating to speak to largely self-selected and actively interested audiences who typically respond with excellent questions and comments. I have participated in such programming for shows ranging from Cleveland's WCPN's exceptional "Stream of Ideas" to KJZZ-Phoenix's "The Show" and several New Hampshire-Pacifica talk shows.

In a well-attended September 2021 forum, I presented for OSU's Kirwan Institute for the Study of Race and Ethnicity a talk titled "The Fictions and Facts About Critical Race Theory." Many of the questions from the audience focused on "What can I do?" I have many answers on a variety of levels. Those answers allow me to connect the different individuals, institutions, and groups with whom I speak and to whom I contribute. Collaboration and connection-making have been fundamental to my values and conduct since at least high school.

That forum also marked my first formal, 45-minute talk in more than four years. I began by introducing my orange shirt from Canada that proclaimed "Every Child Matters." I wear it or my "Read Banned Books" t-shirt or my "I'm With the Banned" sweatshirt for all online appearances (see Figures 1.1 and 1.2).

These engagements across media are satisfying personally, professionally, and politically. They also lead to making contacts and new friends among members of the media, political officials and advocates, and others who contact me in response to my essays and appearances.

The online posting of the video of the Kirwan Forum led an incredibly talented Columbus high school senior to contact me. She was engaged in a senior project on critical race theory and requested my input, leads, perspectives, criticism, and sources. We had an exhilarating conversation. I have taught few university students as inquisitive and desiring of intellectual challenge as she was.

My publications led other high school and college students to request my help. Such experiences are a valued addition to teaching in continuing my life with literacy.

In another social media-age connection, my relatively short-lived participation in Robert Reich's Substack subscriber site led to a connection with Pittsburgh M.D. and environmental activist Ed Wrenn. Ed in turn steered me to the committed, Pittsburgh-area Battle of Homestead Foundation commemorating the history of labor activism in steel mill towns, such as the one where I worked to earn money for college. For some months, I enjoyed the bi-monthly Zoom breakfast meetings. The group was welcoming to an ex-Pittsburgher and former summer steelworker.

My influence, impact, and personal satisfaction from these activities are more direct and quicker than from scholarly publishing, much more like a good class but without the real and artificial constraints of university environments. Neither grading nor "Rate My Professor" is anywhere in play.

Publishing activities flow almost naturally into others, some of them more novel. Although before my retirement I had occasionally assisted newspaper, radio, and television reporters and editors, I began to reach out regularly to local and national journalists offering historical counsel and contemporary leads. Most ignored my emails; one local reporter actually responded, "Research would interfere with my objectivity." She is now a local NPR radio talk show host.

Some welcomed my reaching out. This included the producer of *The New York Times'* podcast *The Daily*. A *Washington Post* media reporter, to whom I had written to point out errors in an article in June 2021, contacted me in late September when writing a follow-up to the original report (see Jeremy Barr, 2021, for the follow-up story.) Some reporters in Columbus have become my colleagues. I assist them with background, depth and comparisons, and more detailed information on their subjects.

For a time, I participated actively on *The Columbus Dispatch* readers' online comments feature, adding perspective and fact-checking. In frustration, after experiencing insults and ignorance, I stopped because contrary to stated policy, the paper's moderator refused to police racist, sexist, xenophobic, and transphobic hate speech. I have better uses of my time, other forms of public education. I have not missed the activity. Not long after, USA Today/Gannett suddenly disabled the feature without notice or explanation.

I occasionally comment on specific articles and opinion essays on *The New York Times* and *The Washington Post* sites. *The Post* is the best. Comments are posted immediately, checked only by artificial intelligence (or algorithm) for offensive language. In sharp contrast, *The Times* continues to be moderated—avowedly at least—by humans. This results in comments occasionally posted almost immediately but others after one or two days—after the specific piece no longer is open for responses and sometimes never.

In part, for a time, I shifted my online commenting and posting energies to the American Historical Association's discussion threads. Discipline is mandated and enforced by moderator approval of all posts on a given thread. Although there is occasional disinformation to correct, the content and conduct is professional.

At my initiative, the editors promptly initiated a new thread on "divisive concepts in history" when I began to turn "censorship" toward critical race theory nondebate issues. After that, I was active on a thread about "history as social science or humanities." As in other activities, this led to making new friends, including Mark Tauger, of West Virginia University, and Kevin Johnson, formerly of Southern Arkansas State University. I have influenced curricular decisions at universities and supplied references and critical perspectives to others.

As with reporters, some Ohio legislative aides ignore me, especially those affiliated with the Ohio Democratic Party and its candidates. A few welcome my offers of assistance and contributions and exchange with me by email or telephone. This includes state Democratic legislative representatives and staff and Democratic U.S. Senator Sherrod Brown, who sends my wife and me handwritten thank you notes in response to letters to the editor. Former Republican Senator Rob Portman (who retired in 2022) and former Representative Troy Balderson only responded with irrelevant, often dishonest form statements, when they responded at all. More recent, gerrymandered Representative Joyce Beatty's Democratic office does not respond to me. City of Columbus officials are completely unresponsive once they learn that a resident expects responsible action and democratic representation.

The year 2021 brought an unusual opportunity: meeting and deciding to assist as a senior advisor to Morgan Harper, the progressive, young, Black, female candidate for Ohio U.S. senator. A mutual friend brought us together in late summer, not long after Morgan formally announced her candidacy. Harper is the first political candidate with whom I have worked directly and personally since I "got clean" for Eugene McCarthy in 1968.

The daughter of a single mother, she was adopted by a schoolteacher after nine months in foster care. After winning scholarships to Columbus Academy, Tufts University, Stanford Law School, and Princeton University, she worked in the Consumer Financial Protection Bureau during President Obama's second term. She commenced on a political career with a broadly based, democratic, inclusive agenda that appealed to me. I enjoyed aiding her on historical and general perspective and issues.

In part because of the expanding readership of my regular "Busting Myths" column in *The Columbus Free Press* and in part because each new relationship leads to another, I commenced a political relationship and friendship with Joe Motil, a longtime, progressive, Columbus activist and 2023 candidate for mayor. I now also coordinate with Bill Lyons, environmental and civic activist and community bill of rights leader. I link them to OSU students and recent graduates who are committed to climate and environmental actions.

*The Columbus Free Press* also led to my friendship with retired journalism professor and Ohio politics writer Jack Hartman, who I linked to my expanding group of political associates. Unfortunately, Jack died from cancer in 2023.

My writing about Columbus, Ohio, also attracted the attention of Al Thompson, a Philadelphia-based national sports journalist and activist against steroid use by young athletes. Al leads the national group POYS (Protect Our Youth From Steroids), lobbies successfully for federal legislation, and exposes the malfeasance of Columbus' trademark bodybuilder event, The Arnold Classic.

## At Home in Columbus

My writing and activism with respect to the city of Columbus and OSU have led directly to more varieties and levels of personal engagements and relationships. My wife and I have lived since 2004 in a 110-year-old historic house in the University District (UD) adjacent to but independent of OSU, a 10-minute walk to my former office. We purchased the house despite warnings about the neighborhood from some university faculty and staff. Our university-linked real estate agent thought we should purchase a house in a well-to-do suburb.

Once a mixed area of single-family owner-occupied homes, homes that housed student boarders typically with homeowners, and small boarding houses, over a period of decades the UD transformed through a major decline in the number of owner-occupiers and a massive expansion of students living in large and small dwellings owned and/or managed by large landowners and property managers with the collusion of the city of Columbus and Ohio State University (Cox, 2021; Manovich, 2018; see also my essays on the University District listed in the Appendix.)

For two decades, along with our neighbors (especially Kay Bea Jones and her late husband Chris Zacher), Vicki and I urged OSU to take responsible action and actively promote safety, orderly behavior, and civility in the UD. Over that period, OSU actually reduced its already limited role. Unlike universities such as the University of Minnesota and the University of Pennsylvania that are known for their leadership in active, responsible neighborhood relationships and constructive programs, OSU leads by neglect and slogans. At a time when many universities and colleges purchase nearby older homes to transform into theme houses, from those housing religious groups to those housing pre-professional and social justice oriented students, OSU refuses.

In recent times, OSU's Office of Student Life proclaims "the residential experience" and "the exceptional student experience." They thoughtlessly extend their slogans for on-campus housing required for two years to absentee-landlord-owned off-campus housing, among "60,000 students. 100 countries. One University District." The off-campus UD does not house 60,000 students. Nor do "students from 100 countries" attend the university. They do not all share "The Exceptional Student Experience."

An August–September 2021 blip in crime in the University District—not a "spike," as the then-president and local media shrieked—(reflecting a citywide wave) sparked excessive media coverage and student-parent fears. (Halperin, 2021;

Hendrix, 2021; Rivers, 2021). OSU responded late, inconsistently, and ignorantly. After an awkward silence, then OSU President Kristina Johnson responded with alarm, new safety slogans, and poorly conceived, often irrelevant new "policies." They did not engage long-term homeowners who have far more to lose (and one of whom was stabbed to death in her home in September 2023). (See my essays under Ohio State University in the Appendix.)

In fall 2021, as football season began with large, out-of-control, loud, drunken, and trash-strewn (all violations of city laws) student parties almost 24 hours a day on game day weekends, my neighbor and I had several revealing conversations with Columbus police officers who responded to our reports of nonemergency legal violations. They told us about their personal fears of large groups of students, the limits of their actions, their lack of necessary resources, and their misunderstanding of OSU's legal responsibilities and property ownership. Some of the same officers told me two autumns later that the assistant city attorney police liaison ordered them "not to enforce the law" or "issue citations" in the UD. This followed orders to zoning code inspectors not to enforce their laws, escalating great risks to all residents and especially to the young students. The goals are to protect the interests of the private property owners and, contradictorily, the reputation of the university. The conflicts are countless.

This set of intersecting circumstances prompted several responses. Also influenced by conversations with the more responsible, student-renter neighbors, I first wrote about the situation in "The Decline of a Once Vital Neighborhood: Columbus' University District" (2021f) and "Columbus' University District: Students and the Institutions That Fail Them" (2021i). In 2022, I broadened my scope to explore wider, ever-more-contradictory connections among Ohio State, the city of Columbus, and private property owners within the overall scope of interrelated city governmental and public university failures.

Exasperated with OSU's increasing neglect combined with obfuscation and dishonesty, these outrages led me to write a strong plea to Columbus City Attorney Zach Klein and city council members in mid-September, with copies to major media. I urgently called on the city to enforce its existing laws immediately regarding noise, trash, public drunkenness, parking, and landlords' responsibilities—and review and update them.

I emailed the letter with supporting documents on a Saturday afternoon. I included among the recipients three responsive city council legislative aides with whom I was acquainted. I suspect that helped my cause.

To my surprise, on Monday morning, Zach Klein's assistant confirmed receipt and stated that a serious response was forthcoming. That afternoon, Klein emailed me. His office arranged a Zoom meeting with me and 10 senior staff including a police commander and police liaison, the heads of code enforcement and zoning, a representative of the community engagement team, city attorneys, and legislative aides.

That meeting exceeded my expectations—and, within a few months, misled me. Beginning with "please call me Harvey," I began with a 20-minute overview of the situation. Questions and reports on city actions in progress followed. Unlike many of my university experiences, no one was then defensive; no one attempted to rebut my statements. We had a frank exchange and, in everyone's estimation, what seemed to be a constructive first step.

The following day three participants followed up with comments and further questions. Initially committed to the then developing matter were city neighborhood engagement representatives, zoning and code enforcement officials, the 311 customer service office's coordinator and staff, some legal personnel, and the then district police commissioner. Several informed me that in city hall I was referred to as a "civic leader." (In OSU's administration building, I have been told, "your name is mud.") My city status was short-lived.

In the meantime, two administrators in OSU's large and disorganized office of student life (but not lives) reached out to me. At first, they appeared to respond honestly, openly, and supportively to my strong statements to their vice president and the university president. (The latter refuse to either engage me or respond at all. Before long, the president, later ordered to resign, forbid most administrators and communications staff to interact with me.) Two people, one a new associate VP and the other a longtime, off-campus engagement manager, each spent hours with me airing issues, seeking my views, and seemingly enjoying the company of a retired senior scholar and professor who lives in a student neighborhood and interacts with his neighbors.

Typically, these meetings, aimed at promoting constructive change, took place around my dining room table, sometimes only with city representatives, sometime only with OSU's, sometimes with both. Personal relationships developed, for a time at least, from the political and academic in the specific context of place.

However, these conversations stopped abruptly without warning or explanation in March 2022, shortly after I connected OSU's Office of Student Life with an assistant city attorney assigned as liaison at my request to the city attorney. Apparently due to a command from the OSU president's office, or her handlers, all cooperation and communication ceased. That is "the OSU way" of rejecting constructive criticism and a perceived threat to its hegemony.

Before long, all city personnel and all OSU personnel above the level of academic deans including non-academic staff ceased communication. This included the new provost, now president of Boston University. She came to my house for advice until the short-termed president ordered her to stop.

Little progress occurred since the initiating meeting in early October 2021 and my first connections with the city in early spring 2021 reversed. That is "the Columbus way," coupled with the OSU habit. Neither neighbors, neighborhoods, homeowners, nor student renters count. (See my essays under Columbus Past and Present and Ohio State University in the Appendix.)

~~~

Surrounded by undergraduate student renters in our neighborhood, my wife and I engage them on our daily walks. I find that I miss talking to college-age people, although I do not miss classrooms or office hours. We found ourselves eager to meet the many students with "pandemic puppies" or service dogs in training.

We became acquainted, became friends with some, offered a variety of advice and information from trash collection, recycling, and zoning laws to academic and career advice and tips on spring break travel. They are at first surprised by the interest of a retired OSU professor and a former staff manager in them as people, and then excited by our conversations about their studies, plans, and questions.

This speaks to OSU's failings in "student life." It reflects the disconnection and loneliness of students among a population of more than 65,000 (for more on these topics, see my articles "Universities Are Not Giving Students the Classes or Support They Need," 2022t, "Busting Myths: Recreating Universities for the 21st Century Without Repeating the Errors and Myths of the 20th Century," 2022v, and "Busting Myths: How Universities Fail Their Students: The President May Be 'Born to Be a Buckeye,' but the Students Are Not," 2022y).

With some students, I developed a more sustained social and working relationship that lies in between academic advisor and older friend. With engineering senior Justin Kim, for example, I assisted in a variety of ways on his project to develop an online platform and app to help self-published authors promote their books.

With recent architecture and urban and regional planning graduate Brett Wedding, I conducted an informal seminar on urbanism and urban history. With recent graduate Matthew Snyder, conversations ranged from his social and environmental studies and his aspirations to study environmental law to the state of the nation and the world. With recent graduate Joseph Glandorf, conversations centered on environmental activism, OSU, and Columbus. On Columbus and Ohio politics, a colleague at Notre Dame connected me with then senior and now law student Jack Wilson, who plans a career as a progressive lawyer. Finally, with my second cousin Liam Gallagher, who graduated in computer science, and his then friend Jeanelle Wu, a new graduate in materials science engineering, the topics are boundless.

These are among other, briefer segments in what my wife and close friends teasingly but also admiringly dub "Harvey U," which offers the following: free tuition; no debt; very small classes; mutual teaching and learning; inclusivity of age, degree level, experience, and rank; and historical grounding. We began with four "seniors at Harvey U" in 2022–2023 and grew to six first-, third-, and fourth-year students in 2023–2024 (see my article "I'm Retired but I'm Still Running My Own Unofficial University," 2022aa). Potential "applicants" contact me from around the world.

I continue writing about OSU, its failed responses to crime, and the University District. That is the responsibility of a retired, knowledgeable professor who cares about the university's students, faculty, educational mission, and role in the larger community. That work led directly to two new books: *Reconstructing the "Uni-versity" From the Ashes of the "Mega- and Multi-versity"* and an edited collection of original essays, *Scholarly Lives in Transition, 1960s to 2020s and Beyond: Misunderstood and Untold Paths in Shaping the American University.*

Retirement "work" has an impact—and rewards.

*Figure 1.3. Bill Lyons, Harvey, and Michael Wilkos, three of 12 participants in the Columbus Reform group, October 2022.*

## From Historian of Literacy, Children and Youth, and Cities to Contemporary Politics, Politicians, and Diverse Activists

With respect to literacy, direct personal relationships continue. I assisted my former doctoral student Di Luo of the University of Alabama with final preparation of her 2022 book *Beyond Citizenship: Literary and Personhood in Everyday China, 1900–1945*; aided in the continuing scholarship on literacy in Turkmenistan of former doctoral student Victoria Clement; helped with former graduate student David Bwire's application for permanent residency status; consulted with fellow retired historian Mary Cayton on her project on newspaper readership in late colonial and early national America; collaborated with OSU history of the book colleagues Sarah Neville and Alan Farmer; communicated with Notre Dame professor John Duffy; kept in touch with Syracuse University's Patrick Berry; and maintained contact with sociologist of communications Jeff Pooley; among many others. For a Cambridge University Press editor who made a special appeal, I made an exception to my decision to no longer review proposals and books.

As my "teaching outside the box" expands, I consider a variety of forms of collaboration with colleagues and students. They are wide-ranging, from writing about the literacy myth in relationship to prison literacy and education with longtime colleague Patrick Berry and discussions with recent friend Bob Eckhart and former football star Maurice Clarrett about Maurice's prison education; to comparative research on literacy studies, communication studies, and disciplines and interdisciplines with Jeff Pooley; to exploring public social sciences and humanities with longtime colleague and fellow scholar of interdisciplinarity Professor of Sociology Jerry Jacobs at the University of Pennsylvania. I learn from all these relationships regardless of differences in age and position.

A final example underway reiterates the intersectionality of the historical moment. It pivots around my younger colleague at Ohio State University, then Assistant Professor of Comparative Literature and Comparative Studies Ashley Hope Pérez, who is author of three young adult novels as well as several scholarly articles. Ashley's most recent novel, the national prize-winning *Out of Darkness* (2015), based on a historical event in a small Texas town in 1937, was banned at least temporarily by school districts in Texas, Utah, Indiana, and Florida, among others. The false charge of "obscenity" was based on one paragraph willfully misread and taken out of context by radical, right-wing activists who hadn't actually read the novel (the historically unprecedented "new illiteracy").

When I learned about Pérez' situation from a local newspaper article in recognition of "Banned Books Week," I reached out to her. We began to correspond and soon met over a lengthy lunch. I urged the OSU and Ohio Conference American Association of University Professors (AAUP) and the state ACLU chapter to issue strong public statements of support. That process began.

My wife and I provided intellectual, social, and moral support for Ashley and her young sons. In addition, Ashley and I have published jointly authored opinion essays in Utah (Pérez & Graff, 2022), Texas, and Indiana newspapers. Our historical and literary interests also intersect in probing the complicated and typically misunderstood practices and processes of reading across ages and cultures.

Perhaps less surprising than my renewed collegiality based on learning and teaching across ranks, ages, and levels of experience is my counseling a growing number of colleagues preparing for their retirements (for more on these efforts, see my "A Post-Retirement Career as a Public Academic Meets the Moment's Need," 2021h, "Teaching Outside the Box," 2022q, "Academic Collegiality is a Contradictory, Self-Serving Myth," 2022l, and "Collegiality Needs a Reboot," 2022o).

## Success and Limits

I increasingly recognize that I am refining the knowledge and skills that I had practiced over decades in the university. I now translate them to public *and* private arenas and have a discernible impact on opinion and policy.

I am quoted, cited, reprinted. I receive positive responses from people I know and strangers who contact me. Many colleagues, former students, and friends respond to my essays. There is also occasional hate mail, of which my favorite if mystifying example is, "You are a socialist who supports white slavery in China."

Historian Steven Mintz from the University of Texas at Austin wrote to me, "Your scholarship models what I am calling for. Your work was never of purely antiquarian interest. It spoke directly to policy issues and theoretical, methodological, and conceptual debates. Your recent writings, it seems to me, build on that foundation" (personal communication, August 2021). He also applauded my work on literacy in two columns of his Higher Ed Gamma blog on *Inside Higher Ed*.

Former AAUP President Hank Reichman (2022) reprinted part of one of my essays on sloganeering by universities in "Per Aspera ad Astra" on the AAUP's *Academe Blog*.

My former graduate school professor, colleague, and friend of more than 50 years, Natalie Zemon Davis, wrote to me, "What an impressive list. I've been reading (or in some cases, i.e., critical race theory, rereading) your essays. Your public voice is so important, Harvey. May it be heard loud and clear and be effective. In solidarity" (personal communication, December 27, 2021). Historian of American education and another friend for almost a half century, Paul Mattingly, wrote, "You are standing at the bridge. Let me stand with you," (personal communication, January 18, 2022). Later he wrote, "A terrific essay, one which meets the long-standing definition of a true hero (Odysseus): 'one skilled in ways of contending'—the all-time best definition of . . . a liberal arts and science education" (personal communication, April 10, 2022).

A younger, mid-career colleague, Chris Hager, commented,

> I have enjoyed watching your retirement from afar. . . . More than once I've thought to myself, *this is what college faculty should all be doing, all of the time! And this is what the labor model of modern higher education is not allowing them to do! One has to retire to begin doing what is rightfully one's job!* . . . I'm glad of and grateful for the thought-provoking reflections of yours that I've been able to read. (personal communication, June 16, 2022)

At the same time, I am aware of the limits of my work. Some right-wing and conservative academic voices, and perhaps some more moderate ones, question or condemn my post-retirement professional activities that are no longer university-based. Contradictorily, they do not object to activist, conservative, and right-wing faculty members' public positions on history, humanities, the social sciences, education, the sciences, and health and medicine. They call that "free speech."

Some label me "partisan," although I do not represent any party. Superficially and contradictorily, others allege that I am violating the "terms of objectivity" and "traditional professional standards."

To them, I reply firmly that they apply a flawed, incomplete, contradictory, and self-serving definition and conception. Trained and experienced scholars have *always* combined professionalism and objectivity with responsible activism.

If the self-appointed critics continue to fuss, I point to right-wing scholars still affiliated with universities who regularly violate established standards for objectivity. The right-wing complaint is uninformed at best, and hypocritical at worst (for more on this topic, see, for example, my "The Best Scholarship Is Political but With No Ideological Stamp," 2022u, "Humanities Could Change the World—If Only They Could Change Themselves," 2023g, "Lessons for Becoming a Public Scholar," 2023h, "Speaking Out on the Israel-Hamas Conflict Doesn't Mean Taking Sides," 2023j, and "Scholar Activism Doesn't Require Taking Sides," 2023k).

Going public is constantly a learning experience—a continuing education as I think about it. So far, it is a satisfying and rewarding retirement "career." It combines the best of the scholarly without the constraints and contradictions of the university or narrowly defined professionalism. I recommend it. The urgent challenges of our times demand it (for more on how I am responding to this demand, see my "A Post-Retirement Career as a Public Academic Meets the Moment's Need," 2021h, "A call to colleagues: Speak out and support children, teachers, librarians, and free speech—and the present and future of your own institutions, too," 2022n Teaching Outside the Box, 2022q, "I'm Retired but I'm Still Running My Own Unofficial University," 2022aa, and "Learning Through Teaching," 2022z).

~~~

Sadly, 2021 meant tributes to four deceased, longtime friends, colleagues, and collaborators. I decided to dedicate *Searching for Literacy* (2022e) to them:

- My acquaintance since 1968 and close friend and colleague from 1979 Jan Reiff at UCLA ("Celebrating Jan Reiff," UCLA history department tribute page, May 24, 2021)
- My decades-long colleague Mike Rose, also at UCLA, with whom I shared literacy and many other interests (see my "Guest Post: Remembering Mike Rose in Person and in Print," 2021b)
- Fellow graduate student, colleague, and co-author Alison Prentice, retired from York and Toronto Universities in Victoria, British Columbia ("Tribute to Alison Prentice," Ontario Historical Society)
- Friend, colleague, collaborator on literacy and other things, and tennis partner Jerry Zaslove of Simon Fraser University

## People and Places

Relatedly and intersectionally, Vicki and I maintain, renew, and expand our connections with many people. The same retirement emphases that stimulate my public education campaign also propel these personal movements.

Among them are old and new friends, colleagues, former students, and neighbors. Those in Columbus visit with coffee or their lunch and bring takeout dinners (or we pick up takeout and meet at their homes). Sometimes friends' dogs join us. In late 2021 we discovered a favorite: picking up freshly made waffles from Winston's Coffee and Waffles food truck and bringing them to our house.

Over more than 40 years, we had many cats and three dogs, two of them for 16 and 15 years, instead of small humans. For us, it was the right decision. But over the years, and in an intensified way now, we have a growing group of "surrogate" grandchildren, without the mixed pleasure and agony of raising our own children. They are the children of younger colleagues and former students.

The kids, aged 2 to 12, eat, chat, perhaps read a bit from our collection of progressive children's books, and then play with our four generations of robot pets. Beginning in 2013, the robot dogs (Tekno, Golden Pup, and Laughing Dog), robot cats (Little Cat and Tuxedo Cat), a robot "intelligent elephant" (Ellie), and a robot velociraptor (Veli) took the place of our last dog McDonald, a West Highland white terrier who lived with us in San Antonio and Columbus. The retired champion was 15 and died with an implanted heart pacemaker.

We chat with the "grandkids" in living and dining rooms, meet in parks for play dates, root for six- and eight-year-olds' soccer teams, read books, and collect large and small items (often "free gifts" from wildlife and environmental groups) to give them. We buy them writing pads, colorful calendars, and age-appropriate books. And from them, we buy Girl Scout Cookies. One named caterpillars in her back yard Harvey and Vicki. Several of them make art for us and send us letters.

We gave a solar-powered robot kit to one six-year-old, aspiring physicist (it only operates 30 minutes each day when the sun is at a certain angle. That is fine with him). I discuss social justice with a six-year-old and think about police with a five-year-old. For the holidays in 2021, we gave each household a copy of the superb children's book from the 1619 Project *Born on the Water* (Hannah-Jones & Watson, 2021). Together, we've proved that one can enjoy having grandchildren without having children first.

Retirement adjustment and the Covid-19 pandemic combined to stimulate me, and us, to seek new friends, rekindle dormant relationships, and thicken long-standing connections. These friends, relationships, and connections range widely over huge distances and more than five decades to include high school, college, and graduate school classmates, teachers, and professors and their families; professional colleagues; former undergraduate students and especially doctoral students from three universities; former neighbors; physicians; and friends from all of the cities in which we lived. Adding to those numbers are at least three generations from around the world of literacy studies scholars; historians of education; members of the SSHA (dating to 1976); urban historians; historians of childhood, youth, and families; and interdisciplinarians.

Returning to my theme: the intersections of the personal, the political, the academic, and place are far too many to count or categorize. They are my life with literacy and my continuing education.

# Chapter 2. First Formations: Early Years in Pittsburgh, 1949–1963

I was born in Pittsburgh, Pennsylvania, on June 19, 1949, on Juneteenth long before the American people and state and federal governments recognized that date. It was also Father's Day. Although I was the firstborn, my father joked that my arrival "ruined" his Father's Day. Jokes were not Milton M. Graff's strongest suit.

My mother, Ruthe Galanty Graff, was raised in Sharpsburg, an immigrant mill town across the Allegheny, one of Pittsburgh's two rivers that come together to form the Ohio River at the downtown Point State Park, also called the Golden Triangle. My father grew up in Braddock, a steel town along the Monongahela River on Pittsburgh's other side.

Both grew up in small shopkeeping, largely immigrant, Jewish families that served their predominantly eastern and southern European industrial communities. My father was first-generation American; his parents migrated from eastern Germany. My mother was one-half first-generation American from Russia via Argentina and one-half third-generation American, the descendant of post-Revolution of 1848 German Jewish immigrants.

My father was the first in his family to graduate from college. He received a degree in business administration from the University of Pittsburgh (Pitt) where he was a member of predominantly Jewish fraternity Sigma Alpha Mu. He then served in the U.S. Army Quartermaster Corps in the South Pacific during World War II. He took quiet pride in his service but seldom spoke about his wartime experiences. His only memento was his Bronze Star. He did not repeat the words of patriotic veterans. After the war, he joined the family jewelry business in Braddock.

My mother attended Pitt for one year. She briefly flirted with left-wing movements of the postwar moment. Later taking a few courses in her 50s, she regretted that she never completed her bachelor's degree. Throughout her life, she struggled with insecurity, anxiety, and depression, with counseling early in the marriage. I have no doubts that her story explains in part my own history. It was never discussed at home, early or later. I would like to know more about her experiences.

I grew up with insecurity and anxiety. When I was diagnosed as clinically depressed as a graduate student in Toronto in 1972–1973, my father did not want my mother to know. As part of his longtime marital practice of protecting her, he insisted that we speak in code about "my project" on our telephone conversations and visits.

Affecting my psychological development from an early age, my mother's fears intertwined inseparably with the financial insecurity that befell the new family when my father was hospitalized with tuberculosis in my second year. During the time I grew up at home, she regularly cited examples of wealthy individuals and families, referring frequently to lawyers, physicians, and big businessmen (no women mentioned in the 1950s and 1960s) as exemplars to her children.

Ironically or not, I became a history professor and my younger brother a popular music journalist. We both grew up to write articles and books, albeit in quite different realms of expression and construction. Despite her contradictions, my mother and my father believed that their child-rearing succeeded, and they took great pride in us.

A similar contradiction marked our family environment. My parents were unrelenting in their commitment to fundamental honesty. My brother and I were punished by losing regular privileges if we were caught telling an untruth. At the same time, my mother spent most of her adult life lying about her age. On one hand, she was the proverbial Jack Benny "39" for decades. On the other hand, when voicing a supposedly exact age, she typically shaved several years from the total. A sign of the times, womanhood in transition, or . . . ?

In another sign of the times, mother also rhetorically held up my father as the ultimate arbiter of authority and punishment in the household. This represented a tacit threat in his absence during the daytime. On his part, I believe, my mother's psychological history combined with long-term financial insecurity led him to support her quietly. Given the period, at the least, these issues were never discussed with or in front of the children. The 11-year age difference between my brother Gary and me exacerbated those gaps and silences.

Among my early foundations were a deep faith in the value and necessity of education at least through college; Conservative Judaism; hard work; financial carefulness and security; and respect and fairness for all others. Despite limited resources, my family subscribed to two daily newspapers, weekly and monthly adult and children's magazines, and some book clubs. I grew from *Highlights* to *Boys' Life* and *Sporting News*. Achievement in traditionally literate ways was emphasized. Studying hard and doing well was expected, enforced, and rewarded.

My parents' traditional political liberalism derived from their immigrant industrial-town origins, transition from Orthodox to moderate Judaism, their families' Depression-era experiences, the New Deal, World War II, and Roosevelt-Truman postwar free-world hopefulness. If they passed their anxieties about status and financial security to me along with the imperative to always strive to succeed even at personal cost, they also instilled a commitment to education, equality, fairness, justice, and democracy.

The "origin" story my parents told me is that they met on a date arranged by a former fraternity brother. They fell in love and married in October 1947. After a train trip to New York and Quebec City for their memorable honeymoon, they purchased a home, and my father opened a jewelry business in the nearby town of Greensburg. (For their 50th anniversary, Vicki and I led them along with my brother and his family back to Quebec City.)

First Formations 51

Figure 2.1. Milton and Ruthe Graff, at marriage, 1947.

Figure 2.2. Milton and Ruthe Graff, pregnant with Harvey, 1949.

Figure 2.3. Harvey at age 1, 1950, sitting on a ball.

I arrived 20 months after their marriage. According to family lore, we lived happily for more than a year. But between my first and second birthdays, my father was diagnosed with tuberculosis. He was confined to a Veterans Administration (VA) hospital in Pittsburgh for the better part of the next year.

My earliest memories begin at the time of my father's TB. Dad's hospitalization necessitated radical changes. My parents sold their new family home and business, losing their financial independence and security for decades. My mother and I moved into my grandmother's small apartment on the east side of Pittsburgh near Highland Park. We were supported by the GI Bill, the VA, and my mother's family's hardware business in Sharpsburg, managed by her younger brother and my grandmother. My mother's younger brother, my Uncle Sonny, was the big brother that I otherwise lacked. These events permanently marked my personality development, mental health, and need to achieve.

My early visual memories are associated with occasional visits to see my father in the VA waiting rooms, my grandmother's apartment and nearby public parks, and the family hardware store which also sold toys. For years, I was spoiled by my uncle and grandmother as the family "guinea pig" for new toys. My parents were unhappy about that, long a source of low-level family conflict. My grandmother also introduced me to *The New York Times* Sunday edition at a pre-reading age, initiating a lifelong habit. I long recycled copies of the paper by sharing them with friends and neighbors.

With my father's cure and release from the hospital during my third year, the long search for stability and security recommenced. It continued into my adulthood and my parents' middle to late-middle age.

We resettled in Pittsburgh, not Greensburg. At that time, it was an exciting city, in its iconic and contradictory passage from a dying Steel City to a "model," "new," white-collar, high-er tech town. It was a historical and a future aspirational urban center. It laid the foundation for my love of cities.

The 1950s and 1960s saw the redevelopment of a high-rise downtown at the Golden Triangle. The site of Fort Duquesne and significant in the French and Indian Wars, this is where shining towers cast shadows over the remains of Revolutionary War encampments. New baseball and football stadiums did not yet occupy the center city beside the rivers. Landmark bridges were under construction parallel to old ones. Downtown was still vital; distinctive neighborhoods had thriving shopping and community centers.

The three of us moved into a two-bedroom apartment in a middle-sized complex on the western edge of the predominantly middle-class and substantially Jewish Squirrel Hill neighborhood. We were not far from the Homestead Bridge to another steel town famous for its mills and great strikes across the river from Pittsburgh. I worked in those aging factories in late-adolescent summer jobs to earn money for college. My father returned to work in his brother-in-law's jewelry business in Braddock. My mother stayed home with me.

*Figure 2.4. Harvey at age 5, at Beechwood Gardens Apartments, 1954.*

When I turned three, my parents sent me to full-day nursery school at the local Jewish Community Center for the next two years. Early for the time, it was a mixed experience both in their motivations, as I understand them, and my socialization and learning.

The impetus illustrated their recognition of the importance of beginning schooling early. At the same time, I was not ready for two years of full-time, often boring and sometimes unpleasant interactions with teachers and classmates. I suffered burnout before the time of kindergarten at age five. I remember episodes of discipline for my acting out or intransigence.

Kindergarten at age five in the nearby elementary school was a first step toward my life of learning. Two major memories dominate. The first is punishment and a report to my parents for my acting out in class once or twice. Punishments from spanking or paddling to standing alone in a cloakroom or corner were still common if beginning to dissipate. Criticism and then banning of such punishments came in the 1960s. The other memory is of being an experimental subject in both the Salk and Sabin polio vaccine trials, conducted by the University of Pittsburgh School of Medicine. My family was resolutely pro-vaccine.

As I turned six, we relocated to the other side of Squirrel Hill during the summer between kindergarten and first grade. We moved into one unit of a four-plex on a moderately quiet street one block from Linden Elementary School, where I spent the next eight years. In the mid-1950s, this was a "good," middling, White, and safe neighborhood with many families and their baby boom generation children. We played tag, war games, softball and whiffle ball, basketball, and hula hoops in the streets and backyards that often intersected with each other. We shot cap guns and watched westerns on television.

After mixed educational and social experiences in the first two to three grades, I settled in as a student and was tracked into advanced programs. This was a transitional period for public education, unclearly caught between mild progressivism with its selective tracking by tests, teachers' recommendations, and parental pushes and more traditional, rigid curricula and discipline.

Calls and more active pushes for equity and equality across boundaries were beginning softly in this mixed period after the landmark 1954 Brown v. Board of Education Supreme Court ruling that "separate but equal" is not equal but before the mid-1960s civil and voting rights legislation and court rulings. Fearful White resistance to integration, especially through resegregation by suburbanization, was beginning (for more on this topic, see my "The Nondebate About Critical Race Theory and Our American Moment," 2022d).

In grades one and two, I had occasional discipline problems (and was threatened with paddling on my rear end by the school principal in the unenlightened mid-1950s). There was a more serious but telling dispute between a second or third grade teacher who thought I was left-handed because of the way I practiced cursive handwriting—unsatisfactorily in her estimation—and my mother and pediatrician who were certain that I was not. I remained right-handed. More signs of the transitional times. My life with literacy had begun.

By the end of third grade, I was more comfortable in the advanced stream. Among my memories are the struggle to move from painfully neat printing to legible cursive script and to begin studying elementary French from an Italian American teacher. When Miss P's students got to high school, we were immediately identified by our Italian-inflected French accents.

I remain impressed by my singular status in our third grade 1956 mock presidential election. It was my first and lingering awareness that I was different politically. I was the only one in the class who voted for Adlai Stevenson, the

Democrat, against Ike—Dwight David Eisenhower—the Republican incumbent and commanding World War II general. It was also the first of many times that my candidate was not victorious and I was in the political minority.

My next political lesson was my 11-year-old's enthusiasm for the boyish and then seemingly charming JFK's successful candidacy for president in 1960. Both his "the new frontier" and "Ask not what your country can do for you; ask what you can do for your country" slogans rang loudly to a self-aware preteen. John Kennedy was the last candidate about whom I was excited until I "got clean for Gene" McCarthy as a college freshman and sophomore. I also recall watching Alan Shepard's first suborbital flight in 1961 on a then-large-screen TV in the school auditorium.

From an early age, I was taught racial, ethnic, and gender (long before that word was in play) equality, equity, and tolerance. These teachings came from a combination of explicit parental statements, family and peer examples, liberal democratic values, moderate Judaism, and my own experiences.

The mill town bases of both sides of my family contributed to an expectation of regular, friendly, and respectful interactions with ethnically, religiously, and racially diverse people. My mother's family's hardware store long employed Black skilled workers and served a largely Italian American clientele. My father's family's jewelry business in Braddock served an eastern and southern European and increasingly racially mixed population.

My family employed periodic (every few weeks) Black house cleaners and laundresses/ironers for my father's business shirts and undergarments, an idiosyncratic taste and sign of the times. Although I am cautious not to exaggerate or romanticize our closeness, these workers were treated and we interacted respectfully, "like friends." Or at least that's what it seemed to a growing child and adolescent. Always on first-name basis, we shared family news. They inquired about my schooling, sports, and the like. They regularly reported on the doings of their own families who occasionally would come to pick them up from work. Some attended my Bar Mitzvah at age 13.

I recall the occasion on which my mother decided that I should learn to play the piano. She felt no need to consult me when she purchased a used piano. I was about eight or nine years old and had absolutely no interest in the second- or third-hand baby grand that overcrowded the dining room. After a few months of my unwavering refusal, she sold the cumbersome object to our house cleaner's church for $25.

In retrospect, this limited but important degree of personal experience compensated at least in part for the fact that our residential neighborhoods and public schools were almost completely segregated. The former determined the latter in the early years between the landmark 1954 Brown v. Board of Education Supreme Court decision and the partial changes wrought by the civil rights struggles and irregular residential change of the 1960s.

Two daily Pittsburgh newspapers papers arrived each morning and evening, *The Pittsburgh Press* and the *Pittsburgh Post-Gazette*, along with my grandmother's *The New York Times* on Sundays. *Readers Digest Condensed Books* came quarterly; we read them occasionally. *Life* and *Time* magazines filled the mailbox and the coffee table. *Boys' Life*, *Sports Illustrated*, and then *Sporting News* replaced *Highlights*. By my teens, I began to buy my own books, a habit that got out of hand by graduate school and after, leading my wife and me to buy houses large enough to hold our books, construct built-in bookcases, and reinforce foundations after inspection by structural engineers.

A few shelves of books occupied a place in the living room behind the black and white TV. I was encouraged to read regularly and, as a teenager, encouraged to buy books from local Squirrel Hill booksellers. It was an active, traditionally middle-class, White cultural set of traditionally literate print spaces. In high school, I began to turn my reading to the then New Left. Most—but not quite all, especially in the mid-to-late 1960s—kinds of music were tolerated, if not always appreciated.

Less manipulative but supportive was the long-distance support of Uncle Charles, my grandmother's older brother. He was an international oil company and diamond mining engineer who lived in New York City with his wife Marion. Charles was the "black sheep" of the family. First-born and educated at Carnegie Tech (later Carnegie Mellon University), he left Pittsburgh instead of remaining to help finance his younger brothers' educations. He assisted a Belgian exploration company in developing colonial resources in the then Belgian Congo where he knew kings and tribal leaders.

He and his little sister Bertha (my grandmother Nan to the world) remained close. From a distance, he actively loved and supported me. For more than 15 years, he mailed me a monthly check for $10. When I visited him in New York City (including a memorable lunch with Vicki on our first trip together to the city), he and Marion gave me hand-me-down luggage, briefcase, neck ties, a miniature set of Shakespeare's works that Marion won as a private school girl, and scarves for Vicki. He enthusiastically encouraged my education. The Shakespeare set resides on the mantle in my study.

Regrettably, elementary school was the last time that learning about science interested me. Eighth grade physics left me uninvolved and distracted. Then and later in high school, as with so many other U.S. school children, the problem was in large part poor teaching combined with poor textbooks. For my cohort, this problem was exacerbated by our status between traditional science texts and instructional styles and the new, post-Sputnik, innovative and active approaches that began in the early 1960s. These approaches appeared under various abbreviations, such as BSCS for biology, PSSC for physics, and often as "project" or "new" biology, chemistry, physics, and math.

I was partly lost and partly turned off by the many "news" combined with off-again, on-again instruction. Some of us learned to play bridge quietly in the back corner of our seventh grade biology class taught, literally, by Miss Mildred Hinderer. At least as often, the old appealed to me more than the new. This continued through high school science and off and on with math, although I learned to fool instructors with integral calculus equations and such.

Innovative and transitional social studies and English/language arts classes proved more to my liking and abilities. In retrospect, those subjects and their often young and innovative teachers who emphasized primary texts laid the foundations on which my best high school and university history and social science and high school English teachers built. The personal, the academic, and the place—with the political beginning its influence—began to emerge in my first four to eight years of schooling and increased steadily. At first, history and the social sciences followed behind languages and math in their appeal to me Clearer links between understanding myself and my world in contemporary and historical context developed in high school. My life with literacy developed.

Nonacademic subjects deepened my understanding negatively and positively. I inherited my mother's inability to carry a musical tune, although I like to sing or hum. In third grade music class, the old-fashioned teacher ordered me *not* to sing and positioned four of us presumed talentless students in the classroom's four corners. This left a small but lingering scar, leading me to do most of my singing in showers. My wife tells me that in my 60s and 70s, I more often carry a tune.

My music teacher's small slap to my young ego was countered by the school's participation in the Pittsburgh Symphony's Young Peoples Concerts series. We were bused to the concert hall several times a year to hear the renowned symphony led by remarkable conductor William Steinberg play the classics.

Another treat was a class outing to an early live recording of *Mr. Rogers' Neighborhood*, the iconic, early public television children's program. I appeared on the still-new TV screen. The program originated at Pittsburgh's pioneering WQED station before PBS television and NPR radio were organized.

Health class—physical education and hygiene—was worse than music. Taught by the coach, hygiene was contentless, especially in any material that might actually help a child of, say, 8 to 13. Anatomy, physiology, sexuality, or disease transmission were seldom if ever mentioned. In gym, Coach did his best *not* to instruct or instill an appreciation of either physical prowess or exercise. He had no organized school teams or leagues to actually coach despite his title! His specialty was shooting underhand baskets standing by himself in any open basketball court.

By the sixth to eighth grades, the fault lines of my hierarchical and competitive social worlds emerged: the combined intersections of the overlap of the social, cultural, and educational realm, revealingly close to the economic, and internalization of the subtle and overt pressure to achieve. Following chapters will reveal how this played out, especially in the academic and social tracks. It is a lifelong dynamic and dialectic and set of contradictions, not at all exceptional to my experiences.

One crack in that wall of intersections appeared with the required seventh and eighth grade, one-half-day-each-week, woodshop and mechanical drawing class—aka "prevocational training" for nonvocational students. We walked a moderate distance from Linden Elementary School to another school in a neighborhood more mixed along class, ethnic, and racial lines just outside of Squirrel Hill.

The official premise of going to these classes was that we were learning valuable life skills and also an introduction to working manually. The experience was all but useless, other than reinforcing nonvocational preferences and prejudices. The small prizes we made in these classes that our families displayed typically in kitchens were wall-mounted notepaper roll holders and little three-legged stools that we laboriously fashioned and proudly presented to them. Cooking and home economics, required for the girls in our class, would have served me much better. I had no choice, of course.

My early foundations embraced family, friends, play, and religious education in addition to public schooling. We were a close-knit family, often mixing with grandmother and mother's younger brother, many aunts, uncles, and cousins, as well as neighbors. At times, I felt closely connected; at other times, more of an outsider, especially as my intellectual and political interests developed and as a competitive and sometimes inhumane teen social life developed, a pattern of conflicts and contradictions to which I became accustomed.

My father worked long hours, often falling asleep in the living room after dinner with the newspaper on his lap. He was not athletic, barely able to help me when I was young mount my two-wheeled bicycle without its training wheels or throw a baseball.

In my late elementary and middle school years, my mother had not yet returned to her own forms of work. As I moved into middle school grades, she gave up awakening early to serve me breakfast and see me on my way to school. I missed that but never complained. At about that time, I learned by myself to replace shirt buttons that fell off—very poorly. Housekeeping duties were never my mother's forte, a disaffinity I inherited.

Mother did greet me at the door on my return home in the afternoon. Together, mother and dad were no-nonsense about the priority of my studies, which came before play, setting a lifelong pattern. They were not inflexible, but they were firm, their expectations for excellence clear. I felt both implicit and explicit pressures. To their credit, they did not succumb to the excesses of my grandmother who rewarded each "A" on my report cards with $1. That left a small but unfortunate sub- or semi-conscious imprint.

My street and the adjoining blocks were full of children approximately my age. We were the baby boomers, the postwar American generation, overflowing, primed for achievement, and often pushed beyond fair expectations and trapped in social, cultural, and economic contradictions of the times and place. The lines between friendly contests and divisive, fun-destroying competition were thin, often brittle. I learned this in neighborhood games of tag, whiffle ball, and basketball and in my short time in both Cub Scouts and Little League. I was not a joiner. I did not follow the leader well. This tendency marked my college and graduate school experiences and my scholarly career.

Soccer on the school field at recess was one informal, less competitive respite. Little League, from which I dropped out quickly, was not. My pseudo big brother

Uncle Sonny tried to pass on his passion for golf, basketball, and tennis. As soon as I was able, I walked the golf course with him on weekend mornings. I played golf for a few years with junior-sized clubs that he gave me, bicycling to the nearby public course. Eclipsed by tennis, it didn't stick. An early interest in tennis long proved satisfying. As a teen, I often played at my family's modest swimming club, continuing illegally after they ended their membership, and with schoolmates.

My early teenage competitive experiment was short-lived. The thin lines between fist fights on the street and in organized boxing sessions at the Young Men's and Young Women's Hebrew Association were another element of this culture of competition. My continued interest in sports fell into individual sports and noncompetitive play rather than team sports. I enjoyed watching the major sports championships on television and occasionally in person.

Especially pleasurable were the broad interests across the family and throughout the community in Pittsburgh's iconic professional baseball team, the Pirates, and football team, the Steelers. My father and uncle splurged on tickets for games, including season tickets for the Steelers as I approached and into my teen years. I often attended games, bundled up for late fall weather, with them or with schoolmates.

Both teams were led by stars like the Pirates' outfielder Roberto Clemente and the Steelers' sports-betting quarterback Bobby Lane, with almost equally outstanding players on both teams, such as baseball players Dick Stuart and Dick Groat and footballers John Henry Johnson, Jimmie Orr, and Ernie Stautner. Among the strongest memories of my childhood is the Pirates' 1960 seven-game victory over the heavily favored New York Yankees. Bill Mazeroski's and Dick Stuart's game-winning performances are frozen in the eyes of Pittsburghers. Some of the plays are etched in the annals of sports history. Some years are best forgotten.

~~~

Other formative experiences and memories surround my haphazard religious education. Our family proudly identified as recently immigrated American Jews, more culturally than religiously observant. When my active bachelor Uncle Sonny finally married Janet, a non-Jewish woman, in the mid-1960s, she converted to Judaism with instruction at a Reform temple.

My parents continued the orientation of their upbringing as Conservative or moderate Jews, as opposed to more liberal Reform or much stricter Orthodox Jews. Although they had been raised in more traditional synagogues, my parents chose the Conservative Tree of Life synagogue not far from our house and near my elementary school as their decades-long base. (This was the site of an antisemitic mass murder in 2021.)

The cultural slang for their orientation—"three-days-a-year Jews"—described our practice. Religious attendance was mandated for the High Holy Days: the autumn celebration of the Jewish New Year called Rosh Hashanah (on the distinctive Jewish calendar), and the Day of Atonement called Yom Kippur. The latter is a day of prayer and fasting. I fasted inconsistently as a child and teen and never again after my first year in college when I fasted and then proceeded to get drunk like a typical, 18-year-old college freshman! My religious attendance and practice substantially stopped after my Bar Mitzvah at age 13 and effectively ended when I left home for college other than close friends' and families' celebrations. Learning about the multiple meanings of Israeli Zionism and the troubled history of Israelis and Palestinians helped to push me away, long before the events of October 7, 2023, and their aftermath.

Following parental ideals, I began weekly Sunday school sessions during my mid-primary-school years and Bar Mitzvah (or for girls Bat Mitzvah) classes, led by the synagogue's cantor, several years before my 13th birthday. That is the date for the ceremonial passage to "man- or womanhood" in the Jewish faith.

Neither set of classes appealed to me. They were a chore, with a dominating emphasis on memorization, softly but uncompromisingly compelled by my parents. The Sunday school curriculum was murky at best, a confusing mélange of Jewish history, Old Testament Scriptures, moderate rather than zealous Zionist support for Israeli independence and a Jewish state, and an insufficient bit of comparative religion.

*Figure 2.5. Harvey at age 13, Bar Mitzvah, June 1962. Photo by Wolowietz.*

This admixture is summed up well practically and symbolically in the substantial number of trees planted in my name in Israel through contributions from my few dollars a week allowance in reward for household chores and small exercises in familial fundraising. I left Sunday school shortly after I was Bar Mitzvah'ed, resisting pleas and invitations to continue on to the "college of Jewish studies" for high school-age students and beyond. I had no interest. If narrowly defined religious belief and practice never appealed to me, a deeply felt ecumenism and "faith" in and respect for all religions and all persons did. That is not insignificant.

The Bar Mitzvah experience among middle- and upper-middle-class, urban and suburban Jewish families is long and complicated. It is much more than a religious rite; it is a time of joy, accomplishment, stress, and competition among young people entering their teen years and puberty and their families. For my circle, based largely but not exclusively in Squirrel Hill, Linden School, and the Tree of Life synagogue, it began before the 13th birthday. For the baby boom cohort, the immersion was multi-year.

It commenced with the Bar and Bat Mitzvahs of older cousins and siblings, Hebrew school for our preparations, seventh and eighth grade dancing classes to prepare for the new teens' parties that were inseparable from the larger constellation of events, and a full year of events during which each of us turned 13.

I recall with laughter more than 60 years later the silly Genevieve Jones, our local middle-aged dance teacher. Leading by hilarious personal exhibition, she tried to take 12-year-olds experiencing coeducational, heterosexual, awkward, and sometimes stressful and competitive early adolescence through the two-step, four-step, waltz, jitterbug, and close and distanced partnering. New to our era were the Twist, Pony, Freddie, Hitch-Hike, Loco-motion, and Mashed Potato. Among the countless moves of the times were the Shimmy, Swim, Boogaloo, Bristol Stomp, Chicken, Drag, Hully Gully, Jerk, Monkey, Strut, and more. It was a lot to learn and practice. I had the great and loving assistance of my older cousin Sharon, who lived two blocks from our house.

A seemingly never-ending cycle of Saturday morning (and for some Reform Jews Friday evening for girls' Bat Mitzvahs) services at which the Bar or Bat Mitzvah boy or girl read from the Holy Torah, chanted a bit, and made a little speech thanking everyone and calling for peace and happiness, occupied my 13th year. These were shared, celebratory moments that occupied part of almost every weekend.

After large, catered luncheons, parties often with disk jockeys (on rare occasions a small band) playing the tunes of the day with occasional hits of the past for parents and relatives occupied Saturday evenings. Bar and Bat Mitzvah was a Saturday (or Friday and Saturday for young women) spectacle as we struggled to outdress, outdance, and be cooler than the other 13-year-olds.

These were the showpieces of the rite of passage for the principals and their associates. They were intensely competitive for parents and 13-year-olds. This was the end of elementary school, for most the end of formal religious education, the experience of puberty and early adolescence, and more: a heavily weighted and freighted time.

For my family, the Bar Mitzvah season came less than two years after the birth of my younger brother Gary on November 7, 1960, JFK's election date. I was 11. My parents' unusual family planning, with more than a decade between the births of their two sons, was never discussed with me. I was surprised but joyous to welcome a lovable little sibling and become a big brother after more than a decade as a sometimes-lonely only child. After his first year or so, with his crib in my parents' bedroom, he shared my bedroom.

A sign of the times in gender norms and expectations, my father resisted baby care. At 11, I changed diapers and dealt with the soiled diaper pail in the days before disposable diapers. Within a couple of years, I was declared the "built-in babysitter" whose family obligations took precedence over his emerging, adolescent social life. I was not pleased about that.

My little brother and I were always close, limited by physical separation when I left home for college at 18 and he was not yet 7. He learned mixed lessons from me. His observations taught him to exclaim, "damn it" ("dammit," in his memory), when his building blocks tumbled down. I taught him to go on strike—in Spanish, no doubt an influence from Cesar Chavez' organizing for immigrant farm workers. And his term of condemnation was "that's riskusking" (translation: "that's disgusting"). The sentimental little fellow cried when I departed for college and later cried at the airport when my future wife and I left after visiting Pittsburgh.

My achievements were at first a problem for a younger brother to counter. But as he grew into his later high school years, his talent for journalism began to shine. Editor of the Allderdice High School newspaper, he was also a stringer for *The Pittsburgh Press*. Graduating journalism school at the University of Missouri where he also wrote for national newspapers, he accepted a position as popular music critic for the *Detroit Free Press*.

Not long after Gary's arrival, without much discussion in front of me at least, my mother returned to work for the first time since marriage. The example of the Bar Mitzvah year and the success of my events stimulated her to put her shingle out as a social consultant. This not-quite profession preoccupied her for the next few decades. Working with caterers and florists; stationers and calligraphers; owners of social halls, restaurants, and country clubs; even car and van renters; and the like, she planned social events, most of them weddings and Bar and Bat Mitzvahs.

Her never-quite-successful business venture could dominate the household. Long before cell phones, mother managed to tie up two phone lines simultaneously with her solicitations, negotiations, and consultations. I recall evenings and weekends in which my father and I, with a little help from young Gary, prepared bags of paper rose petals for wedding guests to throw at newlyweds in lieu of the rice that was banned in sanctuaries, wedding halls, and hotels. The paper petals stuck together in their manufacture. They needed to be fluffed out in the clothes dryer, then counted and packed in small plastic bags tied with tiny plastic bows. The guys in the house did not enjoy this task. A decade later on visits to my family, Vicki made corrections to calligraphy on invitations and name cards.

I also recall my first social date in my late 12th or 13th year with a female neighbor and eighth grade classmate named Bess. I played ball with her brothers and their dog. My father drove us to a local movie theater on a Saturday afternoon. After the film, we went out either for ice cream or pizza. I am certain that there was no touching, not even holding hands. At that age, as well as I can recall, girls and boys were more or less equal, except for competitive sports and who paid. That soon changed.

My 13th year, and this second chapter, ends with elementary school graduation in June 1963. I have no distinct memories of this event. That summer we moved back to the other side of Squirrel Hill to a duplex with our first owner-occupied house since I was an infant. It had separate bedrooms for my brother and me. Happily, it was only four blocks from Taylor Allderdice High School where I started on the pre-collegiate, advanced track the day after Labor Day in September 1963.

# Chapter 3. Coming of Age in Pittsburgh, Squirrel Hill, and Taylor Allderdice High School, 1963–1967

Life changed in too many ways to remember or recount with my transition from 8th to 9th grade and from my K-8 elementary school to a large (more than 3,000 students) 7th to 12th grade public high school in Squirrel Hill. Built in 1927, almost 40 years later it was the newest public high school building in Pittsburgh. Reflecting the neighborhood, it was by far the best academically but among the worst athletically. Extending through my college years at Northwestern University, that was another sign of the times.

That passage into high school brought all the personal and symbolic weight that the myths of social psychology and the fictions of "great transitions" convey. I see clearly how my teen years combined inseparably and uncomfortably the best and the worst of the process of growing up in 1960s middle-class, urban America (for more on growing up in America during this time, see my *Conflicting Paths*, 1995a).

Whatever its idiosyncrasies, the second stage of my pre-adult life formation lay in a series of intersecting conflicts. The seminal writings of the social psychologists that emerged in the same period underscored and elaborated on these conflicts. Chief among them were Erik H. Erikson (1950, 1968), Kenneth Keniston (1965, 1968, 1971), and David Elkind (1981, 1984, 1987). Also influential were sociologists Glen H. Elder, Jr. (1974/1999), James S. Coleman (1961), and Coleman and colleagues (1974) and historian Joseph F. Kett (1977). Documentarian Frederick Wiseman's film *High School* (1968) brilliantly and controversially captured the in-school dynamics.

Not surprisingly (especially to readers familiar with my historical work), conflict and contradiction ruled and integrated my social framework and personal experience (see my works *Conflicting Paths*, 1995a, *Growing Up in America*, 1987a, and *The Literacy Myth*, 1979c). Three are most vivid in memory and my experiences: in-school, often related to achievement but also social cliques and conflicts; common intrafamilial stresses; and extracurricular, organized, and disorganized teenage social life.

In a nutshell, I was successful in my classes and tests but never the top student. At home, I experienced regular, implicit, and explicit pressures to succeed and was told of too many examples, especially from my mother, of wealthy lawyers, doctors, and businesspeople (all male of course). Socially I was never unpopular but never very popular. I had friends and a few girlfriends but was not part of the "cool" and the "in" kids. At times, I was satisfied and comfortable, at other times, insecure, anxious, and depressed. In retrospect, I can see how the latter two pressed on the former as I took steps, at best semiconsciously, toward my developing life with literacy.

There are many lenses through which to view these events. They are interconnected not only with each other but also with the epochal 1960s. Shelves of books have been written about one or another of the many 1960s, including the memoirs of Mickey and Dick Flacks (2018) and Paul Lauter (2020) and the intellectual autobiography of Russian historian Lewis H. Siegelbaum (2019), noted in the Introduction (for the best recent introduction to the era, see Kevin Boyle, 2021, and its references; see also the literature I cited in the Introduction).

The historical political context of the time is inescapable, even overdetermining. For some but not all, this was the radical, rebellious 1960s. The usually noted defining events began with John F. Kennedy's 1960 election and his 1963 assassination in Dallas. At the moment that JFK's death was announced, I was sitting in a miserable "new" geometry class whose ineffectual instructor did not know what to do in response to the news broadcast on the PA system by the school principal. A bright and idiosyncratic classmate (a future professor of political economy in Texas) calmly lectured the rest of us about the history of presidential assassinations, one of his interests that was unknown to the rest of us.

To a social historian, the origins of the period lie in the New Deal, the aftermath of World War II, and the contradictions of early civil rights struggles inextricably interrelated to segregation and racism (see my "The Nondebate About Critical Race Theory and Our American Moment," 2022d). The context of the time includes the great moments of the civil rights movement: President Truman's integration of the armed forces and arming of Black soldiers after World War II, school desegregation, boycotts, beatings, marches to Selma, Freedom Rides, murders of activists in Mississippi, Civil Rights, Voting Rights, and other legislative triumphs of Lyndon Johnson's "Great Society." There are also western democracy's battle against Soviet communism; the space race; the struggles for immigrant rights; the early growth of the feminist and LBGTQ movements; the diverse counterculture of radical youths; and the early, organized, anti-Vietnam War movement with the Port Huron Statement, the University of California at Berkeley free speech rallies and sit-ins, and the founding of Students for a Democratic Society (SDS) and Mobilization Against the War (MOBE).

Until college, I experienced much of this on the national evening news, daily newspapers, and weekly magazines like *Time*, *Newsweek*, and *U.S. News and World Report*. There were some influential occasions of direct personal and learning experiences, too. Most memorable was the mid-1960s national grape boycott, launched by the United Farm Workers with Cesar Chavez in support of the largely Mexican American immigrant workers' rights to organize for a living wage and humane treatment. From its California origins, it spread nationally. The lawyer-father of a school and neighborhood friend took his slightly younger son and me to the local Giant Eagle grocery store to protest the sale of nonunion grapes and to picket on a Saturday. That was my first organized protest. Among the consequences: I lost my taste for raw grapes forever.

This was my first activist experience. It was memorable and educational. Early interests and my limited adolescent involvement in both the civil rights and antiwar movements stimulated me. So too did the foundational role of Pittsburgh in both labor history and Black history. Together, they created expectations for union activism that were dampened by my summer union membership experiences with the Amalgamated Iron, Steel, and Bridge Workers in 1967 and the United Steel Workers in 1968 while laboring to earn money for college.

Reflecting my age and idealism, I took a date to a union meeting, only to witness a near fistfight over planning for the upcoming Fourth of July picnic. It was not the lively discussion of the political economy of unionism and activism for which Sally and I naively hoped.

Among the underpinnings for almost all versions of the 1960s was a relatively healthy economy for many (though certainly not all) that fueled the broad middle class. Massive, monopolistic, corporate capitalism was spreading but did not reach the heights of the *fin-de-siècle* and after. Socioeconomic critics like Ralph Nader had more powerful microphones and larger audiences than their successors would find by the 1990s and later.

Labor unions were perched precariously at their historical height. Simultaneously, the college-educated, white-collar, often professional middle class expanded significantly. It was a great era for public university, college, and community college foundations and growth—and their contradictions (among many sources on these topics, see Mattingly, 2017; my forthcoming *Reconstructing the "Uni-versity" from the Ashes of the "Mega- and Multi-versity"* addresses these topics as well).

Urban deconcentration and suburbanization accelerated with hopefulness for the predominantly White, middle-class, two-parent families who could afford to pay or borrow for postsecondary education. Public schools were just beginning to be challenged on both real and false grounds of decline and charges of either genuine racial discrimination, especially in the suburbs. Busing for school integration in the wake of efforts to make good on the promise of the landmark 1954 Brown v. Board of Education ruling that "separate but equal" is not equal prompted protests from White people in cities and suburbs.

Toward the end of the decade, when my younger brother's cohort was threatened with being bused away from neighborhood public schools, my generally liberal mother spoke about picketing the Pittsburgh Board of Education. I told her that I would disown her, at least rhetorically. She did not follow through, nor was my brother bused.

The social and cultural dimensions of the often exaggerated, incessantly caricatured 1960s are exciting and divisive. The culture—along with the politics, society, and economy—reflected a complex blend of the novel and the historical: a search for the new within the parameters of the ever-changing past. Of course, I did not understand this until I got well into my graduate studies and after.

Rock music of the 1960s exploded from the various combinations of gospel, jazz, blues, folk, rock and roll, and British roots and invasion. My generation, along with those a little older and younger, loved it. Our parents did not. They grasped onto the final days of Frank Sinatra, Frankie Lane, Perry Como, Eddie Fisher, Harry Belafonte, Johnny Mathis, Nat King Cole, Sarah Vaughan, Ella Fitzgerald, and Duke Ellington. Ed Sullivan's iconic TV show became a barometer of change.

We listened, hummed, sang, swayed, and danced, and we purchased 45 rpm and increasingly 33 rpm, long-playing albums from record, grocery, and department stores. I received my first pocket-sized transistor radio when I was eight or nine years old. Personal devices in their early forms literally amplified pop music, widely broadcast on AM frequencies. Small audiotape cassettes and players increased its surrounding presence. As mentioned in the preceding chapter, dozens of dance steps and moves competed for our uneven, often unbalanced, talents. Pittsburgh's own DJ Porky Chadwick on the Black rock channel WAMO became a national influencer. He was "the Daddio of the Radio."

A list of the dominant emphases in popular musical culture only begins to convey its widening presence and influence. The historical legacy ranges from 1920s–1940s folk and pop to late 1950s Elvis Presley and Sam Cooke; also significant were Black artists Odetta, Ray Charles, B. B. King, Little Richard, James Brown, The Temptations, Smokey Robinson and the Miracles, Marvin Gaye, Aretha Franklin, Diana Ross and the Supremes, Ike and Tina Turner, the Jackson Five, and Stevie Wonder.

Before and beside them are two or more generations of folk singers from Pete Seeger to The Weavers; Woody Guthrie; The Kingston Trio; Phil Ochs; Tom Paxton; Buffy Sainte-Marie; Judy Collins; Gordon Lightfoot; Arlo Guthrie; Peter, Paul, and Mary; the Mamas and the Papas; Chad and Jeremy; Simon and Garfunkle; Bob Dylan; Joan Baez; Joni Mitchell; Laura Nyro; and The Lovin' Spoonful.

They were joined by the new pop music that combined the so-called "British invasion" (influenced by American blues, folk, and rock) and Americans: the Byrds; the Beatles; the Rolling Stones; Freddie and the Dreamers; the Dave Clark Five; the Beach Boys; Jimi Hendrix; Crosby, Stills, Nash & Young; and so many more.

Music is the best known of the defining cultural thrusts of the era. Fiction and nonfiction literature are also key ingredients, characteristics, and influences. From about 10th grade, I began buying books and reading outside the curriculum and beyond the shelves of *Readers' Digest Condensed Books* at home and assigned texts in high school.

Influential then and later among fiction works and their authors were women and Black writers—sometimes more or less jokingly (unlike in 2021–2022) "banned in Boston"—including Harper Lee's *To Kill a Mockingbird*, Doris Lessing's *The Golden Notebook*, Sylvia Plath's *The Bell Jar*, Mary McCarthy's *The Group*, and James Baldwin's *The Fire Next Time*. No less important were Joseph Heller's

*Catch-22*, Henry Miller's *Tropic of Cancer*, J. D. Salinger's *Franny and Zooey*, Richard Yates' *Revolutionary Road*, Anthony Burgess' *A Clockwork Orange*, Ken Kesey's *One Flew Over the Cuckoo's Nest* and *Sometimes a Great Notion*, Edward Albee's *Who's Afraid of Virginia Woolf?*, Thomas Pynchon's *V* and *The Crying of Lot 49*, Kurt Vonnegut's *Cat's Cradle*, and William Styron's *The Confessions of Nat Turner* (on book banning, see my essays "The History of Book Banning," 2021p, and "Book Banning Past and Present," 2022a).

Expanding and diversifying influences of nonfiction works made important contributions to the era. The most influential, some of them soon classics, included Betty Friedan's *The Feminine Mystique*, Malcolm X and Alex Haley's *The Autobiography of Malcolm X*, Rachel Carson's *Silent Spring*, Helen Gurley Brown's *Sex and the Single Girl*, Michael Harrington's *The Other America*, Ralph Nader's *Unsafe at Any Speed*, Anaïs Nin's *The Diary of Anais Nin*, Claude Lévi-Strauss' *The Savage Mind* (English translation), and James D. Watson's *The Double Helix*. I read some of them in high school and some in college. I also began to read history, politics, and sociocultural criticism outside of my classes, discovering the New Left and revisionism before they acquired those names. Most of these books remain on my bookshelves, documenting formative phases of my life with literacy.

Films, mainly at indoor theaters until we began to earn our driver's licenses at age 16 and borrow the family car to fill drive-in theaters, were basic to our entertainment and cultural formation. Long before "media literacy" competed for space in course rosters and journals, we teenagers were aware of the inseparable interactions of print, film, and audio, among other media. Even without Harold A. Innis' (1951) and Marshall McLuhan's (1962, 1964) influences, let alone cultural studies, we grappled with the challenges of reading and writing about different modes of expression. This is how I began to define literacy in graduate school and continuing (for discussion and references, see my *Searching for Literacy*, 2022e.)

Movies mainly from large American studios, but increasingly from Europe, helped to define the age and our ages. These years saw me passage from viewing *en famille* to same gender-same age outings and then to heterosexual dates. Reflecting the same currents as politics and literature, the great films of the first two-thirds of the 1960s included *A Raisin in the Sun*, *To Kill a Mockingbird*, *The Manchurian Candidate*, *A Hard Day's Night*, *Dr. Strangelove or: How I Learned to Stop Worrying and Love the Bomb*, *8½*, *Repulsion*, *Cool Hand Luke*, *Bonnie and Clyde*, *The Graduate*, and the iconic James Bond films. French and Italian films barely scratched the mass market or came to the attention of teens. They became among my joys beginning in college.

The music, fiction and nonfiction books, and films of the era all reflected the social and cultural politics of war and peace; struggles for civil rights and racial equality; feminism and gender equality; political economics and the environment; and cross-cultural connections. The sexual revolution and the women's movement were increasingly visible along with calls for peace and justice as I entered and moved through high school.

These many currents combined, sometimes smoothly, sometimes contradictorily, in the rapidly growing and distinctive bodies of political, social, and cultural commentary and criticism that characterized the times. At first, the emerging critical schools were reminiscent of currents of the 1930s which had largely but not completely paused during the 1940s–1950s.

The 1960s were marked by criticism across professions and disciplines from such distinctive figures as Paul Goodman, Saul Alinsky, Herbert Marcuse, early Paulo Freire, Malcom X and other Black activists, and the emergent New Left and feminist movements. They appeared in both longstanding and new publications like the *New Left Review, Dissent, Radical America, In These Times*, and the older *The Nation* and *The New Republic* and publicized in *The New York Review of Books*. Frequent concerns included critiques of social inequality, racial discrimination, public education, state and federal policies, mainline conservative and liberal values, and sexual and gender mores. This was a great age for independent journalists across the world. They increasingly defined my extracurricular reading and writing as I moved through high school to college.

In the pre-social media and pre-internet age of print dominance, the messages were amplified regularly and widely. By about 10th or 11th grade, English and American New Left historians began to catch my eye. In the mix were Michel Foucault and the modern French heirs to Marc Bloch and Henri Lefebvre and the English Marxists like E. P. Thompson and Eric Hobsbawm.

The connections between these currents and their articulation, my high school education, extracurricular activities, and personal development are inextricably and complexly interrelated. They shaped my expanding and deepening uses of literacy.

~~~

Enter the hallowed halls of Allderdice High School with me in September 1963, after a summer working as a deliverer, counter clerk, and soda jerk at a local drugstore for a few dollars an hour. Because of my age and the small size of the neighborhood establishment, I delivered by bicycle. I partially compensated for the meagre pay by snacking freely from the soda bar. Just before school started, we moved houses from one side of Squirrel Hill to the other.

Allderdice is a quite large, public, city school, known widely for its academics. In the third quarter of the 20th century, it held more than 3,000 students, including the grades seven to nine junior high division. It often finished closely behind elite private schools in the Philadelphia area for the most National Merit Scholars, Finalists, and Semifinalists in Pennsylvania. As a very good, very White, and very middle-class urban school, it was academically stratified into two tracks: the advanced, college-bound and the vocational streams. The first was comparatively large and the latter small. The vocational track students attended another facility part of the school week for the necessary training equipment.

As an incoming advanced-track student successfully graduated from eighth grade and expecting to attend college for at least one degree, I was excited. I recall my disinterest and displeasure in the traditional chemistry class after "new" elementary school courses. Between the text and the teacher, the "new" geometry was also a total loss. English, civics, and French brought more pleasurable and productive memories along with expansion of my reading and writing abilities.

Ninth grade social studies were a tantalizing harbinger of courses to come. Working closely with "Project Social Studies" at then Carnegie Tech in Pittsburgh and without a printed textbook, my teacher presented a comparative and cross-cultural course. Almost 60 years later, I recall an exciting unit on the European Renaissance (to which I returned the next years in World and Advanced Placement European History) and a photo essay assignment that I conducted with a classmate at a local arts center.

This was 1963–1964. Not yet conscious of it, I was learning the critical common elements of reading and writing across subjects and different modes of understanding and communications. Failure to recognize the challenges and complexities of literacy more generally was promoted in grossly exaggerated versions in the proliferation of proclaimed "new literacies" a few decades later. That was not the rhetoric of the 1960s. My classmates and I were introduced to reading and writing across print, pictures still and moving, and early "new media" even before the "age of Marshall McLuhan."

With exceptions mainly in math and science, my teachers were young, talented, personable, and keenly interested in their students. A number worked with faculty at the University of Pittsburgh and Carnegie Tech on experimental history, social studies, and literature curricula. Some pursued Ph.D.s and Ed.D.s. Most had M.A. or M.Ed. degrees. In their classrooms, competition was under control and participation encouraged, almost demanded. Ninth grade was satisfying in fair measure because it did not yet carry the academic or the social stresses that came with pre-college 10th through 12th grades—punctuated with PSAT and SAT exams and our more complicated and organized heterosexual social life.

Tenth grade was different. On the one hand, there was the disorganized and inequitable adolescent fraternity "rush." Our high school cliques were much less organized, less impressive, and less offensive than the collegiate. But there was some prestige to belonging as well as new "brothers" to "assist" 14-year-olds in mastering the tools of active, mid-teen socializing with both young males and females. Although I was interested in one of the two or three predominantly Jewish associations, I was not invited to pledge. This was a moderate blow to self-esteem and to my confidence in obtaining invitations to parties and beginning heterosexual dating.

On the other hand, my classes were much more inviting and exciting. Most crucial at the time and for my future was World History for advanced-track students, a precursor of Advanced Placement courses in the next two grades. My teacher was Bruce Forry who also taught Advanced Placement European History to the 12th grade. He was my first academic model and example. (I refrain from using the traditional term "mentor" because my female colleagues convince me that, in their experience, it is inseparable from power relations; see my "The Power of Models and Examples in Education and Higher Education," 2023e). It is no exaggeration to state that between the two courses, Bruce (as I later began to call him) laid the paving stones that led—with some twists and turns—to my undergraduate history major and then to graduate school, my M.A. and Ph.D., and more than 40 years as a history professor.

I well recall my chatting with him at my 40th high school reunion, the only one I attended, and informing him that he was responsible for the central course of my life from age 15 to that moment. In June 2022, I reached him by telephone to tell him about this book. He was delighted! In April 2023, Vicki and I treated him to a memorable three-hour lunch on a visit to Pittsburgh. Some learning and teaching relationships are lifelong.

In Forry's classes as well as in 11th grade Advanced Placement United States History and advanced track and AP English classes, we read college-level texts supplemented with many primary documents, much like good college courses. These exceptional instructors introduced them to us and demanded that we practice advanced literacy skills across diverse texts and media.

I first read Karl Marx, Friedrich Engels, and *The Communist Manifesto* in high school history courses. I was introduced to classics of ancient, European, and American history and civilization. Another sign of the times was the absence of Asia, Africa, South America, and Canada in these courses. My only non-western high school or university course was the timely, special Vietnam seminar at Northwestern University. Graduate studies in Toronto introduced me to Canadian history and literature, but at 75, I am still learning about other parts of the world. Doctoral students taught me about China and Turkmenistan, for example, and over decades, colleagues across disciplines taught me about their subject areas. That learning continues in retirement.

Hand in hand with the focus on advanced texts, a few monographs, and primary documents—in English and literature courses, too—classes were primarily seminar-style discussion sessions with our chairs arranged to form a circle. Although that formation assisted a bit of "collaborative" work on in-class exams (for which Forry once reprimanded me), it overwhelmingly boosted our engagement, involvement, interactions, and active learning. I still remember Forry's unusual ability to cross his legs at the knees and have the crossed leg's foot flat on the floor! At least as important were challenging writing, library, and out-of-school research projects and papers. I was well prepared for university.

As I grew older, I increasingly regretted the substantial failure of high school (as well as grade school) science and math courses. As in elementary school, they irregularly alternated between traditional and "experimental." Among the textbooks, classroom exercises, teachers, and my own developing interests, I turned away from science by about eighth grade and math after 10th grade algebra II and partly through 11th grade calculus. Grade 11 physics was my last high school science course (followed by two quarters of uninteresting, lower-division astronomy to meet my only college math and science requirement in my first year at university). I faked my way through Astronomy I and II by intimidating the teaching assistant with equations learned in high school calculus.

In high school I enjoyed and did well in Algebra I and II, while geometry failed me, repeating a pattern from elementary school. I also did well in 11th grade calculus, which was less well taught. The teacher nominated me for a national math exam, and to my surprise I finished in the high percentiles, winning a certificate of achievement. Combined with my algebra classes, that class provided the basics to fool my way to a passing score on the AP calculus test and college credits. That was the last math class I took, not counting informal instruction in statistics in graduate school.

The final, important high school contribution to my growth was active participation on the school debate team, especially in grades 10 through 12. The debate coaching was poor. None of us, all teenage boys with no probable cause for suspicion, wanted to share a motel room with our young Latin teacher-sponsor on road trips to away events. I benefitted from the debate practice in learning to organize both arguments and evidence. Our team did relatively well, winning some local and regional tournaments.

The annual debate topics, which I no longer remember, were stilted versions of current events. Our abilities and those of our opponents, whether local, from across state, or from neighboring states, varied widely, as did our knowledge and preparation. I did well, benefited from the verbal practice, and gained needed self-confidence. In the pre-internet age, for sources I drew on newspapers, weekly and monthly magazines, and library materials. I recall opponents quoting their own fathers and fabricating their quotations.

I also participated in the seemingly relevant Student United Nations. My experience in Student UN is memorable much less for its content than for the regional and the national assembly at Georgetown University in Washington, DC, and for dates with some of my female UN ambassador associates.

My semi- or extracurricular activities during high school included boring but valuable typing class in summer school around 10th grade at about age 15. Many readers, like so many of my students and younger colleagues, will find it impossible to believe that their elders wrote papers, theses, dissertations, and even books on manual and electric typewriters, long before word processors and personal computers.

Shortly after typing class came a summer school driver's education course in preparation for turning 16 and eligibility for a Pennsylvania learners' permit followed by written and then actual driving examinations with an official inspector. Most of my peers and I took the course in large part to reduce if not completely eliminate the stress and conflict of parental instruction and practice driving. The course was poor, the practice driving more useful. The hills of Pittsburgh are challenging. I side-swiped the rear corner of a parked car in making a right turn up a hill the first time I took the family car out by myself!

~~~

At least as seriously, my classmates and I shared an intense process of researching, identifying, and visiting candidates for college application and attendance. Onsite visits, mail solicitations, and lots of informal chatter accompanied investigating scholarships and loans, essay writing, and completing applications. Without websites and common applications for admission and financial aid, researching schools and scholarships and applying to them occupied, indeed characterized, the final year and a half of high school. For the advanced track in particular, this complicated set of activities was at least as important as preparing for SAT tests, AP exams, and graduation. Especially in the pre-internet and pre-personal computer age, at times it was a full-time activity for the entire household.

Although conversations started earlier, including the vexed question of leaving home or attending Pitt and living in the dormitories (one of my father's occasional money-saving propositions), a full-family focus (with the exception of six-year-old Gary) began during grade 11. With the inconsistent and not especially knowledgeable help of the high school guidance counsellor and a bit of assistance from a private college consultant, we identified a large handful of private and public institutions that included long-shot, Ivy League universities and safe Pitt and Penn State. A group of primarily private universities constituted the most attractive targets. Costs were an overarching issue.

During the summer before my senior year, we made the ritual, middle-class family driving trip to visit a range of campuses mainly in Pennsylvania and New York . Cornell, in Ithaca in New York's lovely Finger Lakes region, was particularly attractive, until I visited a second time the next winter on an alumni-sponsored bus trip and was startled by the frozen, wintry campus (despite attending a Beach Boys concert). I visited Northwestern University just outside of Chicago earlier during a Key Club (my major, nonacademic, extracurricular service activity) national convention in downtown Chicago.

The application process was a family affair. Before today's common application form, my father and I completed seemingly endless application and financial aid forms. I wrote essays about one or more of my desires to attend a particular university, the meaning of my life and times, or what I wanted to be if and when I grew up. This was not a major intellectual challenge. My father laboriously typed the forms and essays on our old, manual Underwood typewriter on the dining room table, while my mother struggled to keep us more or less organized and fed.

In winter 1967 I was named a National Merit Semifinalist, but not a Finalist with scholarship. In early spring 1967, the yesses and nos and financial aid offers arrived by postal mail. When all was added and divided and we learned the state of Pennsylvania's scholarship and loan allocations, the winner was Northwestern.

My family drove me with my recycled footlocker, new suitcases, and new stereo player to Evanston in September.

~~~

In the meantime, my teenage social world partly overlapped and grew out of late-elementary-school relationships and their expansion in the age 13 Bar and Bat Mitzvah whirlwinds. These relationships continued in my first terms in high school. Based in part on longstanding and new friendships, the changing social environments and psychophysical development deepened conflicts and contradictions.

High school hallways, classrooms, the gymnasium during basketball games and occasional school-sponsored dances, and the wall on the edge of school grounds where the smokers hung out quasi-legally, including me (I smoked from age 15 to 37 as the son of two smoking parents), were among our scholastic social environments. A second primary location for me at this time was the "Jewish Y" in Squirrel Hill, the sponsor of sports events, clubs, and some dances. A third was private homes with varying degrees of parental supervision where we hung out, danced to popular music on record players in family dens or living rooms, and surreptitiously squeezed and kissed in partial hiding, sometimes halfway in closets. A fourth, less frequent but more prominent spot—especially for those in the fraternities or members of the expensive golf and country clubs—were the social halls of those organizations for dances with disc jockeys.

Social life had complicated, largely unwritten rules. It was riddled with competition and conflicts. This included clothing and shoes. Girls were attentive to the boys' shirts from Gant (with little hanger loops on the back) and Brooks Brothers. Penny loafers from Brooks Brothers were all but required for the cooler guys and some gals.

Denim blue jeans were a point of contention. At times, they were permitted as proper or even expected attire, at other times not. Unlike today, no one had a beard or mustache. Hair length for boys was also grounds for conflict. Being a good dancer and to a lesser extent a good kisser (we were not skilled in practicing or evaluating that) were advantages. So too were displays of family wealth, including a car at age 16.

My social life embraced all-boy activities, from tennis and basketball to bicycle rides and miniature golf. I gave up my uncle's passion for golf in favor of tennis between ages 12 and 13. We attended baseball and football games both professional and at Pitt, watched movies, and hung out with the guys and with the gals. Beginning to drive at age 16 expanded our field of play. A few high school male buddies remained my close friends for a few years.

After age 13 and especially 15, my social life included heterosexual gatherings, often in groups. Sometimes they were small, such as double dates, and increasingly single-couple pairings. One female friend whom I did not date, Gail, living today just outside Philadelphia, remains close after almost 60 years of shared classes, points of view, and some social spheres. Another, Ava, a year younger who also attended Northwestern, is my intellectual property rights attorney, largely paid with copies of my books.

By age 17 or 18, I had more "serious" girlfriends. I had two fairly long-lasting relationships, Sally and Carol. Sally was my age, a friend of a friend and also of family friends who lived in a former mill town across the river. She was an intellectual soul mate, another highly intelligent overachiever from a middle-class Jewish family.

I recall one date, with my parents away on vacation, when we met at my house after I finished my shift at the summer steel mill job. While I showered and dressed, Sally shopped for dinner groceries and then prepared our meal. Other dates took us to lovely Pittsburgh parks in summer evenings to lay in the grass with her head on my chest or my lap as we watched the moonrise and the stars come out.

The last time I saw Sally was her autumn 1968 weekend trip to visit me as a sophomore at Northwestern University when she was a second-year student at the University of Michigan. We had resumed dating the previous summer. She stayed in a women's dorm with my high school friend. We had a pleasant time in downtown Chicago and walking the beaches next to the Evanston campus. In the pre-internet era, we lost contact. I sometimes wonder what became of lovely, intelligent Sally.

Carol, a year younger, was my second high school sweetheart, to use a phrase that perhaps captures the transitional and contradictory nature of the mid-1960s. Sweet and companionable, she was not, and did not attempt to be, Sally's intellectual equal. Attending Allderdice, she lived in an apartment with her divorced mother in nearby Shadyside. She had ready access to her mother's Volkswagen Bug and taught me to drive a manual stick-shift car. I recall spending a wintry New Year's Eve at my house celebrating with and even dancing with Carol and my parents.

Our happy relationship continued for almost two years, including my first year in college, until I felt the need to break up following her high school graduation. I remember her mother's displeasure with me.

Another sign of this transitional era was the physical nature of our relationships. We actively "made out" and explored each other's bodies, often in each other's bedrooms when our respective parents were away. Sally and I made out in the expansive but empty Pittsburgh public parks. We kissed and hugged passionately.

For our ages and circumstances, we loved each other. We were free with each other—but only up to a major point. Never did we consummate a full act of sexual intercourse. We came close. That awaited college relationships.

~~~

The final installment in my teenage preparations for early adulthood and the further transition from high school and home to life away at university is my work experience. My parents encouraged but did not mandate summer jobs until late in high school. They made no mention of part-time work during school terms for either high school or college.

I toyed with a newspaper route by substituting a few times for short periods for vacationing friends. After 10th or 11th grade, I worked part-time with another person cleaning ceiling panels for a bowling alley. The following summer I worked in a local pharmacy's soda bar and made deliveries on a bicycle.

Serious summer work began immediately after high school graduation when I spent that symbolic, transitional period day-laboring in a steel mill just across the river from Pittsburgh in historic Homestead. The job connection was a family friend who was a business executive for the dying steel manufacturer.

*Figure 3.1. Harvey at age 18, Taylor Allderdice High School Yearbook, 1967.*

Having no choice, I worked swing shift from late afternoon to almost midnight. I manually moved steel slugs with a metal pole from one conveyer belt to another line, repeating the same task over and over. I often requested Darvon pain relievers from the factory dispensary.

The two months plus were eye-opening and deeply educational. I was one of only two college students among a demographically, ethnically, racially, and gender diverse workforce. There were many Vietnam War veterans, but my peace symbol taped to my hard hat prompted little comment other than generally good-natured humor.

Older workers good-naturedly joked about and with the youngsters. The "college boys" quickly bonded and even made a long-weekend vacation trip to Atlantic City. We were more often teased as objects of curiosity than ridicule or scorn. Political or cultural comments were mainly sarcastic. This side of the 1960s is seldom remembered.

More noticeable were the visible drug and alcohol use on the job, in restrooms, and at breaks; the quiet racial coexistence; and the strength and equality of the women among the unionized workers. Occasionally, other workers treated the "kids" to an Iron City or Duquesne beer at a nearby bar. It was quite a learning experience about far more than the kind of work that I was socialized to disdain and deeply desired to avoid. As in other summer jobs, I learned much more about workers as fellow human beings than only to confirm my need to attend college. I learned about myself and "other" others.

A final anecdote before we leave for Evanston and college. While I was working at the mill, I was visited at home one afternoon before work by two Pittsburgh-area resident, Northwestern University juniors or seniors "pre-rushing" me for their fraternity. This is another mark of the times. These two young men had absolutely no idea of what to say and what to make of an 18-year-old, Jewish young man—theirs was not a Jewish legacy house—earning money for college by working in a steel mill. Fraternities and sororities then as well as today were highly segregated by religion as well as social class, race, and ethnicity.

This provided my first lens into the then temporarily declining so-called Hellenic or Greek (fraternity and sorority), Midwestern, Protestant culture of Northwestern undergraduates. In part because of oversized student populations and limited housing alternatives, "Greek life" later rebounded nationally and at Northwestern. Despite some academic, pre-vocational, and theme or value-driven "houses," fraternities and sororities remain sites of separation, competition and conflict, drunkenness, and sexual assault.

# Chapter 4. Northwestern University and Chicago: Higher and Wider Learning, Inside and Outside Classrooms, 1967–1970

In mid-September 1967, at age 18, I moved into a two-student, one-bedroom dormitory room, with toilets and showers down the hall, in unadorned, immediate post-World War II Bobb Hall. One of three on north campus across Sheridan Road from the iconic clay tennis courts and the old gymnasium, my first-year residence hall was clustered among the other men's dormitories and fraternities. Women's residences concentrated on south campus, to protect young women from their male peers. The 1960s arrived late in Evanston and Northwestern University.

Northwestern is a private university founded in the small, suburban Chicago city of Evanston just north of the city boundary. Its origins date from the mid-19th century when John Evans led a group of business executives in establishing a coeducational college in the quiet Methodist-founded town. Evanston was the future home of Emma Willard and the national Women's Christian Temperance Union. Only private clubs sold alcoholic beverages in 1960s Evanston. Memberships, though, were cheap.

By the 1960s, NU was in a self-admitted time of transition. Well into the 1950s and early 1960s, with a number of other private universities, Northwestern had a rigid policy of limiting the admission of Jews, Catholics, Blacks, and other "minorities"—in other words, quotas. It actively recruited relatively moderate- to higher-scoring, middle- to upper-middle-class high school class presidents, star athletes, and homecoming queens and kings from Midwestern towns. It had a well-deserved reputation as a high-middle-ranking party school with academic aspirations and with non-winning sports teams other than tennis and golf.

In the early- to mid-1960s, following a well-publicized fraternity hazing death by drowning in Lake Michigan *and* a quest for higher rankings, Northwestern embarked on a period of rehabilitation and rankings-climbing. It actively recruited nationally a more diverse student (and faculty) population. It succeeded more rapidly with eastern and western Jewish, Catholic, and Asian American students than with members of other underrepresented groups. NU promoted itself as more open, liberal, and diversity-seeking (not yet *the* word of that day). My acceptance and admission were one small part of a time of change. The approximately 70 Black students who were enrolled that year were a university record and a source of official discomfort (for more on the experience of Black students at Northwestern during this era, see Northwestern University Libraries, n.d.).

The university I entered had a long road to travel. I confronted antisemitism during my brief encounter with fraternity rush. Racism, sexism, misogyny, homophobia, and xenophobia were rife, from casual speech to unwritten policies, although we lacked the words of the following generations. Fraternities and sororities were rigidly segregated along all visible lines plus social class as well as sited on opposite ends of the campus.

Discrimination was both blatant and subtle. The visibly small number of Black students, prompted by the civil rights movements and led by the first Black student council president—a future lawyer—held a strike and occupied the administration building in spring 1970. The official university history issued under the names of a retired professor of economics and the just retired provost in 1975 grossly misrepresents the Black students and student activism more generally (see Harold F. Williamson and Payson S. Wild, 1975; compare with Graff, Northwestern University Archives and Library, oral history interviewee on student activism in late 1960s, Sept. 18, 2023, and my "Lessons From the 1960s: Paths to Rediscovering Universities" 2023a).

I began my studies at Northwestern with a year's credits from successful scores on Advanced Placement exams in American and European history, English, and calculus. At that time, colleges were less money-hungry than later, so I was awarded a full year's credit and sophomore standing as well as exemption from introductory courses. Intellectually and financially, that was a great boon. In retrospect, my assessment is more nuanced.

On one hand, passing out of first-year requirements and most large lecture courses and moving directly into upper-division courses was a huge benefit. It led to important faculty-student and peer relationships. It hastened my path to graduate school and the professorate. It saved a year's expenses. On the other hand, another year of personal maturing would have benefited me. I recognized that by the end of graduate school.

Mid-century mores that restricted the location, physical posture, and hours for male and female student interactions especially in dorm rooms were beginning to change. Formal parietal hour rules were eliminated the preceding year. This meant that during a dorm party, a fellow first-year female could visit my room. But I was not allowed to visit a room in a women's dorm. The battle for gender equality was halting and slow.

For all the talk of the counterculture and the sexual revolution, in the late 1960s at Northwestern, male residents of north campus, mainly fraternity members and new chapter pledges, annually marched to south campus where they screamed for women students in dorms and sororities to "throw us your panties." This sorry tradition was called a "panty raid." By my second and third years, more and more women and some men students vocally opposed the tradition, protested to the university administration, and picketed it. But it was not canceled. Participation diminished. The women's revolution came in bits and pieces, contradictorily, to Evanston, original home of the Women's Christian Temperance

Union. My future partner and wife spent her first year at Northwestern in Frances Willard Hall on south campus.

My assigned first-year roommate and I had exchanged only one introductory postal letter in advance of arrival at our shared destination in the pre-email age. Without computer matching and email, Glenn and I were not a good fit. An intending philosophy major from the Chicago suburbs, he took his dirty laundry home to his mother to wash only twice a quarter. The room acquired a distinctive, uninviting odor. Over the span of three quarters, we had little to say to each other. I quickly abandoned my first instinct of taping cutouts of *Playboy Magazine* nude photographs around the doorway. My 18-year-old consciousness awakened step by step.

Fortunately, I quickly made new friends with David, a classmate from Akron, Ohio, in the room next door and Harris, from Long Island, New York, on the other side. Harris introduced me to *The New York Review of Books* to which I subscribed for decades. He and I shared our copies of *The Nation* and *The New Republic*. His roommate from Colorado introduced all of us to fresh spring water beers from Colorado, before Coors became associated with the political right and the object of criticism and boycotts.

David and I shared a room and then an apartment for the next two years before I graduated in three years. The son of a Firestone Tire executive, he was a pre-law political science major. Another friend for the next several years was Ed, a six-year combined B.S.-M.D. student from Lombard, Illinois. Ed's first-year roommate was quarterback on the NU Wildcats football team, the closest I came to any connection with the typically losing Wildcats teams. He was not very tall.

With the exception of a handful of private, preparatory school graduates, all of the several hundred 18-year-olds in Bobb Hall (and more in other first-year dorms) had to adapt to new comfort zones and new habits for their first extended period away from home. This was not easy. Self-discipline does not come easily at age 18.

For reasons that I cannot recall, I was elected president of Bobb Hall for the year. This was not an onerous task, but I took it seriously. One of my first actions was contracting with an affiliate of the Chicago mafia to rent a pool table for the basement recreation room. I also coordinated coed "mixers" with the student heads of women's dorms.

In another sign of the shifting times and my political awakening, with the cooperation of the Dean of Students, I led a successful effort to amalgamate the men's and women's residential organizations into a single, campus-wide association. That left us with an extra mimeograph machine and file cabinet. (Younger readers, note that a mimeograph was an ancestor to Xerox machines and then computer-driven printers for producing multiple copies.) I promptly donated them to the struggling campus Students for a Democratic Society (SDS) group. It was years before male and female residences were fully integrated across campus or within individual dormitories.

My activist leanings were emerging; so too were the breath of acquaintanceships across campus and beyond first-year students. Some friendships lasted throughout my years at Northwestern and well beyond.

Different interests and affinities competed for our time. Eighteen- to 20-year-olds adjusted unevenly to making individual course choices and schedules. For some students—especially in the Technological Institute (Tech) programs, largely engineering or pre-med—there were no choices other than, importantly, general education requirements that were then university-wide with a moderate amount of choice. For liberal arts and science students like me, choices were abundant, sometimes overwhelming. We usually had options among different courses to meet given requirements across a range of electives. We were encouraged to range widely, sample, and experiment.

Despite myths to the contrary, there was not even a veneer of required "great books" to read. My AP credits gave me great freedom. Northwestern was a good place to take advantage of curriculum choice. After my first year I had the steady, responsible, and interactive advising of Lacey Baldwin Smith, professor and distinguished scholar of British history as well as suggestions of other professors and fellow students. (See essays listed in the Appendix.)

Even before the beginning of orientation for first-year students and then classes, fraternity and sorority rush for new student pledges began. As mentioned in Chapter Three, I met with two fraternity brothers at home in the summer. Rush was high-pressure with the various houses segregated not only by race but also by religion broadly cast, social popularity, athletic prowess ("jocks" versus the rest of us), more or less controlled social activity, and less explicitly family income and social class. And it was indeed rushed at the beginning of our first year in college.

Prospective pledges were demeaned and intimidated. With other Jewish and underrepresented students, I was more or less ignored by all but the three Jewish-related frats. Despite having a legacy to one of them from my father's membership more than 30 years earlier, they did not appeal to me in part because of their own class differentiation and their muddled views on religious separation and political awareness. In other words, both "sides" offended me.

Fortunately, late-1960s currents promoted the legitimacy of acting affirmatively by removing oneself from rush. We called it "de-rushing." For several years, it was not uncommon. Along with some of my new dorm friends, I de-rushed and never regretted it. Others "de-pledged" after joining but not completing the often vile and inhumane rites of initiation. Among the campus legends was the account of how one nationally well-known fraternity's pledging rituals led to the drowning of a pledge tied to a rock in Lake Michigan in the late 1950s or early 1960s—and how the university President J. Roscoe Miller blocked all efforts to investigate, prosecute, or suspend his own former fraternity.

A third course of adjustment was based in either or both the dorms or fraternities (to a lesser extent publicly at least in sororities on south campus): drinking alcohol excessively outside the bounds of parental homes. Then and later, it was often said that one of the first year of college's central tasks was learning your limits. This was certainly my experience. Within a year, marijuana came to my rescue.

Because of its conservative religious roots, Evanston was a "dry" town with no open sales of alcohol. Booze, so to speak, was available for purchase across the counter only in Chicago, across Division Street, the town's southern boundary. Legal sales were limited to those aged 21 or older. Undergrads, especially first-year students who also lacked cars of our own, especially when not fraternity or sorority pledges, were "rescued" by friendly dorm "counsellors."

Most often graduate students supplementing their research or teaching assistantships—unlike older undergraduates working for only room and board several decades later—these counsellors comforted their younger charges, made us happy, and in the case of our second-floor grad student in English, also supervised and gently controlled our underage drinking. My immediate circle appreciated Phil's generosity and supportiveness.

Alcohol consumption was one form of experimental learning. Before the end of the first year, I was able to drink almost a fifth of whiskey and still walk. I began to transition from Canadian to Scotch spirits. I remember drinking far too much on Yom Kippur in October 1967, the last time I ritualistically fasted. My drunken stupor led to violent vomiting while trying to sleep off the effects. For our cohort, alcohol and before long marijuana were inseparable from relaxation, socializing, partying, dating—and maturing.

On quiet Thursday, Friday, or Saturday evenings, in not-too-chilly weather, if there were no organized dorm parties or campus events, the nonfraternity pledges would drink awhile and then stand on the side of Sheridan Road, aka US Route 42, which extended through campus between Chicago and Wilmette. High school junior and senior girls from suburban Evanston, Wilmette, Winnetka, Skokie, and other nearby towns would drive the family car up and down the road selecting Northwestern first-year men to pick up for brief "dates." The "townies" and the frosh "roadies" might just chat or make out a little. This was not "free love" but another transition from high school to college and a rickety bridge between the separated south and north campuses and on- and off-campus life.

~~~

Of course, there was formal education. Happily, I was exempt from many if not quite all requirements, a boon to advancing reading and writing or college literacy. I recall a few relatively useless required courses. Among them was Introduction to American Government, an 8:00 am lecture course in which I regularly dozed, my drooping hand leaving a crooked line trailing down pages of my notebook. This course helped me finalize my decision to continue with history and not follow the path to law school that my parents occasionally promoted.

A one-quarter course of French was taught by a graduate assistant. Two wasteful quarters of astronomy were taught by the semi-notorious J. Allen Hynek, who widely supported beliefs in UFOs. I passed by intimidating my TA with fake answers to quizzes and exams based on inventing equations derived from high school calculus.

Returning home at end of the first quarter, I was fitted with my first pair of eyeglasses. Two and a half years later, I led my partner Vicki to her first ophthalmologist's examination and prescription for her first eyeglasses, for which I paid.

For my one-year physical education requirement, I took one quarter each of tennis in the fall, handball taught by an ex-football player who body-slammed us around the court in winter, and in the spring horseback riding (for an extra $25). I was the only male and the tallest in the class. I was assigned the largest horses, although I was probably the least competent rider. Between the two factors, I often either fell off or was gently thrown.

Other, fully or partly elective courses were far more appealing and stimulating. Quite literally, they were formative. Early among them was my future history advisor and second history model Lacey Baldwin Smith's two-quarter British history sequence and former TV quiz show host Bergan Evans' renowned two quarters on western literature. Not a scholar, Evans was an excellent lecturer, always filling the many-hundred-seat Tech Auditorium. This course was neither required for all nor filled with "canonical" works. Other first-year classes included sociology and anthropology courses that were neither memorably good nor bad.

Sometime during my first year, I discovered The Grill—the moderately disreputable food center in the basement of Scott Hall, the old student union in the traditional classroom area. Stopping there to study between classes, I would meet and chat with campus activists and dissidents who contributed to its bad reputation. I had coffee or lunch there rather than trekking back to the Elder Hall cafeteria on north campus. This added to my new rhythms and circles, expanding beyond the first-year dorm and classrooms, adding new readings through these connections. A small chapter in my expanding life with literacy.

From my Bobb Hall presidency from which I supplied SDS with its first mimeograph machine, my developing activism extended to personal associations with the not-well-organized group. Our causes stemmed from the national effort launched in 1962–1963 by Tom Hayden's Port Huron Statement and the Berkeley campus Free Speech Movement to enact university reform and student rights campaigns. These associations provided the grounds for the anti-Vietnam War and peace movements a few years later and led to my marching in Chicago and my service as a Midwest coordinator for MOBE (Mobilization to End the War in Vietnam).

Greater involvement with civil rights campaigns led to membership in Students for SCLC (Southern Christian Leadership Conference) that was spreading from its southern roots, volunteer work in the Black community, and marching in downtown Chicago with Jesse Jackson (both of us so much younger). I was welcomed among the genuinely racially mixed activists of the later 1960s.

*Figure 4.1. Harvey with a classmate's new baby, Northwestern University, 1969.*

Winter and spring 1968 brought more new friends and acquaintances. Some were fellow novice activists and campus radicals in preparation. They often overlapped with the most brilliant students. Two of our leading intellectual lights co-edited two books of essays by nationally recognized New Left scholars before their graduation. One of them, Rod Aya, became an internationally known historian; the other, Norman Miller, a lawyer. With equally engaging peers, we took the same classes including the landmark Vietnam Seminar and the Senior Honors Seminar in history in 1969–1970. A number completed Ph.D. or law degrees.

With other new friends, especially Bill and Marcia, contacts in the residence halls association led to long-lasting connections well into our respective post-graduate studies and sometimes beyond. For a time, I dated a classmate from the Pittsburgh suburbs whom I had met in high school debate tournaments. After a busy fall and winter quarter, David, Scott (another resident of Bobb Hall's second floor), and I rendezvoused in Cincinnati where David drove us to explore Mammoth Cave in Kentucky. It was eye-opening if dark.

Spring quarter 1968 is forever etched in my mental and visual memory because of the assassinations in April of civil rights crusader Martin Luther King, Jr., and in June of Robert F. Kennedy, younger brother of JFK and candidate for U.S. president. I remember standing with Ed on Northwestern's human-made extension of its campus into Lake Michigan on the day of King's murder. Looking south past downtown, we scanned for signs of a city burning. We spied glimpses of flames miles away.

In the spring I was also engulfed in Eugene McCarthy's progressive, anti-war, Democratic presidential campaign. At that point, he competed against Robert F. Kennedy and Vice President Hubert Humphrey. McCarthy was the most liberal and most appealing to young people (including many activists, like me, still too young to vote).

We cut our unruly, semi-hippie hair and "got clean for Gene." I cleverly led McCarthy to victory in Northwestern's every-four-year mock presidential convention. Close friends and I bused to campaign door-to-door in the farmlands of Indiana and Wisconsin. We were sometimes met by farm owners with shotguns in their hands and sometimes by smiling residents who greeted us with photos of young campaigners like us in *Time* and *Newsweek*.

It was quite a learning trip. Alas, it ended with disappointment and disillusion with Richard Nixon's and Spiro Agnew's defeat of Humphrey and Ed Muskie in November. I sympathized with close friends including a female sociology classmate from the Boston area. My disillusionment and disaffection with formal party politics lasted for years. Ironically, when Vicki and I first voted in a presidential election in 1972 at the U.S. Consulate in Toronto, we cast our "hanging chad" ballots under a formal portrait of sitting President Richard M. Nixon, prior to the Watergate revelations.

~~~

Northwestern's rich campus culture was central to my education. My love of French and Italian films derives from campus film festivals and premieres. Concerts in the old Cahn Auditorium in Scott Hall included not only mediocre, pop boy bands but also Joan Baez, Joni Mitchell, and Laura Nyro. There were productions from the excellent theatre program and many fine lectures and seminars by scholars and political leaders. I remember a small group discussion meeting on gun control with Senator Birch Bayh of Indiana and a session with the then-current British Labor Party leader.

We were encouraged to visit Chicago and acquaint ourselves with its world-class resources and institutions—in addition to civil rights and anti-war marches. Not yet an object of fear and loathing to residents of quiet Evanston, it was a short, inexpensive subway ride from campus to the downtown Loop. Frequent visits included the grand Art Institute of Chicago, the Field Museum of Natural History, the Shedd Aquarium, the Museum of Contemporary Art, the south side Museum of Science and Industry, as well as movie theaters and performance halls. So much was affordable even to undergraduates on scholarships and loans a half century ago.

We also browsed the outside windows and sometimes inside the grand department stores of the Loop and along Michigan Avenue. The holiday windows were their own attraction. So too were the downtown movie palaces and moderately priced restaurants. The Art Institute and the movie houses were compelling sites for dates in the late 1960s, often followed by walks along Michigan Avenue, Grant Park, and the Lake Michigan shore. Our haunts increasingly included the then-iconic Old Town and Lincoln Park with its petting zoo just north of downtown and Greek Town's appealing ethnic restaurants just west of the Loop. On rarer occasions when someone had a car, we would visit the substantial Brookfield Zoo on the outskirts of the city.

After Vicki and I became inseparable in 1969 and 1970, we visited museums, downtown, and Old Town. And we reveled in concerts in west side Chicago music halls where we heard Ten Years After with guitarist Alvin Lee and blues legends Muddy Waters and Howlin' Wolf. We also heard Tim Hardin at his prime, the Turtles, the Animals, and various jazz greats.

I returned home to Pittsburgh for the summer of 1968 to spend a second year working in steel production, this time in a different plant that concentrated on fabricating large construction pieces, including sections of bridges and structures. My job was scraping old paint and then repainting large segments with special paints. It was less wear and tear on my young body. It was also a less interactive workforce than the previous summer.

Summer socializing featured time with high school friends Ron, Gail, and David P., who died tragically young. Attending different universities in different cities and towns, during the "summer of love" we shared our experiences, our new discoveries, passions, and dislikes. Given the times, these often focused on current politics. We also reveled in comparing the similarities and differences in our education across history, political science, English education, and pre-med. That was itself a form of learning.

Summer 1968 was a crucial period in American cultural and political history. Wisely or not, my Northwestern friends and I decided that the Woodstock music festival was only a pipe dream. We met instead in Atlantic City for its reputedly "great international" music event. I would be surprised if any reader heard of that tepid festival at the local horserace track.

Wisely, in retrospect, I decided against returning to Chicago for the mass protests at the Democratic presidential nominating convention where Mayor Richard Daley did his best to undermine urban democracy and stoke violence between the Chicago police and the diverse protesters who messily combined political partisans, anti-war and civil rights activists, hippies, and "Yippies." I watched the convention, the protests, and the police violence, as well as the Soviet invasion of Czechoslovakia, on national television in my parents' living room.

Despite the presidential election, fall quarter was relatively quiet. Returning to Evanston in September 1968, David and I settled into a room with a bunk bed in Latham House, a university-owned, independent men's residence on south campus across from the new administration building and a few doors from a dry cleaner and the iconic deli called The Hut. We made new friends including a future suitemate and engineering major named Jerry from central Illinois.

I also acquired my first pet who extralegally cohabited with us. Never permitted a cat or dog as a child at home, I longed for a small creature to love and to love me. I named the sweet, domestic, orange tabby cat "god" (dog spelled backward—I was 19). Although he loved to rise with the sunlight and greet either sleeping David or me first thing in the morning, he fit well into his limited, illegal state. He delighted in meeting female students and loved licking other people's ice cream cones or their ice-cream-covered lips.

His veterinarian sent postcards that stated, "your god is due for his distemper shot." At the end of the academic year, he retired to Ed's Lombard, Illinois, home where the Catholic family renamed him Tiger. He lived a long, contented life with his new name before cancer took him.

As occupants of a university-owned and -managed student residence, we were required to pay for a university board contract and take our meals at the nearby cafeteria of Willard Hall, a dorm for female first-year students. I was not happy with the arrangement in principle, but I was extremely dissatisfied with the food.

Being an occasionally fearless young radical with grand visions and "ways with words"—to borrow from my future colleague and friend Shirley Brice Heath (1983), I launched with David a food strike in protest. Knowing that the 18-year-old female students were unlikely to acknowledge or support our effort, I created a media event. In advance of the strike, I sent letters to the student-run *Daily Northwestern* announcing the event and to the Dean of Students communicating our demands. The morning broke with a lead story in the paper.

As to participation, the strike was a total bust. Perhaps five male students joined David and me. As a media event, it made me briefly a campus celebrity. Most importantly, the dean immediately freed me from my board contract. Returning my payment, he requested that I never dine in a university residence hall again. I happily agreed. I had won.

~~~

Second-year classes were even more stimulating and satisfying than in my first year. Following Bergan Evans' introduction to western literature was a compelling, large lecture course on modern European literature in translation taught by two senior German professors, Meno Spann and Erich Heller. The reading was exhilarating, the lectures gripping, the learning expansive and deepening.

At the same time, paralleling the courses in my history major were further courses in my developing sociology minor. In several second-year courses, I read the social science classics from Karl Marx and Friedrich Engels to Emile Durkheim and Max Weber, a smattering of works by members of the Frankfurt School, C. Wright Mills, and more contemporary works such as David Riesman and Christopher Jencks' *The Academic Revolution* (1968). Little did I know how well I was preparing to be a comparative, new social historian on the one hand and a pioneering interpreter of literacy on the other hand.

Among my classes was visiting professor of American history Jesse Lemisch's exciting, state-of-the-art course in new, revisionist, social and cultural U.S. history. Lemisch's research on Revolutionary-era sailors and urban workers was part of an emerging tradition then known as "history from the bottom up." This course introduced us to the then "new social history" that sought novel perspectives, questions, conceptualizations, sources, and methods to develop a much more inclusive history. Various "new histories" within a decade or so for some time substantially remade much of U.S. and in time world history (for more on this topic, see my *Undisciplining Knowledge*, 2015a, and literature cited there; see also Chapter Five and beyond).

In Lemisch's and others' classes, we read and analyzed the seminal works of the first half of the 1960s and earlier as well as their advisors' preparatory scholarship. These included Oscar Handlin's *Boston's Immigrants* (1941) and *The Uprooted* (1951); Bernard Bailyn's *Education in the Forming of American Society* (1960) and *The Ideological Origins of the American Revolution* (1967); and on slavery, Kenneth M. Stampp's (1956) *The Peculiar Institution* and Stanley M. Elkins' (1959) *Slavery*.

The next generation of "new historians" led with Stephan Thernstrom's (1964) pioneering quantitative study of a Massachusetts working class community's social mobility, *Poverty and Progress*, Herbert G. Gutman's (1977a, 1977b) reconstruction of slavery and then labor history (1961, 1974), and Eugene D. Genovese's recreation of "the world the slaves made" (1969, 1974). Later Genovese, Thernstrom, and influential New Leftist historian Christopher Lasch (1965, 1969) turned rightward.

In early modern English history, I read Peter Laslett's (1965/1984) *The World We Have Lost: England Before the Industrial Age* (the third edition published in 1984 discussed my first book *The Literacy Myth*, 1979c, completing a circle). A second-year course on modern French history taught by Robert Bezucha presented important precedents to and influences on the United States' "new social history" in the historiography of France. This list of historiographers began with Marc Bloch, who wrote *The Historian's Craft* (1963). He was followed by Henri Lefebvre, who wrote *Everyday Life in the Modern World* (1971), and also in the 1960s the Annales School flourished under Fernand Braudel, who wrote the three volume *Civilization and Capitalism, 15th-18th Century* (1992), and Emmanuel Le Roy Ladurie, who wrote *Montaillou* (1978).

Concurrently in Lacey Smith's and the new modern English history professor William Heyck's courses, I read the keystones of the dynamic, often but not always Marxist-inflected, histories by Christopher Hill, *The Century of Revolution* (1961) and *The World Turned Upside Down* (1972); E. P. Thompson, *The Making of the English Working Class* (1964) and "Time, Work-Discipline, and Industrial Capitalism" (1967); and Eric Hobsbawm, *The Age of Revolution* (1962) and *Labouring Men* (1964).

A further mark of this historiographical revolution under way lies in the fact that I first read some of these seminal works in geographic and chronologically defined courses and then again in the two-quarter-long senior honors seminar (and some again in graduate seminars). In that honors seminar, we also read the kindred historical sociology, Barrington Moore's *Social Origins of Dictatorship and Democracy* (1966) and Charles Tilly's early works, such as *The Vendée* (1964). Revealing in retrospect, I reread many of these seminal works under different rubrics in my first two years of graduate school. That is a fundamental lesson in the uses of literacy, to borrow a phrase from the English pioneer of what became cultural studies Richard Hoggart (1957). I encountered Hoggart along with Raymond Williams (1958) when I began to study literacy and its history in 1971–1975.

Equally significant, with a few key exceptions, I was taught by younger professors who were among the first generation of "new historians" and in most cases liberal to moderately left in their orientation. Their fields encompassed U.S., British, European, Latin American, and Asian history and sociology. The joint instructors of the senior honors seminar were an Asianist and a Latin Americanist who had been roommates at Harvard University, Jock McLane and Frank "Pancho" Safford. They focused on new scholarship from the northern and southern hemispheres, respectively.

If my undergraduate historical training had a major limitation, it was the absence of non-western studies. This is at least as much a result of my choices as the discipline's and for far too long the modern American university's shortcomings.

With my major interest in British history, I applied to Queen Mary College, University of London, to study early modern English history for a junior year abroad. I was accepted but was not allowed to use my state of Pennsylvania scholarship funds outside the United States. I then decided to graduate in three years. In retrospect, I have conflicting thoughts about that. On one hand, it was sensible not to spend an additional year taking undergraduate courses. But on the other hand, an additional year of maturity—growing up—would have been a wise choice for my future. So much for historians' hindsight.

~~~

Looking forward, perhaps the most significant moment in my second year at Northwestern takes me back to the Willard Hall cafeteria. Unknown to me, before my food strike, a first-year student from Portland named Esther developed a crush on me. We had barely spoken. After the strike, when I was no longer present in the dining hall, she worried that I was not eating enough and decided to bring food "care packages" a few times a week to my residence about two blocks from her dorm.

Given the tricky social circumstances, Esther enlisted her close friend Vicki to accompany her. The complication was that I wasn't attracted to Esther, but Vicki and I had a partial or beginning connection. This led to several casual double dates with my roommate David paired without his consent with Esther. Kitten god liked both of them, indiscriminately licking their ice cream cones or ice cream-covered lips.

By spring Vicki and I were dating casually but not exclusively. I recall some ventures into Chicago and a trip to the then-innovative Brookfield Zoo in a car borrowed from a senior friend. By the end of spring quarter, the relationship was hanging in the air without a clear direction.

For spring break 1969, David and I traveled to the Bahamas for a holiday with the collegiate masses. It wasn't particularly enjoyable. My major memory involves hitchhiking back to our hotel after dark from another party and discovering the driver's hand moving up my knee. I asked him to stop the car, and I exited.

Spring quarter marked another pre-professional step. All of my advisor Lacey Baldwin Smith's doctoral students were abroad doing doctoral dissertation research. This left him without a teaching assistant for his British history survey. He asked me to conduct two discussion sections in exchange for independent study credit. I prepared under his supervision. The sections went well; I enjoyed it. It was my first experience teaching history in a university. It was transformative.

I returned home for the final summer from mid-June to early September 1969. For this season of the first flight to land astronauts Neil Armstrong and Buzz Aldrin on the moon, I left the steel mills to work in cultivated nature in the Pittsburgh public parks as an assistant supervisor for high school-age, "junior gardeners." This job was a political appointment via a friend of the family.

Less taxing, more relaxing, healthier, and safer than the mills, it paid a little less. Some of the older workers were friendlier than the teens, who resented their slightly older supervisor at least on some days. My most lasting impression was the respect I felt for the deep wisdom and humanity of an older, not formally educated, Italian American, lifelong park worker named Angie. Through a summer of lunch and work break conversations, he introduced me to what I would later interpret as the limits of formal literacy education and the powers of intelligence. The academy remains resistant to those concepts despite several generations of pioneering scholarship into the strength and depth of oral cultures—and the limits of literacy by itself (see, for example, Nathalie Zemon Davis, 1975, among many others.)

~~~

Vicki went home to work in accounting for Des Moines, Iowa-based Pioneer Hybrid Corn Company for the first half of the summer between her first and second years at Northwestern. Drawing on my social consultant mother's connections, I sent flowers for her July 14 Bastille Day birthday through a local florist. She later told me that the flowers immediately led her to question her impression that I was a highly intelligent but overly cynical young man. She now suspected a streak of romanticism.

In late July, I made a preplanned, weeklong trip to Chicago to see Northwestern friends in Evanston. Among other liaisons, I arranged a date with Vicki. She returned to campus for the second half of the summer to continue her work-study job in the psychology department while living at the Evanston YWCA (and learning from her roommates to shoplift without getting caught). We had a fun evening in downtown Chicago. That date and my "romantic streak" created a path that she followed when we returned for the fall 1969 term.

As soon as I returned to Evanston, Vicki met me at my four-person suite in the former married student apartments that were minimally converted into upper-division student housing on south campus with men and women living on alternating floors. She carried a large, stuffed leopard and claimed that I had promised to pay one-half its price. I had no recollection of any such commitment. But it matched my leopard bedspread and pillow. She also had a leopard print jumpsuit, scarf, coat, and hat. I never paid that share. We later bequeathed the leopard to the toddler daughter of one of my University of Texas at San Antonio graduate students.

*Figure 4.2. Harvey and Vicki L. Wells, first photo, Evanston, 1969.*

Vicki was there to stay—for the next 55 years and counting. As we agreed to intercourse, I asked if she had a prescription for oral birth control. She did not. Together we decided that was a mandatory next step, another sign of the changing times. Prescriptions were available through the student health service, a recent innovation.

Vicki joined our suite of four registered, fee-paying male residents including David and Jerry from Latham House, an illegal cat named Penelope (from one of Vicki's summer YWCA roommates), an illegally unboarded kitchenette, and an illegal extension phone in the back bedroom. Although she officially shared a room with another student in a different women's residence, she became an extralegal fifth roommate who shared my single bed and the bathroom. There were occasional tense moments and noisy times, especially with the somewhat troubled fourth legal roommate Winston, but we coped more or less amicably.

Four of the five of us, plus Penelope, often hosted small gatherings and parties. Spread across the beds, desk, table chairs, and the floor, some of the group drank beer, whiskey, or Scotch, others smoked marijuana, and one good friend meditated, all to the latest or classic rock, blues, or folk music. He went on to complete a Ph.D. at Maharishi University. These were intense but not rowdy or loud affairs.

*Figure 4.3. Harvey, Vicki, and kitten Penelope, with Northwestern friends Laurie, David, and Dean, 1969–1970.*

Penelope loved the parties. Not only was she quite sociable, but also she loved to stick her head deeply into glasses of whiskey and lick up the tailings. She even appreciated having pot smoke blown in her face. Alone with Vicki and me studying, she alternately entertained us by doing acrobatic tricks on the rungs of ladder-back chairs or annoyed us by repeatedly retrieving wads of paper we tossed into the wastebasket in that age of pens, pencil, and paper.

On rare occasions, Vicki and I escaped to sleep on the sofa in her work-study boss' office suite. At other times when we needed a respite, we slept in her half-empty dorm room. But the janitorial staff in the women's residence were much more hostile to my presence than the personnel in my building were to Vicki's. Of course, in the late 1960s, university cleaning employees made the men's residence hall beds but not the women's. The sympathetic staff in my building also provided extra clean sheets at the appropriate time of the month. It was quite an adventure, one that neither of us would contemplate repeating.

~~~

Third and final year was intense. I convinced Vicki to major in anthropology, which she loved, as she occasionally contemplated a future career. Her political and cultural radicalization progressed, under my influence and tutelage. She continued to work part-time for the self-promoting psychology professor who imagined himself a one-person educational transformer, leading with widely advertised all-A classes, another sign of the times.

My courses were demanding but stimulating. That fall I participated in the Vietnam Seminar, taught by a young, liberal historian of Japan, John "Jock" McLane. The self-selected seminar members comprised an exceptional and lively intellectual circle. I was not the only future professor. I also recall a first-rate course in German history by Professor James Sheehan, who was soon recruited by Stanford University, and an independent study in social theory with a sociology professor.

The most important activity of that quarter was selecting potential graduate programs in history and making applications. With my intention to concentrate in modern British history, Lacey Smith and I spent hours in his bookshelf-lined, historic Harris Hall office pouring over the printed *American Historical Association Guide to Departments of History*. I was a high- but not the highest-ranking student with strong recommendations.

Together we developed a list of aspirational, selective but possible, and safe programs. They ranged from Harvard, Columbia, and Penn on one end, to SUNY at Stony Brook and UC-Santa Barbara on the other. In the competitive middle were UC-Berkeley, University of Wisconsin-Madison, and the University of Toronto.

I also searched for fellowships. Lacey Smith nominated me for a highly unlikely Rhodes Scholarship, which were then all male and all but required athletic distinction. I also applied for a Woodrow Wilson fellowship. Completing applications, drafting self-promoting and aspirational essays, and requesting letters of recommendation occupied much of that quarter.

Several months of waiting, more and less patiently, followed that whirlwind of activity. During winter quarter as a finalist for the Woodrow Wilson fellowship, I traveled to Indianapolis for a personal, grueling interview with a panel of professors, some of them trying to impress each other more than question me. That was another learning experience.

Vicki and I each returned to our families for winter break, having agreed to tell our parents about our attachment and commitment to stay together. My parents were surprised. My father asked if we had to "get married quickly"—in other words, was Vicki pregnant? He was also hesitant because she is not Jewish. My mother asked, "Is it Laurie?"—mistaking a close female friend for my inseparable girlfriend and roommate.

Vicki's parents were far less open to our connection and contemplation of our future together. Immediately after her brother's elaborate wedding to his college girlfriend in a small Iowa town, Vicki asked her father if he was ready for another wedding, perhaps the next summer. He responded strongly: definitely not!

Her reactionary, antisemitic father informed her that "Jewish boys only want one thing from Christian girls." (He had said the same thing when she was in high school about what Black boys want from White girls.) Her parents beseeched her to either break off the relationship or at least temporarily withdraw. Their illogic was that "separation would prove the strength of your love."

Rendezvousing at O'Hare Airport to spend New Year's Eve at a still-vacationing friend's apartment, we compared notes. We quickly dismissed these reactions and further confirmed our commitment by making passionate if uncomfortable love on the living room floor.

During the 1969–1970 school year, Vicki and I began another long-lasting friendship with a women's independent hall resident and fellow student named Laurie. The friend of Ava Kirschenbaum (now Doppelt), another student from Taylor Allderdice in Pittsburgh, Laurie and I first connected over politics and music. It was a social relationship. As Vicki also established a friendship with Laurie, the three of us often cooked dinner together in the dormitory's student kitchen. We also often ate out together. We remain in contact with Ava and her husband Art Doppelt, fellow Northwestern history graduate, who live in Florida.

On more than one occasion, another resident stole our uncooked food from its containers. We responded by purchasing a lockbox, but first baked brownies laced with chocolate Ex-Lax in each portion. The culprit stole those brownies but took nothing after that.

Laurie, Vicki, and I formed a close, collegial, and generational relationship. One year my junior and Vicki's age, Laurie grew up on Long Island in a family of furriers. Among her unique possessions was a rabbit fur coat resplendently dyed to resemble a watercolor painting. Often joined by her high school friend Dean, a student at a Wisconsin liberal arts college, we smoked pot while listening to contemporary music. We also drafted "the great American novel." Laurie came across the manuscript five years later and entrusted it to us. It was buried for years in my

Northwestern files. I found it recently when cleaning out that file cabinet. Let's just say it was far from "great"! Laurie became a public defense attorney practicing in Peoria, Illinois; we later learned that she died tragically young.

Much like fall 1969, winter quarter 1970 was consuming. It included my bout of mononucleosis. The two-quarter-long, senior honors seminar in history dominated my schedule while I waited to hear from graduate programs. Its first half focused on reading 20th-century historiographical classics (like those listed previously) and, in consultation with our subject area advisors, defining our honors thesis topics, questions, sources, and approaches.

For me, this meant instructive, encouraging sessions with new modern English historian Bill Heyck. My interests and his guidance settled on "the anti-socialist response to the first Labour Party government in Britain, 1924" as the subject of my thesis. That led to seemingly endless hours in the lower level of the old, about-to-be-vacated Deering Library reading both microfilms and decaying print copies of *The Times* of London, parliamentary papers, and especially political cartoons in the weekly magazine *Punch*, one of the innovations of my approach. Unknown to me, I was learning to use my literacy to read and interpret graphic expressions long before that became a scholarly fad and then an established subject across disciplines.

For spring break, Vicki accompanied me to Pittsburgh to meet my family for the first time. We followed this with a brief trip to New York City (using a free pass on a Greyhound bus). This was her first venture east of Chicago, first sight of the formation of the Ohio River at Pittsburgh's Point, and first views of the Atlantic Ocean and the Big Apple.

Despite their reservations about Vicki being Presbyterian, for my parents, it was all but love at first sight. One of them remarked, perhaps in jest or not, that she was a much nicer person than their eldest son! Young Gary jumped at the chance to have a big sister. Grandmother and Uncle Sonny and his young family joined in. Vicki immediately fell in love with Pittsburgh's defining hills and older neighborhoods, although never with driving across them.

In New York, we stayed in the apartment of our good friends from Northwestern Bill and Marcia. Slightly older, Bill was in Columbia Law School while Marcia pursued graduate work in African studies. We gleefully roamed about the city. Surprisingly, Bill and Marcia's small apartment on the Upper West Side contained an old rocking chair which barely fit the space. They offered it to us because a mutual friend was driving back to Chicago from NYC and had room to transport it. That chair accompanied us from Evanston to Toronto, Dallas, San Antonio, and Columbus. Today it sits happily in a corner of our master bedroom holding clean pants and shorts (see Illustration 13).

We returned to Evanston for our final quarter at NU before my graduation and Vicki's completion of one-half of her bachelor's degree. During the early spring, Vicki's parents visited Chicago and met me. As we anticipated, it did not go well. Vicki's more accepting mother said little. But her father's hostility, even fear, was transparent. Jewish, intellectual, left-leaning politically, with longish hair, a mustache, and bell-bottom trousers, I represented all that was wrong with America (pronounced Amurika).

Those sentiments receded only slightly over the decades. Her father Keith's antisemitism made no rational sense; he was among the first U.S. troops to enter German concentration and extermination camps including Dachau. Such is the power of origins, religious culture, ignorance, and fears of difference.

More generally, it was a great time of anticipation and life-phase-defining plans. On one hand, I labored successfully with my honors thesis, renting a state-of-the-art IBM Selectric typewriter on which we took turns typing the final draft. In those years, I drafted long-hand on yellow legal pads and revised on the typewriter. By my second year in graduate school, I transitioned to drafting on our portable electric typewriter. Personal computers were almost two decades in the future.

The honors thesis draft was accepted without reservations or much revision. That was quite satisfying. On the other hand, future-shaping news came in bits and pieces. I was awarded a Woodrow Wilson National Fellowship that paid most expenses for the first year of graduate school. I was elected to Phi Beta Kappa, the national academic honorary society, and I received word that I would graduate with high honors in history.

The final decision was most crucial: graduate school and financial support. The acceptances came in as expected; the significant differences were the offers of support. A few of the middle- and lower-ranking programs offered teaching assistantships in lieu of fellowships. My advisors and my own instincts deemed this a treacherous course for beginning graduate work.

I faced another large decision. The year was 1970; I was about to turn 21. The Vietnam War was far from over. The military draft for young men actively continued. My draft lottery number was 103, not a safe space.

The sum total of factors led Vicki and me to select the graduate program in history at the University of Toronto in Canada as the best option. It had a first-rate history department with well-known, modern British scholars of the 19th and 20th centuries and deep strengths in European history. I was not yet a draft dodger or deserter, but we decided, with my family's concurrence, to take preemptive action. Vicki would complete her bachelor's degree, working part-time as she had at Northwestern, and we would then decide on her next steps in Toronto.

Those factors came to a crescendo in May and June of 1970. Following the May 4 National Guard killing of four student protesters and wounding of nine others at Kent State University in Ohio, like a great many other campuses, Northwestern exploded. U.S. aerial bombings in Cambodia were revealed a few days earlier. We were active along with many other NU students in blocking Sheridan Road, ripping up the pavement to isolate the campus temporarily from the outside world.

Despite the objection of Republican-leaning business students and some fraternity members, the student body supported a strike against the university and a cessation of classes for more than a week. During that time, all but a tiny number of professors avoided their offices in support of the students. I was active on the history department faculty-student reforms committee that developed. When classes resumed, the university gave all students the option of taking a "T" for the quarter instead of a letter grade.

~~~

Family resistance led us to postpone marriage for another year and to continue, as was becoming increasingly common, cohabitation. I attended my graduation in Northwestern's basketball arena in part because my parents, 7-year-old brother, and grandmother drove to Evanston to attend and to take us out to celebrate. Many graduates, including me, taped peace symbols to the tops of our caps. It was a happy, satisfying weekend. Everyone was proud of and happy for their son, brother, grandson, and partner.

The final two months in Evanston encapsulated the past and the future. We moved from our campus residences to the third story of a lovely old house in the middle of an older section of town. The rental apartment was furnished. On the first floor lived a slightly older couple—a lawyer with Northwestern University Law School, his artist wife, and the first of their two children. We immediately became friends. We remain in touch with John and Dianne Shullenberger more than 50 years later and have several of Dianne's art works on the walls of our house.

Vicki continued to work as a research assistant in the psychology department. I embarked on another new summer career. With no other option for summer-long paid work, I applied for a commercial driver's license and drove an Evanston Red Top taxi from mid-June through mid-August.

Less physically taxing than steel mills or parks, it was a miserable job. Drivers had to pay far too much of our receipts to the company for overpriced gasoline in exchange for the use of the vehicle. To my surprise, many passengers either did not tip or tipped poorly, worsening the problem of low take-home pay. I began to remind passengers that tipping was customary and expected.

I learned experientially that a taxi could intimidate most other vehicles with the major exception of Chicago city buses and that there were more crazy drivers on the roads than I imagined. A final learning experience: I wrote a short exposé article titled, "To drive a cab." I sent it to *The New Republic* and quickly received my first of many formal rejection letters.

In July we flew to Toronto for a few days to begin searching for prospective places to live near the university. Staying with friends of friends, we delighted in the haunts of our impending home. We spent a few memorable hours attending a University of Toronto Varsity Blues football game. Not only was the quarterback not much taller than I was, but the game bore minimal resemblance to games played in major American college football conferences like the Big Ten, where Northwestern occupied the lower rungs except in tennis and golf.

We excitedly returned for our final weeks in Evanston. Renting a U-Haul van to carry our few belongings, we drove to Toronto in the latter part of August, completing a formative phase of our lives and beginning the next with great expectations.

*Figure 4.4. Harvey in rocking chair in Evanston apartment, July 1970, sketched by Vicki.*

# Chapter 5. The Great Canadian Adventure, the New Social History, and Beginning to Study Literacy, 1970–1975

Newcomers to Canada, Toronto, and the University of Toronto, Vicki and I arrived in the city in late August 1975. With our belongings in the small rental van, including bookcases and a pole lamp liberated from Northwestern residence halls and the New York City rocking chair, we rented an apartment and found furniture quickly. Having no car, we located within walking distance of the University of Toronto's prominent, central city location, also on the excellent subway and bus lines.

We were fortunate. A landlord had a tenement, railway flat-style, second-floor, one-bedroom apartment with room for my study above a Mac's Milk convenience store and a men's clothing shop on Bloor Street, the city's major east-west thoroughfare. A short walk from the U of T, in 1970 it was an affordable $120 a month. We rented four rooms of furniture for $10 per month with an option to buy for $100 after one year. A new Canadian kitten we named Hamilton (after the Ontario industrial city that I began to study) joined us later in the year.

Not long after arrival, I took a bus to Niagara Falls, New York, and a taxi to the American Friendship Bridge. I walked across the bridge to apply for the legal status of Landed Immigrant. In Canada, this status does not have the stigma of the U.S. Resident Alien designation. I also gained free health care in Ontario (OHIP or Ontario Health Insurance Program, a policy of the incumbent Progressive Conservative Party) among other benefits. Vicki applied from within the country.

As I prepared to begin my first seminar in 19th-century British history, a social psychology seminar as a foundation for anticipated further research on British anti-socialism, and an independent study in modern European history, I fretted over whether I should wear a tie or blue jeans and carry a briefcase or wear a backpack. I quickly withdrew from the narrowly focused psychology seminar, the professor of which had no interest in reaching out to other disciplines.

Vicki tediously negotiated with the admissions office of the university about her standing at the U of T after two full years at an American university. The problem was that Ontario required grade 13 for college-bound students, a vestige of late-blooming, Canadian progressive education. She finally found a responsible staff person who granted her credit for grade 13 for her first-year classes at Northwestern and credit for a first year at Toronto for her second year.

This left her with two years to complete a general bachelor's degree. Thinking increasingly about a teaching certificate and at least a first career in teaching, she switched her major from anthropology to geography—a major subject in Canadian schools as in Great Britain, unlike American. She found a part-time job as a Kelly Girl temporary bank teller, trained to substitute at any of Canada's five national banking systems and assigned to banks all over the city. A long-term assignment was at a bank located between our apartment and the U of T. She held this job for the next three years.

Thus began our first year in Toronto, city and university. My eager but reserved enthusiasm rapidly declined. My efforts to begin a constructive, tutorial relationship with my anticipated advisor, the 20th-century British historian, failed. I found him intellectually and personally unresponsive. I later learned that he was hard of hearing in one ear but did not admit it or take corrective steps. I also learned that I was the 11th student who attempted to work under his supervision. Only one completed his degree. I was not to be the second.

At the same time, the seminar on Victorian history proved disappointing. As was too often the case in Toronto's history department, professors crammed seminars around crowded tables in their offices. To say that this class was uncomfortable physically as well as pedagogically is an understatement.

Author of one exceedingly long book, an interminable, day-by-day chronicle of the Aberdeen Coalition government of 1852–1854, the senior professor was not current with the exciting new social, political, cultural, or economic histories to which I had been introduced at Northwestern. He was an unskilled seminar leader. I recall one student regularly falling asleep until the back of his head hit the wall behind his chair, when he would jarringly but briefly awaken.

As a new student with both typical anxieties and deeply rooted self-doubts, I sought this professor's counsel. Dismissing my concern about the missing scholarly references in the course syllabus, he assured me that, based on my oral participation, I was doing fine. All I needed to do was go to the library, read one book each day for the next two years, and take my qualifying doctoral exams. That was not the explanation or the reassurance that I needed. But it was, and remains, a troubling element of faculty-student relationships.

Fortunately, I became quite friendly with one of the several Americans in the class. Originally from New Jersey and a former graduate student at the University of Wisconsin-Madison, Bob had been drafted, inducted into the U.S. Army, and then deserted to Toronto. Bob and his wife Dena, a high school teacher and later a graduate student, Vicki, and I quickly become close friends. Bob was a year ahead of me in the program. We remained good friends for decades. As a university press editor, he later published one of my books and prompted me to start two book series in interdisciplinary social history.

One day in November, over lunch in the old library's eating area, I shared my dissatisfaction and self-doubts. I admitted to developing depression. Bob said to me, "you should meet the young guy up the street." I did. That meeting fundamentally changed the course of my life.

My first efforts to find psychiatric treatment for depression also came in Toronto while I was in graduate school. The group therapy sessions were unsuccessful, but the doctor prescribed a low dose of Vivactil, which I took for many years as a maintenance-level antidepressant.

The "young guy" was Michael B. Katz, a historian of American education and society. A 1966 graduate of the Harvard Graduate School of Education, Katz held a joint appointment in history of education and history at the University of Toronto. He was located in the Department of History and Philosophy of Education in the shining, new but unaesthetic Ontario Institute for Studies in Education's (OISE) 12-story building on the northern edge of campus on Bloor Street. I made an appointment to meet with him the next week.

Vicki and I met together with the 32-year-old associate professor in his eighth-floor office. Recently tenured, he published the landmark, revisionist history of early 19th-century Massachusetts common school reform, *The Irony of Early School Reform* (1968). That book transformed the history of education in the States. He then initiated Canadian history's first quantitative social history project focused on the industrial city of Hamilton, Ontario, in the 19th century (see Katz, 1975).

With a little assistance and support from Vicki, I explained my predicament. Michael listened closely. At the end of my presentation, he picked up his office phone and called the head of graduate admissions for OISE and asked if I could transfer from history to history of education with my Woodrow Wilson fellowship. The immediate response was "yes."

I successfully completed my first semester in British and European history courses and looked toward a new professional beginning. Katz's history of social structure seminar was undoubtedly the most consequential course I ever took. We read and in some cases I reread the modern classics: Peter Laslett's *The World We Have Lost* (1965/1984); Lawrence Stone's *The Crisis of the Aristocracy* (1965) and his seminal articles in *Past & Present*, such as "Literacy and Education in England, 1640–1900" (1969); Charles Tilly's *The Vendée* (1964); in European history, E. A. Wrigley's *Population and History* (1969) and *Nineteenth-Century Society* (1972); in colonial American history, John Demos' *A Little Commonwealth* (1970), Kenneth A. Lockridge's *A New England Town the First One Hundred Years* (1970), and Philip J. Greven Jr.'s *Four Generations* (1970); and in 19th-century American history, Stephan Thernstrom's *Poverty and Progress* (1964) and others. This was among the most active periods in modern historiography.

Katz was an exceptional seminar leader, alternating his own introductions, student presentations, constructive critical questioning, opportunities for rethinking and restatement, and interchange among the group. After my disappointing and frustrating first term, the seminar was challenging, exhilarating, and both personally and intellectually fulfilling. Collegial relationships that began in that class continue to this day across Canadian, Australian, and American borders.

Friendships from a second-year seminar and one from a final-year graduate seminar that I taught also continue. Those connections were central to my graduate education and own career over more than 50 years. Katz along with Natalie Zemon Davis and Jill Ker Conway did not so much teach us but show us through their example and their intellectual but collegially humane expectations (for more on relationships like these, see my "The Power of Models and Examples in Education and Higher Education," 2023e).

Katz required each student to complete a seminar project using the census, tax rolls, and city directory database that he was carefully building for his Hamilton (Ontario) Project (later renamed Canadian Social History Project). Reflecting the early days of the "new" quantitative social, demographic, family, and urban history, students transferred the data from primary sources in print or microfilm to handwritten forms and then to 80-column IBM punch cards. A mechanical card sorter aided data analysis. Over the next few years, we shifted to computer analysis of batches of cards with their information transferred to magnetic tape (for more on this type of research being conducted at the time, see Thernstrom and Sennett, 1969, and Tilly and Landes, 1971).

My earlier interests and experiences, new historical currents, and sociopolitical currents surrounding widespread criticisms of schooling and its relationship to inequality fortuitously collided. Having read Lawrence Stone's (1969) immediately classic *Past and Present* article "Literacy and Education in England, 1640–1900" and a lesser-known but more rigorous study by Roger Schofield (1968) of Laslett and Wrigley's Cambridge Group for the History of Population and Social Structure, "The Measurement of Literacy in Pre-Industrial England," I decided to do a pilot study of literacy in 19th-century Canada (and North America) based on the evidence of an unusual question about literacy and writing on the 1861 Census of Canada. In 1971, I had no idea that, literally and transformatively, my life with literacy was beginning.

Among other findings, I demonstrated that the census data were reliable and inseparably related to the history of education, social structure, ethnicity, race, age, and gender, as well as immigration and socio-economic development. Not only was it a pioneering seminar paper, but it also led directly to my master's thesis (Graff, 1971b) and in turn my first three scholarly articles by the completion of my third year as a graduate student: "Notes on Methods for Studying Literacy From the Manuscript Census" (1971a), "Approaches in the Historical Study of Literacy" (1972a), and "Towards a Meaning of Literacy" (1972b).

While I was immersing myself in historical literacy studies in a relatively narrow framework, with Katz' advice I also studied the history of education in Ontario and pursued a reading course with another faculty member in the history of European education—encountering Philippe Ariès' (1962) *Centuries of Childhood* on the history of childhood, and Stone on families and literacy, especially his *Family, Sex and Marriage in England, 1500–1800* (1977), among other important works.

At the same time, Vicki also broke new ground in her studies and our consequential mutual relationships. Among the most significant and long-lasting impacts was her enrollment in 1970–1971 in the first course offered in Canada on the history of women. The instructors for the two-semester course were pioneering, early modern French cultural historian Natalie Zemon Davis and

Australian-born historian of American women Jill Ker Conway. Both became our lifelong friends. Jill later became the first female president of all-women Smith College, and Natalie held Princeton University's most prominent chair in European history (for more on these relationships, see my "The Power of Models and Examples in Education and Higher Education," 2023e).

By all accounts, including Vicki's, this was one of the great undergraduate courses of modern history. Unlike most team teaching, both instructors attended and participated in every class meeting, with one commenting, responding, or raising questions about the other's lecture. Both instructors joined interested students for a brown bag lunch after class. The teaching assistants became notable scholars of women's history in their own right. Vicki explored the medieval and early modern witch trials in England and Europe for her first term paper.

I also studied with Natalie and Jill. Natalie published a landmark essay on literacy and oral reading in early modern French popular culture in her collection *Society and Culture in Early Modern France* (1975). We consulted with each other about our research projects while I was a second- and third-year doctoral student and she was a tenured professor. She was welcoming, supportive, and helpful. Until her death in September 2023 at 94 years old when she was still writing history books, she retained her friendship and interest in my writing and Vicki's and my lives. I took a formal seminar with Jill on 19th- and 20th-century American intellectual and cultural history. That led to friendship with both Vicki and me until her death.

Vicki and I developed social relationships and close faculty-student friendships with these professors and their spouses. In my first term as Katz's advisee, he asked me to babysit his young children several times when he and his new, second wife Edda went out. We also socialized with Michael and Edda over the years. During our final travels in Canada, just before moving to Dallas, Texas, in late summer 1975, we visited his family when they spent several months exchanging houses with a colleague at the University of British Columbia in Vancouver.

We invited Jill and her husband John, a former Harvard professor called back to Canada to accept a distinguished chair at the new York University in north Toronto, to a cheese fondue dinner served on a tablecloth spread over the living room floor of our Bloor Street West apartment. In 1972, John sincerely consulted us about whether he should, or could, call students by their first names instead of Mr. and Miss. We also saw Natalie and her mathematician, political-activist husband Chandler socially and at campus events.

Jill often took me to lunch at either a Kensington Market kosher deli where we ate chopped liver on bagels or at U of T's musty faculty club. We both preferred the former. She also served on my dissertation committee and wrote fellowship and job recommendation letters.

We long continued our friendships with both couples. We visited Natalie in Berkeley, where she moved from Toronto in the mid-1970s to teach at the University of California at Berkeley. We stayed in touch as she accepted an endowed chair at Princeton and through her retirement and move back to Toronto to live full-time with Chandler. He was long barred from the United States after he was fired by the University of Michigan, imprisoned, and then exiled. This followed accusations of communism by Joe McCarthy and the House Un-American Activities Committee in the 1950s.

We visited Jill and John at their country cottage in western Massachusetts while Jill served as the first female president of the historic, all-women's Smith College. We remained in contact with her after John's death and her move to Boston and MIT in the later 1980s until her death a few years ago.

Another defining moment of the first year in Toronto was my Pittsburgh draft board's order for me to appear for a physical examination prior to a call for enlistment in the armed forces. My parents consulted an attorney. With the assistance of a longtime family friend and M.D., I appeared for the examination carrying a back brace—I long had back problems—and physicians' letters about my back and my flat feet. This was the knowledgeable, fortunate, middle-class approach to avoiding the draft. I failed the physical, leading to celebrations in Pittsburgh and Toronto among my family, peers, and friends.

During summer 1971, Michael Katz employed both Vicki and me as research assistants for his Canadian social history project. Vicki coded data, and I read contemporary newspapers recording names and their contexts to compile a database for computer analysis. She also continued her work as a bank teller and was one of the first tellers trained in new, online banking technology employing mainframe computers, she reminds me. We enjoyed our first summer in Toronto with its many outdoor and indoor attractions and musical venues.

~~~

More dramatic, or melodramatic, were the consequences of our decision to marry in Toronto at the end of July—a story for the ages, and the aged. We aimed for ecumenical neutrality. We asked a fellow graduate student, an Anglican priest, to perform a secular service in the chapel at historic Hart House, the University of Toronto's equivalent of a student union. Derwyn gladly accepted. We reserved the chapel and gained permission to cover the cross at its front with a plain, velvet cloth. We ordered a modest arrangement of flowers. Vicki found an original, peasant-style, designer gown with empire waist, puffed sleeves, and eyelet lace for $45—the most she'd ever spent on a dress—and I purchased a brown suit.

All was on schedule until my father unexpectedly telephoned three weeks out and announced, "I'm not coming unless you have a rabbi."

This out-of-the-blue threat completely threw us. Most Jewish rabbis will not conduct a mixed marriage without the non-Jewish partner formally converting. We did not agree with that, and, regardless, it was much too late to begin that process. Scrambling, we searched for a Reform rabbi in Ontario, upstate New York, northern Pennsylvania, and eastern Michigan. None were available.

Finally, a friend of a friend led us to Rabbi Abraham Feinberg, the elderly rabbi of a large Reform synagogue in Toronto. Feinberg was in California visiting his son, but his secretary made tentative arrangements including an interview upon his return. The son, an M.D. in San Francisco, found a growth on his father's leg. He removed it and sent the Rabbi home to Toronto for a skin graft.

Feinberg interviewed us in his Mount Sinai Hospital room. We learned that he was renowned. Originally an American radio crooner in the 1930s, he was long known as Toronto's "Red Rabbi." He was the first theologian in Canada to bring Martin Luther King, Jr., to his pulpit in the 1960s. More recently, he traveled to Hanoi with Jane Fonda, Tom Hayden, and other anti-war activists to meet Ho Chi Minh—the Marxist-Leninist prime minister and then president of North Vietnam. He proudly displayed the cane that Ho presented him.

We had a most pleasant conversation. Rabbi Feinberg agreed to perform a nondenominational ceremony on Saturday evening, July 31, 1971. The location, however, was undetermined, pending his time of release from the hospital. A few days in advance, the Rabbi's assistant informed us that we were one of three couples he would marry in his hospital room that weekend. We canceled the priest, chapel, flowers, and handful of nonfamily friend, classmate, and professor guests.

Meanwhile, my mother surreptitiously met with Feinberg, seeking additional consolation for her misgivings about her son's impending marriage to a non-Jew. We learned years later that she had also consulted her Pittsburgh rabbi. All this despite her immediate affection for Vicki. Sectarianism runs deep on all sides.

Vicki's parents, younger sister, and sister-in-law traveled from Des Moines, Iowa (her brother was on a U.S. naval ship in the Mediterranean), along with my parents, 10-year-old brother, and grandmother from Pittsburgh. Our families gathered in the hospital's 10th-floor waiting room just after 7:00 p.m. My brother sneaked into the facility between my father and me, because he was too young for visiting. Due to limits on the number of visitors, we slipped into the rabbi's room in ones and twos.

By 7:30, we were all assembled. My family was happy, having had their way. Vicki's parents looked as if they were at a funeral, wondering why they hadn't made their own demands. My brother and Vicki's teenage sister, who were the ring bearers on either side of the hospital bed, were happy.

At the appointed hour with the minute hand on the clock ascending according to Jewish tradition, Feinberg telephoned the hospital operators and requested them to "hold my calls." He performed a brief, nondenominational ceremony that emphasized the historical and theological bonds between Judaism and Christianity. Presenting us with both a Province of Ontario legal certificate and his own document decorated like an illuminated manuscript, he declared us married.

Leaning over his bed from opposite sides, we embraced and kissed. We adjourned to the vicinity of Hart House where each of our fathers snapped poorly focused photos, one set overexposed, the other underexposed. The evening ended with dinner in the private dining room of our favorite Scandinavian restaurant with close friends Bob and Dena joining the families.

With the wedding night itself unremarkable, Gary slept on the living room sofa of our apartment. Lacking both time and money, our honeymoon consisted of daily tickets to the Canadian Open tennis tournament in Toronto. Vicki joined me in the stadium after work at the bank each day for about two weeks. Most memorably, the English Canadian audience loudly booed the singing of the French language version of the national anthem at the peak of English versus French cultural and political conflict.

Given the lack of a large ceremony or parties and the neutral location, gifts were few. My father provided our rings, bringing us a selection from his jewelry store from which to choose. My mother gave Vicki a strand of cultured pearls to wear with her wedding dress. Noteworthy, reflecting the times, were the gifts of two waterbeds. We sold them because the floors in our tenement apartment could not support the weight. Upon advertising, they sold immediately.

We lived in Toronto during what many residents and observers then and later consider the city's golden age. The city achieved North American, indeed worldwide recognition as a thriving, vibrant, and growing city. It became a desirable place to live and a tourist attraction. As a metropolitan area, it gained attention for its lakefront location, multi-borough city and suburban government structure, and striking, new, double-tower city hall (see, for one introduction, Doucet and Doucet, 2022).

For young students with limited resources, Toronto was an affordable playground. Living on fellowships, scholarships, research assistantships, part-time work, and a small monthly check from my family, we were comfortable. Weekly groceries—including one meal of rib-eye steak plus hamburgers, hot dogs, spaghetti, and macaroni and cheese—cost $9.00. We served fellow students and favorite professors cheese fondue or baked lasagna.

Within walking distance west on Bloor Street was a cluster of eastern European, Greek, Indian, and French restaurants, anchored by the famous Honest Ed's Warehouse semi-discount store. Dinner at our favorite Hungarian spot cost $2.50 each for a delicious plate of noodles. Hungarian "Bull's Blood" (Egri Bikaver) red wine was little more than $1–2 per bottle. A birthday or anniversary splurge at one of the French restaurants ran about $25 with cocktails and wine. For Vicki's U of T graduation, for example, we dined memorably at L'Aubergine.

Slightly farther away to the south and east was the iconic, historical Kensington Market, another favorite. On the edge of Greek, Italian, and Asian neighborhoods, this was originally an eastern European settlement area. It was home to delis, cheese shops, and butcher shops where one could purchase a live chicken and have it slaughtered to take home to cook. We did not do that.

A good walk beyond that took us to the Art Gallery of Ontario or downtown. To the east was the university. Walking farther took us to the Bloor and Yonge Street area, with bars, restaurants, many stores, and movie theatres south on Yonge Street. That was a Saturday afternoon jaunt.

A bit northeast was Yorkville, a centrally located, somewhat upscale and hip shopping, dining, entertainment, and residential area. We enjoyed eating, drinking, window-shopping, and visiting the lovely home of fellow OISE-Katz graduate student and dear friend Alison Prentice, her physicist husband, and their two young sons. Alison became a founder of the field of Canadian women's history.

We co-authored a volume called *Children and Schools in Nineteenth-Century Canada* (1979) for the pioneering school curriculum project called Canada's Visual History of the National Museum of Civilization (then called National Museum of Man). This was my first formal foray into public history. Sadly, Alison died in 2021 after a battle with cancer.

Toronto had lovely parks and an excellent, inexpensive, clean, and safe public subway, bus, and streetcar system. There were unfortunately also occasional, but increasing, racist outbursts directed at Black West Indian and sometimes East Indian immigrants or citizens, as well as young hockey players tripping over their sticks going to and from games.

We easily walked to Queen's Park just beyond the U of T campus for a stroll past the historic provincial parliament or a visit to the Royal Ontario Museum of history and archaeology. We could also take the streetcar and then a short ferry ride to Toronto Island. A longer subway and bus ride led west to lovely High Park and the small but charming zoo where I first fell in love with West Highland cattle (or "shaggy sheep cows"). On our first trip to Scotland in 1974, I met the natives.

Even as students, we could afford to attend the excellent Toronto Symphony and the ballet as well as occasional jazz and popular music clubs and concerts. More cosmopolitan than almost all U.S. cities, foreign films were readily available. At the university, visiting lecturers were common.

At home on Bloor Street, Hamilton, our rescued cat, frolicked with squirrels in the parking lot behind our building (one of whom scratched on the back door one day to ask if Hamilton could come out to play. He did). That is, when he wasn't tearing open freezer paper and devouring a defrosting raw steak. That episode left him uncomfortable for days. The sweet kitten sometimes sat beside my portable electric typewriter as I wrote papers, allowing the carriage to advance precariously close to his head. He loved to snuggle with his humans and also left teeth impressions on the corners of book pages and scratch marks on the spines of 33 rpm vinyl records.

Living as noncitizens, we were less engaged in politics than I had been in Evanston and Chicago. In part, this reflected my disillusionment with party politics after 1968 and my captivating encounter with the new histories. Canadian friends and colleagues participated in the growing, left-liberal, New Democratic Party (NDP). Even as landed immigrants, we benefitted from the social welfare programs of the ruling Ontario Progressive Conservative Party. The political, academic, and place intersected inseparably.

In my graduate education, the role of social theory in historical interpretation and what would later be called the "history wars" over interpretation, methods, and sources took the place of personal activism. This was an intense period of intellectual conflict over modes of interpretation and theoretical presumptions. Grounds of controversy were often confused along lines of stereotypical false distinctions oversimplified into right, center, and various "lefts," also known as conservative, liberal, and different versions of Marxism. There was much side shifting.

Among historians, the major rightward movement of colleagues Eugene Genovese and Christopher Lasch grabbed attention. This became a formative part of my education. Antonio Gramsci and Karl Marx—in historical context— were profound influences, often through leading scholars such as E. P. Thompson, Eric Hobsbawm, and Barrington Moore, along with historical materialist anthropologists, sociologists, linguists, and literary theorists.

Vicki and I and our fellow expatriates followed the anti-war movement, the Watergate scandal, and Nixon's threatened impeachment and resignation. We cast our first votes in a presidential election at the U.S. Consulate under a portrait of Richard Nixon in November 1972. We unhesitatingly voted against him.

~~~

Year two of the Canadian adventure was equally gripping and fulfilling. For Vicki, it was the second and final year of undergraduate studies as a geography major, preparing for her one-year College of Education B.Ed. teacher training program. A course in philosophy of language enthralled her. We became friendly with her Portuguese-born professor and his girlfriend. At one point, he confessed that he wanted "to sleep with both of us." We declined.

Vicki also learned a great deal from a team-taught, interdisciplinary course on "community." A historian, a sociologist, a political scientist, and an urban studies professor joined in this lecture and discussion course that featured the instructors responding to and debating each other's presentations. The students were involved actively.

Combining the required projects for that course along with two geography classes, the centerpiece of Vicki's school year was a series of three interrelated original research projects on Toronto's historic Kensington Market district. She conducted two field studies of its store distributions, ethnic relationships, trade areas, and functional interactions, interviewing residents, shop owners, and visitors. Vicki gained permission to conduct extensive research on the district's history and changing population and submit the paper for two courses.

Borrowing sources and methods (without computers) from Katz's Hamilton Project, she examined city directories, historic maps, and other records. Assisted by historians, geographers, and sociologists, she practiced the "new social history" that Michael was developing and I was learning. The result was a unique undergraduate project and an impressive set of papers, which all earned "A" grades. Regrettably, we did not think to publish them.

My studies and Katz's advising led in several interrelated directions at once. Financial support shifted from the Woodrow Wilson fellowship to OISE/University of Toronto funding, Hamilton Project research assistantships, and then a Canada Mortgage and Housing Corporation (CMHC) dissertation fellowship for urban studies.

My first task for the fall term was completion of my master's thesis on literacy and social structure in mid-19th-century Hamilton. Katz kindly read the first complete draft handwritten on yellow legal pages, the one and only time I asked a professor to do that. Because the field was novel and limited, Katz mailed copies of the final version to Lawrence Stone at Princeton and Roger Schofield at Cambridge University. Stone responded to Katz briefly and peremptorily.

In contrast, Schofield wrote a long, handwritten letter directly to me, blending praise and thoughts about future directions. Not surprisingly, it was Schofield with whom I met when we visited Cambridge in 1974. We became colleagues and good friends, staying briefly in each other's homes in London and Dallas, respectively, until his premature death in the mid-2010s.

I also prepared two articles based on my master's thesis for the *Urban History Review* (1972a) and *History of Education Quarterly* (1972b). In fall semester I registered for Michael's signature seminar on the history of American education, the subject of his dissertation and landmark first book, *The Irony of Early School Reform* (1968), and the primary reason for Toronto's hiring him in two departments. Well taught, it was not only the grounding in the field that I needed for my research and degree, but more importantly it was also a thorough introduction to the intertwined roles of social theory, ideology, ongoing revision of historical interpretations, sources and methods, and interpretation.

Educational history was in a period of transformation with the impact of the new social history and quantitative methods—and the concurrent, powerful revelations of contemporary critics and new school reformers. Key contributors included Paul Goodman (1960, 1964), Jonathan Kozol (1967), Paulo Freire (1970a, 1970b, 1970c, 1973), and documentary filmmaker Frederick Wiseman with *High School* (1968). Scholars' and social critics' writings intertwined unusually closely and productively.

Katz was a founder of what was called "revisionism" in American educational history and history more generally. It was sometimes extremely divisive, leading to outrageous attacks especially by Columbia Teachers College historian Lawrence Cremin's students like Diane Ravitch. Always promoting her own books, Ravitch (1978) took every opportunity to "revise" the "revisionists," violating scholarly standards in the process. Katz responded in "An Apology for American Educational History" (1979), later expanding on this response in Chapter Five of his book *Reconstructing American Education* (1987).

Other Cremin students also contributed to the divisiveness in unscholarly ways, negatively affecting both the developing field and young scholars. Other historians took sides for quite different reasons, some of them more overtly political or ideological than historiographical. I was soon attacked for being either or both Katz's student or a "second generation revisionist" in one of the confused, awkward formulations.

Katz's history of education seminar gave me another opportunity to conduct an experiment in social historical research. Introduced in several courses to the emerging field of family and children's and youth's history and the sociology of the life cycle, I studied the early life course of children and adolescents in Boston in 1860, using the U.S. manuscript census. Influenced by pioneering social psychologists like Erik H. Erikson (1950, 1968), Kenneth Keniston (1965, 1968, 1971), and Glen H. Elder, Jr. (1974/1999, 2003), social critics Goodman (1960, 1964) and Kozol (1967), and the emerging context-shaped "life course" conceptualization, as well as historical studies, I estimated stages of childhood and adolescent development and dependency in a seminar paper published later that year as "Patterns of Dependency and Child Development in the Mid-Nineteenth Century City" (1973b).

This was my fourth article as a graduate student. Although I did not know it then, it prefigured my volume *Conflicting Paths: Growing Up in America* (1995a); decades of teaching the history of growing up to undergraduate and graduate students across disciplines; and public work with television, radio, museums, and historical societies.

In accord with the best of historical revisionism or reinterpretation—ignored by its ideological critics—Katz taught us that history could and should be part of social criticism and crafting sounder, more equitable policies. History is an applied and theoretical discipline. That does not compromise its integrity or objectivity, as long as it is carefully researched, fact-based, and objectively interpreted. To assert otherwise advances false, often distorted dichotomies (for more on this, see Katz, 1987, and my *Undisciplining Knowledge*, 2015a).

Given the transformations in historical practice and Katz's central position, my doctoral orientation was another sign of the times and the place. Michael taught us that basic scholarship, strong conclusions, and what we later called "applied knowledge," or public and applied history, were consistent, not contradictory. Advocacy and objectivity are not opposed. He made clear in seminars, workshops, project meetings, over lunch or dinner, even in conversations in the sauna after our squash games that the crucial factor lay in always doing one's homework: complete research, thorough analysis, clear interpretation and argument, all as part of application. And, too often ignored, understanding the argument and evidence of those whom you engage critically (for more on these ideas, see my "The Best Scholarship Is Political but With No Ideological Stamp," 2022u, and "Lessons for Becoming a Public Scholar," 2023h). With respect to Michael's historical writing, this stance defined his "revisionism," first in American educational history, then urban social history and history of families, followed by the history of poverty, social policy, and social institutions.

Katz's history of social structure and history of U.S. education courses provided a firm foundation that continues to guide me. History of American education, with both its historical and contemporary readings, took me several steps closer to my dissertation and my academic future. Together, they established an early draft of my historical research, interpretation, and pedagogical practices. They previewed my selection of major topics for more than 45 active years and in general terms throughout the continuation of my life. Following Katz's tutelage, I was prepared to make major contributions to a sizable number of fields of study that cross disciplinary, topical, chronological, methodological, and interpretive grounds.

Briefly put, these fields are the history of literacy and the field of literacy studies; the history of children, youth, women, and families; the history of cities; theory and method in the humanities and the social sciences; and interdisciplinarity. It is no simplification or exaggeration that all these interests had their makings in my first years of graduate school and my relocation from British history to Katz and the new social, comparative, and quantitative histories, with developed interests in U.S., Canadian, and European history in the modern era.

Together the then new histories create a critical conceptualization and application of historical research and teaching to better understand both past and present and their inextricable interconnections. They aim at a fuller, more accurate, and more convincing set of interpretations that recognize the centrality of contradictions. And finally, new and better questions.

Each of these broad topics led to at least one of my major books, in some areas several of them; many articles, lectures, and conference sessions; and lecture courses and seminars, undergraduate and graduate. With literacy, my intersecting fields of interest contributed to the construction of innovative programs across disciplines and other demarcations. They led to cross appointments, course cross-listings, and working with graduate thesis and dissertation students in different departments and colleges. They led to three cities—Dallas, San Antonio, Columbus—three vastly different public universities, and three distinct experiences. Critically, they are interconnected and inseparable from the four forces of this life history: the personal, the political, the academic, and place—cities and universities.

~~~

I also audited a research seminar in European social and demographic history taught by the pioneering historian Edward Shorter, who soon published an influential but controversial history of the family in Europe (1975). Although I chose not to do a research project, the class broadened my methodological and comparative understanding.

Shorter studied at Harvard with the leading historical sociologist Charles Tilly, author of *The Vendée* (1964) about peasants during the French Revolution and *As History Meets Sociology* (1981) and co-editor with David Landes of the fundamental *History as Social Science* (1971). Tilly and Shorter co-edited the landmark Academic Press book series Studies in Social Discontinuity in which the book from my 1975 dissertation *The Literacy Myth* was published (1979c). From our first meeting in a University of Toronto men's room in 1974 while Chuck was presenting a series of seminars, he proved a faithful guide, linking me to a generation of his own University of Michigan history and sociology students. Some of them, led by Mary Jo Maynes and Leslie Moch, remain colleagues and friends to this day. Many of those contacts were forged at the early meetings of the SSHA in the mid- to late-1970s.

At Katz's suggestion, I also completed a reading course with a philosophy professor who grounded me in the philosophy of history. Providing me with a lasting education that few practicing historians have, I recall that this philosopher took pride in the fact he had read 10 entire works of history as the basis for his dissertation. That was an unusual number even for a philosopher of history.

My required course work concluded with a seminar on Ontario history by pioneering Canadian historian Maurice Careless, at Katz's and fellow student-colleague Alison Prentice's suggestion. I had researched and published on the history of 19th-century Ontario but lacked a comprehensive foundation. Careless' seminar provided that. It also gave me an opportunity to explore literacy in rural Ontario. That seminar paper was published as "Literacy and Social Structure in Elgin County, Canada West" (1973a).

Careless was an exceptional Canadian historian. Although well into his career, he was rare among his colleagues. Not only an outstanding scholar, he was also supportive, not threatened or falsely nationalistic in the face of new historical methods. Unlike his peers, he understood that the new histories were not "American imperialism" but reached Canada more directly from the Sixieme Section of the Sorbonne in Paris (to Montreal and Quebec) and the Cambridge Group in Great Britain than from the United States.

Also, unlike other Canadianists in the Toronto department, he saw Katz and his students, like me, Alison, and Susan Houston, as colleagues rather than aliens. (see Chad Gaffield, 2020). For the next three years and after, Maurice encouraged and supported me intellectually and personally. Periodically taking me to lunch at the faculty club, he advised me on dissertation research and job possibilities, wrote letters of recommendation, confirmed my credentials as a historian of Canada, and served on my dissertation committee.

~~~

The final pillar of my graduate "training" was less formal: the regular, informal seminars of Katz's Hamilton and then Canadian Social History Project. This experience instilled in me a lifelong commitment to interdisciplinarity inseparably combined with collaboration and collegiality across ranks and ages. I practiced this in various ways throughout my career (see Graff, 2022l, 2022o, 2023e).

We met every other week in the project's work room, around a table tennis table at which a few of us played vigorously at lunch time—especially Canadian historical urban geographer Michael Doucet, Australian geography teacher turned graduate history student Ian Davey, and me. With the net down, the table tripled as a lunch table and seminar table. In retirement, we three, and a few others, remain close colleagues and friends.

Katz led a stable core of students, faculty, and staff. We included Ian Winchester, a younger philosophy professor with a strong interest in historical methods; project assistant John Tiller, an American draft dodger; historical geography student Doucet; history of education student Davey; me; for shorter periods Bruce Tucker and Mark Stern from U of T history department and Haley Bamman from history of education; and often York University urban historian Peter Knights, who brought his cans of carbonated soda in padded mailing envelopes to keep them cold. From time to time, we had more distant visitors including Ken Lockridge from Michigan and Egil Johansson from Sweden. Katz's fellow urban historians and close friends, author of *Town into City* (1972) Michael H. Frisch from the University at Buffalo and Ted Hershberg (1981) of the University of Pennsylvania's Philadelphia Social History Project also visited.

Often Katz presented a draft of a new working paper. That was his method for working through the voluminous database step by step. The drafts varied in completeness and polish but were always thought provoking. Occasionally, we graduate students presented our work. I paraphrase Katz's remark in the Acknowledgments to his 1975 *The People of Hamilton, Canada West* that the project meetings were the best seminars that any of us had attended in a long time.

The project group presented an informal model that I later adapted for use with Dallas history, the more formal Dallas Social History Group, and a children's studies program at KERA TV, all in Dallas; interdisciplinary and cross-division literacy studies at UT-San Antonio; Teen Chicago at the Chicago Historical Society (now Museum of Chicago History); and in fullest development, LiteracyStudies@OSU at Ohio State University beginning in 2004. I continue to use the model informally with colleague/friends across disciplines around the world and with Ohio State University undergraduates in what we humorously call "Harvey U" (for more on "Harvey U," see Graff, 2022aa).

~~~

Vicki received her Bachelor of Arts degree at the end of spring 1972. Toronto's ceremony depended heavily on British traditions: She literally knelt on a velvet cushion at the feet of the Governor General, who tapped her shoulder with a sabre. I watched with flowers to present to her.

In addition to my research assistantship with the Hamilton Project and Vicki's work at banks, summer 1972 included a brief vacation at a tennis camp and a driving tour around the lovely lakes of eastern Ontario in a rental car. Our landlord reluctantly informed us that we had to vacate and relocate by the end of the summer because his daughter needed a place to live. A few weeks' search located a one-bedroom apartment set just below ground level about a mile north on Bathurst Street in a medium-sized, older building with a central courtyard. Across the way from my classmate Michael Doucet's and his wife Natalie's apartment, it was quieter than Bloor St. with shops but not restaurants close by. Mike became a major figure in urban historical geography and a faculty association leader at Ryerson University in Toronto. Hamilton the cat approved; he had safer spaces to play. It was a positive trade-off (except for a voyeur masturbating on our windows) and start to year three of the Canadian Adventure.

Vicki progressed through classes and practice teaching, acquiring her Bachelor of Education degree and certification in elementary grades and high school geography. In the spring of 1973, Branksome Hall, the elite, private school for girls, hired her. Although only a beginning full-time teacher, she had the credentials to be appointed head of history and geography.

~~~

Largely forgotten today, the late 1950s and 1960s witnessed a rediscovery of the "crises of literacy." This stood out among the failures of schooling especially but not only for members of underrepresented racial groups, poor people, inner-city and rural residents, immigrants, females, and members of different linguistic groups. Paul Goodman (1960, 1964), John Holt (1964, 1967), Jonathan Kozol (1967), and others published landmark works that were partly ethnographic and observational and partly liberal to left social criticism.

As usual, outside of English departments and especially writing programs, reading attracted far more attention than writing as educators and social scientists took reading as the key indicator of literacy. With rare exceptions, rhetoric and writing instructors seldom inquired into reading or accessing meaning as opposed to expressing meaning. This is one of many strains among the literacy myths.

In the 21st century, an endless series of "new literacy myths" proliferates. I have lists of hundreds of proclaimed "literacies" including financial, racial, and media. Most are forms of marketing. None stand independently as actual literacy. These steps backward fill the chronological and intellectual gap between recognition of the power of the "literacy myth," the impact of the New Literacy Studies that formed in the 1970s–1990s, and the more recent proliferation of "many literacies."

~~~

Inseparable from debates about inequality, discrimination, and expanding civil rights on one hand and the recurring "reading wars" about early instruction (phonics versus phonetics in various formulations), educational ethnographies, and new interests of linguists with its field in periodic ferment on the other hand, more scholars explored and exposed the inseparable intersections of reading *and* writing in their social *and* historical contexts. Those central dialectical relationships were only slowly institutionalized. International educational criticism and activism by Paulo Freire (1970a, 1970b, 1970c, 1973) and others from Brazil to Cuba and the Cuban national literacy campaign powerfully added to the mix.

First-, second-, and third-world ethnographies exploring learning, language, and social psychology in contexts of daily life began to spread (see Arnove and Graff, 1987/2008, and Graff, *Searching for Literacy*, 2022e).

Progressive-to-left literacy critics and the pioneers of what became known and partly institutionalized as cultural studies propelled new attention to what Richard Hoggart called "the uses of literacy" in his classic 1957 book of that name. This accompanied Raymond Williams' 1958 landmark *Culture and Society* among his many related works. In the late 1960s and 1970s, these interpretations were influential across disciplines including history, anthropology, and literature.

Increasingly, texts *and* their readers and writers were conceptualized as interactive elements. No one "variable" was independently determinative. Perhaps most importantly, *literacy by itself* was less often seen as independently transformative irrespective of other life and contextual circumstances. Historians like E. P. Thompson (1964, 1967) brought this eye- and mind-opening new theoretical and empirical approach to audiences across the world and across disciplines. The power of some degree of literacy within collective cultures balanced the limits of literacy by itself. With this understanding, many negative representations of slaves, women, immigrants, and young persons began to change. In economics—whose modern conceptions of "investment in human capital" prized and priced literacy and education highly—Italian economic historian Carlo M. Cipolla raised modest doubts in *Literacy and Development in the West* (1969).

At the same time, in opposing major works in communications under the shadow of proliferating "new media," popularized, often slogan-based, universalistic, and relatively data-free generalizations about the independently transformative power of individual access and uses of reading and writing across media, especially print, overflowed. This was central to the burgeoning field of communication studies. It reinforced the elitist and classist views that inflated expectations of the direct consequences of reading and writing central to certain influential literary approaches to antiquity through the Renaissance and the Enlightenment.

Ironically, the "Toronto School" of communication theory promulgated these views widely, prompted by Harold A. Innis and Marshall McLuhan, based at the University of Toronto. Innis' more scholarly 1951 *The Bias of Communication* was a serious study compared to his younger colleague McLuhan's uncritically repeated, caricatured best sellers, *The Gutenberg Galaxy: The Making of Typographic Man* in 1962 and *Understanding Media: The Extensions of Man* in 1964. The gendering was no accident.

At the same time, classicist Eric A. Havelock's *Preface to Plato* (1963) and early modern philosophy scholar Walter J. Ong's *Ramus, Method, and the Decay of Dialogue* (1958) further emphasized academically appealing (and self-promoting) exaggerations of the necessarily independent determinative power of print and individual access to text. Arithmetic misrepresentations of the presumed impact of multiple typographic printing after Gutenberg pushed this further. Elizabeth L. Eisenstein's paeons to printing began to appear in journal articles.

Multi-volume praise-songs to print followed in the 1970s and 1980s. For example, sustained documented criticism from different perspectives by Anthony T. Grafton ("The Importance of Being Printed," 1980) or me (*The Legacies of Literacy*, 1987b) made little impression against the history and humanities mythmaking of Eisenstein's 1979/1980 *The Printing Press as an Agent of Change*. Eisenstein's inattention to both reading and writing and lack of direct evidence of printing specifically as "an agent of change" were powerful. Human agency and human difference played little role in her analysis. Eisenstein's "printing myth" supplemented "the literacy myth." Human uses of reading and writing attract insufficient attention.

Long-standing elitist traditions amplified these elements into grand endorsements of "literary canons" and "great books" curricula. Surprisingly few classroom teachers or literary critics asked about how students actually read and make meaning (for more on this topic, see, for example, my "Myths Shape the Continuing "Crisis of the Humanities," 2022s, "The Inseparability of 'Historical Myths' and 'Permanent Crises' in the Humanities," 2022b, and "Opinion: The Persistent 'Reading Myth' and the 'Crisis of the Humanities,'" 2023d).

What I named "the literacy myth" at end of the 1970s was amplified for decades by well-known Cambridge anthropologist Jack Goody (1968) and Toronto educational psychologist David R. Olson (1994), who later followed McLuhan as head of what was named the McLuhan Center at the U of T, and their students and colleagues. Quick to make sweeping transhistorical assertions, neither Goody nor Olson did historical research nor followed an emerging two generations of reorienting research and interpretations.

For whatever reasons, Olson had no interest in discussing literacy, its study, or its interpretation with me, a doctoral student two floors down in the Ontario Institute for Studies in Education building. Nor did McLuhan's center down the street. Similarly, Goody and his associates did not exchange views with Roger Schofield, Peter Laslett, Anthony Wrigley, nor their students like David Cressy and Rab Houston at Cambridge University. As I first learned at Northwestern and would see in each of my university appointments, interdisciplinarity is always bounded (I discuss this at length in *The Literacy Myth*, 1979c, several of the essays in *Literacy Myths, Legacies, and Lessons*, 2011/2023c, *Searching for Literacy*, 2022e, and *Undisciplining Knowledge*, 2015a).

For me, the multiple elements of what is sometimes called "dissertating" twisted and turned in a challenging intellectual context. My dissertation research, drafting, submitting chapters first to Katz, rapidly receiving constructive criticism, and then revision occupied center stage for the next few years. When I prepared my first drafts and sent them to Katz at Princeton, where he was a fellow at the Institute for Advanced Study writing *The People of Hamilton* (1975), he cautioned me, "not so hot off the typewriter." Taking several deep breaths, I listened to him. That was another chapter in my life with literacy.

As I progressed with analysis, writing, and revision, I continued to publish articles that developed data not fully exploited in my dissertation. These papers derived from the comparative research and the database I compiled on the cities of Kingston and London in addition to Hamilton: an original exploration of mid-19th century manuscript gaol (jail) registers that provided information on inmate literacy to test past and present presumptions of a direct relationship tying illiteracy to criminality. I also examined a manuscript on employment pay registers from the eastern Ontario lumber industry. (See my "Crime and Punishment in the Nineteenth Century" (1977a), "Towards a Meaning of Literacy" (1975), "Literacy in History" (1975a), and "Respected and Profitable Labour" (1976b).

Each of these subprojects explored larger questions in the theoretical and empirical literature with new empirical quantitative and qualitative evidence. Neither Katz nor my other committee members presumed that any one primary source including quantitative data stood alone. I divided my time—by direction and design—between coding data and the computer center, university library, and both Province of Ottawa and National Archives in Toronto and Ottawa, respectively. I also explored records in Hamilton and Kingston, Ontario.

In general terms, my dissertation "Literacy and Social Structure in the Nineteenth-Century City" (1975b) was an unprecedented, multi-dimensional set of investigations into literacy's social, economic, cultural, and political relationships in the middle decades of the 19th century with an urban base. From many sources and perspectives, some quantitative, others more traditional, I reinterpreted the role of literacy in lives, work, social and geographic mobility, family, growing up, schools, criminality, economic development, and communities. While the quantitative data were primarily Canadian, my evidentiary and interpretive base included the United States and England, cross-border, and trans-Atlantic dimensions.

Among many arguments, I maintained that largely self-reported indicators of literacy (compared to other recent studies that made assumptions about literacy based on ability to sign one's name) seldom had a simple and direct association with social origins; social, economic, and occupational standing; crime and punishment; children's schooling; age and gender; or indicators of cultural participation. My contexts crossed sociocultural, quantitative and qualitative, humanities and social sciences, and history and theory boundaries. This was interdisciplinarity in the arts and sciences in the 1970s (for more on this approach, see my *Undisciplining Knowledge*, 2015a, and "Literacy Studies and Interdisciplinary Studies: Reflections on History and Theory," 2012).

Encapsulated in the title to the book version of my dissertation, *The Literacy Myth* (1979c) represented a sustained critique and reinterpretation of normative, ahistorical, and universalist approaches to literacy in actual lives as lived. My new understanding of the past continues to directly inform comprehension and actions in the present and future. Those are among the reasons that the articles coming from my dissertation research and later books have been influential (for reviews of the current state of the field, see my "The New Literacy Studies and the Resurgent Literacy Myth," 2022c, "*The Literacy Myth* at Thirty," 2010a, *Literacy Myths,*

*Legacies, and Lessons*, 2011/2023c, *Searching for Literacy*, 2022e, "The Shock of the 'New' Histories," 2001/2005, and with John Duffy, "Literacy Myths," 2008).

As my dissertation progressed, I also wrote about the strengths and limitations of the manuscript census as a basis for historical research and understanding in "What the 1861 Census Can Tell Us About Literacy" (1975c). Along the path of my dissertation, summer 1973 provided another adventure and set of exceptional learning experiences. I attended the second year of the Newberry Library summer institute in social, demographic, and family history in Chicago, with fellowship support from the Spencer and Mellon Foundations. An outgrowth of Richard Jensen's Family and Community History Center, the institute provided unusual tutelage in new historical methods for advanced graduate students and younger professors. Colonial demographic and family historian Daniel Scott Smith joined his University of Chicago at Illinois colleague in teaching the course.

I was more prepared and my research farther along than many others in the program. For me, the greatest benefits lay in conversations with Jensen and especially Smith and in making the acquaintance of fellow social historians. Several of them became long-lasting friends, from Kathryn (Kitty) Sklar, then at Michigan, to Judith Smith, a student in American studies at Brown, later a professor at Boston University and Boston College. At the end of three weeks, we were each awarded a certificate. My career-long relationship with the Newberry Library commenced.

Although I had only completed three years of graduate studies, I accepted an invitation to teach a summer seminar on the history of American education in the Graduate School of Education at Northwestern University. Vicki flew to meet me as I moved from the near north side of Chicago to our old stomping grounds in Evanston. I substituted for Northwestern's historian of education Robert Church while he spent that summer away from campus. Our cat, Hamilton, was scheduled to accompany Vicki. But as a Canadian-born nationalist, he ran away instead. In fact, he absconded in retaliation for being neutered.

The summer seminar was a positive experience. I had not taught since I was an unofficial teaching assistant as a Northwestern undergraduate. The course went very well. The students were diverse, able, and interested. Some became our summer friends. Equally importantly, we delighted in returning to Evanston and Chicago and took advantage of the opportunities for food, music, and the arts.

Driving a rental car back to Toronto in August, we stopped to visit Ken Lockridge in Ann Arbor, Michigan. I had developed a friendship with him originating in our respective research on the history of literacy. He was completing an important book, *Literacy in Colonial New England* (1974). For some time, he joined my models and examples.

~~~

We returned to Toronto for the 1973–1974 academic year. I resumed my research with the support of the CMHC urban studies fellowship. Working hard, I completed the greater part of my basic primary and secondary research.

Vicki began to practice her secondary school teaching skills. She particularly enjoyed field trips with her students to observe the geographic formations of the Niagara escarpment. For variety, we sometimes chaperoned school dances, shaking our heads at the young prep and military school dates of Branksome Hall's students.

More often, we socialized with our cohort of graduate students and their partners. We dined in or out together, drinking inexpensive Hungarian and Yugoslavian wines (and boycotting Canadian and New York vintages); attended film screenings, concerts, and with our Australian classmate a tennis tournament featuring Rod Laver; and played "Dictionary" with exceptionally intelligent people. We've never laughed as hard as we did during those evenings.

A coed group of students and a young professor played squash one morning each week, followed by a collectively prepared brunch. A small group of graduate students played highly competitive but joking tennis: a big-serving Canadian Chad Gaffield, Australian Ian Davey, and me. Both Chad and Ian went on to notable careers in Canada and Australia, respectively. Chad headed the Social Sciences and Humanities Research Council of Canada and held a Canada research chair at the University of Ottawa, while Ian led the education faculty and served as a leader at the University of South Australia in Adelaide.

~~~

The summer of 1974 brought another adventure. After contemplating and saving for several years and some hemming and hawing by me about finances and completing my dissertation, we made our first transatlantic trip. It was predominantly but not exclusively for pleasure, the first of many that combined business and pleasure. We embarked for six weeks to England, Wales, and Scotland. A first and final week in London bookended four weeks on the road in a rental car.

Ever since my first sparks of interest in British history as a teenager, I longed for this trip. We went with a lengthy wish list ranging from historical and cultural sights to many lesser-known recommendations of friends and colleagues. The *Blue Guide* along with *England on $5 and $10 A Day* were our primers. The six weeks exceeded our expectations.

We spent our first and last weeks in the small, moderately priced, and comfortable The George Hotel in Bloomsbury within walking distance of the British Museum, the University of London, and Georgian terraced, gently curving streets with welcoming restaurants and bars. Many young adults roamed the area. We were 24- and 25-year-old kids in a candy shop, lapping up famous and lesser-known sites in and around the city.

Along with almost all the museums and parks, trekking to Highgate Cemetery to pay homage to the tomb of Karl Marx was among my first imperatives. The previous week, we learned, vandals had knocked down the iconic, upper torso sculptural monument from his grave. We boated on the Thames and bused to Windsor Castle. Happily, my undergraduate advisor, Lacey Smith, was serving as assistant to the cultural attaché at the U.S. Embassy. We had lunch with Lacey and his family in the garden of his lovely rental house.

We then picked up a rental car at Heathrow Airport for a four-week exploration of southwestern, central, northern, and northeastern England, eastern Wales, Glasgow, Edinburgh, and the Scottish Highlands and islands. The locals with whom we spoke considered us absolutely crazy Americans for driving so much. As the sole driver at that time, I gradually mastered navigating "the wrong way on the road" and steering from the right-hand seat. Vicki guided me with road maps and signage. We searched out inexpensive hotels, bed and breakfasts, and rooms to rent, on occasion paying extra for a bath or gas heating. It was an adventure and sometimes a comedy.

As tourists and scholar-in-becoming, we first explored Oxford and Cambridge. In Cambridge, Roger Schofield led us to his personal favorite sights, including the Clare College library where he showed us Sir Isaac Newton's handwritten notes in an early printed book. At Oxford, we dined at the famous The Swan on the river. I briefly and awkwardly punted on the river.

Heading west toward Land's End, we toured Devon's and Cornwall's towns, cathedrals, and countryside. We began our checklist of seeing 18 of the 21 Church of England Cathedrals. We delighted in Devon clotted cream. From there, we journeyed to eastern Wales and a hike through Snowdonia National Park, then to the historic midlands for more walks and touring the locations of classic 19th-century novels. Ever the historian plus one, we sampled the cities where much of the early Industrial Revolution took place and the lovely border country. The cities and industrialization ranked high among my historical interests.

Scotland was among the high points of the trip (and future visits) from its highlands to the lowlands. We fell in love with Edinburgh, its Old Town, Castle Mount, and New Town. Our guidebook led us to the zoo with its iconic, 11:00 a.m. parade of penguins (which we returned to see again several decades later). A world-class walking city.

From the city to Loch Ness without sighting a monster. And to the highlands and via ferry to the Hebrides Islands with spectacular scenery, ancient remains, cozy bed and breakfasts, inviting cafes, and outstanding Scotch whiskey. The hills, lakes, and herds of West Highland cattle and sheep walking along and crossing the roads remain vivid in my mind. A final week in London and home.

Vicki began her second year teaching geography at Branksome Hall. I turned toward completing my dissertation and beginning a fraught job search in one of the worst job markets in history (see my "Finding a Permanent Job in the Humanities Has Never Been Easy," 2023f). OISE had no undergraduate students, so assisting in courses was not an option for job preparation. At their request, I taught the graduate seminar in American educational history in Katz's absence during my final year. I also continued as the Hamilton Project's graduate research assistant.

All went well. Among my students was a first-year doctoral candidate named Chad Gaffield, who became a lifelong friend and leading Canadian historian. He sometimes accords me more credit for his success than I might deserve.

More generally, looking over my graduate education and the next years, I also wrote "Introduction to 'Literacy Studies in Sweden'" (1974), "Counting on the Past: Quantification in History" (1976a), and "Selected Bibliography: Urban, Social, Sociological, Demographic, and Quantitative History" (1976c). As I completed my dissertation Katz said quietly to me, "You have enough graduate student articles, Harvey." I am sure he was right.

~~~

There is one further dimension of my graduate training, an aspect that is insufficiently appreciated and remains too rare. These are the substantial extracurricular opportunities and general professional experience that I received. Their breadth and depth reflect the times, the place, the fields, and my advisors and multiple models. Chapter One reflects the culmination of this process.

As a graduate-only department, history and philosophy of education drew less exclusive and formal lines among many (but not all) faculty, students, and staff than most units. The 1960s and 1970s were also a time of greater acceptance and tolerance. At least partial equity within organizations was encouraged more than in most periods before or after.

At the department level, from my first year to my last, I served as a member of its inclusive general assembly. At various times, I sat on departmental committees for admissions and admissions policy, faculty and chair searches, orientation, evaluation, research and development, programs and graduate studies, nominations, and the library. While some of this activity was more pretense and self-congratulatory on the part of the tenured faculty than substance—especially as related to hiring, promotion, and finances—it was a great learning opportunity that was invaluable preparation for my future faculty roles and responsibilities. I also served as a consultant to the Canadian Social History Project from 1973 to 1975.

My professional preparation extended beyond the department and the university. At least as consequential was early involvement in professional societies and their annual meetings. I attended my first American professional meetings at the department's expense in 1973: convenings of the American Educational Research Association and the History of Education Society. I began my friendship with Paul Mattingly, a historian at New York University (sleeping on his hotel room sofa at the History of Education Society meeting a year later). Our lengthy personal and professional relationship continues.

The 1970s were a pioneering period for student members on committees and boards, which for me included the following:

- Editorial board of OISE-based *Interchange: A Quarterly Review of Education* (1974–1975; corresponding editor, 1975–1976; consulting editor, 1985–present)

- Executive committee of the Canadian Association for American Studies (founding student member, 1972–1975; program committee, 1974)
- Program committee, Division F Historiography, American Educational Research Association (1973)
- Steering and program committees, Canadian Population Studies Group (1974–1976)

Finally, I was encouraged or invited to present my graduate student research and also chair sessions at both student and regular professional meetings. These included the Little Community Conference, primarily for graduate students, at Brandeis University (1972); History of Education Society, Chicago (1973); Canadian Association for American Studies, Ottawa (1974); and Canadian Historical Association, Edmonton (1975). At each event, I made new acquaintances and initiated long-lasting friendships.

Michael Katz's 1974 relocation from the U of T/OISE to York University in north Toronto constituted a minor hiccup for my program but a major obstacle for the future of the Hamilton-Canadian Social History Project. Michael's younger colleague Ian Winchester became my Toronto supervisor of record, but Katz remained my principal advisor in practice. He continued to return my drafts almost immediately.

~~~

The school year of 1974–1975 was not the time to search for academic positions, especially in the humanities and the social sciences. Despite recent myths, the academic "job crisis" is not new. There was a "job crisis" in every decade since World War II. Professorial positions were exceedingly scarce as I completed my degree.

Vicki and I preferred to remain in Canada, but on the one hand, there were almost no positions to which to apply, and, perhaps more powerfully, on the other hand, there were rising currents of Canadian nationalism and negative backlash to the over-hiring of often-mediocre Americans during a period of university expansion in the mid- to late-1960s. I recall one Canadian history department asking Maurice Careless if I knew *any* Canadian history! At least one of my handful of on-site interviews deteriorated into an uninformed debate about social and quantitative history and an ignorant attack on my advisor.

I plugged on, writing, revising, reading job ads for positions in Canada and the United States, applying and applying. In the spring, the just-opening campus of the University of Texas at Dallas asked me if I was interested in applying for a tenure-track cross-appointment in history/humanities and social science. I applied. Not long afterwards, I was invited to an interview, not on campus, but in a hotel room at the Toronto airport. I met with the new dean of arts and humanities. A former nun, the founding faculty dubbed her "the flying dean." Shortly afterward, she offered me the job.

We hesitated. Not only was our preference to remain in Canada, but Dallas, Texas, and a brand-new branch of a large, public university system gave us pause. We knew little about Dallas beyond its public images, dominated by the 1963 Kennedy assassination and the Cowboys football team. They were not appealing. Too many images turned out to be more accurate than not. In the end, the combination of a tenure-track position, a city rather than a college town, and the self-promotions of a supposedly distinctive, indeed unique, interdisciplinary university settled the matter. We celebrated, sometimes with friends who brought us funny hats that they thought evoked the Wild West.

In July, our first trip to the West Coast of Canada and the United States, to Vancouver, British Columbia, and San Francisco, California, marked the end of our Canadian adventure. Planning to take a train with viewing cars through the Canadian Rockies, we flew to Calgary only to find the Canadian National Railway running 24 hours late. We shifted to a bus via Banff and Jasper National Parks. We had booked a room in the University of British Columbia (UBC) dorms, empty of students for the summer.

With its lovely downtown, historic neighborhoods, and majestic waterfront, Vancouver was smashing. Coincidentally, the Katz family spent the summer there, exchanging their Toronto house for a house near UBC owned by a friend and colleague. We explored the city and its beaches together.

From Vancouver, we took a ferry to quaint Victoria on beautiful Vancouver Island. From there a flight to San Francisco, another city where we experienced love at first sight. A full five days took us from Golden Gate and Fisherman's Wharf to Haight-Asbury, Muir Woods, Berkeley, and Stanford. We visited Natalie Davis in her new abode in Berkeley. Like Vancouver, this was the first of recurring visits and increasing familiarity.

Returning to Toronto, we prepared to move. We resolved the problem that my dissertation typist had stopped without completing her job by alternating typing the remaining pages between us. All responsible parties approved the final draft and confirmed a date for an October formal defense. Tradition held that summer defenses were inconvenient for the faculty. My U of T business wasn't quite complete.

# Chapter 6. A Not-So-Great Migration to Big D, Dallas, Texas: New Frontiers, New University, New City, 1975–1979

Seen for the first time, Dallas together with the University of Texas at Dallas were a shock. Because I was interviewed at the Toronto airport and hired by telephone and mail, they were a new frontier to Vicki and me. They required radical adjustments that took years. That adaptation becomes another major set of experiences that documents the continuing intersections of the personal, political, academic, and place. In part, it led to a decades-long teaching, research, and public service project that culminated in the publication of my book *The Dallas Myth: The Making and Unmaking of an American City* (2008a).

Our physical move south and west was unpleasant. We rented an AMC Gremlin (a relatively new, early hatchback model) to test drive as a candidate for our first car purchase—a requirement for living in Dallas. We did not need a car in Evanston-Chicago or Toronto. When we reached Oklahoma and were required to pay a toll to drive on barely paved highways, I was ready to turn around and head back north. When we arrived in Dallas to learn that our possessions had been removed from their moving van at the border and delayed for up to two weeks, we both were ready to return to Toronto.

We persevered. With limited possessions, we moved into our two-story, townhouse apartment in a moderate-sized complex with requisite small swimming pools and laundry rooms, not far from the university, north of the city of Dallas boundary. On the west side road of North Central Expressway (US 75), The Timbers apartments sat across the highway from the major Texas Instruments plant. With our belongings delayed, we purchased air and foam mattresses, sheets, and towels to camp out in our bare abode and negotiated with the moving company and insurance agents. In time, our possessions arrived safely.

We purchased a new AMC Gremlin for cash from our savings from fellowships and Vicki's teaching job, a first and only experience. Not long afterward, we added our first dog, a brindle mix of Australian and cairn terrier puppy we named Morgan, after the leading character in a 1960s British alternative film. He was a wonderful member of the family, but he tragically died at seven months after swallowing a chicken bone he found near a garbage can. We had no better luck with cats in that townhouse. One pregnant stray we took in—black with white paws, named Soxy—died shortly after giving birth to two kittens, who also died. Two other cats succumbed to the heavy traffic leaving the highways.

Lacking Texas teacher certification, Vicki found employment in a nearby preschool. Not having driven since a teenage car accident, she took driving lessons to regain her license. Her first attempts at driving with me instructing her were not healthy for our relationship.

~~~

Both Dallas and the university were full of surprises. Their newness and their size—this was Big D and the University of Texas *near* Dallas—were major elements. So too was their underdeveloped, unfinished, and incomplete state. Both were physically, politically, socially, and culturally disorganized, disconnected, and immature (see my *The Dallas Myth*, 2008a).

The major theme of this chapter, the first phase—1975–1979—of our long relationships with Dallas and UT-Dallas (UTD), is radical adjustment to an often-alien environment. I soon learned, and relearned, that UTD weighed heavily on my psychological vulnerabilities. Universities do this (see my "Colleges Must Learn From Sports Figures About Mental Health," 2021e, and "Academic Collegiality is a Contradictory, Self-Serving Myth," 2022l). After almost five decades I can attest that my struggles—and the support I found at home, among colleagues, and eventually from three differently trained, excellent psychiatrists in three cities—made me a better teacher, graduate advisor, colleague, and person. If that's contradictory, it is also fundamentally human.

Both Dallas and UT-Dallas were dominated by origin and alternative reality myths—as in the Dallas Myth and the Dallas Way—that I explicated formally and documented in my book on the subject and in my teaching. For Big D and UTD, bravado and ceaseless self-promotion are attempts to hide an abiding sense of insecurity and inferiority. This derived in part from their backward sense of origins and patterns of emergence. Dallas long loved to claim, absolutely falsely *and* profoundly ahistorically, that it has "no reason to exist," because it was not a port city. It does sit on the banks of the Trinity River and an early cross-country horse and wagon trail.

UTD developed backwardly. It was first a Ph.D.-granting graduate institution in the sciences—following its foundation as Texas Instruments' research department—gradually adding other graduate programs, juniors and seniors, and later first-year students and sophomores. For both UTD and Dallas, people were their greatest asset and their most unappreciated quality, institutional management and integrity, their least.

After several decades of observation, research, teaching about the city, supervising student local history research, an array of civic involvements, reflection, and time away in Chicago, San Antonio, and Columbus, I completed *The Dallas Myth: The Making and Unmaking of an American City* (2008a). To help set the stage, I quote from *The Dallas Myth*:

> The ninth largest city in the United States, Dallas is exceptional among American cities for the claims of its elite and boosters that it is a "city with no limits" and a "city with no history." . . .

Dallas looms disproportionately large in the American imagination. Yet it lacks an identity of its own.

I published the book with an out-of-state university press to general applause beyond the pens of representatives of Dallas institutions, many of whom did not open the book before condemning it. Many other Texas publications and academics praised it. Not only did I need mental, temporal, and physical distance from the city, I needed intellectual space. In between leaving Dallas and completing the book, I authored other books and articles on literacy, the history of growing up, and social science history. Multiple dimensions of distance are central to my journeys including my own uses of literacy.

Arriving in Dallas mid-August 1975, before the opening of the first school year for most of the overwhelmingly new university campus, knowing virtually no one except a distant cousin in a suburb, and with a brand-new car, we explored. Like much of the city, UTD was under construction. There was little to see on the substantially newly built, flat, and plain, almost treeless campus dominated by parking lots. My fellow faculty members were just arriving from around the United States and abroad. Outside the sciences, the entire "founding faculty" of about 130 was new.

As chance, job markets, different challenges, and developing opportunities had it, this was the first of the three public universities at which I taught from 1975 to 2017. The first two were new, branch campuses of a huge hierarchical, unequal, and disorganized state system, each located just beyond the city boundaries of two of the three largest cities in Texas.

The third was the huge, main campus of *The* Ohio State University in Columbus, the state capital and now the 14th largest city in the nation. Despite their many differences, they were all poorly managed public universities whose promise was never realized, in part because of inadequate leadership. In each, the administration led by sloganeering (see my "An Education in Sloganeering," 2015b, "The Banality of University Slogans," 2022f, "Slogans Are No Substitute for Concrete University Policies and Programmes," 2022h, and "Sloganeering and the Limits of Leadership," 2022i).

UTD emerged from its seeds as a research center established by the three founders (thus that ubiquitous campus word "Founders" and the names of the three new buildings—Johnson, Green, McDermott—of 1975–1976) of the huge Texas Instruments computer corporation, first to conduct industrial research and then to train technicians. The center developed in the 1940s but was formalized as the Graduate Research Center of the Southwest or Southwest Center for Advanced Science (SCAS) in the early 1960s, and construction of Founders Hall, the primary science building, began in 1962 as the center moved from its location on the Southern Methodist University (SMU) campus in the separately chartered, upper-class, overwhelmingly white University Park within north central Dallas (The University of Texas at Dallas, n.d.-d).

SCAS became UTD in the late 1960s to early 1970s. It was a graduate school and research center in the sciences with some distinction in computer science, geoscience, space science, math, and physics. Faculty came from top graduate programs and laboratories in the United States and abroad, and students from wide ranges. Among its claims to fame was its collection of moon rocks from early lunar explorations.

The words on the UTD website today reflect the Dallas Myth or the Dallas Way far more than UTD's or SCAS' history: "UT Dallas continues to build a future as bright as its beginnings, preparing graduates for leadership roles in science, engineering, business, research, the arts, government and the global community" (The University of Texas at Dallas, n.d.-b). It was founded as an R&D center for private industry.

Closer to reality is another statement on the university's website:

> A Dynamic Past: In the 1960s, Eugene McDermott, Erik Jonsson [a future Dallas mayor] and Cecil Green saw promising young Texans leaving the state to pursue education while their company, Texas Instruments, recruited out-of-state talent to work at their Dallas-based headquarters. (The University of Texas at Dallas, n.d.-c)

The myth recycles:

> Hoping to create better higher-education opportunities in North Texas, the trio established the Graduate Research Center of the Southwest—the foundation for what will become The University of Texas at Dallas. Rooted in an entrepreneurial spirit, UTD has grown into one of the nation's top public research universities. (The University of Texas at Dallas, n.d.-c)

And:

> Created by bold visionaries and tech pioneers, UT Dallas has nurtured generations of innovators in its first 50 years. Our creativity and enterprising spirit has been—and will continue to be—UT Dallas' guiding light. (The University of Texas at Dallas, n.d.-a)

"The foundation for what will become." "Generations" in 50 years. "One of the nation's top public research universities." No, on all counts.

By the late 1960s and early 1970s, the new graduate center became complicated and expensive. The founders arranged to transfer it to the state of Texas and the University of Texas System as a branch campus with upper-division (juniors, seniors) and graduate students, with first-year students and sophomores coming later. The state assumed management and funding. Texas Instruments donated the land.

The pitch to the state was marketing and promotion in the Dallas Way. No ordinary university like the nearby University of Texas at Arlington and other branches of the system anchored in Austin, UT "near" Dallas was to be "interdisciplinary" and unique. This was a catchy notion of the time that was never defined nor put into practice. "Interdisciplinary" disappeared from the university's rhetoric and organization—except for cost-cutting reasons of staffing and support—before long.

More than almost anything else, the slogan struggled to provide an identity, no matter how insubstantial or false. It cut costs by avoiding the budgeting of separate disciplinary departments and staff—that is, infrastructure—with unintegrated schools instead. It attracted students uncertain about their intentions and for the first decades both unprepared and confused about UTD rhetorics and realities. No less importantly if contradictorily, it lured a first-rate, overwhelmingly young faculty just out of graduate school. Another founding faculty member once said, "Aren't we all someone famous' best student?" About the junior faculty, he wasn't wrong.

Scheduled to open as "a university" in fall semester 1975, a campus had to be built around the lonely plain Founders Building on the suburban prairie and a substantial founding faculty hired by a new, inexperienced, and unqualified administration. Additional buildings named for the three founders were constructed quickly to accommodate science, social science, education, human development (i.e., psychology), arts and humanities, business, the inadequate library, scant physical education, and the physically and intellectually distant administration. There was no on-campus housing nor were there competitive collegiate sports teams for decades.

~~~

The UTD way is synonymous with, indeed derivative of, the Dallas Way. Both imitate without acknowledgment. "Reading" UTD was quick and easy. Dallas was a bit more complicated. In 1975, I was unfamiliar with the local lexicon of the contradictory, conflict-ridden "Dallas Way" and "Tales of Two Cities," aspirational and real, new and old, developed and undeveloped, urban and suburban, rich and poor, White and Black, and also brown. Concluding my 25-year struggle to understand Dallas in multiple contexts, *The Dallas Myth* (2008a) presented a historical interpretation of the development and consequences of ideology, power, social and cultural relations, urban forms, and geographic location (for additional reading on this topic, see *The Dallas Myth*'s bibliography, Patricia Evridge Hill, 1996—Hill was my doctoral student, and Warren Leslie, 1964/1998; contrast these sources with ahistorical and misconceived Robert B. Fairbanks, 1998, and vanity-press, coffee-table, anti-historical Darwin Payne, 1994).

Even with an orientation, Dallas is a hard city to "read." It is less difficult to navigate physically. We quickly learned our way around its freeways to its attractive, expensive, in-city residential areas University Park and Highland

Park surrounding Southern Methodist University (SMU); Lakewood with small waterways including White Rock Lake; sections of Old East Dallas, Oak Lawn, Turtle Creek, and Oak Cliff; and its uncontrolled, repetitive suburban sprawl. Downtown's West End and Deep Ellum long struggled to become entertainment districts. More established and appealing were the early, open-air shopping center Highland Park Village, Greenville Avenue in East Dallas, Oak Lawn, and parts of Oak Cliff.

Across the two phases of our life in Dallas, 1975–1979 and 1981–1998, we developed a number of favorite haunts. As explained in Chapter Eight, we renavigated, renegotiated, and readjusted by relocating to Old East Dallas just north of Downtown, far from the suburban university site.

Dallas was quite a good restaurant town. We had many favorites. Ranking high among them was the iconic Sonny Bryan's BBQ, where luxury limousines and beat-up pickups sat side-by-side until the daily smoked meat ran out, on weekends before noon. Other favorites included the many varieties of Mexican and Tex-Mex that we learned to eat and to love, led by seafood specialist Café Cancun. Among our haunts were The Grape, Dallas' first wine bar; a little Greek spot on Lower Greenville in East Dallas; the pricey, fine-dining French Room in the Adolphus Hotel and The Mansion; and the local coffee and French bakery chain La Madeleine. Dallas was short on high-quality Asian restaurants. Of course, there were also many excellent cooks among our friends and colleagues.

For films, we all but lived at the independent Inwood Theatre in Inwood Village in University Park. Downtown was a developers' domain but a design disaster. Each of the swelling number of skyscrapers underperformed its predecessor. Downtown housed the good but not world-class Dallas Museum of Fine Arts, modern Symphony Hall, and later the architecturally more attractive Nasher Sculpture Garden. Nearby Fair Park with a good natural historical museum and the Dallas Cowboys' original stadium (the Cotton Bowl) was appealing when neither the state fair nor football season was underway.

The fact that smaller, historical rival Fort Worth had a more attractive, interconnected, and livable urban center, with superior cultural institutions to Dallas, did not sit well on the eastern side of the Trinity River. That did not fit with the Dallas Myth or the Dallas Way. With its equally iconic Angelo's Barbecue and excellent St. Emilion for special occasions, Fort Worth did not need a myth. Its stockyards creatively redeveloped, it had no shame in being a former cow town with the world-class Kimball Art Museum. Dallas was not too far a drive to Austin, San Antonio, and the Hill Country, or to the charming, small towns of East Texas, or even Houston. We visited all of them.

Depending on one's perspective, Dallas' status as one of the most racially and ethnically segregated cities in the country with a long history of violence and prejudice is either central to the Dallas Myth or an aberration from it. I experienced more face-to-face incidents of antisemitism and encountered more personal or indirect racial and ethnic discrimination there than anywhere else I have lived or visited. For a non-practicing Jewish sociocultural historian, I experienced another chapter in my continuing education. Some discrimination was superficial, even trivial, repetition of inherited cultural rhetoric. Some had career, indeed life-threatening consequences. It is critical but tricky to understand the similarities and differences.

Shop clerks casually referred to "being Jew-ed." Students from rural Texas informed me that I was the first Jew they had ever met. One young woman was relieved to see that I "didn't have horns," and told me so. Realizing that her intentions were not cruel, I bit my tongue and nodded. She frightened me more when she began to drop to one knee in the front row of my lecture while I quoted Jonathan Edwards preaching during the 18th-century Great Awakening in colonial America.

~~~

In early September 1975, UTD's first semester, its founding faculty, the first generation of undergraduates, and a smattering of graduate students all arrived. An inspiring young faculty assembled. More than a few of them remain our friends 50 years later.

Unnecessarily opaque UTD was harder to negotiate than the metroplex itself. This was partly by promotional design but even more by poor physical design and administrative incompetence. My own location on the campus at the time was indicative. As a social science historian, hired by the School of Arts and Humanities as a history and humanities professor, because of my specialties, I was also cross appointed to the School of Social Sciences. For the first year, I was housed within the latter until the provost ordered me, for no reason beyond convenience, "back to where you are budgeted." So much for even the thinnest veneer of interdisciplinarity in practice.

This "crossing" led one particularly ignorant but self-styled, interdisciplinary, tenured arts and humanities professor to ask me, "Do you speak in numbers?" She later voted against my early tenure because of her British antisemitism and her professional limitations. Her doctoral degree was in education, not history or American studies.

Two of her British antisemitic colleagues joined her on the School of Arts and Humanities faculty. The oldest had migrated to the US to take a faculty position in New England, the other two for graduate studies in education. Two had been denied tenure in their previous institutions; they were among the few "senior"—i.e., tenured associate and full—professors at UTD. Their small numbers in comparison to the numerical dominance of assistant professors magnified their power. They wielded it unfairly, unprofessionally, anti-intellectually, and inhumanely.

As with all my research and teaching across the humanities and social sciences, personal experiences deepened my multiple forms of understanding and responses. Similar to other prejudices that lead to bias, discrimination, and destructive actions, antisemitism derives from fear based on ignorance. I learned this in studying nonliterates, and children and adolescents, as well as within universities: whatever contradictions arise. Almost 50 years later, I take pains to distinguish antisemitism from common allegations and distortions surrounding support for innocent Palestinian as well as Israeli lives. Support for innocent Palestinian lives is neither antisemitism nor anti-Israeli genocide.

~~~

That was how the tenured faculty cookie crumbled in the formation of the UTD faculty hierarchy. Intolerant of difference in general, this intolerance included conflicting attitudes toward interdisciplinarity, the new university's founding self-promotion but not what it actually practiced. Not surprisingly, UTD was ill-prepared to open its new doors when the founding fall term began. Disorganization and lack of readiness reigned from the top down. This was all but debilitating to a young faculty, many of us in our first or second full-time positions with no more than a year or two of full-time teaching experience, and to a predominately older, nontraditional student body.

On average, the students were in their mid- to late-20s, older than I was. Many were military veterans and married women with older children resuming their interrupted schooling. Some were highly motivated, committed learners lacking in self-confidence and college skills. When the opportunity to get to know them outside the classroom arose, Vicki and I made friends.

I recall the challenge of preparing undergraduate lectures for the first time. My experience lay in seminars, especially at the graduate level. None of the faculty had any knowledge about students' ability levels or preparation. No one at the university thought to inquire about this or brief us.

My responsibilities included teaching introductory seminars; first courses for history majors; general U.S. history and social history; the history of children, women, and families; and later the history of literacy; the history of cities; and public history at both undergraduate and graduate levels. Over time, my circle of graduate students developed, adding a layer of commitment and pleasure. We socialized with many of them and remain in contact with quite a few.

Smaller classes were easier to manage, although an interactive seminar format was novel to almost all of them. The new library was unable to support instructional needs as well as the uncertainty and discomfort of students transferring from community colleges or returning to college after a lengthy hiatus. Unprepared for expected problems, life at UTD was one disorganized challenge after another.

~~~

My University of Toronto formal dissertation defense briefly interrupted my first semester in early October. I flew back to Toronto, staying with the Katz family, ready for my oral presentation and questions. I was not prepared for what followed.

Ritual dominated the University of Toronto in many ways. Most dissertation defenses took place in a symbolic chamber (sometimes jokingly called "the Star Chamber") in Massey Hall, the men's graduate residential college overseen by Robertson Davies, a famous Canadian novelist. Large, high-backed chairs surrounded the room. My supervising committee and I gathered around a smaller, more informal, collegial table in the center. The formal rules are typically set aside. The chairperson is appointed from an outside department and had no relationship to the candidate. Their role is limited.

Unfortunately, my designated chair was a newly appointed professor of English who was attending his first U of T defense. Unfamiliar with the rules, he stopped repeatedly to reread them. He was unwilling to accept the words of more experienced colleagues or move the proceedings along less formally, as the others repeatedly urged. This created an atmosphere that none of us desired.

Matters worsened when the external examiner (Ken Lockridge from Michigan, my literacy colleague) led off the questioning. He began to read his written evaluation, planning to ask me to respond. The chair stopped him, stating that the rules did not explicitly authorize such a move. (Nor did they prohibit it.) General bickering ensued. This ended with Ken starting to ask a question orally but then shifting to his written statement.

When the chair was not obstructing the proceedings, all went well. The questions were responsible, relevant to my text, and constructively put. That is, until the chair's turn arrived. Normally, I later learned, the appointed outside chair does not ask candidates questions. To ask questions is not considered appropriate.

Despite his obsession with the rules, the subject matter of literacy interested him as a 19th-century literature scholar. Having read only the dissertation abstract and not understanding that his views represented the very misconceptions I was refuting, he began to make ignorant and irrelevant remarks. Together my committee members cut him off. They excused me so the committee could make its final decision.

The worst was yet to come. Although there was unanimity about the quality of the dissertation and my successfully passing the oral examination, the chair retreated to the written rules. The committee wished to dispense with a formal, written vote, but the written guidelines did not explicitly address that. For a full half hour, I sat increasingly nervously in the hallway wondering what the hell was going on.

Eventually, Michael Katz joined me. He congratulated me heartily and then proceeded to condemn the chair in no uncertain terms. No one looked at the chair when Katz guided me back into the room for congratulations.

Treating me to lunch, Michael and I did our best to laugh about the experience, which was unique for him, too. The atmosphere brightened, particularly when Michael informed me that he and his wife Edda were hosting a "surprise" party for me that evening at his house with my friends, fellow students, and some of my professors. I remember that occasion well, during which I telephoned Vicki in Dallas to share the news.

~~~

Returning to Dallas, my first semester (and UTD's) was intense. Neither the institution nor I nor many of the students were prepared for either the expected or unforeseen challenges. Many but not all could not be anticipated. Student uncertainty, often-weak skills, and background was one matter; my inexperience and that of many of my fellow first- or second-year full-time instructors was another. The inadequacy of the physical site, the library, the support services, and worst of all the near total lack of leadership were unexpected and impossible to correct.

The unexpected gap in ability between the majority young, untenured faculty and the much smaller number of associate and full professors—almost all of whom had been denied tenure in their former universities—was itself crippling to responsible faculty development, mentorship, and collegiality. That was inseparable from senior leadership at college and university levels. My major guides were slightly older, more experienced, fellow untenured colleagues (for my reflections, see "Academic Collegiality is a Contradictory, Self-Serving Myth," 2022l, "Collegiality Needs a Reboot" 2022o, and "Ignore the Books," 2022r).

Most helpful was my colleague and immediate friend, modern European cinema and psychohistorian Paul Monaco. He first assured me that I was not as poor a lecturer as I seemed to think and that I needed to give myself an opportunity to practice and learn. He also gave me basic suggestions from his longer experience. He had taught full-time for several years between his M.A. and Ph.D. studies.

Paul and I later obtained a grant from the Mathematics Social Sciences Board (MSSB) of the National Science Foundation to host a pioneering conference on quantitative history and psychohistory in 1977. We published the papers as *Quantification and Psychology: Toward a "New" History* (1980). Paul was one of our closest friends in Dallas before he moved to Montana State University. He remained a good friend until his death.

Steve Weissman, another older and more experienced colleague and friend, was a political scientist for whom UTD was his second job. He counseled me on teaching, and we had long conversations about our research. Those talks and sharing our writing go on today. Steve, his wife Nancy, their son Daniel, and their dog were among our closest social companions. I occasionally accompanied Steve in his role as assistant coach for Daniel's Little League baseball team. Daniel is now a professor of psychology at the University of Michigan.

We supported Nancy's efforts to expand her social work career into singing gigs. After Vicki accidentally injured her left hand in a collision with a glass door, she used her insurance settlement to purchase a guitar. She began to write songs. On "All I Need," she collaborated with Nancy, with Vicki writing the lyrics and Nancy the music.

Vicki wrote scores of songs and poems on many themes. She also pursued guitar lessons on various instruments in Dallas and Chicago. In Toronto she had bought a kit and in Dallas started to build a dulcimer, but in five decades she never completed it. In 2023, she published her 1979 feminist manifesto, "We Do These Things," in the *Journal of Expressive Writing*.

My collegial support and friends group included political scientists Steve Weissman, Bob Bradley, Paul Peretz, Ric Hula, and Marvin Cohen; sociologist of gender Paula England; anthropologist of Caribbean immigrants Alex Stepick; linguist of indigenous peoples Leanne Hinton; and joining us a bit later German historian Jerry Soliday and art historian Deborah Stott. Jerry was my sole colleague in social history. All were social friends. Only Soliday and Stott completed their careers at UTD.

Bradley, Cohen, Hula, and I ended days in the office and classrooms with rounds of racquetball and occasionally tennis on UTD's minimal sports facilities. These relationships captured the special qualities of the founding faculty. In general, political science is not among the disciplines I hold in high esteem, but these founding faculty members were special. As with others among the first cohort of professors, many did not remain at UTD, some by choice, others by termination—which was uncommonly frequent. My close friends straddled that line.

Because of the lack of structure, the largely empty, rhetorical promotion of cross- and interdisciplinarity, and my early involvement with faculty activists, my circle of colleagues and potential friends expanded to include people in human development and education, general studies, and the sciences. I, and then we, developed special friendships with geologists, physicists, chemists, and biologists. I learned from them. They expanded my life with literacy into new domains. We collaborated in limited faculty governance and occasional movements for reform.

More than a few became close, personal, and social friends. We watched some of their children grow up. This was partial compensation for the limited visons of my home bases in the Schools of Arts and Humanities and Social Sciences. I can now say that that limited vision applies to academia in general—full of contradicting, incessant, self-promoting rhetoric (this is the subject of my forthcoming book , *Reconstructing the "Uni-versity" from the Ashes of the "Mega- and Multi-versity"*).

My close collaborations included members of the School of General Studies. Dean Carolyn Galerstein and I quickly recognized our common interests in the status of women, one of the foci of her programs and of her extracurricular activities. Carolyn invited me to participate in public advocacy work in Dallas, speaking at the Women for Change, Inc., Dallas, seminar on education in fall 1975, for example. Together we organized a conference at UTD on women and public policy in 1976 and published its proceedings and a follow-up report: *Women and Public Policy* (Galerstein & Graff, 1978). A Texas Committee for the Humanities program and then a publication grant supported us. This was the first of many public history and humanities projects throughout my years in Dallas (for more on these public projects, see my "Lessons for Becoming a Public Scholar," 2023h.)

With respect to women in Texas, my activities also included service with my colleague Paula England as university representatives to the workshop on women in higher education at Texas A&M University in 1978. We learned that the issues for an urban, officially designated research university were vastly different than those at more rural and lower-level institutions. I also contributed as a consultant to "It Made a Difference": Women in Texas History Project (1979–1982).

I worked closely with an instructor and staff member in the School of General Studies, Ruthe Winegarten. A longtime friend, Ruthe began studying for her Ph.D. in humanities, but I counseled her to drop out because scholarship was not her métier, and a graduate humanities degree was not a prerequisite for her intended career path. She moved to Austin and conducted groundbreaking oral histories and archival projects of Texas public women, especially pioneering Democratic woman governor Anne Richards.

Not only did I lunch frequently with these people, but Vicki and I also socialized with them, their partners, and families. I fondly remember taking disco dancing lessons with political scientist Bob Bradley and his wife, French literature scholar Carolyn Herrington, at the local community college. (She later became a professor and Dean of Education in Florida and Missouri.) I was probably the worst dancer among the four of us, but that did not limit our fun. We still laugh about that.

In our third year and thereafter, my circles expanded to include Southern Methodist University and later University of Texas at Arlington colleagues. Several became long-lasting friends, and in 1981 they also became founding members of the Dallas Social History Group that I built when I returned to UTD after two years on research leave in Chicago. Dan Orlovsky, SMU's Russian historian who had been Jerry Soliday's student at Harvard, has been a close friend and colleague since 1978.

With revealingly few exceptions, relationships with tenured faculty differed. A chip on the shoulder—combined with a sense of failure and sometimes inferiority—was a common badge. So was a sense of comparative insecurity and easy intellectual intimidation. Few of them had interest or ability in professionally assisting their younger colleagues in a setting where that was an imperative need. That should have been a prerequisite for tenure at a new, self-styled, nontraditional endeavor. But there was no visible or recognizable plan. Founding deans, provost, and president had no relevant experiences or sense of professional responsibility.

This was seen most dramatically in the high rate of turnover among the founding faculty. Some of it was by choice. Some secured other faculty posts. A few, like our friend political theorist Marvin Cohen, opted out of academia for a successful career in administering social philanthropies. Denied tenure from his unconscionable entry rank of untenured associate professor, Steve Weissman successfully combined a career in federal government and nonprofit sector research and writing. Both used the skills and knowledge learned in graduate school.

Some losses resulted directly from the actions of the tenured faculty. As should be expected from the foregoing, the founding faculty's areas of expertise did not always align with student knowledge or interest. For example, too many musicologists and folklorists were hired. Not surprisingly, their courses did not attract enough students to move forward. In one way or another, they were either "counseled out" or terminated before their third full year was completed. In most cases, they did not know that this form of firing was possible in the UT System.

Even more professionally irresponsible was the "third-year massacre." In the University of Texas System and other universities, untenured faculty undergo their first formal review of "progress toward tenure"—that is progress made in research, teaching, service, and a nebulous category called "collegiality"—during their third (or elsewhere fourth) full year of service. In many universities, this is often an initiation rite, relatively perfunctory, resulting in a neutral recommendation, sometimes very positive, and occasionally offering specific recommendations or cautions.

During UTD's third year, 1977–1978, several assistant professors were summarily terminated. External input was almost never sought in these early reviews. The rationale for negative recommendations was seldom stated explicitly. The effects on morale, including my own, cannot be exaggerated. What I did not know was how accurately these decisions foreshadowed my early tenure review the next year.

~~~

My excitement at having a new job, many stimulating new colleagues and friends, and a newly minted Ph.D. degree turned to anxiety and depression as the interminable first semester rolled on. I considered leaving UTD temporarily and contemplated seeking alternative employment. I felt trapped between the perennial questions: Is it them? Or is it me?

In the new year, a friend (the wife of a new friend in geoscience) suggested that I contact a local psychiatrist she knew. I did and found the first excellent therapist that I ever encountered. Trained first as a pediatrician, Bobby Gene Black was a fine psychiatrist as well as a companionate and knowledgeable human being. In addition, he was a likeable "Texas Old Boy." He treated me, and also Vicki a few times, for the better part of the next few years.

He also confirmed that UTD had immediately established itself as a source of business and concern among his professional community. (I later learned that my final university, Ohio State, had a similar reputation and impact on business in the local psychiatric community.) Among many other insights, Bobby Gene led me to understand the familial roots of my insecurities and depression and how schooling and then professional demands weighed heavily on them. This understanding had great value to me personally, my primary relationships, and my teaching and graduate supervision.

Therapy and greater self-understanding helped enormously—not only at work but also at home. As I grew in self- and other understanding psychologically,

I was better able to deal with my problems, on the one hand, and to turn my attention more effectively across my new campus and city, on the other. With this rejuvenation, Vicki's personal support, and the assistance of our circle of colleagues and friends, I renewed my commitment to teaching, research, and the public. Despite the stress of the environment and the demanding workload, my teaching broadened. My research blossomed. I also secured external support in the form of fellowships and grants-in-aid, and my public history collaborations increased.

As a product of Michael Katz's Hamilton/Canadian Social History Project and finding the history of Dallas a wasteland, I initiated the Dallas Social History Project, which ran from 1975–1979, with support from the School of Arts and Humanities. I applied for a major grant from the National Endowment for the Humanities, but the proposal was not funded. This was the age of "social history projects" of which only a few led to substantial publications, but several developed databases and archives for teaching and interested citizens (see my "The 'New' Social History and the Southwest," 1978e).

Working with two graduate humanities research assistants paid by UTD research grants, Alan R. Baron and Charles Barton, we compiled and published the first comprehensive bibliography on the city, *Dallas, Texas: A Bibliographical Guide to the Sources of its Social History to 1930*( 1977, 1979). At the same time, 1976–1978, I collaborated with School of Social Science colleagues in a research group on school desegregation, White flight, and busing in Dallas

Working with the Dallas Historical Society and the Dallas Public Library, I taught the first regular, for-credit course on Dallas history in the city's history. With the support of my dean, the course included a bus tour of the city, led by one of the city of Dallas' urban planners. We had sessions at the Dallas Historical Society and in the Texas and Dallas collections of the Dallas Public Library. The overwhelmingly suburban students were surprised and attracted by the sights of the city. Several asked, "How much do houses cost in this neighborhood?"

The distinguished Texas political journalist Mollie Ivins—who dubbed George W. Bush "shrub" and who often commented on Dallas and refused to write for the conservative *Dallas Morning News* when the *Dallas Times Herald* went out of business—spoke to the class. Each student completed a primary-source research paper. It was an immense success.

The Dallas history course and the Dallas history project spanned the academic and the public spheres. A product of my interconnected political and academic values and experiences, Michael Katz's example, and my understanding of Dallas' and Texas' needs, my commitment to history in the public realm expanded. Later in the 1980s, I introduced a graduate seminar on public history, many of whose enrollees were full-time professionals seeking to reframe or change their roles and responsibilities.

In addition to my work on women's issues with Galerstein and Winegarten, I cooperated with the Texas Committee for the Humanities (TCH), the state-based affiliate of the National Endowment for the Humanities. I served first as UTD representative to its conference on humanistic perspectives on public policy in San Antonio, 1976, and then as a general consultant. I also served as consultant, humanist, and presenter for the following TCH-sponsored events, among others:

- Southern Resource Center, Dallas, project on the Community Development Act of 1974 and the East Dallas community (1976)
- Conference on quality education for Black students in Texas, Austin (1976)
- Fuerza de los Barrios, Fort Worth, Trinity River Project (1976)
- Texas Coalition for Juvenile Justice Reform, program on status offenders (1977)
- Collaborative approach to services for the elderly, University of Texas Council of Presidents (1977)

Some of my professional outreach activities were more explicitly historical than others. Beginning in 1976, I consulted with state, regional, and local historical societies and groups. I joined the Dallas Public Library's advisory board for the humanities resources information system project (sponsored by the NEH, National Science Foundation, and TCH); humanities involvement group (1977–1979); and later served as advisor to the Dallas and Texas history division (1984–1989). I contributed "Basic Education" (1978a) and "Youth" (1978g) to *Issues and Alternatives: A Guide for the Policy Maker*. As president of North Texas Phi Beta Kappa in the next decade, I inaugurated an annual lecture on "Culture in the City" in cooperation with the library.

With the Dallas Historical Society, I was consulting historian (1976–1989), member of the advisory board for "A Return to the Neighborhoods" Project (1977–1979), and historian and speaker for their seminar on community history (1982). With the city of Dallas, I served on the Historic Landmark and Preservation Committee's historic marker taskforce (1977–1981), publicity taskforce (1981–1985), and archives committee (1983–1988). As a published professional historian, who also wrote opinion essays for the *Dallas Morning News* and advised KERA, an NPR affiliate, I also wrote brochures for these historic landmarks from 1977 to 1985:

- Swiss Avenue Historic District
- Old Fair Park Fire Station
- Union Station
- Cedar Springs (Oak Lawn) Fire Station
- Federal Reserve Bank
- Trinity Methodist Church
- Miller Shingle Style House
- South Boulevard/Park Row
- Saint Paul United Methodist Church

- Ambassador Hotel
- Melrose Hotel
- Majestic Theatre
- Cedar Crest
- Magnolia Building
- Fair Park

Of these brochures, the one about Union Station remains widely available (see Graff, n.d.).

I also advised a Dallas-based, local public policy consulting group, Kaplan, Gans, and Kahn (1976–1978), and the Division of Humanities at Eastfield College of the Dallas County Community College District (1978). I did not know that this diverse work would culminate in writing and publishing *The Dallas Myth: The Making and Unmaking of an American City* (2008a). That took personal and historical time.

At the same time, responding to the same factors—the always-developing intersection of the personal, the political, the academic, and place—my scholarly relationships expanded as my career took firmer shape. No doubt I was responding to my advisors' examples and sponsorship, the intellectual and professional isolation of UTD, the expanding professional organizational opportunities of the mid- to late-1970s, and the social, cultural, and political currents of the times. All of these dynamically shaped me. Living as an intellectual in Dallas carried its own imperatives.

As I have reviewed my files, I find it difficult to grasp the range and depth of my commitments. At the time, I was learning to teach well, beginning what would eventually become the major history of Dallas, and completing the transformation of my dissertation into *The Literacy Myth* (1979c). Not only were my courses new preparations, but the history program, the school, and the university made substantial demands on new, untenured faculty. In retrospect, I now see how each element mutually (if not always consistently or consciously) shaped and reshaped the others. But during those years, I could not see the intersections of the personal, political, academic, and place.

~~~

My first years at UTD included membership in the Schools of Arts and Humanities, Social Science, and General Studies/Interdisciplinary Studies and on the graduate faculty in Education. At the university level, I served on the Council on Teacher Education, Teacher Certification Review Team in History and English, and the Task Force on the Role and Scope of Teacher Education. I also contributed to various women's studies committees, the Association of Women Faculty, and several Dallas research groups. Those commitments flowed from my early upbringing, high school, and especially college and graduate school learning experiences.

In the School of Arts and Humanities, I was a member of the Ccommittee on Teacher Education, the Faculty Agenda Committee and parliamentarian, and various search committees. This was a considerable workload for an untenured faculty member. Little credit for either salary increments or tenure accrued for service. The novelty and lack of leadership at UTD exacerbated both complications. Yet, it was a valuable if uncoordinated form of professional socialization and preparation.

Beyond the university, the city, and the state, I consulted for the new *Journal of Family History* bibliographic project (1977–1979) and reviewed, served on panels, and consulted for the National Endowment for the Humanities from 1977. I served on the Nominating Committee for the History of Education Society (1976 and 1979), as a coordinator for the Southwest Coordinating Committee on Women in the Historical Profession (1977–1979), and as a regional network coordinator for the new SSHA (1976–1984). From its inception, the SSHA became my regular intellectual and social home away from home. I was awarded a plaque for consecutive attendance through the first 43 meetings.

The inaugural annual meeting of the SSHA took place in November 1976. In time, it led to my 1999–2000 presidency for the 25th anniversary and 2000 presidential address, "The Shock of the '"New" (Histories)': Social Science Histories and Historical Literacies" (2001/2005). Many of my longtime colleagues, collaborations, and friendships began at SSHA meetings. Throughout my career, I organized sessions with my graduate students at SSHA, History of Education Society, History of Childhood Association, and Conference on Composition and Communication (CCCC). This is what Michael Katz and Jill Conway taught me.

Most of my scholarly activity in this period focused on literacy and its history. I delivered invited lectures at the University of Western Ontario, Southern Methodist University, and the University of Chicago. Internationally, I spoke at the Time, Space, and Man Interdisciplinary Symposium on Microdemography in Historical Perspective at the University of Umeå, Sweden, in 1977. I also chaired sessions at the History of Education Society in Cambridge, Massachusetts (1976), Toronto (1977), and Chicago (1978) and at the Southwestern Social Science Association in Houston (1978).

The presentation in Sweden in summer 1977 was one highlight of a spectacular visit to Sweden, Norway, Denmark, and The Netherlands made possible by a guest scholarship from the Swedish Institute and support as a guest scholar at Umeå University. This stemmed from my collaborations with Egil Johansson and his students and colleagues and with Ken Lockridge since graduate studies.

Vicki and I flew to Stockholm and then traveled to the historic university town of Uppsala, where Ken Lockridge and his Swedish girlfriend (later wife) loaned us her apartment. We toured the university with its magnificent gardens and library used by centuries of scholars. We made day trips to see the many sights of Stockholm.

From Uppsala we boarded a train to Umeå, home of the northernmost university and Egil Johansson. Egil was a pioneering historian of Swedish literacy who discovered remarkable educational and demographic parish registers. Egil was my friend and colleague since I was a graduate student. I presented lectures and seminars and met with faculty and graduate students at Umeå. We spent a night in Finland visiting one of the data input centers of Egil's demographic database, whose support was part of the Swedish federal government's welfare state. The Finnish hotel's bar featured a local band singing Beatles' songs in English whose words they clearly did not understand.

In Umeå we experienced the arrival of the northern summer in mid-June. Seemingly overnight, the sky transformed from ordinary darkness and light to almost constant daylight. The Swedes' behavior changed accordingly, often in the streets. Lightness, in all its dimensions, filled the sky and the atmosphere. It was a singular delight.

The international Time, Space, and Man Symposium focused on historical demography in Umeå came next. An array of the finest European and North American researchers made presentations. They included my advisors, models, and friends Roger Schofield, Chuck and Louise Tilly, Ken Lockridge, Tony Wrigley, Michael Anderson, and Egil Johansson. I met others from Sweden, Europe, and elsewhere, some whose work I knew and others whose work I would soon encounter. Egil, Ken, and I ensured that literacy's history took its proper place in the historical demographic matrix.

At the end of the conference, with a Eurail Pass, Vicki and I took trains around much of Sweden from the south to the west and north, crossing the Arctic circle to Narvick in Norway, and then down the majestic fjord coast for a few days in beautiful Oslo. We took an overnight train across southern Norway to lovely Bergen on the west coast, then back to Oslo. From there to delightful Copenhagen and an overnight train to Amsterdam for five striking days. Back to Dallas and the work that awaited each of us. Although we were not yet 30, it was the trip of a lifetime, to that point.

~~~

Back home, I returned to preparing *The Literacy Myth* (1979c), my first monograph and what is known as the "tenure book." For the first two to three years after completing my dissertation, I was not ready to revise it into a publishable book. That transformation was still a mystery, and I was preoccupied with many substantial adjustments to Dallas, UTD, teaching undergraduates, and early work on the history of Dallas. I fretted anxiously about *not* writing the book.

At the same time, I was garnering the resources I needed, completing remaining research, acquiring funding, and, without realizing it, intellectually contemplating the revisions to come. In effect, I was preparing to turn my dissertation into a book. Much of that occurred during the summers of 1977 and especially 1978.

My aspirations and more concrete plans to be a productive scholar required both UTD and especially external research support. Untenured faculty had no paid time off, and UTD had no sabbatical or research leave until more than 15 years later. Our low salaries forced summer teaching.

I applied for and was awarded grants and fellowships from the National Endowment for the Humanities in 1976 and the American Council of Learned Societies in 1978. The funding for my Swedish visit in 1977 also advanced my scholarly knowledge of the history of literacy and gave me meaningful opportunities to present my ideas. Together, the research assistance and funding partly freed me from summer teaching during my pre-tenure period.

This support directly assisted me in publishing more articles about literacy. New studies included material that did not fit within the covers of my dissertation and some threads outside the scope of my intended book. Looking forward to future teaching, research, and writing, I began to write about the new social history more broadly. As my scholarly vision widened and matured, I wrote "The 'New Math': Quantification, the 'New' History, and the History of Education" (1977b).

I also made early contributions to the just-beginning study of the history of criminality with my publications "'Pauperism, Misery, and Vice': Illiteracy and Criminality in the Nineteenth Century" (1977c) and "The Reality Behind the Rhetoric: The Social and Economic Meanings of Literacy in the Mid-Nineteenth Century: The Example of Literacy and Criminality" (1978f). In the perspective of "the literacy myth," I examined the accepted and the unexamined and the documentable relationships between literacy and criminality. I critiqued traditional, normative conceptions of direct, unmediated relationships and argued for new interpretations. "Crime and Punishment in the Nineteenth Century: A New Look at the Criminal" (1977a) broadened the lens.

Writing about literacy more generally, I strived to establish the lines of a larger context and conceptualization with "Literacy and History" (1978b) for the International Institute for Adult Literacy Methods in Tehran, "Literacy Past and Present: Critical Approaches in the Literacy/Society Relationship" (1978d), "Literacy: How Many Views?" (1978c), "Literacy, Education, and Fertility, Past and Present: A Critical Review" (1979b), and "Interpreting Historical Literacy: The Pattern of Literacy in Quebec—A Comment" (1979a). Without quickly recognizing it, I moved ever more closely toward *The Literacy Myth* (1979c).

A first foray combining my graduate studies in the "new urban history" that included Katz's project, my teaching, and my new interest in the largely unexplored history of Dallas was "The 'New' Social History and the Southwest: The Dallas Social History Project," (1978e). I did not complete that extremely long-term project until I published *The Dallas Myth* (2008a) 30 years later, a decade after leaving Dallas and several years after leaving Texas. There are lessons for younger (tenured) scholars in that necessary three-decade space of time.

After more than two years of fretting about not writing the "dissertation book," key pieces fell into place. Among the most compelling was my conception of a "catchy" *and* memorable title to precede the mundane dissertation title. This was *The Literacy Myth* (1979c), which prefaced the subtitle *Literacy and Social Structure in the Nineteenth-Century City*.

In the summer of 1978, I was not aware that I would soon add a phrase to common usage of scholars and students of literacy and that the core of my reinterpretation would have a transformative impact on conversations about literacy past, present, and future. Based in interdisciplinary comparative social history, education, and social sciences, my relationships with other fields across the arts and humanities including writing and reading lay in the future. Major intersections accompanied, indeed were inseparable from, the emergence of the New Literacy Studies in the 1980s and 1990s. Rhetoric, composition, and writing studies had to respond to the larger discoveries made by me and my colleagues (see the following for discussion and references).

A historical note to readers younger than 50 or 60 years old: I both drafted and prepared final copy on *typewriters* for all of my high school, undergraduate, and graduate writing and for my first single-authored books and edited books until the early 1990s. We purchased our first home computer—a not-quite-portable Osborne with a separate, viewable monitor sitting atop it—at that time. A file in the word processing system WordStar held a maximum of about 20 pages. UTD provided personal computers to its faculty a year or two later. Electronic processing, other than on typewriters with magnetic card readers, was not possible until the next decade. That transformed—in part—our lives with literacy.

I wrote almost all of the final draft of *The Literacy Myth* (1979c) relatively quickly during the summer months of 1978. After securing Michael Katz's comments, I sent the manuscript to Chuck Tilly to consider for his state-of-the-art series Studies in Social Discontinuity. Tilly approved the draft and asked for a few revisions, including "a sketch of daily life" for literates and illiterates in 19th-century cities.

He also asked why I had not replicated the basic quantitative analysis with more sophisticated multivariate methods. I referred him to my later "famous footnote" that explained that just as I set out to do that in 1977–1978, I learned that the UTD computer center lost the magnetic tape of my data and that the OISE/U of T center had relocated and had lost my backup tape in the shuffle. So much for historical certainty and digital permanence.

Tilly promptly recommended publication to Academic Press, the series publisher. My first book editor Eliot Werner took responsibility. He supervised final copy preparation, permissions, and copyediting. The press announced publication for September 1979. I recall the excitement and mixed pleasure of preparing final copy. *The Literacy Myth* (1979c) is the only one of my pre-retirement books that Vicki had the time to edit. She now edits often.

When the final page proofs arrived, we took turns reading them aloud to each other. We both lost our voices. In the pre-computer and pre-text-programs age, we laboriously prepared the index on 3" x 5" cards arranged on the living room floor. That was the one and only index I prepared myself. Vicki's memorable observation as her partner's first history book, full of numbers and tables as well as illustrations, went to press was "Wondering is better than knowing." There was never a doubt about who was the historian in the house.

During this time, the unit that my graduate school colleague Alison Prentice and I prepared in 1975, *Children and Schools in Nineteenth-Century Canada/L'école canadienne et l'enfant au dix-neuvième siècle*, for Canada's National Museum of Man's Canada's Visual History Series, which included a historical guide and slides for use in schools and universities, was published (1979, rev. ed. with CD-ROM, 1994). That was another line on my curriculum vitae and argument for tenure in 1979.

So were the award of a National Endowment for the Humanities full-year fellowship at Chicago's Newberry Library (1979–1980) and a Spencer Foundation Fellowship from the National Academy of Education (1979–1982). I proposed to draft a general history of literacy in the western world, published as *The Legacies of Literacy: Continuities and Contradictions in Western Culture and Society* (1987b). In 1978–1979, I saw these volumes as the culmination of almost one decade's research and writing. Those awards and the firm new research proposal solidified my case for early tenure in spring 1979 with the fellowship research year in Chicago upcoming.

~~~

Once again, UTD defied expectations, reason and logic, and professional precedents. The faculty "ad hoc committee of my [tenured] peers" divided on my case. Ad hoc is an anachronistic academic distraction. As mentioned earlier, one of the members of the committee was a British antisemite, and another a biased observer of one class session. The first had been denied tenure at their earlier institution and the other newly tenured at UTD on a slim record. The only other social historian on the faculty, a tenured associate professor, was not appointed to the review committee despite his expertise and his desire to serve. He was most qualified to evaluate my research and teaching. The entire disreputable endeavor derived from antisemitism, dislike of challenging new scholarship and nontraditional approaches despite the self-promotion of the institution, and personal and professional jealousy.

The external member of the committee was dumbfounded by the unprofessional, biased, and personal opposition. The case against my promotion rested on "doubts about his collegiality" and questions about teaching based on one in-class observation. They ignored all other evidence, including my scholarship, teaching evaluations, and service.

The author of the unbalanced classroom report later commented to others, "Graff was saved by the Jewish mafia," referring to one female professor of literature and one female professor of Spanish. The comment was sexist as well as antisemitic. These members of the committee ignored my record and both internal and external recommendations. The reasons why remain too obvious to state. The case was unusually egregious but not unique.

The committee forwarded a confused, contradictory, and divided recommendation to the Dean of Arts and Humanities. The Dean was the third British antisemite on the faculty, also denied tenure in his earlier position. The university-wide faculty Committee on Qualifications (CQ) voted unanimously in favor of my tenure. The provost and president followed the Dean's muddled inaction with the president "not recommending tenure and promotion at this time," adding an unexplained comment that "there are doubts about your tenurability."

Along with the greatest number of my colleagues and friends at UTD and elsewhere, I was furious. As we packed for the year in Chicago, we resolved to do our best never to return to a faculty position at UTD nor to live in Big D again.

~~~

*The Literacy Myth* (1979c) was published shortly after Vicki and I moved to an apartment leased by and less than two blocks from the Newberry Library, across from a historic "Speaker's Park" known for its radical, political, and pro-union speeches and rallies over more than a century.

It should have been an auspicious time for us, but it was muted. After my editor Eliot informed me that he had the first copy of my new book from the printers, I eagerly waited by my Newberry Library fellows' mailbox. I had to wait a few days because it was the first book he had taken through the entire process from first submission to final printing. He took that copy home for the weekend! After it arrived the next week, my new colleagues joined in celebrating its publication.

*The Literacy Myth* (1979c) did quite well in the short and the longer term. It was named a *Society* magazine Book-of-the-Month, nominated for several professional book awards, and discussed at a session of the SSHA in 1981. It was excerpted in *Journal of Reading* (Jeanne Shay Schumm & Maruerite C. Radenich, 1984), Malcolm Kiniry and Mike Rose's *Critical Strategies for Academic Thinking and Writing* (1990, 1993, 1997), and textbook anthologies. A plenary session marked its 30th anniversary at the Expanding Literacy Studies International Interdisciplinary Conference for Graduate Students at The Ohio State University in 2009. Its influence continues across disciplines and around the world. It brought the importance of the critical new history of literacy to the attention of many fields and subfields. A fourth edition with new materials was published in 2023 in the WAC Clearinghouse Landmark Publications in Writing Studies series (Graff, 1991/2023b).

That impact reverberates in the many opportunities I have had, and continue to have, to reflect on my interpretations, their importance and influence, and my revisions in a series of essays and lectures:

- "Literacy, Myths, and Legacies: Lessons from the Past/Reflections for the Future" (1993a)
- "Literacy, Myths, and Legacies: Lessons from the History of Literacy" (1994b)

- "Literacy, Myths, and Lessons: Keynote Address" (1991a, 1994c)
- "Assessing the History of Literacy in the 1990s: Themes and Questions" (1995/2009a)
- "Literacy, Myths, and Legacies: Lessons from the History of Literacy" (1995/2007c)
- "The Persisting Power and Costs of the Literacy Myth: A Comment on Literacy, Economy and Society: Results of the First International Adult Literacy Survey (IALS)" (1996/1997b)
- "Literacy's Myths and Legacies: From Lessons from the History of Literacy, to the Question of Critical Literacy" (1993b, 2001c, 2001d)
- "Literacy Myths," with John Duffy (2008)
- "The Literacy Myth at Thirty" (2010a)
- "The Literacy Myth: Literacy, Education and Demography" (2010b)
- "The Legacies of Literacy Studies" (2013)
- "Em busca do letramento: as origens sociais e intelectuais des estudos sobre letramento [Searching for Literacy: The Social and Intellectual Origins of Literacy Studies]" (2016a)
- "Interview with H. J. Graff & B. Street" (Ana Maria de Oliveira Galvão et al., 2016)
- "The New Literacy Studies and the Resurgent Literacy Myth" (2022c)
- "Harvey J. Graff: A Tribute," (Duffy et al., 2024)
- *Searching for Literacy: The Social and Intellectual Origins of Literacy Studies* (2022e)
- A new edition of *The Literacy Myth* published by the WAC Clearinghouse (1991/2023b)
- 45th anniversary marked at the May 2024 Expanding Literacy Studies/ HJG Reunion at Ohio State University

~~~

Along with psychologists Sylvia Scribner and Michael Cole's *The Psychology of Literacy* (1981), anthropologist Shirley Brice Heath's *Ways with Words: Language, Life, and Work in Communities and Classrooms* (1983), and anthropologist Brian Street's *Literacy in Theory and Practice* (1984), *The Literacy Myth* (1979c) laid the foundation for the New Literacy Studies, a major revision of our understanding of literacy across disciplines among other boundaries.

# Chapter 7. Interlude: In Exile at the Newberry Library and Chicago, 1979–1981

Following the disheartening debacle of my early tenure denial, Vicki and I distanced ourselves from the University of Texas near Dallas. The clash with the speedy acceptance and publication of *The Literacy Myth* (1979c) and award of both a National Endowment for the Humanities Fellowship to the Newberry Library in Chicago to research and write *The Legacies of Literacy* (1987b) and a Spencer Fellowship from the National Academy of Education was too great.

We were also tired of living on North Central Expressway in the middle of nowhere and Vicki's moves from preschool to one private elementary school after another as several went out of business (one still owes her back pay). We subleased our townhouse to a visiting professor and rented a U-Haul trailer to tow the possessions we needed for what we expected to be one year in exile (or retreat) in Chicago. The interlude from Dallas and full-time teaching turned into two years.

En route to Chicago in August 1979, we stopped first in Columbia, Missouri, to see my brother Gary. He was a second-year journalism student writing for the school newspaper and also contributing as a stringer to national dailies. From there we stopped briefly in Peoria, Illinois, to see our old friend from Northwestern and co-author of "The Great American Novel," Laurie, now deceased, who was then a public defense attorney.

Arrival in Chicago and at The Newberry Library brought optimism and energy. Settling into new spaces, even if temporary, away from UTD and Dallas was liberating. Those spaces extended far beyond the physical. Both the Newberry and our small apartment were within walking distance of restaurants and shopping, Lincoln Park, the Loop and downtown, even Old Town. In contrast to Dallas, we did not use the car often. Of course, the Chicago area was our own "second city."

My goals were threefold: to gain a much-needed personal and professional respite from UTD and Big D, to search for another academic position, and to write my general history of literacy *The Legacies of Literacy* (1987b).

The Newberry was a welcoming professional and personal environment. I had several professional acquaintances from SSHA meetings and the 1973 summer institute, especially Daniel Scott Smith and Richard Jensen, both of the University of Illinois at Chicago. Jensen also served as director of the Newberry's Family and Community History Center. Soon after our arrival, he offered Vicki a position as a typist—for a higher salary than she had earned as a full-time teacher in Dallas. After one year she was promoted to administrative assistant, working closely with Jan Reiff, the center's associate director. For Vicki, this position marked the beginning of her transition from teaching to office administration, architectural marketing and promotion, and manager of editorial services for the American Heart Association.

The heads and assistant directors of the Renaissance Center and the Cartography Center center at the Newberry were also welcoming and supportive of my research and writing. Harriet Lightman of the Center for Medieval and Renaissance Studies, a historian of European women, and her husband George Huppert, an early modern Europeanist at the University of Illinois at Chicago, continue as our close friends. We watched their daughter grow up, ice skate, earn her Ph.D., and in 2022 give birth to her first child.

Other colleagues teaching in the area, Newberry-affiliated researchers, and instructors in the summer program included Robert Church at Northwestern; John Craig at the University of Chicago; Sue Hirsch and Lewis Ehrenberg at Loyola University; at the summer institute Marge Murphey, Bill Cronon, and Walter Licht; and Jon Butler at the University of Illinois Chicago.

My fellow fellows were friendly, supportive, and collegial. The distinguished medieval social historian and historian of children and families Barbara Hanawalt occupied the neighboring carrel in the book stacks reserved for those of us who typed our manuscripts (in the pre-personal computer, pre-laptop, and pre-iPad era). Barbara was a fellow SSHA founding member and early president (and future Ohio State colleague). With Barbara's philosopher of science husband Ron Giere, we shared a love of good food, wine, and jazz. Barbara and Ron were also excellent cooks and Ron a wine connoisseur. (We resumed those connections in Columbus in 2004.) Along with Barbara and Ron, Ellen Dwyer, an American historian from Indiana University, became our lifelong friend.

An old and new colleague, Jan Reiff, a fellow student in a British history course my second year at Northwestern and now a fellow urban social historian, prepared a celebration dinner when *The Literacy Myth* (1979c) arrived. She had an apartment in the same building as ours where we often cooked dinners together. As a graduate student at the University of Washington, she learned the art of Asian cooking. We also watched major sports events together including the memorable gold medal victory of the U.S. men's hockey team in the 1980 Winter Olympics. As well as Vicki's boss and my urban social history colleague, Jan quickly became one of our closest friends until her sudden death in 2021. (See my "Celebrating Jan Reiff," UCLA history department tribute page, May 24, 2021.)

With these friends and other fellows, we enjoyed the spaces and the haunts of Lincoln Park, Old Town, the Near North, downtown and the Loop, Grant Park, and Evanston. We savored the tastes of restaurants like Greek Town's The Acropolis, Diana's, several French spots around town, Chicago deep-dish pizza—especially at Gino's on Rush Street, Michelina's, and several Thai and Vietnamese places. Vicki and Jan marched in a historic Women's Day March in downtown Chicago in 1980.

I played indoor tennis on Sundays in Evanston with one local fellow and his friends. Chicago's denser, more defined, and connected urban form was such a welcome change from Dallas' not "new" and not quite "Sunbelt City." Dallas, in fact, is an overgrown, southern Midwestern—not Southwestern or Sun Belt—town (see my *The Dallas Myth*, 2008a).

~~~

After settling in, I began to prepare my fellowship-sponsored history of literacy in the western world. My goals were ambitious; my scope was encompassing. Not only was there no general history of literacy in the western world, but the sum of the existing parts also drew much on what was becoming accepted to many scholars as what I termed "the literacy myth." That is: reading, writing, and especially movable typographic printing as "agents of change," in Eisenstein's (1979/1980) words, or in anthropologist Jack Goody's, "the cultural significance literacy" (1968, p. X). Each was viewed, with little direct primary evidence, as an independent variable irrespective of historical social, cultural, political, or economic contexts, from the invention of alphabets, to forms of schooling, to reading and practice in writing, to the aftermath of Johannes Gutenberg.

I proposed to synthesize interpretively, chronologically, and geographically disconnected research in new terms that greatly extended and adapted my perspectives on the 19th century. For this study, published as *The Legacies of Literacy: Continuities and Contradictions in Western Culture and Society* (1987b), time and space were critical concerns. My dialectical approach with its emphasis on complexity and contradictions was underscored in the words of the subtitle. I offered an alternative to the conventional, traditionally reflexive emphasis on change and simplistic causal connections. I devoted unusual attention to the origins of writing, alphabets, and communication systems, the interrelationships of reading and writing, and the pre-Gutenberg eras. Changes cannot be understood without understanding origins and continuities. Human actors are key variables in my narratives.

Acknowledging the strengths and the limitations of my sources and arguments, I presented my synthetic reinterpretation in four parts:

- Part I: Setting the Stage—The origins of literacy, from writing to literacy, and from Athens to Rome and beyond
- Part II: Before the Printing Press—"The light of literacy in the 'Dark Ages'" (5th to 10th centuries); New lights of literacy and learning (11th to 13th centuries); Ends and beginnings (14th to 15th centuries) including humanism, Italian Renaissance, and England
- Part III: An Old World and a New World—Print, protests, and the people—printing, revisiting Renaissances, and Reformations; Toward Enlightenment, toward modernity
- Part IV: Toward the Present and the Future—19th-century origins of our own times; Today and tomorrow—revisioning literacy

The Newberry had many of the sources I needed. Its interlibrary loan specialist helped to secure the rest, and I made a few excursions to Northwestern's and the University of Chicago's excellent libraries in Evanston and Hyde Park, respectively. In that environment, with interested and supportive colleagues, my writing went well. *The Legacies of Literacy* (1987b) put my reinterpretation of the 19th century's transformative experiences of literacy and illiteracy into a new and unprecedentedly factual, comprehensive, and comparative framework.

My later book *Searching for Literacy: The Social and Intellectual Origins of Literacy Studies* (2022e) completed my almost half-century-long project across disciplines and interdisciplines. My edited collection of essays, *Literacy and Historical Development: A Reader* (2007b) collected the most important secondary sources (see also Arnove and Graff, 1987/2008, and Graff, *Literacy Myths, Legacies, and Lessons*, 2011/2023c).

Reading and writing six days each week, I completed an overly long draft of a two-volume manuscript by the time we returned to Dallas in August 1981. Revised with editorial assistance into one long volume, it was published in 1987 by Indiana University Press. Sections were translated into several languages. It appeared in its entirety in Italian in three volumes as *Storia dell'Alfabetizzazione Occidentale* (1989). Chapters continue to be reprinted. The few negative reviewers clearly did not read the entire text.

*The Legacies of Literacy* (1987b) was discussed at a session of the SSHA in 1987. It was awarded the American Educational Studies Association Critics Choice Award in 1987, received a *Society* magazine book-of-the-month designation, and was nominated for several book awards. Excerpts are included in textbooks. It remains unique among the literature.

As I conceived this project, which I then shortsightedly expected to complete "my life with literacy," I viewed it as the centerpiece of a trio of inseparable projects. While at the Newberry, I also prepared two companion, edited books. With *Legacies*, they constitute their own reference shelf.

I envisioned the project of *Legacies* as a multilayered whole for scholars, students, and other interested parties including librarians and educators. Forming the core of a course syllabus was among my goals. These books are *Literacy in History: An Interdisciplinary Research Bibliography* (1981a) and *Literacy and Social Development in the West* (1981c), a collection of the major secondary studies (see my 1986a for the Italian edition). This was superseded by *Literacy and Historical Development* (2007b).

With the freedom of the full-time fellowship and no other writing obligations—and the supportive collegiality of others in my community of scholars and friends—I also published articles. Some focused on literacy; others explored more general historiographical, methodological, and theoretical issues. On literacy, they were "Literacy, Jobs, and Industrialization" (1981b), "Scrivendo un libro sulla storia dell'alfabetismo occidentale" (1980c), and "Reflections on the History of Literacy" (1981d; the Portuguese translation, "O mito do alfabetismo" was published in 1990). On more general but related topics, I wrote a review of *Historical Studies of Changing Fertility*" (1980a) and a review of *Theoretical methods in social history* (1980b).

I wisely and profitably decided not to spend my fellowship year(s) in professional isolation. I was escaping UTD, after all, not my profession, intellectual interests, or friends and colleagues. I remained an untenured assistant professor, so I needed to "sell my wares" and build my curriculum vitae. Maintaining my commitment and involvement was in itself liberating.

On invitation, I presented lectures and seminars about the history of literacy at the University of Chicago (1979 and 1980), the Newberry Library (1979 and 1980), the University of Toronto and the Ontario Institute for Studies in Education (1980), and, while a visiting professor in July 1981, at Simon Fraser University and the University of British Columbia in Vancouver.

I also spoke about the history of literacy at the SSHA (1979 and 1980), by invitation at the University of Pennsylvania (1980), the Conference on Literacy in Post-Reformation Europe at the University of Leicester in England (1980), the Library of Congress Center for the Book and the National Institute of Education's History of Literacy Conference (1980), the American Antiquarian Society's Conference on Printing and Society in Early America (1980), the Bard College Conference on Crisis in Literacy: Cultural Hard Times (1981), and Simon Fraser University's SITE Program on Literacy (1981).

My service to scholarly publishing expanded with membership on the editorial boards of the *History of Education Quarterly* (1979–1983) and *Historical Methods* (1987–1989). I also assisted the State University of New York Press (1979–1985) and Garland Publishing (1979–1981) as a consultant.

Conversations with a fellow graduate student, colleague, and friend from Toronto Bob Mandel (later university press editor and director) led to my launching the first of two book series that I edited. This was the Interdisciplinary Perspectives in Social History series of the State University of New York Press, for which I served as general editor (1979–1985). It ended in 1985 with only a few titles in print. Our next effort at Indiana University Press had much greater success and impact.

Staying busy, I also served as a consultant to the "It Made a Difference": Women in Texas History Project (1979–1982); on the advisory board of scholars for Potomac Educational Resources, Inc., a research and consulting group for educational policy and public history (1979–1987); and on the Newberry Library Renaissance Conference's advisory committee (1981–1982). Also at the Newberry Library, I contributed as fellow, research associate, member of the fellowship committee and later fellowship reviewer and associate of the Family and Community History Center (1979–1981). Unlike at UTD, my collegial service was appreciated.

On the national and international level, I advised the *Historical Atlas of Canada* (1979–1982), the U.S. President's Commission for a National Agenda for the Eighties (1980), and the National Institute of Education (1980). I was also a judge for the Chicago Metro History Fair (1980) and a consultant for the Illinois Humanities Council (1980–1981). Intersectionality continued despite the constraints of my temporary fellowship standing in Chicago.

~~~

Enjoying our self-imposed exile from UTD and Dallas, Vicki and I spent a splendid week before Christmas 1979 on the beautiful French and Dutch island of St. Maarten in the Caribbean. This was our first West Indian trip together. We returned to spend Christmas and the New Year with our Chicago friends.

Fighting residual anxiety and signs of depression, I found a competent psychiatrist in the northern suburb of Wilmette. Vicki and I coped off and on with marital difficulties but never considered counseling or separation. Over our 55-plus years together, we have successfully confronted our share of struggles, learning and growing together along the journeys.

~~~

Among the most pressing tasks of 1979–1980, and then 1980–1981, was the challenge to find another academic position. We did not want to return to UTD for another biased and illegitimate tenure review. Or to live in Big D. I immediately launched an intensive job search. As in 1974–1975, the market remained bare. I applied as widely as possible for tenure track and continuing tenured and untenured associate and assistant professorships in history, education, relatively undefined forms of "general studies," and administrative positions for which I met the basic qualifications. In 1979–1980, I had several interviews for history and education positions but received no offers. One minor university in New Jersey's search for an almost completely undefined position was so confused and chaotic that they invited me to visit and present seminars to faculty and graduate students twice. I am still waiting for their decision after 45 years.

As we reached the middle of spring 1980, Vicki I and decided that we could not return to Dallas. My Spencer Fellowship from the National Institute of Education provided some funding; Vicki was promoted to administrative assistant with a raise; and I was offered a visiting adjunct professorship in history to teach a graduate seminar at Loyola University of Chicago's downtown center, just a few blocks from the Newberry. That was a fine experience. More than one student commented that the course was "more like a real grad seminar" than other classes they had taken. A limited return to the classroom benefitted me as well.

I wrote to UTD, requesting a second year's leave. The dean of Arts and Humanities did not hesitate to grant my request. We found a first-floor apartment on quiet Armitage Avenue near North Avenue in the culturally rich and historic Old Town neighborhood. Moving most of our furniture, we put other contents of our Dallas townhouse, including my books, into storage and returned from Dallas to Chicago in August 1980.

*Figure 7.1. Harvey and Vicki moving to Chicago for second year at Newberry Library, 1980.*

Vicki's job, my writing, the graduate seminar, and my job search continued in the 1980–1981 academic year. Vicki took guitar lessons at the nearby Old Town School of Folk Music. I had more interviews in several fields including for an assistant deanship at a distinguished private university. I visited a few institutions that seemed even less appealing than the University of Texas near Dallas.

For some positions, I was too productive and advanced a scholar. For others, my qualifications exceeded guidelines for untenured faculty, but the universities were not able to appoint with tenure. For some schools of education, I was too much of a historian.

Finally, in spring 1981, a major public university in Boston offered me a very desirable position. It was a cross-appointment in American studies and history that also carried the role of program head for the former. Everyone was excited.

As I drafted my strongly worded letter of resignation for UTD, the Massachusetts university's administration informed me that the state of Massachusetts had gone bankrupt. It was a great shock. University officials and the faculty were disappointed and deeply apologetic. The position disappeared and the offer vanished. We had no choice but to return to UTD and Dallas. As we faced that unpleasant reality together, we vowed to redesign my relationship with the university as well as our connections to the city in as many ways as possible.

~~~

I had one final respite before we made the return drive. During the preceding winter, a professor and program director from Simon Fraser University (SFU) in

Vancouver, British Columbia, Canada, tracked me to the Newberry. As program head of English and liberal studies at SFU, Jerry Zaslove read *The Literacy Myth* (1979c) shortly after publication. He wrote to share his enthusiasm for the book and also to invite me to teach a special, interdisciplinary summer school seminar and present a lecture on the history of literacy.

UTD informed him that I was no longer affiliated with them, despite the fact that I was on regular fellowship leave. Fortunately, Zaslove persevered. He contacted my publisher, who led him to me in Chicago. I gladly accepted his offers, and a splendid three weeks in beautiful Vancouver followed. Jerry became my friend and tennis partner on my semi-regular visits for decades, until his 2021 death. I also lectured at the University of British Columbia. On both campuses, I saw a few colleague friends and met others. This eased the strain of my return from exile.

In August, we drove back to Texas. Oklahoma's state roads had been upgraded between 1975 and 1981. We began to plan our reorientation and to reorganize our approach to and lives in Dallas.

# Chapter 8. Dallas and UTD: Negotiating a Return and Beginning Again, 1981–1998

Despite the dark cloud of our prior experience with the University of Texas near Dallas and Dallas, we chose to reapproach both with new and different attitudes and strategies. To a considerable extent, we succeeded. Readjustment was a matter of navigation and negotiation, experiment and trial. It required rebuilding and reconnecting but most importantly exercising control over as many matters as possible. In a few words: redirecting the tangents of the intersecting forces.

First, we relocated within the city of Dallas, far from the northern edge of Dallas County where the university sat, beyond the fringes of the city on the Richardson-Plano border. Given our four-year history and the locations of other colleagues, we settled in the older and more developed area known as Old East Dallas.

Temporarily staying with our friend Donna Soliday, we scoured the classified newspaper ads searching for a place to live and for a dog, preferably a Scottish terrier or a similar mixed breed. We found a two-bedroom, two-bathroom, second-floor apartment with space for a study and my books. It was in a duplex on a main but not overly busy street, within a few blocks of shopping and restaurants on one side and a small park on the other side. It lay between the active, Lower Greenville shopping, restaurant, and nightlife district and attractive White Rock Lake. It was just north of downtown, where Vicki found work.

Just after we left Donna's suburban home and moved into our apartment, she found a cairn terrier puppy on her front doorstep. She knew immediately that he was meant for us. Without alerting us, she took him in and spent the next few days searching her neighborhood for notices about a lost dog. Finding none, she happily presented us with the adorable young pup as a homecoming gift.

We named him Harrison for the Scottish isle of Harris. He remained part of our family for the next 16 years through good and bad health, sometimes with companion cats. Among Harrison's favorite activities was, after pooping, picking up a stick, sometimes a large one, and bouncing along the sidewalk carrying it. We called this "playing rompity."

He made friends all over the neighborhood. About a week after we took him home, Harrison escaped from the small, fenced area beside the house. We were at work and didn't know. Surprisingly, the local postal carrier recognized him and delivered him to our landlords, who lived on the first floor.

~~~

Second, after being a full-day, Monday–Friday, 8:00 a.m.–5:00 p.m. office rat in graduate school, my first four years at UTD, and two years at the Newberry

Library, I stopped going to campus every day. I worked at home several days each week. I went to UTD only on teaching days and for mandated meetings. Otherwise, I read, wrote, and prepared classes—on a newly minted personal computer beginning in the early 1990s—comfortably and mostly without interruption from my home study, sometimes interrupted by lunch with UTD or SMU friends.

To renegotiate and renavigate commuting from near the city center to the suburban campus on city streets and a busy expressway, I formed a carpool with other faculty members and some graduate students who lived in the vicinity. In this decidedly un-Texan move, no one drove more than one day each week or less, and with companions. Still a smoker, I was forbidden from lighting up in the cars. When I finally stopped smoking in 1987, I was hugged, especially by my carpoolers, and told that I smelled much better! The carpool continued for most of the years until I left Dallas in 1998.

*Figure 8.1. Harvey in UTD office, 1980s.*

Third, I—and we—chose not to obsess about tenure or to allow related concerns about my future at the university to influence me or us unnecessarily. The two years in exile gave me perspective, comparative context, and personal understanding and growth. Several factors, including the breadth and depth of my welcome back to UTD by the rank-and-file across campus and our quickly established and growing network of colleagues, graduate students, and friends, added to my confidence.

Fourth, in a variety of often intersecting ways, I redesigned my relationships with UTD and the Dallas area more broadly. This ranged from expanding my research and advising into the city's past and present in preparation eventually to write an original book about Dallas, to encouraging and supervising student research into the city's history, expanding my involvement with public and private institutions and groups including leadership roles, and collaborating with reporters from the *Dallas Morning News* and reporters and producers at the local NPR/PBS affiliate KERA radio and TV.

I was connecting many dots that constituted public history and public humanities: the personal, political, academic, and place (for more on these activities, see my "Lessons for Becoming a Public Scholar," 2023h). I also taught a pioneering graduate humanities seminar on public history; a course on Dallas; other courses on urban history as well as on the history of literacy, U.S. history, and the history of children and youth; and graduate and undergraduate introductory approaches and methods courses.

Upon my return, I also founded the Dallas Social History Group. We usually met monthly at the more or less central location of Southern Methodist University's Dallas Hall. With a broadly defined approach, the group brought together historians, other humanities professors, and a few social scientists from UTD, SMU, the University of Texas at Arlington, and occasionally other Dallas and North Texas institutions. Some UTD doctoral students joined us. The group continues for more than four decades, even after I left the city. Its regular participants repeatedly confirmed the value it added and the needs it fulfilled for them.

Fifth, and no less important, Vicki made basic career decisions. Her earlier experience with Dallas schools combined with her office work at the Newberry influenced her to seek office-based administrative work in downtown Dallas not far from our residence. One commuter in the household was more than enough.

After discussing possible positions with the city of Dallas, she accepted a job as a marketing assistant with an architectural firm. When it ended about a year later, she became marketing coordinator and then director of communications for a larger architectural firm. She held that position for about six years before moving to the American Heart Association's national headquarters, which had relocated to Dallas from New York City in 1975.

~~~

Returning to UTD represented a contradictory return to an old academic home and an alienating environment. Little had changed materially other than more faces gone and fewer new ones added. But I had changed. That manifested in my professional and personal conduct and my relationships. My earlier experience strengthened most connections, outside of the administration and a certain minority of the tenured faculty.

I was a stronger teacher at all levels. While never one of the world's great stand-up lecturers, I was satisfactory to almost all students in larger lecture courses in U.S. history, the Dallas history course, and an interdisciplinary course on the history of children, youth, and families in American history. I experimented with visual media including classic and experimental films, writing assignments, and group projects.

For years in formats large and small, I developed large undergraduate courses and graduate seminars on "growing up in America," with extensive use of memoirs, novels, films, visual slides, and scholarly texts. In effect, I was teaching literacy across media. Prompted by Michael Katz's research in the 1970s and a published seminar paper on the stages of adolescence in 1860 Boston (Graff, 1973b), my interests evolved into *Conflicting Paths: Growing Up in America* (1995a), an original interpretation of more than 500 first-person accounts and other historical materials covering more than 200 years. It became a standard source. At the same time, I have not yet earned back my $10,000 advance on royalties.

The smaller classes I taught included introduction to history and historical methods, urban history, and social history, with their appropriate-level research projects. With growing interest nationally and internationally in my major areas of research and teaching and with the growth of online academic publishing venues, I shared both syllabi and discussions about pedagogical approaches and projects. These activities constituted a valuable set of additions to my *curriculum vitae* and annual review reports (see my "Doctoral Seminar in the History of Ideas," 1986c, "Teaching the History of Literacy at the University of Texas," 1994d, "Using First-Person Sources in Social and Cultural History," 1994e, "Interdisciplinary Explorations in the History of Children, Adolescents, and Youth," 1999a, "Teaching and Historical Understanding," 1999b, "Growing Up in America," 2001a, "Teaching [and] Historical Understanding," 1999c, "Teaching the History of Growing Up," 2008b, and with Joy L. Bivens, "Coming of Age in Chicago," 2004).

As the pseudo "interdisciplinary" humanities Ph.D. program grew, I developed a coterie of advisees whose interests crossed historical and literary studies. I originated new seminars on the following topics: introduction to interdisciplinarity in the humanities, the history of literacy, urban social history, and an unusually stimulating seminar on public history. In that course, especially self-selected, often older professional students conducted research relevant to their employment activities, possible extensions of their work, and their expertise in various public realms. It was exemplary public humanities and history.

My future books *Conflicting Paths: Growing Up in America* (1995a), *The Dallas Myth* (2008a), and *Undisciplining Knowledge: Interdisciplinarity in the Twentieth Century* (2015a) all connected with each other and advanced between my graduate education and successive decades of teaching. Both consciously and unconsciously, lifelong connections inseparably intertwined my education, teaching, and research, never one in isolation from the others.

I co-taught two courses on women and gender, one historically based with a philosopher of women and gender (Nancy Tuana, now at Penn State), the other on women in literature with a professor of European literature (Lillian Furst, who moved to the University of North Carolina and is now deceased). They were powerful chapters in expanding education for both the instructors and students. The seminar with Tuana met in the early evening. The group quickly decided to rotate responsibilities for preparing dinners to share during the mid-session break. At the end of the semester, we produced a book of the recipes.

I also co-taught an exciting, experimental seminar called Crises in Expression and Representation, focusing on the 17th and early 20th centuries with an extraordinarily wide-ranging art historian and specialist in visual literacy and the book arts, Johanna Drucker, who has recently retired from UCLA (see Drucker and Graff, 1991).

A full professor at the time, I felt that I struggled to keep up with the second-year assistant professor, previously a book artist. Several years ago, from her endowed chair in information sciences at UCLA, the author of the landmark *Graphesis: Visual Forms of Knowledge Production* (2014), confessed: "Harvey, I was scared shitless every class." Johanna and her companion cat, Punky, hosted me in Austin, Texas, that summer while I did research for *Conflicting Paths* (1995a) in the Barker Historical Collection at UT-Austin. We remain in regular contact.

For several years, my group of graduate students met regularly with me, rotating among our living and dining rooms. We read important texts or presented portions of dissertations and theses in progress. The longer-lasting participants included Cathy Civello, Martha Burdette, Sally Ramsay, Jill Milling, Patricia Hill, and Soledad Jasin. (Sally and Jill died tragically and prematurely not long after completing their dissertations from a horse accident and lung cancer, respectively.)

I vividly recall a meeting of this group the afternoon before my tenure decision was announced, and I remember their responses when I shared the positive results. Among master's students, Martha Burdette (who studied English and education), Tony Fracchia (a high school history teacher), and Darryl Baird (a photographic artist) all became and remain good friends. For years Tony and I played tennis, never counting points. We wagered cartons of yogurt. Since I left Texas, he keeps me informed about Texas and Dallas politics and foibles. We make small, inexpensive, humorous wagers on the major tennis tournaments.

My graduate students were exceptional. Not only did they form a close-knit, mutually supportive, cross- and interdisciplinary intellectual and social group, but also most of them completed their degrees (two finishing master's degrees with me and their Ph.D.s elsewhere). Several women moved from high school teaching to graduate studies (nontraditional academic career paths such as these are explored in my forthcoming edited collection of original first-person essays,

*Scholarly Lives in Transition, 1960s to 2020s and Beyond: Misunderstood and Untold Paths in Shaping the American University*).

Most practiced their academic profession at one level or another, in colleges or other environments. Several published books based on their dissertations, an accomplishment almost unheard of for students in this program. Patty Hill published her dissertation as *Dallas: The Making of a Modern City* (1996) and had a successful career as a professor of history and department chair before retiring recently from San Jose State University. She assisted me with my Dallas research, and we jointly collaborated on the reprinted edition of Warren Leslie's *Dallas Public and Private* (1964/1998). Cathy Civello published *Patterns of Ambivalence: The Fiction and Poetry of Stevie Smith* in 1997. Some also achieved tenure, although one returned happily to high school teaching.

In a multidisciplinary humanities graduate program, students cross many lines—more, in fact, than most faculty members. My group, I state without hesitation, was special. They all became personal and family friends. Vicki and I remain in regular contact with them, scattered all over the country. We also remain in communication with several of my master's students and a few undergraduates.

*Figure 8.2. Harvey with new Ph.D. Patricia E. Hill at UTD graduation, 1990.*

Another special relationship is with Cindy Maciel-Reyes. She was secretary in the Arts and Humanities College master's office when I returned from Chicago. Cindy then became a full-time student. We're not certain if she took a formal undergraduate course with me or not. After Cindy completed her bachelor's degree in art, Vicki hired her to work on preparing visual materials for the promotion of architectural projects. Cindy and her mother brought us wonderful, homemade Mexican food. She later moved to the Austin area, worked in Austin, married, and raised two children. We write and talk regularly.

With the rise and increasingly constructive early use of the internet, I began sharing my more innovative syllabi online. I published "Doctoral Seminar in the History of Ideas" (1986c), "Teaching the History of Literacy at the University of Texas" (1994d), "Reading and Writing the City" (1996c), and "Crises in Expression and Representation" (Drucker & Graff, 1991). I also contributed urban graduate and undergraduate course syllabuses to the Urban History Association's *Syllabus Exchange* (Graff, 1990) and its *Syllabus Exchange II & Sampler* (Graff, 1993), as well as its H-Urban electronic network (Graff, 1994a, 1995b, 1995d, 1996a, 1996b, 1997a, 2000, 2001g, 2002b, 2002c). These contributions led to many new connections with faculty members, graduate students, and some universities both nationally and internationally.

When I returned to UTD in autumn 1981, the British dean who opposed my early tenure strongly cautioned me against an immediate re-review for tenure. I could not oppose him, of course. My review was postponed until the 1982–1983 academic year. It was another irrational struggle with my opponents repeating their decreasingly persuasive and undocumentable slander.

This time the faculty ad hoc committee favored tenure by a substantial majority as did the university-wide Committee on Qualifications. The dean made a muddled, vaguely negative recommendation.

The overflowing dossier advanced to the provost. He was not happy to have the case before him again. Senior professors across the campus wrote or called him in my support. UT-Dallas' one Nobel laureate, Polykarp Kusch, who retired from Columbia University where he had also been a provost, telephoned the provost and admonished him for his delay of several years in promoting me. (Every major UT campus tries to employ one Nobel Prize winner, almost always retired from major east- or west-coast universities.) Some of the senior faculty demanded that I be immediately promoted to full professor based on my record.

The (melo)drama came to a crescendo when the provost summoned me to his office on the day before his final decision was due in April 1983. I vividly recall our sitting at a small table in his large office. Both of us smokers, we more or less blew smoke—of one kind or another—in each other's faces. I refused to be intimidated. The provost, Alex Clark, began by telling me how irritated he was to receive Kusch's admonitions. I calmly replied that "untenured faculty in the university have no direct way to respond to unfair attacks and illegitimate uses of the review process." He nodded. He hemmed and hawed a while and then began his test for me.

His decision apparently rested on how calmly and responsibly I responded to a seemingly neutral question for which he had no basis for evaluation. He asked me to explain in terms he could understand how a social historian like me fit in and contributed to a graduate humanities program that emphasized at least rhetorically the history of ideas. It was an easy question, one I had thought about since I had joined the faculty. But I realized immediately that the provost's opinion rested not on the contents of my response but on how seemingly professional, balanced, and low-key my answer would be.

At the end of this awkward meeting, as we shook hands, the provost told me that my letter would be with the others in our mailboxes the next morning. That was Thursday. Along with colleagues, graduates, and friends in Dallas, across the country, and around the world, we spent that evening in suspense.

On Friday, I waited until mid-morning to drive to campus. I did not want to stand beside my cubbyhole of a mailbox waiting for delivery. When I arrived around 11:00 a.m. the provost's letter was waiting. Anticlimactically and three years delayed, I was promoted to associate professor of history and humanities and awarded academic tenure.

Overwhelmingly, the response I received to this news when I shared it combined relief and celebration. In this pre-internet and pre-social media age, I made many telephone calls and asked friends to call others. There were parties large and intimate, baked cakes, congratulatory cards and letters, both immediately and over time.

Although UTD colleagues shared my relief and satisfaction, my dean and one of my antisemitic opponents were forever silent. The other, the shrillest of the British antisemites, knocked on my office door, interrupting a long-distance telephone call to give me insincere congratulations. They said to me, "Prove him [the provost] right." I replied, "I have already more than done that." They turned on their heels and walked away. We seldom spoke. More than a decade later, after they had finally published their first book, I held my nose, bit my tongue, and did not oppose their promotion to professor. Ironically, the outside evaluator in that case asked in writing, "How did this person ever gain tenure?"

I was promoted to full professor within four years. That promotion occurred, with a perfunctory review, in 1987 as *The Legacies of Literacy* (1987b) appeared in print. Along the way, new colleagues like European cultural historian Michael Wilson became lifelong friends. Royce Hanson, a political scientist, and Brian Berry, a renowned geographer, interacted with me on Dallas matters.

Beyond encouraging a greater sense of accomplishment, freedom, and professional security, my tenure prompted Vicki and me to purchase our first home in Old East Dallas not far from our apartment and the local, informal shopping center. On a moderate-sized lot, it was a three-bedroom house with two and a half bathrooms that had been relocated from a lakeside site and reassembled. It was one block north of our close friend from SMU Dan Orlovsky's family.

We did not know then that the weight of my too-many books would lead to structural problems with the foundation and require expensive repairs. Later, before we purchased our future homes in San Antonio and Columbus, we had structural engineers inspect the likely candidates. They stopped us from bidding on houses that were not prepared for my admittedly excessive scholarly baggage. They also told us where to reinforce floors and where *not* to locate bookcases, valuable lessons not taught in graduate history programs.

Harrison now had a yard to play in. He developed a special relationship with felines. Stray cats followed him on his walks. Three littermates in particular, who had been abandoned when neighbors moved out, followed him home. One was killed by a car. One who we took in walked shoulder-to-shoulder with Harrison; we named him Shadow. We also adopted his sibling, Topaz, who later died from feline infectious peritonitis.

Our neighbors Gerald and Nancy, my colleague in feminist philosophy, also brought us two kittens. At first sight, they were terrified of Harrison and hid behind books on a bookshelf. The next time Gerald and Nancy visited, they did not bring the kittens, but Harrison looked for them behind the books. Named Orpheus and Nebulous, aka Orphie and Nebbie, they soon joined our family. Sadly, Orphie died not long after adoption. Without her sibling to play with, Nebbie loved to wrestle with Harrison and continued to hide, challenging him—and us—to find her.

With a relatively small faculty, an excessive and inefficient bureaucratic organization, and administrative incompetence, the UTD faculty continued to be overwhelmed with service and teaching responsibilities. This is *not* how to develop a new, supposedly interdisciplinary university with a young faculty. Nor is it an acceptable path for a mature institution with a seasoned, experienced teaching, administrative, and ancillary staff.

My assignments in the School of Arts and Humanities mushroomed after my tenure in 1983. Over the next 15 years until I left the university in 1998, I served on and chaired search committees, served on college steering and interdisciplinary studies committees, as community college liaison, on the graduate studies committee, on faculty ad hoc review committees (for which I also served as chair), on the committee on grants and development, on the Cecil Green lectures committee, on core curriculum committees (for which I also served as chair), and on the library development committee, among others. At the same time, I served on multiple university-wide committees (these are listed in the Appendix). I also served as consultant and instructor for the NEH implementation grant, "The Art of Translation in an Interdisciplinary Curriculum: Re-Creative Dynamics in the Humanities" from 1983 to 1987.

No rest for the wicked! But I did my best to help a persistently negligent branch campus—one that refused to learn from its own mistakes or the examples from other universities in Texas or across the nation—function more or less. Of course, I was not alone in that attempt. That is how many institutions struggle to get by. I made new colleagues and friends across the university and beyond along the way.

My time at Vancouver's Simon Fraser University in July 1981 led to continuing relationships, especially with the Institute for the Humanities' director Jerry Zaslove, who became a close colleague, good friend, and tennis partner. From an initial, shared interest in the critical revisioning of literacy in historical perspective and critical rethinking more generally, we repeatedly found common ground.

I returned to SFU to teach summer school in 1982. For several years I consulted with their Institute for the Humanities on conferences and external studies programs. I was also a special arrangements doctoral committee member. Other activities included being interviewed by British Columbia's public educational television's Knowledge Network in 1981, consulting for the SFU Institute for the Humanities' *The Story of Literacy* proposed television series in 1985, speaking at the Conference on the Legacy of J. S. Woodsworth and the Welfare State in Canada in 1988, and in 1993 consulting on the British Columbia Prison Education Research Report by the SFU Institute for the Humanities (Stephen Duguid, 1998).

In Dallas, local engagements widened as I continued to integrate in new ways the academic with the public and the specificities of place. In retrospect, I see more clearly now my lifelong search for constructive and affirming intersections, on the one hand, and on the other hand, my simultaneous teaching and learning within and across disciplines, both in academia and in multiple public spheres (see also Chapter One).

My career as an active publishing scholar with many books and articles on a number of topics but also as a public writer, speaker, and advisor exemplifies these intersections. Public, institutional, and media relationships all reflect intersectionality. Our residence in Dallas for 23 years (with two years plus several additional months doing research in Chicago and nine months in Worcester, Massachusetts) illustrates this well. Looking back, I know that I made a difference. I also learned a great deal about many things—the place, the people, the institutions, the history, and myself.

The most regular and longest-lasting relationship was with the Dallas Social History Group. Meeting my needs and others', I founded the group upon my return from Chicago in 1981 and coordinated its meetings until 1987. I continued to participate until I left the city in 1998. Not only did this group provide an individually *and* collectively needed intellectual space for its members, but it also contributed to professional exchanges and mutual learning first and then friendship. My longtime friendships with UT-Arlington faculty—Leslie Moch, Kathy Underwood, Nora Faires, and Gary Stark—advanced with these contacts.

There were also many Southern Methodist University connections made across the humanities and social sciences, not least among them my friendship with Dan Orlovsky (and his family) from 1977, including throughout the time we were neighbors from 1983 to 1998. At SMU, I was also a fellow of the William P. Clements Center for Southwest Studies in the department of history from 1996–2004 and advisor to the Stanton Sharp Symposium on the History of the Family in 1996. I returned to speak after leaving Texas. In retrospect, I am not surprised that SMU and UT-Arlington accorded greater recognition to my accomplishments than my own employing institution.

I also led the North Texas Phi Beta Kappa Association for members who had been elected by their original universities and were then living in North Texas. I no longer remember what led to my initial involvement. I was soon a member of its special projects committee and the committee on awards (1981–1984). Next, I became vice president (1982–1984) and president (1984–1986). I remember a telephone call on a Sunday morning when we were sleeping late after returning the night before from a European trip. The outgoing president asked me to accept the presidential office. I apparently muttered a sleepy "yes."

I used this position in combination with other public roles to establish the Phi Beta Kappa-Dallas Public Library Annual Lecture on Culture and the City held at the central Dallas Public Library with Phi Beta Kappa's financial support. As founder and chair of the advisory committee, I brought some of the best scholars on urban culture to speak. They included the noted urban historians Thomas Bender and Michael Frisch and a distinguished philosopher. The series ran from 1983 to 1987. My successors did not continue it despite strong attendance, media coverage, and civic needs.

My earlier cooperation with the Dallas Public Library continued as I became an advisor to the Dallas and Texas history division from 1984 to 1989. I was also advisor, coordinator, and participant for the sesquicentennial Symposium on Dallas Past and Present in 1986. With the Dallas Historical Society and Alpha Xi Omega, HRA, Inc. of Alpha Kappa Alpha Sorority, I served as consultant and presenter at public forums addressing the "Black Dallas Remembered" oral history project from 1985 to 1987.

I wrote more brochures for historic landmarks for the city of Dallas until 1985. I also contributed as a member of the publicity taskforce of the Historic Landmark and Preservation Committee (1981–1985), and the Archives Committee (1983–1988). Similarly, I was a member of the Historical Publications Committee for the Dallas Sesquicentennial Commission (1984–1986). As the rare historian looking closely at the city, I published "How Can You Celebrate a Sesquicentennial If You Have No History? Reflections on Historical Consciousness in Dallas," commissioned by *The Dallas Morning News* for the Texas State Sesquicentennial in 1986.

Spreading my public historical outreach, I wrote for the Historic Preservation League's *Historic Dallas* from 1981 to 1983 (see, for example, Graff, 1982a, 1982b) and advised the league's neighborhoods book committee from 1983 to 1986. A collateral connection was service on the advisory board of the Dallas Folklore Media Center (1984–1989) and humanities advisor and speaker for the 1983 symposium "Folklife in Dallas," funded by the Texas Committee for the Humanities. I sat on the advisory board for the Texas history gallery of the Fort Worth Museum of Science and History from 1992 to 1998.

Just as I was using different kinds of visual media in my courses, I also learned more about the use of film and video for history education through consulting and participating on the Dallas County Community College District's and Harper and Row's telecourse, "The American Adventure"—26 half-hour programs for 600 colleges in 45 states and the PBS Adult Learning Network (1985–1986).

An incredibly special and unusual experience for a practicing historian came with my opportunity to perform as an extra in filming the Texas docudrama *West of Hester Street* (Allen Mondell & Cynthia Mondell, 1983). This project focused on the Galveston Movement that shifted the landing of immigrating European Jews from New York City to the port of Galveston, Texas, during 1907 to 1910. This movement responded to rising anti-immigration, antisemitism, and nativism in East Coast receiving areas. The cast and crew flew from Dallas to Galveston where those of us acting as immigrants physically landed from a boat to the shore. We then resettled in Dallas. In technical terms, I was a "featured extra." In at least one scene, my head blocked out the literal signs of the late 20th century. The director-producer team, friends Alan and Cynthia Mondale, did a remarkable job and the film garnered praise around the country. It is an experience that all historians should have at some point in their career, better earlier than later.

On the state of Texas level, in the mid-1980s, I advised the *Handbook of Texas Women* (now available as an online resource at https://texaswomen.tshaonline.org/) and the *Handbook of Texas History* (now available online at https://www.tshaonline.org/handbook). I also served in the late 1980s on the advisory boards of the Dallas Jewish Historical Society and *Deep in the Heart: The Lives and Legends of Texas Jews: A Photographic History* (Ruthe Winegarten & Cathy Schechter, 1990).

As we decided to leave Dallas after more than two decades, I wrote "Comment: Race Between San Antonio, Dallas Like Fabled Tortoise and the Hare" for the *San Antonio Express-News* (1997c). This looked forward first to our relocation to San Antonio and then to completing *The Dallas Myth* (2008a) one decade later.

I extended my relationships with print media and local and national public radio and television. These constitute additional links in the chain that expands today. Before its demise, I assisted the *Dallas Times Herald*, then *The Dallas Morning News*. Later I shifted to the *San Antonio Express-News*, *The Columbus Dispatch*, and the *Columbus Free Press* newspapers, (London) *Times Higher Education*, *Inside Higher Ed*, *The Chronicle of Higher Education*, *The Nation*, and the *Huffington Post*. I long cooperated with reporters from *The New York Times*, *The Washington Post*, and NPR. In my view, all scholars should—with care and intelligence.

My long-term relationship with National Public Radio and the Public Broadcasting System began in Dallas with KERA 90.1 FM and Channel 13. I advised the radio station on news programming, developing a close relationship with reporter Bill Zeeble. With Channel 13, I commented on air on *News Edition* from 1983 to 1986. I served from 1983 to 1985 on the advisory board of *Legacies of the Land: A Tale of Texas* (Martin, 1985), which was funded by the Texas Committee for the Humanities.

My most rewarding involvement with KERA Channel 13 accompanied the publication of *Conflicting Paths: Growing Up in America* (1995a) and the publicity surrounding my popular courses on the history of children, youth, and families. This led the producers to invite me to serve as an advisor for the early 1990s "Family Project." They expanded my role into chief advisor and commentator for "A Better Childhood (ABC) Quiz" (Rob Tranchin & Tom Voight, 1991).

This program won the Katherine Ripley Award for Electronic Media from Planned Parenthood of Dallas; the Matrix Award from the Dallas Professional Chapter of Women in Media; and the Silver Award for Local Programs from the Corporation for Public Broadcasting. Later I was principal advisor and radio commentator for the documentary production *First Steps* (Tranchin, 1992).

I remained highly active outside the university and the city. Most national and international connections and contributions centered on literacy. That began to widen to encompass urban history and children and adolescents. These assignments ranged from consulting on the Fertility Determinants Project at Indiana University (1983), involvement in the University of Southern California's Annenberg School of Communications' Annenberg Scholars Program (1983), and serving on the advisory board of the American Antiquarian Society's Program on the History of the Book in American Culture (1985–1991). Literacy also led me to be advising humanist (1989–1991) and keynote speaker and panelist for the New Hampshire Humanities Council's 1991 "Literacy: Myths and Legacies" Conference (Graff, 1991).

My involvement on urban issues and in urban history expanded to include membership on the board of advisors of H-Urban (Humanities and Social Sciences Online's H-Net Network on Urban History) from the mid-1990s, the international advisory board of the University of Illinois at Chicago's Great Cities Institute's electronic network (1995–2002), and the online seminar "The History of Community Organizing and Community-Based Housing and Economic Development in an International Context" (1995–1999).

Reflecting my interests and expertise in the history of children, women, and families, I was advisor and manuscript reviewer for the special issue on "Feminisms and Youth Cultures" for *Signs: Journal of Women in Culture and Society* (Kum-Kum Bhavani et al., 1998) and member of the board of advisors and project scholar for the documentary *A History of American Teenagers* (Alves, 2001), which was funded by the NEH.

Internationally, I was a member of the United States working group of the International Commission for the History of Social Movements and Social Structures and the International Congress on Historical Sciences (1990). I consulted on the Everyday Literacy Practices in and Out of Schools in Low Socioeconomic Urban Communities Project at Griffith University, Australia, beginning in 1993. In the mid-1990s, I was also a resource member for the UNESCO Institute of Education's Literacy Exchange Network. I commented on the Italian national radio's *America Coast to Coast* several times in the 1980s and on Australian radio during a lecture tour and wonderful holiday in Australia in 1993.

In the United States and Canada, I broadened and deepened my involvement with the still-young SSHA. This culminated in my presidency during its 25th anniversary in 2000. I participated in every meeting from its founding in 1976 until 2015. As a regional network coordinator from 1976 to 1984, I helped to establish the Allan Sharlin Memorial Award for a dear friend taken away by cancer far too young. I was the founding chair in 1984–1985 and committee member from 1984 to 1986. His family and I worked together on this endeavor, which remembers Allan annually.

I organized one or more sessions for each year's SSHA meetings, usually collaborating with my colleagues and close friends M. J. Maynes on literacy, children and youth, and interdisciplinarity; and Jan Reiff on urban history, public history, historical methods, and interdisciplinarity. I brought scholars Michael Katz, Paul Mattingly, Mike Frisch, Sharon Zukin, Michael Wilson, Chris Hager, Jerry Jacobs, John Guillory, Bengt Sandin, Sigurdur Magnusson, several anthropologists, sociologists, linguists, folklorists, and literary historians and critics to sessions, among others.

I also organized SSHA sessions with my graduate students from UTD and later Ohio State, and I organized sessions with my graduate students at the Conference on College Composition and Communication (CCCC). All of my major books were honored with SSHA sessions and some on literacy by CCCCs.

I was elected to the SSHA executive committee 1987 to 1989, then vice president and president-elect from 1998 to 1999. Serving as president in 1999–2000, I created a committee on the future of SSHA as part of the 25th anniversary of the organization. I titled that annual meeting's program, "Looking Backward and Looking Forward: Perspectives on Social Science History." It featured both a celebration and critical stocktaking.

My presidential address continues to be cited and discussed after more than two decades. Published in 2001 (and reprinted in 2005 as part of an edited collection), it is titled, "The Shock of the '"New" Histories': Social Science Histories and Historical Literacies." Consistent with the 25th anniversary theme, the program chairs—my longtime colleague and friend (and former Tilly student) Leslie Page Moch and the first Sharlin Prize winner, sociologist Philip McMichael—and I co-edited a selection of the papers in *Looking Backward and Looking Forward: Perspectives on Social Science History* (2005).

~~~

Many conference presentations and invited lectures in this period focused on literacy. (They are listed in the Appendix.) The history of literacy took me across the United States, Canada, Mexico, Brazil, Australia, and Europe, making acquaintances with people and places. That is among its many benefits. As my international stature and recognition as an interpreter of literacy past and present grew, so did invitations to speak, advise, and write.

As my research on growing up, urban history, and interdisciplinarity progressed, and as I published more on those topics, I spoke more frequently about them, too. I published increasingly often outside the United States and was translated widely. The intersections of personal experience, education, research, teaching, and both university and community relationships propelled my life with literacy, children and youth, cities, and interdisciplinarity.

My research and writing attracted funding. UTD awarded me funds to support my doctoral students. As I prepared to research and write *Conflicting Paths: Growing Up in America* (1995a), I was awarded a Peterson Fellowship by the American Antiquarian Society in 1984, which I declined in favor of a 1985–1986 short-term fellowship from the Newberry Library. I also conducted primary source research at the Barker Historical Collection at the University of Texas at Austin.

My project on the history of growing up originated in a 1971 graduate school seminar paper. It expanded with my teaching about the subject and came to fruition in the 1980s and early 1990s. Not coincidentally, in the wake of the field of the history of the family emerging from demographic, cultural, and social history, children and youth followed as a semi-institutionalized field of study with courses, national and international societies, regular and special conferences, journals, and book series.

In this context, I first expanded my undergraduate and graduate course offerings. Then I edited a collection of previously published essays, designed for classroom use. This became *Growing Up in America: Historical Experiences* (1987a). My new reinterpretation of growing up in American history, *Conflicting Paths* (1995a) also appeared. *Choice Magazine* awarded it the Outstanding Academic Book Award.

I broke the back of drafting the manuscript as an American Antiquarian Society/National Endowment for the Humanities Fellow in 1988–1989. I worked hard while living alone in the AAS fellows' residence in Worcester, Massachusetts. Vicki, Harrison, and the cats stayed in Dallas. We saw each other about once a month. Old friends not far away in Cambridge and a few new friends and other fellows distracted me.

Worcester was quiet and thus conducive to research and writing. By design, my primary research base developed by reading unpublished manuscripts and published first-person accounts of "growing up" mainly in the Texas State and University of Texas archives, the Newberry Library, and the American Antiquarian Society with a briefer stop at the National Archives and the Library of Congress. As in all my projects, interlibrary loan librarians as well as archivists were fundamental.

The book added a much needed, deeply researched, and deeply autobiographical dimension to the project of rediscovering and understanding the myth- and fiction-laden views of growing up. I identified and examined approximately 500 personal accounts from the 18th through the 20th centuries across the geography of the US. My subjects' literacy and my own intersected inseparably. In my conceptual and theoretical framework, I focused on the intersections of changes *and* continuities and systemic differences *between and across* class, gender, ethnic, and geographic distinctions. Interdisciplinarily, and unprecedentedly, I literally "read" the "traditional" first-person primary sources through the lens of a quantitatively and demographically trained comparative social historian.

In my view, other studies exaggerated, and continue to exaggerate, the importance of one set of factors over the others rather than their complicated but richly human intersections. The usual result is a lack of context for recent changes and an overattention to favored and/or underprivileged groups rather than both. I purposefully chose not to include young people of color. In my view, their history demands full, independent treatment before meaningful comparisons can be made. Reading these accounts and constructing their histories are different scholarly uses of literacy in different contexts.

Relatedly, I demonstrated with my large sample that most scholars followed the influential works of Philippe Ariès (1960) and Lawrence Stone (1977). As a result, they failed to first distinguish and then explore the relationships between "childhood" as concept, set of cultural expectations, or "stage of life," and children themselves as quite different human subjects *and* actors synchronically and across time.

In 1991 and 1992, Spencer Foundation research grants allowed me time to complete and revise the *Conflicting Paths* (1995a) manuscript for publication by Harvard University Press. In 1992 I lectured and conducted discussions at the Seminar on Children and the History of Childhood at the department of thematic studies–child studies at Linköping University in Sweden (with Bengt Sandin), and in 1996 I chaired and commented on papers on women and children at the American Studies Association annual meeting.

Writing and publishing continued apace, as I shifted from literacy—which I could never "put behind me"—to children, adolescents, and families; cities; and historical methods and interpretation. Of course, I understand implicitly and practically the inseparable interrelationships between studying and understanding literacy past and present and young persons. My books in these years included the first of several collections of my essays on literacy, *The Labyrinths of Literacy: Reflections on Literacy Past and Present* (1987/1995c), republished by the University of Pittsburgh Press in its Composition, Literacy, and Culture series. I also wrote jointly and then co-edited with my colleague, comparative education scholar Robert F. Arnove of Indiana University, a pioneering collection of essays, *National Literacy Campaigns: Historical and Comparative Perspectives* (1987/2008). Transaction Publishers issued a new edition of *The Literacy Myth* with a new introduction in 1991 (republished by the WAC Clearinghouse in 2023).

∼∼∼

Over these years, I published both scholarly and general interest articles on my major topics and related interests. On literacy, these dealt with the European Renaissance, 19th-century English working-class readers, literacy and libraries, the historiography of literacy, national literacy campaigns, literacy and development, and general interpretive issues. (See the Appendix.) As an authority on literacy, I accepted invitations to write these encyclopedia entries:

- "Illiteracy," *The World Book Encyclopedia* (World Book, 1993)
- "Literacy," *Funk and Wagnalls New Encyclopedia* (Funk and Wagnalls, 1983)
- "Literacy," *The Social Science Encyclopedia* (Graff, 1985/2004)
- "Literacy," *The World Book Encyclopedia* (World Book, 1995)
- "Literacy," in *Encarta* (Microsoft, 1998)

Working toward *Conflicting Paths* (1995a), stimulated by my undergraduate interdisciplinary lecture and film courses and graduate seminars as well as by public engagement on the issues, I published several articles on the history of families and growing up, childhood and early adolescence, and using first-person sources in social and cultural history. (See the Appendix for details.)

Looking toward *The Dallas Myth* (2008a) and grounded in teaching and civic work with urban studies and issues, I wrote "The City, Crisis, and Change in American Culture: Perceptions and Perspectives" (1983) and "How Can You Celebrate a Sesquicentennial if You Have No History?" (1986). I took another step toward *The Dallas Myth* (2008a) when my former graduate student Patricia Hill and I published a new edition of Warren Leslie's (1964/1998) *Dallas Public and Private* with a new introduction.

More general, scholarly publications included critical essay reviews published in *Contemporary Sociology* (Graff, 1986b), *Criminal Justice History* (Graff, 1986d), *Journal of Social History* (Graff, 1987e), *History of Education Quarterly* (Graff, 1987c), *Society* (Graff, 1987d), and *Historical Studies in Education/Revue d'histoirede l'éducation* (Graff, 1991b). Some of these essays appeared in general-interest, socially oriented magazines like *Society*.

Finally, my work as a series editor resumed. The Interdisciplinary Studies in History series published by Indiana University Press with me as general editor began in 1982. With 19 books contracted, 13 were completed before the press and I agreed to stop. With a focus on synthetic, interpretive works by leading scholars, books included studies of immigration and adaptation, rioting, growing old, urban migration, and early modern European culture and society, among others.

I served on the editorial boards of *Historical Methods* (1987–1989), the *Studies in Written Language and Literacy* book series (1992 to present), and *Social Science History* (1994–1997). I was special advisor to the *Wilson Quarterly*'s special section on literacy (The Struggle for Literacy, 1986) and consulted for Indiana University Press and Wayne State University Press.

~~~

Vicki, Harrison, the off-and-on-again cats, and I were much more content in phase two of our Dallas years. Living far from the suburban campus "near Dallas," we resided in a more traditional and settled, inner-city neighborhood. We were close to friends, shops, restaurants, and entertainment. We ate out frequently, saw new foreign and alternative films, and gathered with colleagues and friends. I played tennis (not keeping score) with my former graduate student Tony F., and Vicki enjoyed working downtown, either driving or taking the bus. With two incomes, we were comfortable. We had occasional personal difficulties but nothing out of the ordinary or beyond our ability to accommodate, resolve, and rebalance. Most of the time, we were at peace at least with the elements within our control.

Between my invitations to speak at campuses or conferences and our savings, we traveled frequently. When possible, Vicki accompanied me. We turned professional engagements into holidays, often overseas. I traveled to London in 1982, The Netherlands in 1991, Sweden again in 1992, Spain in 1993, and several times to Canada by myself. Together, we went to Mexico City for a conference in 1982. After a 1984 conference in Bellagio, Italy, Vicki joined me for travel to Milan, Florence, Venice, and Rome. We saw Armando Petrucci and other Italian colleagues socially. The trip was damaged but not ruined when a thief on a scooter stole Vicki's purse the day before our departure home.

Personal holidays also took us several times to nearby Mexico, a variety of cities and towns in Texas, New Mexico, Arkansas, New Orleans, South Carolina, Los Angeles, San Francisco, the Bay area and northern California, Seattle, Alaska, British Columbia, Peru, and Spain. Many of these trips were remarkable, leaving lasting memories. The visit to Alaska included a cruise on a smaller, environmentally friendly ship that anchored close to small islands. We shared a dining room table with an older couple from San Francisco and Sonoma Valley who paid for wine each evening. They owned a small winery in Sonoma, which we visited a few years later, tasting all their products and sharing dinner once again.

Among our three vacation-only trips to Mexico, the highlight was a 1987 train tour from Chihuahua through the spectacular Copper Canyon—larger and deeper than the Grand Canyon—to Los Mochis on the west coast, followed by a flight to La Paz at the southern tip of the Baja California peninsula.

Another memorable holiday was our 1992 trip to Peru. The first week we cruised with a small group in a thatched-roof boat on a tributary of the Amazon River, sleeping under mosquito nets, hiking through jungle mud, walking on ropes and ladders across the tree canopy, exchanging T-shirts for trinkets in Indigenous villages, and meeting a team of scientists from the Smithsonian who were investigating the local bat population and a team of bird specialists from the Cornell Lab of Ornithology. I barely survived the week without chocolate and decent coffee. I fared much better in the Andes Mountains the second week, touring on the train from Cusco to the spectacular ruins at Machu Picchu.

I managed to present Vicki with a cake and bouquet for her 42nd birthday, and she hiked to the summit of Huana Picchu as well as walked across a treacherous log bridge on the Inca Trail that overlooked a steep cliff. With her 35mm SLR camera, zoom and macro lenses, and zoom flash, she took 867 slides during those two weeks.

*Figure 8.3. Vicki and Harvey at a dinner event in the 1990s.*

Again, the trip was almost ruined the night before our departure, this time by a car bomb explosion in Lima—one of the last gasps of the "Shining Path" group near the end of their rebellion. A Swiss couple who lived in Lima were exceptionally kind and helped us return from the restaurant to our hotel, where we reconvened with other tour members. Vicki and I learned that we remain calm in emergencies.

The following year (1993) I was invited to present the plenary address for a conference on literacy and power at Griffith University in Brisbane, Australia. As word spread, I received other keynote and campus lecture invitations. Seizing the opportunity, I negotiated with sponsors and colleagues to extend this two-week trip into four additional weeks with Vicki, speaking at Australian universities including LaTrobe, Adelaide, South Australia, Macquarie, Wollongong, University of Technology-Sydney, Queensland Institute of Technology, and Central Queensland. We did this by exchanging lecture fees and one person's expenses for the expenses of two people.

Because I lost my voice with a case of "Melbourne throat," Vicki actually read my papers for two presentations in Adelaide, one of which was recorded for the public radio system! When I whispered my responses to questions in Vicki's ear, she sometimes took the liberty of revising my words. Male colleagues in attendance were somewhat flustered by this gender role reversal; I commented that all academics should experience it.

In Adelaide we stayed with graduate school friends Ian and Pene Davey and took a small airplane to the remarkable natural habitat of Kangaroo Island; in

Sydney we stayed with literacy studies colleague Jenny Hammond. Between visiting those two cities we toured the red sandstone mountain in central Australia called Uluru—an amazing, Aboriginal sacred site formerly known as Ayers Rock—and the national capital Canberra. After my final lecture in Rockhampton, we visited the northeast Sun Coast and descended in an elevator to the ocean floor to view "fringe reef" sea life.

Through the 1980s and into the early 2000s, we enjoyed whitewater rafting trips to California and Colorado and a sea kayaking adventure to Vancouver Island. I was never an outdoor camper, so we found beautiful locations where we could sleep in old inns and spend the days on the water.

We also visited New York City whenever possible to see sights, exhibits, concerts and shows, new and old restaurants, colleagues, and friends. On one memorable event, I keynoted an international advisory conference on literacy and national policies in the chambers of the United Nations. On other occasions I lectured, presented seminars, attended conferences, or met with editors, and I even had a few job interviews. And of course, we visited family in Pittsburgh, Phoenix, and Detroit. People and place, as always, were inseparable. Significantly, academia often paid the bills.

~~~

In the second half of 1987, we experienced life-changing transitions. Driving back to her architectural firm's downtown office on a late August evening after dinner to complete a deadline project, Vicki's car was hit squarely on the driver's side by another vehicle that missed a red light at the intersection. I was summoned by the hospital, which fortuitously sat on one corner of the intersection.

Vicki was badly injured, although not in life-threatening condition. Her pelvis was broken in multiple places and her collarbone was bruised from the seatbelt, and she also suffered shock. The consulting orthopedic surgeon (enlightened for the time) said no cast or surgery was required. After a week in the hospital, with me visiting before and after classes and a neighbor walking and feeding Harrison, she was released. She spent the next three months recuperating at home with physical therapy, a walker, then crutches, and finally a cane.

Her employer—a large, multinational architectural firm—reluctantly granted her medical leave with insurance coverage. At the end of six weeks, however, they informed her that either she must return to work or lose her position and her insurance. Physically unable to return to her job, she also lacked her doctor's clearance. Fortunately, we were able to shift her to my medical coverage. The firm went out of business two months later.

As Vicki's recovery progressed and she began to seek new employment, she telephoned Larry Joyce, vice president of communications at the American Heart Association's (AHA) national headquarters. The husband of Gail Joyce who had been a secretary and then my master's degree student and graduate research assistant at UTD, we knew him socially. He encouraged Vicki for years to come "take a look" at the AHA, but she never had time. Now she had time. Over lunch conversation, Larry offered her a temporary job as a special projects manager. From this undefined status, she could apply for other positions in theorganization. (On occasions, household conversations stumbled between our two AHAs: American Historical and American Heart Associations.)

The rest, as they say, is history. Working on special projects exposed Vicki to vice presidents and staff in all departments and all aspects of the AHA mission. She applied for and became manager of editorial and media production. She was among the leaders in the transition to personal computers and online databases as well as website production. The work was satisfying, and the responsibilities for promoting heart health and public understanding were gratifying and much more in *and* tandem with her values than promoting designs for large, often unaesthetic structures.

In this position, she oversaw editorial, slide, audio, and video production. She also employed one of my doctoral students, Soledad Jasin—a native Spanish speaker originally from Argentina—as a consultant to edit the AHA's increasing production of Spanish-language materials. For Vicki, as for me, the personal, the political, her knowledge and experience intersected ever more clearly over time. Our separate and joint lives with literacy are ever-expanding. She held the manager position until we moved to San Antonio in 1998; more about that in the next chapter.

Also, fortuitously and finally, I smoked my last Lucky Strike cigarette just before midnight on New Year's Eve, December 31, 1987—less than a month before Vicki started at the AHA. Using Nicorette chewing gum, I stopped cold after smoking one to two packs of unfiltered cigarettes per day from ages 15 or 16 to 37. There have been no discernable health consequences. That is no excuse for this inexcusable part of my personal history.

Our lives continued stably and generally contentedly. Neither UTD nor Dallas would ever truly be home to us. I had a more or less balanced relationship with the university and a solid coterie of close colleagues, fine students, and good friends. But as an institution UTD never matured. Its administration proved incapable of learning. The School of Arts and Humanities is now the School of Arts, Technology, and Humanities, with more courses in video gaming than any other subject, my last colleague still teaching there tells me.

~~~

I remained alert for more interesting, stimulating, and satisfying academic positions. As I gained seniority, there were ever fewer, given general market conditions and the limits of rank. In the late winter or early spring of 1997, I read an advertisement for a position as director of the Division of Behavioral and cultural Studies or Sciences (stated alternatively) at the University of Texas at San Antonio (UTSA).

UTSA's history paralleled UT-Dallas' as a new, suburban, branch campus of an expanding, large, public university system. It lacked the scientific foundation—and the Texas Instruments underwriting—on which UTD was founded. Like San Antonio itself, the university did not suffer from a dominating and distorting "Myth" or "Way" to the extent that Dallas and UTD did. San Antonio did have a significant and visible history and is in most ways a beautiful, richly historic city.

One UTD friend and colleague, a chemist long a leader in the faculty senate, cautioned me that the UTSA faculty senate was new and weak. He was partly correct. But by itself that caution did not weigh heavily on my thinking.

The division encompassed faculty in American studies, anthropology and archeology, history, and psychology. Its history was murky and included a long-term pattern of competition, divisiveness, and dominance by psychology. The future visions, as presented to me, promoted greater integration, interdisciplinarity, equality, and interchange among the four bachelor's and master's degree programs. During telephone conversations with the dean and a curious, personal interview aimed at securing my interest, they persuaded me to undertake my first full-time administrative role. As the next chapter explains, that was a mistake, but likely a necessary one.

I needed to overcome one complication before we could reach agreement. I was finally scheduled for UTD's newly established, very tardy equivalent of a regular faculty sabbatical, called a Special Faculty Development Assignment, for the 1997–1998 academic year. This was my first university-funded research leave in 23 years of service. I felt strongly that I was entitled to have it before leaving for San Antonio.

Surprisingly, both UTD and UTSA administrations agreed. I was granted permission to have the "development assignment" and then immediately depart, an exception to the standard rules. UTSA permitted me to delay my appointment date for one year. The only UTD colleague who grumbled about "fairness" had had the professional leave the year before, which many colleagues thought should have been mine. (He had earlier told me that his tenure review was relatively easy because "they were out to get you.")

I used the year to complete the research for and begin drafting *The Dallas Myth: The Making and Unmaking of an American City* (2008a) and to finish some other writing tasks. No less importantly, it gave Vicki and me the time to prepare carefully for our relocation: get to know San Antonio, search for a house, sell our Dallas home, get acquainted with some new colleagues, and pack my too many books. We succeeded in all of that before driving to San Antonio in two cars with one cat in August 1998. By that time both Harrison and Nebbie had passed away.

# Chapter 9. San Antonio: Flirting With and Separating From Administration, 1998–2004

When I ponder our six years in the Alamo City—when the Battle of the Alamo was not yet declared a triumph of White Texan Americans and a "war for American independence" by Governor Greg Abbott's "1836 Project" and Mexicans were still present in the Mexican-American War (see my "Busting Myths: How Many 'Projects' Does it Take to Obstruct a Truly American History?", 2022m, and "The Nondebate About Critical Race Theory and Our American Moment," 2022d)—I think of the lovely, historical, and diverse city, our Victorian house in the substantial Monte Vista historic district just north of the city center and the River Walk, a group of dear colleagues and friends, and a West Highland white terrier new family member named McDonald. I do not think first of the University of Texas *near* San Antonio or its division of behavioral and cultural studies/sciences.

To make a long story succinct, the personal, political, academic, and place—educational institution and city—intersected in diverse ways, albeit with contradictory parallels between the two suburban branch campuses of the University of Texas System and their adjacent cities, whose names they not-quite-accurately carried.

We left the home of our Dallas friends the Orlovskys, where we and our cat Shadow stayed overnight after our moving van left for San Antonio, on a sunny August morning in 1998. I had only the barest glimpse of what awaited me at UTSA. We drove separate cars for the three-and-a-half-hour trip. Vicki and Shadow arrived several hours after I did. Shadow did not want to leave Dallas (or the safe space under the Orlovsky's porch), and their car stopped for his needs, a nap for Vicki, and lunch. I waited for them and the moving van.

We spent the first days moving in, scouting the neighborhood, and meeting new neighbors. We were delighted with the lovely, late-Victorian house—more than a century old—with turret, wraparound porch with outside ceiling fans, separate rooms for my study and Vicki's office, guest bedroom, and extra bathrooms. It had a deck, guesthouse, and two carports in the back yard. We hired contractors to build bookshelves on the walls of almost every room and reinforced the floor under the one we designated as the "library."

It was more than comfortable. This was important because Vicki now did her work for the American Heart Association remotely from her home office under the Victorian turret. She searched briefly for a San Antonio-based job but quickly learned that the city lacked Dallas' significant sector of headquarters like the AHA or other nonprofit organizations. Not wanting to lose her talents and expertise, the AHA approved her proposal to become their first full-time, off-site employee. They flew her computer to San Antonio with a technician to install it and paid for a second telephone line in the pre-cellphone era. Her AHA tenure lasted until August 2004.

Figure 9.1. Harvey and Vicki's 1896 home in Monte Vista historical district, 1998.

Figure 9.2. San Antonio house book-lined interior.

We also began to explore the city with neighborhood walks, strolling along the Depression-era Works Project Administration's River Walk, the historic King William District south of downtown with novelist Sandra Cisneros' controversial "purple house," the Spanish Mission Trail, and other parts of the city. San Antonio immediately felt more like home than Dallas ever did.

The next week I began my near-daily expressway commute to the suburban campus on the northern outskirts of the city (much like UT near Dallas). Welcomed at first, I moved into the director's office suite and began a positive relationship with my administrative assistant, small staff, and new colleagues. In words that rang loudly, then and later, my assistant repeated that my predecessor informed her that "anthropologists go to the field," "historians write books," and "psychologists do research," in ascending order of significance. That sentiment summarized the situation and circumscribed the arena of competition and conflict I largely unknowingly entered.

At first, I felt cautiously excited about what I then believed to be a genuine opportunity to reimagine the division into a more equal, cooperative, and intellectually interactive and engaging operation of faculty and students. I did not yet know that 1998–1999 would be one of the worst years of my academic life, rivalling my protracted tenure "war" and my first year of teaching's near-drowning.

Cracks appeared in the division's walls quickly. I later learned that one psychologist whose parents lived in Fort Worth and who came to Dallas several times to have lunch with me during the gap year was actually "spying," trying to get the inside track on the new, non-psychologist, and therefore dangerous, alien director.

While several younger psychologists, especially one married couple, were enthusiastic and welcoming (she was head of the undergraduate honors program and invited me immediately to teach a seminar), the rest lobbied me to guarantee budgetary support for their experimental "labs" (tiny interview rooms). I had not yet received a copy of the budget, and other faculty clusters also had legitimate bids.

The former, long-term director—an unproductive psychologist but staunch defender of his flock, especially in the face of the presumed challenge by the new, much-too-scholarly director—intrusively looked over my shoulder and literally listened behind pillars in the hallways. He was sometimes aided in these activities by his former administrative assistant.

Unmistakable rumors and before long repeated, undocumented criticisms— warranted and unwarranted—seeped out first in the hallways and then in faculty meetings. The majority of the dominant psychology faculty feared change and the new, interdisciplinary, humanities scholar *and* social scientist, historian (and book-writing) director. They distrusted me and barely contained their desire to flex their muscles.

In contrast, at least at first, the one faculty member in American studies, the anthropologists and archaeologists, and especially the historians were outwardly supportive and personally welcoming. The social and cultural anthropologists, one and a half of the three archaeologists, and all except the older, more conservative, and typically less productive by simple number of publications historians were eager for greater equity and mutual respect among the programs, curriculum reforms, and support of teaching, research, and service.

The dean—who had hired me and falsely promoted interdisciplinarity and desire for reform of the division and his college—stood by unhelpfully, mainly unresponsively. I never knew what the dean knew, understood, or desired, except that I must always avoid problems for his office and maintain his budget. I recall his ire when I hired a full-time, adjunct assistant professor at a fair, full salary instead of the dean's cut-rate approach. That was another warning sign.

Despite having almost 25 years of university experience, I was an inexperienced and sometimes uncertain administrator with too little knowledge of my new university. Instead of trying explicitly to rally the troops to frame a new agenda and having more division meetings, in retrospect, perhaps I should have gone door-to-door beseeching and reassuring faculty. There was no time for that, and it is not my style. Greater savvy and/or administrative experience might have allowed me to read more of the signs more quickly. Or not.

A perceived personal or programmatic snub to one faculty member in early spring 1999 led to an in-house "revolt." I no longer recall what the incident was. That faculty member soon left the university. Two relatively junior professors, neither of them psychologists, began a door-to-door campaign of personal, nonprogrammatic complaints and character assassination against me. Neither came to me. I learned about their conduct secondhand—a clear sign of the division's culture or lack thereof.

Quickly amplified by the psychologists, the complaints reached the dean. Without consulting me or investigating, he emailed the division faculty, asking each of them to rate my short-duration performance. I had some strong defenders. Some took a middle ground, stating reasonably that it was simply too early for this kind of review to take place.

The dean called me into his office for a brief meeting. Showing me a handful of examples from his polling on his computer screen, he murkily suggested that some unspecified course of action was needed. He then forwarded me all the responses without any identifying information.

I remember my shock. The character assassination was stunning. It far exceeded my imagination in its personal assaults, inappropriateness, and irrelevance. In contrast to UTD's British antisemites, I was attacked as either or both a homosexual or for being inappropriately supportive and tolerant of LGBTQ faculty members in 1998–1999. I was not aware of any such faculty members. There were a few antisemitic slurs and a few comments about my progressive politics and my academic accomplishments. Nothing was directly relevant to my position or performance as division director. Nothing was actually explained, discussed, or documented.

Expectedly, I was assailed for being too scholarly for the division and the university and either unfair to or ignorant of the glories of pseudo-experimental psychology. I admit that it is not a discipline I hold in the highest respect. I may have made a few off-hand remarks, but that in itself was never an explicit issue.

I went home badly shaken. I sat in my second-floor study in tears. And I decided, with Vicki's concurrence and support, to offer my resignation as director to the dean the next day in advance of his formally requesting it, or worse. He accepted. I began to consider what to do next.

My colleagues' responses were predictably mixed. There was immediate outrage and strong support from those who were becoming our friends, especially among historians and anthropologists; a fairly silent, neutral, middle group; and a quite satisfied group across the disciplines, especially among psychologists. I recall the immediate, positive outreach from the younger historians and now longtime friends, Europeanist Kolleen Guy and Asianist Wing Chung Ng, among a few others.

From colleagues elsewhere in the university there was broad surprise and dismay, which I did my best to calm. Bob Bayley and Juliet Langman—my culture, literacy, and language colleagues in the College of Education—voiced strong condemnation of the dean and division and support for me.

It was now June 1999. The spring semester was over; summer school was beginning. I taught one course as planned and prepared to move from the spacious, comfortable director's suite to a tiny faculty office down the corridor. Many of my books went home. I stuffed as many bookcases and file cabinets into the room as I could and squeezed in to sit at my desk with my computer beside me. If I needed a physical representation of my downfall, I had it. Fortunately, supportive colleagues, respected historians, and friends to this day occupied offices on either side of me. Through my personal physician Bradley Kayser, I connected with an excellent San Antonio psychiatrist, Dianne Martinez.

~~~

In some ways it felt like Dallas in 1979, but with tenure, full professorship, and a most satisfactory residence in a desirable area in the center of the historic city—and with my learning experiences of the preceding two decades—it was not the same. The intersections, especially, of the personal, the academic, and place differed markedly. Beginning with the combination of the city and the location of our house, there was a level of comfort and compensation unlike anything in our Dallas years.

We already had a well-developed life separate from university and campus. We had neighbors who became close friends, especially attorneys Kathleen Doria and Ruben Silva, their son Joaquin, and their dogs, three houses away. My fellow literacy scholar and linguist Bob Bayley and his translator-weaver wife Ann Robinson were two blocks away.

Shortly after we settled into our new abode, we began to search for a new dog. Vicki discovered a breeder of pedigreed dogs who was downsizing her stock that she was not using in her breeding program. Among them was a West Highland white terrier named McDonald born in Norway who had won championships—for his good looks, not for his performance arts—and who had papers affirming his award-winning breeding lines.

*Figure 9.3. MacDonald at home in San Antonio, 1998.*

Aside from urinating on a pile of newspapers and a box of my notes that I was unpacking, McDonald quickly became a beloved member of the family for 14 years. His owner offered him to us at no cost as long as we provided a good home and loved him, neutered him, and promised to return him if we were ever unable to keep him. From time to time, she checked on him, and Vicki provided updates.

McDonald cured Ann Robinson's childhood fear of dogs by softly leaping onto the couch and laying his head on her lap. She became his devoted friend, on occasion coming to take him for walks. He was often the center of the student seminar potluck dinners I regularly hosted at home. I don't know who loved whom the most.

A special relationship quickly developed with my physician Bradley Kayser and his wife Gemma Kennedy. At the time of my first checkup, my new San Antonio internist informed me that I was "his first historian." He urged—almost demanded—that I bring him one of my books. I dropped off *Conflicting Paths* (1995a) at his office, and a week or two later he telephoned to say, "I've read your book. I have questions. I'm taking you to lunch." He did. They weren't bad questions, that is, for an internist rather than a historical specialist. At the end of the meal and conversation, he stated, "sign the book for me to keep; your next checkup is free."

We quickly became close friends. We socialized with Bradley and Gemma, got to know their children and attended their Bat and Bar Mitzvahs, enjoyed their annual at-home jazz fest, and more. To this day, Bradley delights in quoting passages from my books to me. I remain awestruck.

There were shops, a particularly good Mexican and other restaurants within two blocks of our house, and accessibility to River Walk, downtown, and a shopping center with a movie theatre that featured foreign and alternative films.

Despite my miscalculation in accepting the UTSA division directorship, we quickly made many collegial contacts and good friends from behavioral and cultural studies and elsewhere in the university as well as from Trinity University near our house. Some remain in communication today. Among those who combined faculty collegiality and personal friendship were Kolleen Guy and Wing Chung Ng. In addition were American historians Yolanda Leyva who moved to UT-El Paso, Jim Schneider and Jack Reynolds both now retired, Anne Hardgrove and Kirsten Gardner, and later John Giggie and Gaye Okoh, both of whom moved on from San Antonio. Anthropologist friends included Jim McDonald, Dan Gelo, and archeologist Laura Levy.

Wing Chung recently reminded me of a "cold soup dinner" that Vicki and I hosted. Each couple or individual prepared a cold soup of their choosing, and a group of about eight people shared them in multiple courses. I hired Wing Chung's then high schooler son Chuck and his football teammate to pack boxes of books when we prepared to leave the city. Chuck and his sister Stella, who was also McDonald's friend, are now adults. So too are Kolleen's children, who completed their college degrees and now live in Europe. Kolleen later joined a university in China affiliated with Duke University.

Reflecting my significant relationships outside the division were Bob Bayley and Juliet Langman in linguistics, as well as Art Vega and Woody Saunders in sociology and political science. In addition, I became well acquainted with Trinity University historians John Martin and Char Miller (soon to leave for Duke and the Claremont colleges, respectively). I occasionally played tennis with Jack Reynolds. And my friend and former student in Dallas, Tony Fracchia, visited with his tennis racket, staying overnight in our guesthouse, sometimes with wife Pearl Garza.

Another friend from our first years at UTD, political scientist Paul Peretz, owned two rental houses in San Antonio, part of his personal retirement fund. Every now and then he came to check on them, staying in our guesthouse. A few times he brought his wife, the outstanding political scientist Jean Shroedel. At UTSA Gender Studies' and my invitation, Jean lectured at UTSA.

These years were marked by memorable travel. As I mentioned in the previous chapter, we often went to the Western states for whitewater rafting and kayaking. International travel featured trips to Sweden around ceremonies and conferences (more about those later) and Spain where earlier I had been invited to speak at conferences. We returned together in 2000 for a Spanish holiday to Madrid, Bilbao and Frank Gehry's new Guggenheim Museum, San Sebastian on the northern coast, and most memorably Barcelona. The latter remains a favorite world city for both of us. I am well versed in "reading cities."

~~~

188  Chapter 9

As in Dallas, but proportionally less given the duration of our residence and the fact that I was not researching or writing San Antonio's history, I was active locally in public history and public humanities. I served on the advisory group for the San Antonio History Website Development Project (funded by a NEH grant to UTSA in 2001) and participated in an experimental graduate seminar titled "Exhibiting Adolescence/Adolescents" in 2004. The course explored different approaches to "exhibiting" adolescents and adolescence museologically, with the cooperation of the Witte Museum's curatorial and administrative staff in San Antonio and the Chicago Historical Society. As in Chicago, I also served as a history fair judge.

As in Dallas and in Columbus, I assisted and contributed to local and national media. This presaged my greater focus in retirement but stemmed from the relationships among the political, academic, and place. With newspaper editor Joe Holley of the *San Antonio Express News*, I advised on reporting and also published "Comment: Race between San Antonio, Dallas Like Fabled Tortoise and the Hare" (1997c), "Comment: City Must Create Own Mold for Public Universities" (1998), and "Alamo City's Different Futures: 'Fast Forward' Left Important Points Muddled" (2001f).

I also advised, consulted, and moderated electronic discussions for National Public Radio's "The Changing Face of America" series that aired on *Talk of the Nation*, *All Things Considered*, and *Morning Edition* from 2000 to 2001 (find information about the series as well as a link to its archives at https://news.npr.org/programs/specials/cfoa/). In print media, I assisted reporters from *The New York Times*, *San Antonio Express-News*, and the *Times Educational Supplement*.

~~~

At UTSA, I was officially professor of history. I was also a member of the doctoral faculty in Culture, Literacy, and Language in the School of Education; doctoral faculty in English in Arts and Humanities; faculty in the Division of Bilingual and Bicultural Studies; graduate faculty in Public Administration (Urban Studies); and faculty in the learning community and freshman seminars for undergraduate studies. My teaching ranged widely from first-year seminars and large lecture courses to doctoral seminars in Culture, Literacy, and Language. Many of my classes were cross-listed.

Specific courses I taught included Introduction to Historical Study; undergraduate and graduate seminars on the history of growing up; cross-listed graduate seminars on the history of literacy and literacy studies; and my least favorite, large lecture courses on United States history. I learned to make do but never truly accepted the latter, taught without teaching or grading assistants or small discussion sections.

In classes with 200 to 300 or more students, I required practice in writing in collaborative group essays with checks to promote participation and reduce cheating. For the only time in my teaching career, I used exams with multiple-choice questions scored by machine readers. I did have assistance in running the cards through the machine reader and compiling the results. I recall holding a discussion in one of these several-hundred-student classes the day after the 9/11 terrorist attacks on New York City, trying to add historical and contemporary perspectives. Military veteran class members aided me.

My graduate students included master's students in history; master's and Ph.D. students in culture, literacy, and language; and master's and Ph.D. students in English. Some of these mostly nontraditional students were excellent. A few were not prepared by prior education or ability for graduate work and needed to be counseled out.

Among my clearest memories is one doctoral student in literacy studies, Michael Campbell, who with his wife Susan and adorable daughter remain our friends. We transferred possession of Vicki's last, large, stuffed animal, a leopard from her sophomore year at Northwestern, to young Lily who is now a graduate of a German university.

I also recall fondly my fall 2003 doctoral seminar students in English 7063 who collectively presented their research on a panel titled, "Reading Critically the Sources of Children and Childhood: Literary and Historical Perspectives" to the American Studies Association of Texas annual meeting in San Antonio. I had the honor of chairing the exciting session, designated at the conference's end as an "outstanding session."

As at UT-Dallas, I continued to contribute nationally to the collective enterprise of improving teaching. I shared graduate and undergraduate course syllabuses on H-Child, H-Education, and SHARP electronic networks.

First as division director and then as professor, I had major administrative responsibilities. Given the immaturity of the institution, the number of other full professors who were reluctant to admit others to their hallowed halls or to accept their fair share of responsibilities is not surprising. I recall being called to testify at my chair's request before a university-wide, faculty personnel committee about why another full professor's listing an article that was not accepted for publication as "forthcoming" was not a legitimate action. It is not.

I recall my surprise when without warning a package arrived for me on campus with my 25 years in the University of Texas System Award. A few years later as I left UTSA came a clock that never worked, my University of Texas at San Antonio Retirement commemoration. There is a message in that gift.

~~~

More significantly and powerfully, the years 2000 and 2001 were etched with lifetime recognitions. In November 2000 in my home city of Pittsburgh, the SSHA celebrated its 25th anniversary. I was president, set the theme for this special meeting, and presented my address, later published as "The Shock of the '"New" Histories': Social Science Histories and Historical Literacies" (2001/2005).

I had the additional pleasure of my parents, still living and in Pittsburgh, sitting in front of the head table with Vicki, Michael Katz, and a group of my closest academic colleagues and friends. Several historians, social scientists, and present and former colleagues who did not usually attend SSHA came that year to share the experience and to honor me.

Eight months later, I was awarded another rare distinction. Linköping University, Sweden, presented me with the Honorary Doctor of Philosophy degree for "contributions to knowledge." Dean Bengt Sandin, a fellow historian of children and youth, surprised me with a long-distance call one morning to ask if I would accept an honorary degree. He did not want to bother writing a formal letter if I would not! I was one of the distinguished scholars from around the world that the university recognized that year.

The honorees assembled in the front row of the elaborately decorated concert hall with university leaders, attired in university-rented tuxedos and with laurel wreaths on our heads. The dean had telephoned me again to ask awkwardly the length of my trousers' inseam.

I will never forget the faculty member, a professor of communication and also a baroness, formally bequeathing me the honor, proclaiming, "Before you, Honorary Dr. Graff, we thought we understood literacy. But you taught us that we did not. Before you, we thought we understood childhood. But you taught us that we did not." Tears streamed down my cheeks beneath the slightly crooked laurel wreath perched on my bald head.

*Figure 9.4. Harvey receiving Honorary Ph.D. from Professor Viveka Adelswärd, Linköping University, Sweden, June 2001. Photo © Masood Khatibi.*

The celebration occupied three days, including a banquet with reindeer steak and entertainment by a male glee club. Vicki purchased a special outfit for the event; we shopped for it in New York City. In addition to my diploma, Linköping presented me with an engraved ring (like a wedding band) and a traditional, formal, silk burgher's hat. I wear the ring but have little occasion to wear the hat.

The day after the ceremony, we visited the baroness and baron's stately manor for lunch. It was the servants' day off, so royalty cooked for their visitors. The university paid full expenses for both Vicki and me. This allowed us to spend a spectacular week in Paris following the Swedish adventure.

*Figure 9.5. Harvey in robe and hood with laurel wreath and Vicki in gown after ceremony.*

*Figure 9.6. Harvey with Dean Bengt Sandin presenting honorary burgher's hat and Viveka Adelswärd at Baron Adelswärd's castle.*

~~~

I did not permit UTSA to interfere with my national and international activities. I needed intellectual stimulation and valued the distraction. In any case, I had too much research, writing, teaching, and collaboration underway.

I continued to hold office in the SSHA and attended annual meetings. In most years, I organized sessions on literacy, growing up, cities, or interdisciplinary themes. I became a consulting editor for *Historical Social Research/Historische Sozialforchung*, a German journal, from 1998. I also served on the scholarly advisory board for LifeTimes/Everyday Life in America: A New Way of Doing History from 2002. My general historiographical essays in these years addressed social scientists, historians, university professors in general, and scholars in education: "Teaching and Historical Understanding" (1999b) and "Teaching [and] Historical Understanding" (1999c).

With respect to literacy, I sat on the board of advisors and was project scholar for the proposed documentary film series, *Rewriting Literacy*, in 1998. I served on the international editorial board of *Literacy and Numeracy Studies: An International Journal*, an Australian publication, from 1998 and the editorial board of the *Journal of Language, Identity, and Education* from 2000 to 2007.

More significantly, I was co-organizer, coordinator, and speaker (with scholars from Sweden, Australia, and Canada and with support from the Swedish Bicentennial Research Fund to Linköping University) for "Literacy, Religion, Gender, and Social History: A Socio-Cultural History for the 21st Century. An International Conference for Egil Johansson," held in Vadstena, Sweden, in May 2002 (coordinated by Bengt Sandin at Linköping University). Egil Johansson contributed to the international advancement of historical studies of literacy from the 1970s. He was my friend, colleague, and host in Sweden for decades.

After the Vadstena conference, Linköping University invited us to attend the ceremony and banquet for its 2002 honorary doctorates. The university again paid full expenses for both Vicki and me. In addition to spending time with Bengt and his family on their farm, this trip allowed us to stop in Iceland on the way home to tour that majestic country. The then young cultural historian Sigurdur "Siggi" Magnusson hosted us in his home city, Reykjavík. His graduate advisor Peter Stearns had connected us when Siggi was a doctoral student studying literacy and Icelandic folk cultures at Carnegie Mellon University. This was another of our several experiences of our lifetimes.

My contribution as a regular voice on literacy past and present grew. I was a featured speaker at the 2000 Conference on College Composition and Communication (CCCC) annual meeting, and again at the 2004 CCCC annual meeting, "Educating the Imagination and Reimagining Education." I regularly shared the podium as a featured speaker with my colleague and dear friend Deborah Brandt. Through CCCCs, I met and became friendly not only with Brandt but also her graduate student John Duffy, as well as Mike Rose, Patrick Berry, and others.

I was also a featured speaker and discussant at the Institute for Literary History and National Conference, "Prospero's Plots and Caliban's Critique: Literacies, Texts, and Nationalisms in the New World," held at Miami University, Ohio, in 2000 and the University of California at Los Angeles' California Center for the Book's forum for print and electronic culture and department of library and information studies seminar, also in 2000.

My books on literacy in these years included *Alfabetismo di massa: mito storia realtà*, in the series "Il Sapere Del Libro" (2002a). Other series authors included Roger Chartier, Robert Darnton, Anthony Grafton, and Donald McKenzie.

I coedited a special issue of *Interchange* with Alison Mackinnon, Bengt Sandin, and Ian Winchester (2003a) that collected papers from an international conference in Vadstena, Sweden, in May 2002 called "Egil Johansson, the Demographic Database, and Socio-Cultural History for the 21st Century: Literacy, Religion, Gender, and Social History." Those papers were later published in an expanded book, *Understanding Literacy in its Historical Contexts: Socio-Cultural History and the Legacy of Egil Johansson* (Graff et al., 2009), with support from the Swedish Bicentennial Fund/Stiftelsen Riksbankens Jubileunsfond, Linköping University, and Ohio State University.

Articles and book chapters on literacy included "The Nineteenth-Century Origins of Our Times" (Graff, 2001e), "Literacy's Myths and Legacies" (Graff, 2001c, 2001d), "Literacy," in *The Oxford Companion to United States History* (Graff, 2001b), "Literacy, Religion, Gender, and Social History: A Socio-Cultural History for the 21st Century" (Graff et al., 2003b), and "Introduction to Historical Studies of Literacy" (Graff, 2003).

Following the publication of *Conflicting Paths: Growing Up in America* (1995a), my multi-level teaching of the history of children and adolescents and my active role in the Society for the History of Childhood and Youth (SHCY) led to my increasing involvement in that growing field . I participated on the executive committee of SHCY (2003–2007) and attended most annual meetings during these and later years, often organizing sessions. I was also on the board of advisors of H-Childhood (Humanities and Social Sciences Online's network on the history of childhood and youth, available at https://networks.h-net.org/h-childhood) from 1998 and the advisory board for *The Child: An Encyclopedic Companion* (Schweder, 2009) from 2001 to 2009.

A special opportunity arose when Marie Scatena of the Teen Chicago Project of the Chicago Historical Society (later renamed the Museum of Chicago History) contacted me in 2001. Marie wrote at the urging of the president of the society, Lonnie Bunch, who knew my book *Conflicting Paths* (1995a). After ascertaining my interest, Marie formally invited me to serve as principal academic advisor, a position I held from 2001 to 2004. This was a unique endeavor which took me to Chicago four times a year for more than three years, including the memorable, final performances and presentations in spring 2004.

Teen Chicago was a multi-year project on the history of teens, oral history, public programming, publications, and transformation of the roles of young people in museums and historical societies. With funding from the Joyce Foundation, Elizabeth Morse Charitable Trust, Chicago Community Trust, Nathan Cummings Foundation, Field Foundation of Illinois, James S. Kemper Foundation, Illinois Humanities Council, and the National Endowment for the Humanities, it garnered a great deal of attention in Chicago and across the nation. It was awarded the American Association of Museums' Excellence in Education Award and Honorable Mention for the Muse Award (Media and Technology) in 2005. The program worked in association with Chicago's NPR station, for which I served as advisor for their series on children and adolescents from 2003 to 2004.

Expertly coordinated by Scatena, the project revolved around a group of Chicago high school teenage students. They did local historical and contemporary research, conducted oral histories, and wrote about their firsthand experiences. I assisted with background, context, questions, and leads.

The result was an impressive, original, historical exhibit at the Chicago Historical Society, an archive, personal writings, and a performance at the end of the project in late spring 2004. The major written project was published in a special issue of *Chicago History* titled "Coming of Age in Chicago" (Bivens & Graff, 2004), for which I was consulting editor, advisor, and contributor.

Writing about the history of growing up continued with "Interdisciplinary Explorations in the History of Children, Adolescents, and Youth" (1999a) and "Growing Up in America" (2001a).

Looking toward *The Dallas Myth* (2008a), which I began to draft, I served on the Urban History Association board of directors from 2002 to 2004 and participated in the conference on The University and the City: Urban Education and the Liberal Arts at Wayne State University in 1999. I also organized SSHA urban history sessions.

My research and writing continued to secure funding. During my tenure at UTSA, I received faculty awards for research and travel. In 2001, the Swedish Bicentennial Research Fund awarded me an international conference grant to Linköping University. In the same year, the SSHA awarded Leslie Moch, Philip McMichael, and me a grant to prepare a collection of papers from the 25th anniversary meeting. The next year, UTSA awarded me a semester's faculty development leave for research to advance my writing of *The Dallas Myth* (2008a).

~~~

My days at UTSA began to end with the arrival of an unexpected letter of invitation from the chair of the Department of English at The Ohio State University late in 2003. She told me about the award of a state-endowed, chaired professorship, the inaugural Ohio Eminent Scholar in Literacy Studies, to the department and the university. Her lengthy letter sought to persuade me of the position's singular importance and opportunity and to solicit my interest. I was surprised and flattered. I recall walking next door to Kolleen Guy's office to debrief and share my mixed feelings of honor and questions.

For several weeks, the department chair, search committee chair, and I exchanged emails and telephone conversations. Given my history with a new position at UTSA and earlier travails at UTD, I responded cautiously. I was concerned about the position's location in the Department of English's Rhetoric and Composition program and about Ohio State being an overly large university in the Midwest, best known for its football team. That caution lessened with OSU's commitment to a full, joint appointment in the Department of History and the chair's promise of institutional flexibility. At the same time, I was biding my time institutionally and professionally at UTSA.

I agreed to visit OSU in early 2004. It was less a traditional job interview than an opportunity to meet one another and exchange initial ideas about the possibilities of the position—and to persuade me. Barbara Hanawalt, my old friend from the Newberry Library in 1979–1980 and regular SSHA colleague, held an endowed chair in Ohio State's History Department. She told me, "the word is: the position is yours to lose, Harvey."

My campus visit was delayed for a few days because of my father's expected death of multiple causes including Lou Gehrig's Disease (amyotrophic lateral sclerosis or ALS) and stroke in late December. Given his medical condition, he very much wanted to pass away. For the family, it was a time of relief and celebration of his life. Vicki and I flew to Pittsburgh to oversee arrangements with my brother Gary, who had taken initial responsibility.

In the first week of January, as the new semester was beginning, I flew to Columbus. I felt no pressure but rather anticipation and great curiosity. The search committee chair graciously met me at the airport and gave me my first of several tours of residential neighborhoods in the campus area. Potential new colleagues were primed to welcome me. It marked a real contrast with all my previous interviews dating back to the mid-1970s. Never before had I been so actively and unreservedly sought for what I had actually accomplished.

I learned that this was the second year of searching to fill the new position. At first, the department looked for a person who would lead to K-12 school linkages. They found no suitable, qualified person. In year two, they elected to "find the best scholar." Their inquiries led directly to me.

For the two departments and the university writ large, the centerpiece of my visit was a public lecture relating "lessons from the history of literacy." Just prior to my presentation, one faculty member stuck her head in the room in which I was waiting quietly and asked, "Is there really only one of you? You've written so many books." The search committee chair, Nan Johnson, then brought me dark chocolate to enhance my preparation.

The lecture was well attended, with an overwhelmingly positive response. The questions were appropriately probing. It was an intellectually positive experience. Campus invited lectures are not always so mutually satisfying.

I met many prospective colleagues at the seemingly endless succession of group meals and meetings. During a driving tour of the university area and learning about my excessive personal library, Chris Zacher, professor of English and longtime director of the Humanities Institute, commented, "Oh, the house next door to ours is for sale. It would hold your books." He drove me past the two houses, and I spied my future, nearly century-old home with its landmark sycamore tree, a ten-minute walk to my Denney Hall office.

The department's job and salary offer came shortly after I returned to San Antonio. Vicki and I were both positively inclined. We negotiated salary and especially support for my research and building a distinctive campus-wide, cross- and interdisciplinary program in literacy studies. OSU also offered a substantial stipend to offset the costs of our expensive move.

Despite some hesitation about returning to the Midwest, the underachieving city of Columbus, and about OSU's size and identification with big-time collegiate football, it was well past time to join a more established and substantial academic institution and leave Texas. A joint appointment in history, the promise of wider connections, and solid support all enhanced the attraction. As it happened, the history department voted unanimously on my appointment before the English department did.

I informed UTSA about OSU's strong offer. Colleagues and a few of my deans were saddened. The provost responded that he would mount a counteroffer. He never did—a fitting conclusion to my UTSA years.

Vicki and I made our first of several visits in April. On these trips, we house hunted, job searched for Vicki, and saw new colleagues and old friends including Barbara Hanawalt and Ron Giere, Randy Roth and Alison Sweeney, Chris Zacher and Kay Bea Jones, and Amy Shuman and Amy Horowitz.

Remembering our habits from the Newberry year and our SSHA meetings, Barbara and Ron predicted that their restaurant-going and communal dinners at home were about to improve. Without family in the area, we regularly dined out on Thanksgiving and Christmas with Barbara and Ron and shared the contents of his wine cellar. Longtime SSHA colleague Randy Roth facilitated campus connections. The early visits and continued meetings with new people made it much easier for me to start quickly in the fall to build LiteracyStudies@OSU.

Similar to the situation with our move to San Antonio, Vicki hoped to continue working remotely for the American Heart Association from Columbus. Before she could make the request, however, her boss informed her that she could keep her job if she were willing to move back to Dallas, contrary to national trends. Because that was not possible, the AHA offered her a generous severance package that helped to cushion the transition. Despite promises of assistance from OSU, Vicki's job search in Columbus continued for more than a year.

Notwithstanding our English department-related realtor's conviction that we should settle in a comfortable middle-class suburb like Worthington or Upper Arlington—not in the campus area within walking distance from my office—we persevered. We house hunted in older residential areas, especially Victorian Village and the University District.

We purchased the University District house next door to Chris Zacher, his architecture professor wife Kay Bea Jones, son Sam then 10 years old, and dog Prince. It was then an 89-year-old, late-Victorian, architect-designed house. Immediately hiring a woodworking contractor to build bookcases throughout the house, we drove one car to Columbus in late July and the second car, McDonald, and ourselves in mid-August. Two moving vans with our possessions, but mainly my books, arrived shortly thereafter.

# Chapter 10. Transitions and Challenges in Mid-Career: The Ohio State University and Columbus, 2004–2017

Moving in 2004 to Columbus, Ohio, *The* Ohio State University, and a Department of English (with joint appointment in History) as the inaugural Ohio Eminent Scholar in Literacy Studies is a complicated tale of opportunities taken then mostly taken away, obstacles generally surmounted or avoided, and unprecedented accomplishments; new and old colleagues, students, and friends; and unexpected experiences. It is a story of great expectations but disappointing endings, followed by new beginnings after retirement.

Overall, in this chapter I disentangle the increasingly complicated contradictions of my life of intersectionality among the personal, the political, the academic, and place in its next-to-final phase. This chapter explores in multiple dimensions the final course of my professional life in pursuit of one form of interdisciplinarity and others. It continues directly and indirectly my life with literacy.

Chapter Ten also follows variations on the theme, and the factual realities, of another poorly managed public university failing to fulfill its promises to me, and to its students, faculty, staff, and taxpaying as well as supposedly benefiting public. This time it was not a new, suburban, branch campus, but one of the largest, flagship, urban, public universities in the United States, a land grant institution 150 years old. Disappointment by an institution of higher education is a recurring element of my life history, an experience central to the history of American higher education since at least the 1950s–1960s mass expansions, if not over more than 200 years. (See my essays under Universities and Ohio State University in the Appendix.)

There is insufficient research on higher education administration, including the internal connections and disconnections at all levels, from university-wide officials to the school or college and departmental levels. This is largely where the "action" for the faculty and students takes place. Understanding may begin with Paul H. Mattingly's *American Academic Cultures* (2017), Michael Fabricant and Stephen Brier's *Austerity Blues* (2016), Christopher Newfield's *The Great Mistake* (2016); and Steven Brint's *Two Cheers for Higher Education* (2018), among a large but uneven literature. I am probing the topic of higher education administration, and proposing changes, in my forthcoming book *Reconstructing the "Uni-versity" From the Ashes of the "Mega- and Multi-versity."*

This not-quite-final "chapter" is at once a story of Vicki's and my joint and individual patterns of resettlement and professional and personal adaptations in middle age. McDonald happily transitioned to the cooler climate of Ohio until his death from heart failure in 2013. (He spent his final months with an implanted heart pacemaker. It was successfully removed and implanted into another animal.) This is also the tale of career completion. I narrate this segment of the journey toward a mixed legacy through a series of eight slices of life, 2004–2017, with more or less explicit lessons from each.

~~~

First, moving to an English department and, even with a joint appointment, leaving the daily grounds and rounds of a history program or department and planning to operate from day one *across* the uncoordinated, disconnected university, I simultaneously left familiar ground and began anew at age 55. For Ohio State, my situation was unprecedented, for most universities, unusual. For myself, I attempted to operationalize dreams that dated back to educational reforms and intellectual aspirations proposed in the 1960s and 1970s.

In a truly cross-campus, interdisciplinary initiative, I sought to build ideas and new connections beyond traditional disciplines and the organizational structure and hierarchies in which they are embedded: departments and colleges or schools. Although insufficiently questioned or contextualized and too often presumed to be "natural," divisions and hierarchies are themselves historical developments (see for example, my *Undisciplining Knowledge,* 2015a, "Interdisciplinarity is Not About the Humanities Aping the Sciences," 2021d, and "History Lessons Can Help Disciplines to Survive," 2021k; see also Jacobs, 2014; Frickel et al., 2016; and Millgram, 2015).

*Figure 10.1. University District home in snow, 2019. Photo by Kay Bea Jones.*

In some ways, my vision was founded in personal and professional history. Michael Katz's Hamilton/Canadian Social History Project was the most direct influence. I was also stimulated by the precedent-setting examples in social science history of Peter Laslett's and Tony (E. Anthony) Wrigley's Cambridge Group for the History of Population and Social Structure (CamPops) at the University of Cambridge, England, and Chuck Tilly's Center for Research on Social Organization at the University of Michigan. The original model derived from the sixième section of the **École** Pratique des Hautes Etudes in Paris led by Fernand Braudel and Lucien Febvre in the 1950s and 1960s, inspired by Marc Bloch and Henri Lefebvre (see Bloch, 1963; Braudel, 1992; and Lefebvre, 1971).

On a personal cum professional level, I came to OSU attempting to achieve what I could only dream about at UTD and UTSA. These universities' immaturity, the fragility of the basic institutional structures, and the instability of the faculty together precluded the bases to establish a cross- or interdisciplinary, campus-wide program or set of programs. They also lacked funding and supportive leadership. The conditions of my hiring and the endowment of the Ohio Eminent Scholar chair provided, for a time at least, just that. In retrospect, my failures to innovate successfully at UTD and UTSA were all but preordained given the youth and immaturity of the universities and the character of their leadership. I understand how their rhetorical promotion and sloganeering—part of their origin myths—inadequately substituted for vision, planning, and direction.

~~~

For years I blamed myself in part for not seeing through the smokescreens or finding pathways around them. That may be too harsh a judgment. My 13 years of active service at OSU underscore that point and the questions it raises. Although I never "escaped" from my foundational role in the New Literacy Studies and the serious historical study of literacy, I expanded my active research first to the history of growing up and then to urban and Dallas history. For decades, I asserted that I was "putting literacy behind me." I failed, but successfully.

I completed *The Dallas Myth* (2008a) in my first years at OSU with research endowment support and then moved to a new mid-course: greater attention to writing about—but not actively conducting new research in primary sources on—literacy and the history of literacy. At the same time, I reintegrated numerous strains of my education, teaching, and writing about interdisciplinarity into work toward a social and cultural history of interdisciplinarity itself. This came to fruition in *Undisciplining Knowledge: Interdisciplinarity in the Twentieth Century* (2015a) on one hand and *Searching for Literacy: The Social and Intellectual Origins of Literacy Studies* (2022e, completed in 2015) on the other hand.

From 2004 until I was forced in 2017 to end the overwhelmingly successful, interdisciplinary initiative LiteracyStudies@OSU, I sought to practice what I had been taught and what I had long preached. In sum, this entailed a unique, university-wide role. I continued my earlier practice of teaching across disciplinary and division boundaries (especially in history, humanities, and education with graduate students from across the arts and sciences), along with other, newer, and original forms of outreach and integration across almost the entire university. This is captured materially and symbolically by my newer scholarly research projects and books, *Undisciplining Knowledge* (2015a), *Searching for Literacy* (2022e), and several new and revised collections of essays.

When I was seeking a publisher for *The Dallas Myth* (2008a), a reviewer and a university press editor led me to the freelance developmental editor Grey Osterud. With a Ph.D. in American history and as a former tenured professor, Grey is an editor whose abilities are not paralleled by any other I've encountered. Not only did she successfully perform final revision and preparation for publication of that book, but she also worked with me on *Undisciplining Knowledge* (2015a) and *Searching for Literacy* (2022e). Grey became a firm and trusted advisor and friend.

Those books, my final academic works as a working professor, confirm how the personal history reported in this book represents the intersectionality I identified and traced over 75 years. This chapter and Chapter One on retirement mark a new beginning in remembering, reflecting, and writing—and exercising literacy and literacies, constituting a not-quite-final review. Despite my retirement, I remain engaged in all of these issues, often in new and different ways.

~~~

Second, to both my surprise and unsurprise, my Ohio State experience confirms many lessons of my Texas years. I have demonstrated elsewhere, in papers published in 2015 and 2021 and continuing, that OSU is one of the nation's leading "Slogan U's" (for example, see Graff, 2015b, 2022f, 2022h, 2022i). I have not attempted to trace the beginnings, but I suspect that sloganeering has been part of *The* Ohio State University—as the land grant charter states—since its origins 150 years ago on land stolen from Indigenous people and under segregationist federal legislation. The five university presidents whom I have known have literally "led" by enunciating slogans without programs, budgets, or timetables. Few if any of their catchphrases bore resemblance to reality.

Slogans in use at OSU have ranged from "Buckeye Nation" (see Booker, 2018) to "One University" (see The Ohio State University Foundation, 2013) for perhaps the most dis-integrated, large public university in the nation. An "Innovation District" of one block with an "Interdisciplinary Research Facility" sits on the western edge of campus (Knox, 2021). The Office of Student Life touts the never-defined "Exceptional Student Experience," as if there were a single one. The "Scarlet & Gray Advantage" plan boasts of debt-free graduation without cutting costs (The Ohio State University, n.d), an arithmetic and logical impossibility.

The university is far too large and disconnected for its out-of-date, inadequate, and overflowing administrative structures, procedures, and communications. Regardless of slogans and research funding, OSU is best known for its football teams. The head coach's salary is almost 10 times the university president's (Szilagy, 2023)—more than enough to employ at least 100 new full professors. At least one Buckeye team booster approved of that decision, in a letter to the *Columbus Dispatch*'s sports page, because hiring more faculty only means adding more "liberals."

Both the Ohio Eminent Scholar (OES) position and my hiring reflect this common thrust toward the entrepreneurial and promotional domains. For both better and worse, I took my position seriously and made my best—and my collaborators' and participants' best—efforts to achieve our goals.

As a historian and a literacy studies scholar, I was warmly welcomed by many but not all of my new colleagues. The English Department was and is deeply divided internally among literary critics, literary theorists, historical and contemporary literature scholars, creative writers, disability studies and gender studies scholars, Black and ethnic studies scholars, and rhetoric and composition—also known as writing studies—specialists. Such divisions are common; their number reflects the size of the university and department, the latter steadily declining over almost two decades. While I was a member of the department, there was no leadership or common direction, no moderation of divisions, conflicts, or competition.

Within the English Department, I was attached to the large, proud, and not particularly disciplinarily integrated concentration in rhetoric and composition. It was symbolically renamed "Rhetoric, Composition, and Literacy" upon my hiring. Some of my courses were linked to literary history and criticism, and I worked with graduate students across divisions and time periods.

Some of my rhetoric and composition colleagues never accepted the "L" being added to their concentration, never accepted having a well-published historian join them, nor me, despite voting for my appointment.

Some of the faculty in literature and creative writing saw no reason that the new OES was either a historian or within the domain of RC and L. Some, not surprisingly, seemed intimidated by my productivity and scholarly reputation. That of course is not unique to OSU or its English department. Over the years, I had more close associates from literature than RCL but more students from RCL and outside English.

My courses were all cross-listed in the department of history and some in other departments. I supervised graduate students and sat on exam and thesis committees across the university but especially in English and history. I agreed, however, that I was obligated to serve on committees only in one department—English.

The Institute for Collaborative Research and Public Humanities (later known as the Humanities Institute and now known as the Humanities Collaboratory) immediately reached out to me. The director Chris Zacher, who lived next door to our house and urged us to buy it, actively recruited me. The Institute long provided office space for LiteracyStudies@OSU's administrative assistant (later associate director) and graduate research assistants until it was forced to leave its old house for smaller, shared offices in a classroom building. The College of Arts and Humanities never recognized the value of its cross-disciplinary institute. Chris, the institute, and LiteracyStudies@OSU collaborated closely for many years, organizationally, fiscally, programmatically, and intellectually. All new initiatives need a base from which to commence, ideally outside a single disciplinary department.

Because of the nature of the Ohio Eminent Scholar position and its endowment, LiteracyStudies@OSU's reach and outreach led to recurrent if not always sympathetic or supportive relationships with the offices of the dean of the College of Arts and Humanities and the Office of the Provost (or Academic Affairs).

It is not unfair to report that only one of my several successive deans, provosts, and presidents expressed any interest in the initiative. A professor in the department of theatre, he said that he learned from literacy studies and from me.

When I closed the program, the dean in office (a historian) along with the provost (an agriculturalist) and several vice provosts personally admitted that the university violated written agreements about the initiative's support and the use of its funds. They nonetheless refused to act in LiteracyStudies@OSU's or the university's own interests. This unjustifiable inaction led directly to the loss of my associate director of a dozen years' full-time position and benefits on which she and her husband depended. After I retired, the dean renamed the state-endowed Ohio Eminent Scholar in Literacy Studies without approval at the university or state level.

This incident stands out among a series of promises made and promises broken. Failures at the department, college, and university level contributed directly to the end of LiteracyStudies@OSU and my earlier-than-anticipated retirement in 2017. Deans, provosts, associate provosts, and department chairs all made positive noises to my face but seldom acted affirmatively, consistently, or kept promises. This pattern took a toll that I finally could not sustain. I generalize, reluctantly, that this reflects much about contemporary universities.

My relationships also included faculty members in several divisions within the large College of Education. My courses on literacy were cross-listed, and I co-supervised master's degree and doctoral students in areas related to both literacy and history of education. Education graduate students were among the most active participants in the literacy studies graduate group (GradSem) that existed for most of the lifetime of the overall program. A majority were former teachers returning for higher degrees. Some were excellent, and we remain in contact.

~~~

Third, LiteracyStudies@OSU at its prime exceeded my own and everyone else's expectations as a campus-wide, interdisciplinary set of interconnected programs and activities. Some faculty and administrators deemed my goals no more than impossible aspirations, or at least unlikely for disconnected Ohio State University. My first English Department chair once commented only half-jokingly, "Harvey, is Ohio State big enough for you?" We achieved national and international recognition and attracted visitors and graduate students. Our doctoral students have done well professionally.

LiteracyStudies@OSU is best conceptualized as a set of interlinked working parts, many of which could stand on their own, but the sum of whose parts was much larger. The program's former website and printed materials stated the following:

> Literacy Studies formed in 2004 as an interdisciplinary working group of the Humanities Institute, under the direction of Harvey J. Graff, Ohio Eminent Scholar in Literacy Studies and Professor of English and History. The intent was to foster a campus-wide conversation and collaborative investigation into the nature of literacy, bringing together historical, contextual, comparative, and critical perspectives and modes of understanding.
>
> The group began its work by inviting distinguished scholars of literacy to share their insights and ideas. They also organized cross-disciplinary forums around central questions, such as the roles of literacy in science and health. The aim overall was to explore ideas about and approaches to literacy and literacy studies at The Ohio State University, where interests and strengths range widely. These initial efforts kindled new institutional and intellectual relationships between different disciplinary clusters and their faculty, staff, and students, from the arts, humanities, and sciences, to education, medicine, engineering, and law…
>
> LiteracyStudies@OSU, now a University-wide initiative supported by the College of Arts and Sciences, the Humanities Institute, and the Department of English, is recognized nationally and internationally as a model of interdisciplinary program development.
>
> LiteracyStudies@OSU initiatives are the result of shared interests and collaborative efforts. The goal is to enable conversation and cooperation across departments, across campus, and beyond. Participation is helping to increase awareness of the complexities of literacy in diverse media and cultural contexts. The dialogue also gives rise to new initiatives and activities, such as the new Literacy in Translation Series. (LiteracyStudies@OSU, n.d.)

Both my previous experiences at purportedly but in fact pseudo-interdisciplinary institutions and my historical knowledge of universities, disciplinarity, and interdisciplinarity taught me that I did not want to establish a department, center, or degrees that were segregated and that would compete or conflict with others (for examples of my thinking about interdisciplinarity, see Graff, 2010c, 2012, 2015a, and 2021d).LiteracyStudies@OSU strived to be a set of intersecting points, and both overlapping and interconnecting spheres.

LiteracyStudies@OSU actively practiced my understanding of reading, writing, and arithmetic applied and adapted across, between, and among all fields of study. We persuaded faculty members, researchers, staff members, and students across the huge university that promulgating their own of the "many" or "endless literacies" was not the road to knowledge, understanding, or collaboration. This was an unparalleled test of my conclusions from decades of research and teaching.

The initiative was self-directed, with the advice and sometimes the consent of colleagues and administrators across the campus. From her first service as my graduate research assistant to administrative assistant and then associate director and lecturer, Susan Hanson deserves credit for her long-term contribution to our success. We sought and received financial and programmatic support from many departments and at the university-wide level.

One category of financial support underwrote LiteracyStudies@OSU. The endowment for the OES chair provided basic funding, although the college never allowed me to see its account balances. Funding included initiative programming grants from the College of Humanities, an award from the Humanities Institute to found and develop the literacy studies working group, and a Colleges of Arts and Sciences interdisciplinary curriculum enhancement award (declined in favor of alternative funding).

In 2006, our third year, we received a grant from the Graduate Gchool to develop the Graduate Interdisciplinary Specialization in Literacy Studies, a graduate student elective minor. As our plans more fully emerged, the next year we received major funding for the initiative from the College of Humanities and additional funds from the Colleges of Ats and Sciences, the College of Art, the College of Biological Sciences, the College of Dentistry, the Department of English, the Department of Entomology, and the University Libraries to support an annual lecture series.

The Literacy Studies working group quickly became a campus-wide initiative. We achieved this through a combination of both overlapping and quasi-independent working groups, public programs and visiting speakers' series, a graduate minor, a university-wide graduate students' interdisciplinary seminar, a student society, and long-standing history of the book and other working groups for faculty and graduate students.

In 2009 we organized the landmark, international, interdisciplinary graduate student conference "Expanding Literacy Studies" that featured keynote addresses by my longtime literacy studies colleague and friend Shirley Brice Heath and me on the occasion of the 30th anniversary of the first publication of *The Literacy Myth* (1979c). Graduate students from OSU and other universities participated in the program under Susan's and my supervision.

Several hundred OSU students and representatives from across the United States and foreign countries participated, more than 300 in all. The printed program filled many pages. One of the respondents to my keynote was an advanced doctoral student from Iceland and Scotland. The conference was one of the highlights of LiteracyStudies@OSU's 13-year history. We celebrated its 15th anniversary with a reunion in May 2024 at the same conference center.

Over those years, our visiting lecture series was extremely popular across the university and beyond. Working on our own model, LiteracyStudies@OSU and different departments shared costs and responsibilities. Noted visitors included scholars whose work contributed to the understanding of literacy from across the disciplines and the globe, including North America, South America, Europe, the Middle East, and South Asia. They included colleagues and friends such as Deborah Brandt, Shirley Heath, Mike Rose, Johanna Drucker, M. J. Maynes, Bengt Sandin, Michael Wilson, Kolleen Guy, John Duffy, Patrick Berry, Andrew Hacker, William Labov, Jon Miller, Ira Shor, David Nord, Lesley Bartlett, Teresa McCarty, Christopher Hager, Elizabeth Moje, Joanne Rappaport, Lawrence Venuti, Suresh Canagarajah, Anne Dyson, Randall McLeod, Cynthia Brokaw, Anthony Pym, Claudia Angelelli, Kate Viera, Laura Mandell, Curt Dudley-Marling, and Frances Cody, among educationists, linguists, language specialists, scientists, medical experts, and many others from the Americas and Western Europe.

The roster remains impressive. Graduate students and faculty met with them in small groups, often over lunch. And the GradSem—the regular, self-directed, organized graduate student seminar—discussed the visitors' work either before or after their visits. Many of the speakers related directly to and were invited by the various working groups.

Working groups were in a diverse, almost dizzying array of subjects. Some were short-lived, while others lasted more than a decade. Their topics ranged from the history of the book (long led by Alan Farmer in English); history of reading; and history of reading, writing, and book arts; to Appalachian literacy; literacy in the arts; literacy in dance; literacy in science; literacy in health and medicine; literacy in translation; and others, most with multiple leaders and long-standing members.

Faculty from across the entire university met to discuss literacy in science and medicine, for example, and attend lectures by visitors. Collaboration with Moritz College of Law colleagues was also stimulating and rewarding.

Hundreds of OSU central- and regional-campus students and scores of faculty members participated over the years. To give a flavor, faculty and graduate student researchers came from English, history, comparative studies, classics, linguistics, East Asian and Near Eastern languages and literature, French and Italian, Spanish and Portuguese, dance, arts, music, architecture, anthropology, communication, geosciences, biology, chemistry, physics, education, law, engineering, medicine, nursing, dental medicine, veterinary medicine, the computer center, university communications, the Wexner Center for the Arts, the Center for Teaching, and University Libraries.

Students were sometimes prompted to participate by their professors and at other times by their own scholarly or more general interests. Substantial numbers came from English, education, history, the arts, health, and medicine, fewer from the social and natural sciences. That followed faculty and disciplinary interests and patterns of collaboration. A few undergraduates joined in, often prompted by attendance in my courses.

Across the many divisions, intellectual and personal exchange, communication, and mutual respect reigned. LiteracyStudies@OSU stimulated course enrollments and attracted doctoral students to active faculty participants including me. I supervised or co-supervised dissertations in English, history, education, and dance.

~~~

Fourth, as my activities in the previous sections of this chapter indicate, I played an active role across campus. In addition to English and history, I was also a faculty associate in the Department of Comparative Studies and a not-quite-formal associate of the College of Education. I was an affiliated faculty member in the Diversity and Identity Studies Collective, Humanities Institute, International Poverty Solutions Collaborative, Mershon Center for International Security Studies, Center for Medieval and Renaissance Studies, Kirwan Institute for the Study of Race and Ethnicity, and Project Narrative.

These activities represent how I put my academic politics into practice. At times, it was intellectually stimulating and rewarding. At other times, it was a drag or nuisance. But it led me to worthwhile acquaintanceships and friends, a number of which continue in my retirement.

The English Department, of course, was most demanding. By assignment or election, I was affiliated with rhetoric, composition, and literacy; American and English literature before 1900; popular culture; and narrative studies. Search committees I participated on included selective investment searches and numerous searches for assistant and associate professors. I also participated on tenure and promotion committees. On at least four occasions, I was nominated (but never chosen) for Graduate or Undergraduate Professor of the Year.

In the Hstory Department I was linked to American and European history, curriculum constellations, and the modern America initiative. I served on the advisory committee for the Center for Historical Research (CHR); the Family, Kinship, and Household: New Perspectives initiative; and on the Popular Culture faculty. But at times, History had difficulty remembering my cross-appointment or physical location down the street.

Consistent with my now "advanced" intersectionality in active practice, I was closely involved with the Humanities Institute. In addition to serving on its Advisory Committee, I advised on the Building Public Space initiative, Working Group on Public Humanities, and the Neighborhood Institute. I had almost non-stop conversations with its longtime director Chris Zacher, next-door neighbor and personal friend until his death in 2019. (I continue to work with his widow, professor emeritus of architecture Kay Bea Jones, on OSU student and University District neighborhood issues. Son Sam completed his Ph.D. in political science at Yale.) I also served on the Civic Engagement committee of the College of Arts and Sciences.

At the university-wide level, my OES position made me a member of the President's and Provost's Advisory Council, composed of faculty holding university-wide, named chairs. We met regularly with the president, provost, and other senior administrators. I knew them all by first name and made my opinions and constructive criticisms known, for better and for worse.

My position also led to appointment to the Ohio State Teaching Enhancement Program (OSTEP) steering committee (and chair for one year)—the Committee to Select Distinguished University Lecturers. And, of course, I was a founding member of the University Council on Literacy Studies.

Less formally but no less importantly to me, I worked with colleagues across campus on the Working Group on the Future of the University and ad hoc working groups revising undergraduate education, reforming general education, and combatting admissions policies that severely harmed the arts and sciences. The collegial knowledge, commitment, activism, and continuing friendships of Randy Roth (History), Steve Rissing (Biology), Alan Farmer (English), Mike Bevis (Geosciences), Creighton Ogle (Mathematics), and others remain with me. Then President Gordon Gee, in his "second coming" at OSU, feigned support of our efforts and fed us lunch, but as was his practice, did nothing (on Gee, see Graff, 2015b, as well as regular news reports on his tenure as president of West Virginia University).

His successors in the presidency, Michael Drake and Kristina Johnson, showed no interest (see Graff, 2022f, 2022h, and 2022i). At OSU, university-wide general education requirements went from one unsupportable, unworkable, and divisive iteration to another, most recently and without acknowledgment attempting a poor copy of the University at Buffalo (formerly SUNY Buffalo) for reasons unknown.

While I was active, the number of mid- to upper-level, highly paid administrative positions grew almost monthly. They seldom had publicized job descriptions. Their rates of increase and ratio of salaries to the faculty's rose exponentially.

My university-wide position, collegial and friendship relations with faculty members across campus (including one engineer, one veterinary medicine specialist, and several in the medical school through my physicians and others), and involvement in reform efforts gave me a unique window, perspective, and involvement with OSU. My experience at other public universities helped to open that window farther. All this helps to shape my forthcoming book, *Reconstructing the "Uni-versity" from the Ashes of the "Mega- and Multi-versity."*

What I see clearly now is an overly large, disconnected, and poorly managed university with many excellent faculty members, students, staff members, and physical resources. The Faculty Senate lacks influence and effective leadership. The AAUP Chapter is ineffectual. On one hand, I worked with others on various reform proposals. On the other hand, adopting a practice I followed to a limited extent in Dallas and San Antonio, and expanded in retirement, I worked with higher education reporters in the daily *Columbus Dispatch* and with OSU student journalists on *The Lantern*, and I offered them perspectives, details, and public data that the university typically (and frequently illegally) denied them. It sometimes led to more acute and insightful articles.

I also wrote opinion essays, a practice that I later expanded. Evolutionary biologist Steve Rissing and I published "Early-College Programs Lack Many Benefits of the Real Thing" (2015). I published the widely discussed "An Education in Sloganeering" (2015b) and "Not a Popularity Contest" (2015c). These publications foreshadowed my retirement roles.

~~~

Fifth, inseparable from LiteracyStudies@OSU, my most compelling experiences and memories of Ohio State are of my students, along with a large handful of close colleagues and friends, with many of whom Vicki and I remain in contact.

Over more than a dozen years at OSU, I taught undergraduate students introductory general education courses on literacy and upper-division courses on literacy, the history of literacy, the history of children and youth, and introductions to graduate research. My undergraduate courses attracted a sizable proportion of nonmajors.

I happily wrote recommendations for law and medical schools, with students achieving a high rate of acceptance. Those former students are now lawyers and physicians. Nick Sincere, Nina Passen, and Blake Taneff immediately come to mind. I only taught one football player; he had trouble keeping his eyes open. Three members of "The Best Damned Band in the Land" (TBDBITL), OSU's marching band, fared better in wakefulness, interest, and achievement. I was able to reward them with recommendations of sights and eating places when they accompanied the football team to the Sugar Bowl in New Orleans. (I formally complained when the band director demanded their release from classes with no advance notice to me or to them.)

Two other undergraduate students merit special mention: Windy Hawkins and Ellen Manovich. Windy was my work-study research assistant in 2007–2009. As a young single mother, she never missed a deadline, sometimes delivering her work to me at home (a few minutes' drive from the office) with her toddler in the car. She completed her second master's degree in health care, and her two daughters do well in school.

Ellen was my finest undergraduate student in almost a half century of teaching. Early in her first semester, as a new student in the University Honors program, a Presidential Scholar, and a member of the nationally competitive rowing team, she scrutinized the History and English faculty rosters and picked me out. She emailed: "I'm a new honors student. They say that I must learn to do research. Will you teach me?" My relationship with her and her entire family continues.

Ellen completed a groundbreaking honors thesis on the history of the University District that abuts the OSU campus. It won the Undergraduate Thesis of the Year award. She also nominated me for Advisor of the Year (with a nomination that brought tears to my eyes). I was awarded the honor. While I recovered from back surgery, she accepted the award on my behalf and brought it to my bedside. Every professor would be honored with such a deeply felt and articulately expressed tribute.

Ellen completed doctoral study in History at the University of Minnesota. She continued to excel, writing an original doctoral dissertation comparing three university districts in three different U.S. cities. I served as external member of her dissertation committee and participated remotely in the final defense.

She taught history at Carleton College and published an article from her dissertation in the *Journal of Social History* (Manovich, 2018). Now on a career pause, she happily raises her young family. As an urban historian, she teaches children to "read the city." Ellen is only one of my former students who delight Vicki and me with photographs of their growing children. Hers are among our "surrogate grandchildren."

At the graduate level, I taught introductory courses in methods and theory including interdisciplinarity and electives on the history of literacy, literacy studies, and history of children and youth. These cross-listed seminars attracted students from a wide range of interests, disciplines, and specializations, making for rich interactions and research projects. As a result, my many thesis and especially dissertation students were a stimulating and diverse group who knew each other and worked collaboratively. Each semester concluded with potluck dinners at our home.

For graduate students in English, History, Education, and Dance, I was a seminar instructor, advisor and supervisor, Master's Examination Committee chair and member, and Doctoral Dissertation director and/or Defense Committee member. I also led the university-wide Literacy Studies GradSem.

Many grad students were active in Literacy Studies, including the 2009 International Student Sonference hosted by LiteracyStudies@OSU. In 2013, David Bwire (Education), Di Luo (History), and Nora McCook (English) formed an SSHA panel on comparative histories of literacy with me as chair and John Duffy from Notre Dame University as commentator. In earlier years I formed sessions with English and education students at the Conference on College Composition and Communication (CCCC), including Kelly Bradbury, Shawn Casey, Michael Harker, Kate White, and Julia Voss.

Many of these students remain in regular communication with me. Almost all who desired tenure track positions secured them. Some have included "literacy myth" in their dissertation, article, or book titles; others have not. Among their books so far are Michael Harker's *The Lure of Literacy* (2015), Kelly Susan Bradbury's *Reimagining Popular Notions of American Intellectualism* (2016), Victoria Clement's *Learning to Become Turkmen* (2018), and Di Luo's *Beyond Citizenship: Literacy and Personhood in Everyday China, 1900–1945* (2022). Their articles are too numerous to list, but they are in such subject areas as composition, digital media, history, art education, education, and dance, among others.

In addition to those I've mentioned, others who stand out, in multiple ways, are Michael Harwick, Cate Sacchi St. Pierre, Envera Dukaj, and Sarah Webb-Sunderhaus in English; William Sturkey, Sarah Kernan, Lisa Zevorich Susner, and Jessica Blissit in History; Caitlin Law Ryan, Ben Johnson, Jamie Teeple, and Suzu Strayer in Education; Rachael Riggs Leyva in Dance; and Vicki Daiello in Art. I am proud of them, their diversity, and achievements. Vicki and I have holiday cards and digital folders with photos of their children, and I have their publications on the shelves above my desk.

I also mention here the graduate students at other universities who benefitted either directly or indirectly from LiteracyStudies@OSU and from my assistance. Two noted scholars among them come immediately to mind: John Duffy, a student of Deborah Brandt at the University of Wisconsin-Madison and now a professor at Notre Dame, author of *Writing from These Roots* (2007); and Patrick Berry, a student at the University of Illinois now on the faculty at Syracuse University, author of *Doing Time, Writing Lives* (2018).

~~~

Sixth is my own scholarship. Despite—or in some important ways because of—LiteracyStudies@OSU and my other university activities, my writing and research proceeded well. A reduced teaching load helped. So did a research fund associated with the Ohio Eminent Scholar position that provided a research assistant and covered some expenses. This dedicated assistance, for the first time in my lengthy career, made a material difference.

For my research, I was awarded a special assignment for a course release in 2007 and in 2008–2010 a grant for Research and Creativity in the Arts and Humanities. I received a Faculty Professional Leave for the 2011–2012 academic year. Except for that year, throughout this period I continued as director of LiteracyStudies@OSU. My former colleague Brenda Brueggeman served as acting director during my leave year.

Completing *The Dallas Myth: The Making and Unmaking of an American City* (2008a) in 2005–2006, I used these funds and the time away from teaching to continue my decades-long project to re-envision our understanding of literacy and begin work toward a history of interdisciplinarity. This was another stocktaking, culmination, and set of propositions, rooted in history, for both scholars and multiple publics.

Beyond LiteracyStudies@OSU, I continued my scholarship and professional activities in literacy studies and the history of literacy. Literacy led to a distinguished lecture at the Mary Lou Fulton Endowed Symposium series at Arizona State University in 2005. At the recommendation of my OSU Moritz College of Law colleague and friend Peter Shane, I served on the Advisory Board of the Communications and Society program of the Aspen Institute for the Knight Commission on the Information Needs of Communities in a Democracy.

I consulted for *The Bedford Bibliography for Teachers of Writing* and served on the advisory board of the Museum of Writing online collaborative project of the Institute of English Studies at the University of London and the Faculty of Information Studies and University Library of the University of California at Los Angeles. In addition, I was a member of the international Editorial Board of the Computers and Composition Digital Press (CCDP) and of the founding EditorialBboard for the journal *Literacy in Composition Studies*.

My books on literacy in the Ohio State years included the edited volumes: *Literacy and Historical Development* (2007b); *National Literacy Campaigns*, co-edited with Robert F. Arnove (1987/2008); and *Understanding Literacy in its Historical Contexts*, co-edited with Alison Mackinnon, Bengt Sandin, and Ian Winchester (2009). I also wrote *Literacy Myths, Legacies, and Lessons* (2011/2023c, foreword by Shirley Brice Heath) and my review and final scholarly reflections on the history of literacy studies itself, *Searching for Literacy: The Social and Intellectual Origins of Literacy Studies* (2022e).

*Figure 10.2. Harvey conducting seminar at host's home, University of Arizona, Tucson, 2008.*

Articles and book chapters in these years included the much-cited "Literacy Myths," with John Duffy in the *Encyclopedia of Language and Education* (2008), "Bibliography of the History of Literacy in Western Europe and North America" (2007a), "Not Your Mother's Literacy, But Perhaps Your Daughter's" with Susan Hanson (2008), "Introduction to Historical Studies of Literacy" (2003), and "Literacy, Religion, Gender, and Social History: A Socio-Cultural History for the 21st Century" with Alison Mackinnon, Bengt Sandin, and Ian Winchester (2003b).

The 30th anniversary of the first publication of *The Literacy Myth* (1979c) stimulated renewed interest and widespread tributes. They began in 2009 with a plenary session at the Expanding Literacy Studies International Interdisciplinary Conference for Graduate Students at OSU with responses from graduate students from several countries.

They continued with a talk in 2010 at the Simon Fraser University Institute for the Humanities on "*The Literacy Myth* Now Thirty Years Old Revisited." A radio interview and my keynote address to the Symposium on Critical Perspectives on Understanding Literacy in a Technological Age at the British Columbia Institute of Technology accompanied it. As always, but with a regularly spreading network and shifting emphases, the personal, political, academic, and place intersected and realigned.

My frequently cited and discussed "*The Literacy Myth* at Thirty" (2010a), "The Literacy Myth: Literacy, Education and Demography" (2010b), and "The Legacies of Literacy Studies" (2013) were part of the anniversary. Among my other contributions in these years were "Epilogue: Literacy Studies and Interdisciplinary Studies with Notes on the Place of Deborah Brandt" (2014a) and "Interview with H. J. Graff & B. Street" (Galvão et al., 2016).

In different venues, I reflected on and extended my interpretations of literacy past, present, and future. As opportunities presented, I sought and developed different scholarly *and* public audiences.

Scholars in Brazil, where one of my earlier books on literacy had been translated into Portuguese, continued their interest. I participated on the scientific committee of the 2010 I SIHELE (International Seminar on History of Teaching Reading and Writing) seminar, "The Constitution of the Field of History of Literacy in Brazil," promoted by Grupo de Pesquisa História do ensino de língua e literatura no Brasil (GPHELLB), and I also participated in the research group "History of Teaching Language and Literature in Brazil" for the Faculty of Philosophy and Sciences' Post-Graduate Program in Education at Universidade Estadual Paulista-Campus Marilia.

In 2013 I engaged with the Scientific Committee for ABAlf's (Brazilian Association of Literacy) conference "The Meanings of Literacy in Brazil: What We Know, What We Do and What We Want?" and the I SIHELE seminar "Methods and Teaching Materials in the History of the Initial Teaching of Reading and Writing in Brazil."

In summer 2014 Vicki and I visited Brazil and had an exhilarating introduction to the country and its scholars, stimulated by my invitation to keynote the IV Colóquio Internacional Letramento e Cultura Escrita (4th International Conference of Literacy and Written Culture) at Minas Gerais, meet with faculty and graduate students there, and also conduct seminars in Rio de Janiero. An award from the federal government of Brazil supported my visit. Ana Galvão, professor at the Federal University at Minas Gerais, was one of the coordinators for my visit and organizers of the conference. Her gracious hosting of Vicki and me contributed to our continuing scholarly collaboration and friendship.

Ana had visited LiteracyStudies@OSU while she and her husband Leo were visiting professors in Illinois. She was one of the interviewers and editors of a memorable and historically significant, joint session with my longtime colleague Brian Street and me about the origins of literacy studies and our respective roles in the development of the field (Galvão et al., 2016). I knew Brian from our appearances at international conferences and his visits to the College of Education at OSU.

Before the conference began, Vicki and I spent three days in historic Salvador da Bahía on the east coast and two days in Brasília, the modern capital city in central Brazil. The former is an incredible city heavily influenced by the vibrant culture of the descendants of Africans transported to the Portuguese colony as enslaved laborers. The highlight of our visit was a bus excursion a few miles north to Projeto Tamar, where conservation volunteers dig up sea turtle eggs and move them to a safer part of the beach. Vicki composed "Tartarugas," a song describing the project's work.

Brasília offered a stunning contrast with its city plan resembling an airplane; discrete districts devoted to governmental, commercial, residential, or recreational functions; and vast, treeless plazas of concrete punctuated with public art and architectural marvels, mostly designed by Oscar Niemeyer and constructed from 1956 to 1960 as part of President Juscelino Kubitschek's "Fifty Years in Five" initiative.

Back to the State of Minas Gerais and the beautiful, historic city of Belo Horizonte, where the university hosting the conference was located. Vicki attended some sessions but also toured museums and photographed the sights around the central square. She joined the participants for many delicious lunches and dinners over several days. In addition to the inaugural lecture on graduate education programs, I conducted a session on the history of literacy.

After the conference, Ana Galvão, her husband Leo, and younger son Tomas led us to the historic gold mining town of Ouro Preto. By happy coincidence, we were all treated to dinner at the mountaintop home of one of her university colleagues in a town where cows roam freely in the streets and mailboxes are painted in delightful designs, including one we called the "Reading Cow"!

In Rio de Janeiro we stayed in a hotel overlooking Copacabana beach with its constant hum of activities and had time for touring. Several professors at the university graciously hosted us. We also shared a wonderful dinner with

Michael Katz's oldest daughter Rebecca and her husband John. I babysat her 40 years earlier. She had grown up to be a teacher and translator in Rio, engaged in social work.

~~~

In 2015 I served on the scientific committee for I CONBAlf (Brazilian Congress on Literacy)—Associacao Brasileira de Alfabetizacao (Brazilian Association of Literacy). I was invited to consult and participate in seminars on interdisciplinarity in São Paulo.

On invitation, I also presented keynote addresses about literacy and its history to these events:

- Western States Rhetoric and Literacy Conference, "Big Rhetorics, Big Literacies: The Discourses of Power," at Arizona State University in 2004
- Conference on "From Woodblocks to the Internet: Chinese Publishing and Print Culture in Transition," at Ohio State University in 2004
- National Council of Teachers of English Assembly for Research Conference, "Literacies Across Time, Space, and Place: New Directions in Literacy Research for Political Action," with Deborah Brandt at Ohio State University in 2005
- Conference on College Composition and Communication (CCCC) annual meeting, "Writing Realities, Changing Realities," in New Orleans, LA, in 2008
- The Symposium on Critical Perspectives on Understanding Literacy in a Technological Age at the British Columbia Institute of Technology in 2010
- The Conference on College Composition and Communication annual meeting, "Writing Gateways," in St. Louis, MO, in 2012

An especially enjoyable invited lecture on literacy took place at the Graduate School of Education and Information Science, University of California at Los Angeles, in 2013. Invited by my longtime colleague and friend Johanna Drucker, her endowed chair's funds paid for my visit. I modified my lecture format and asked UCLA to circulate discussion questions for the audience in advance. I introduced each question with details and perspectives in the place of a traditional presentation.

The night before my lecture, Vicki shared with Johanna and me by email a photo of the newly arrived, mechanical dog Tekno—our first of four generations of robot pets. (They took the place of McDonald, our last canine family member.) Knowing me well, certain that I would not be embarrassed and would take the moment in stride, Johanna used Tekno's image in her introduction. He and I brought the house down. It paved the way to a wonderful discussion.

A memorable dinner with my UCLA friends Johanna, Jan Reiff, and Mike Rose followed. Jan and Mike, tragically, are no longer with us. Both passed away in 2021. They are among the dear colleagues and friends to whom *Searching for Literacy*, 2022e, is dedicated.

*Figure 10.3. Tekno, first robot pet, previewing his virtual appearance at Harvey's UCLA lecture, 2014.*

With respect to the history of children and youth, my writings included "Coming of Age in Chicago" with Joy L. Bivens (2004), "Teaching the History of Growing Up" (2008b), and "The Critical Historiography of Childhood" (2009b).

I participated in the invitational Conference on Rethinking Child Development at the University of California, Berkeley's Center for Child and Youth Policy and Department of History in 2005. This was one of a series of small conferences to bring together historians and social scientists on the subject of childhood. I also served on the executive committee for the Society for the History of Children and Youth and participated in the society's meetings in 2005, 2007 (in Sweden), 2009, and 2011. In 2009 I spoke at the 20th Anniversary Seminar on Child Studies at the Department of Child Studies, Linköping University, Sweden.

Vicki joined me on some of these combined, business-pleasure trips. After the 2007 meeting in Sweden, for example, she and I took a train from Norrköping to Stockholm, an overnight ferry to Helsinki, and a hydrofoil catamaran to Tallinn, capital of Estonia. For this part of the trip—which included a guided walking tour of the old town and its fortified walls—longtime friends Jim Block from DePaul University in Chicago and his wife Ruth joined us. Vicki and I continued by bus to St. Petersburg, Russia, for three remarkable days, followed by three days in Helsinki.

On urban history and the history of Dallas, I participated in the 2006 annual meeting of the Urban History Association in Tempe, Arizona. Michael Katz delivered his presidential address, and we dined together.

*The Dallas Myth* (2008a), with its distant origins in the 1970s, was published in 2008. Attracting local, state, and national attention, it was discussed at a session at the SSHA in 2008. In recognition of the book's publication, I presented the Gartner Honors Lecture at Southern Methodist University in 2010 and in 2011 was invited to speak and confer by the Master of City and Regional Planning graduate program and the Student Planning Association at the University of Texas at Arlington, where I also spoke to the OneBook Program. It was their book of the year. National Public Radio's Radiolab program also interviewed me in 2010 on the origins of cities.

In 2010, Ohio State honored me with the Distinguished Undergraduate Research Mentor Award. In 2011, I was nominated for the Grawemeyer Award in Education from the University of Louisville, and in 2013, I was awarded the first and only award for "unmatched record of attendance at the annual conference of the SSHA, 1976–2013 *and counting.*"

In 2015–2016 I received a grant from the Center for Real Estate, Fisher College of Business at Ohio State to support a graduate research assistant. Chloe Tull and I began an investigation of Campus Partners, OSU's property development arm. Just as the project became revealing—the quasi-independent, quasi-university, quasi-nonprofit, quasi-active, aid-to-private-developers agency was overpaying for university-vicinity properties and selling them to developers at a substantial loss—I had to end it. In typical OSU fashion, Campus Partners refused to allow access to public data. In addition, it had no annual reports. My report, "Disconnecting Gown and Town: Campus Partners for Urban Community Development, Ohio State University," will be published soon.

At the intersection of my studies, teaching, research, and writing since my undergraduate years at Northwestern and especially my graduate school years in Toronto, I focused more directly and formally on interdisciplinarity itself. Its programmatic culmination lay in LiteracyStudies@OSU and the Ohio Eminent Scholar post.

I was an invited speaker at the Scope of Interdisciplinarity Conference at Athabasca University in Edmonton Alberta, Canada in 2008. I previewed some of the book's arguments in letters to the editor "The Troubled Discourse of Interdisciplinarity" (2010c) and "Throwing the Baby Out with the Interdisciplinary Bath Water" (2014c) and a book chapter, "Literacy Studies and Interdisciplinary Studies" (2012).

In 2013–2014 I was awarded full-year, residential fellowships by both the National Humanities Center in Research Triangle Park, North Carolina, and the Center for Advanced Studies in the Behavioral Sciences at Stanford University to complete *Undisciplining Knowledge: Interdisciplinarity in the Twentieth Century* (2015a). Weighing several factors, we chose to accept the Birkelund Fellowship at the National Humanities Center and lived happily in a rented townhouse in Durham across the street from Duke University (where our friend from San Antonio John Martin taught history).

My culminating, preretirement, scholarly statement was my social, cultural, intellectual, and institutional history *Undisciplining Knowledge* (2015a). This groundbreaking study presented an unprecedented history for a topic typically, repeatedly, and mistakenly claimed to be novel. I traced the divergent and contradictory patterns of successes and failures over the decades and across disciplines and disciplinary clusters. My approach explicitly compared two identified interdisciplinary institutional developments in each chapter: genetic biology and sociology from the 1890s to the 1920s, the humanities and communication from the 1870s to the 1960s, social relations and operations research from the 1930s to the 1960s, cognitive science and the new histories from the 1940s to the 1980s, materials science and cultural studies from the 1960s to the 1990s, and, most recently, bioscience and literacy studies.

*Figure 10.4. Plush toy Al B. Tross, co-author with Harvey and Vicki of The Book of Tross: An Illustrated Glossary of Trossical Terms, reading Harvey's Undisciplining Knowledge, 2015.*

Overall, I offered a history for each field, including literacy studies, set within historical, disciplinary, institutional, and comparative contexts. I revealed a complex and contradictory history of change and continuity, achievements and limitations, a variety of paths to multi-, cross-, and what I defined as interdisciplinarity, arguing for the imperative to evaluate rhetoric and realities, plural. Each proclaimed interdiscipline arose within specific historical circumstances; many had an institutional half-life. Almost all fell short of their most grandiose claims. Interdisciplinarity is inseparable from the history of knowledge, disciplines, and higher education.

*Undisciplining Knowledge* (2015a) sometimes provoked upset as I stepped lightly and more strongly on often-fragile fingers and toes. Most offended, revealing their institutionally and intellectually thin skins, have been proponents of so-called "transdisciplinarity," which is itself a logical and intellectual impossibility. But that challenge was among my purposes.

Preparation for this book, perhaps even more than most of my others, reflected varieties of interdisciplinary cooperation and collaboration. I see these varied cooperations and collaborations in my sequential and interactive connections with education, teaching, collegial relationships, conferences, lectures, and publications.

A special case in point is my long relationship with sociologist Jerry Jacobs of the University of Pennsylvania. Jerry and I began our intellectual exchanges in 2009 and continued through the publication of his *In Defense of Disciplines: Interdisciplinarity and Specialization in the Research University* (2013) and my *Undisciplining Knowledge* (2015a) two years later.

Not only do our disciplinary bases differ, but so do our interpretations. Nevertheless, we constructively shared our interests and materials, commented on each other's drafts, wrote book jacket endorsements for each other's books, authored reviews, and participated in conference sessions that featured each other's books. We are close friends and continue to share our work. We may collaborate in the future by writing on disciplines in the public realm.

Responses to *Undisciplining Knowledge* (2015a) continue. Among the immediate ones were a stimulating session at the SSHA in 2015. The participants were sociologist Jerry Jacobs, social and cultural historian M. J. Maynes, historian and computer scientist Jan Reiff, historian and political scientist Bill Sewell, and literary historian and critic John Guillory. The papers and my response were published online as *A Forum on Interdisciplinarity* (Graff et. al, n.d.).

*Undisciplining Knowledge* (2015a) was also honored at a book celebration at the Rochester Institute of Technology in 2016 and featured in interviews with *Inside Higher Ed* (Jaschik, 2015); *A View From the Bridge:* Nature's Books and Arts Blog (Van Noorden, 2015); and *News of the National Humanities Center* (Solomon, 2014), which was excerpted on the History News Network website (Graff, 2014b). I also wrote a complementary article, "Interdisciplinarity as Ideology and Practice," (2016c). I further reflected broadly in "The 'Problem' of Interdisciplinarity in Theory, Practice, and History" (2016b).

Finally, I advised, spoke, and wrote about more general history and humanities issues. In 2007 I conducted a grueling but intellectually stimulating, one-person review of the McGill University Arts Faculty Humanities Program and Interdisciplinary Studies, and in 2008 I was a member of the external review committee for the President's Advisory Board of the Department of History at Carnegie Mellon University.

I served as a reviewer for *Dropout Nation*, a documentary film for the Public Broadcasting Service's series *Frontline* (Koughan, 2012) in 2010 and as a member of the editorial advisory board of *American Periodicals* beginning in 2005. As earlier, I continued to advise, interview, and moderate radio and television news and talk shows. In Columbus, I worked with several *Columbus Dispatch* news reporters.

Related activities revolved around "Politics, Activism and the History of America's Public Schools: A Conference Marking the 40th Anniversary of *The Irony of Early School Reform*" by Michael Katz at the University of Pennsylvania in 2008. *The Irony of Early School Reform* (Katz, 1968) was one of the first books I read in 1971 when I became Michael's graduate student; he was my advisor and guide for more than 40 years. This conference was an incredibly special occasion.

Vicki accompanied me, and several of his graduate students joined us—from my era and more recent ones from Toronto, York University, and the University of Pennsylvania, where Michael completed his career. First appointed to the Graduate School of Education at Penn, he held an endowed chair in History and headed the Urban Studies Program. At my urging Ian Davey came from Adelaide, Australia, and Chad Gaffield from Ottawa, Canada.

I met a number of Katz's recent and current students. Among them was Dan Amsterdam, who began his career at Ohio State University's Newark Campus. Dan, his wife Kate Christman, and children Farrah and Eliot became our close friends. Dan now teaches at Georgia Tech in Atlanta.

Several of Michael's former students, over four decades and three universities, joined me in a tribute/memorial SSHA session in 2015 that I organized following his death in 2014. Leah Gordon, then of Stanford University, now of Brandeis University; Margaret O'Mara of the University of Washington; Mark Stern of the University of Pennsylvania; Merlin Chowkwanyun of Columbia University; participated in "Michael B. Katz: His Contribution and Legacy to Social Science History and Beyond: A Round Table Discussion," which I chaired (Graff et al., 2015).

Edda Katz, Michael's widow, and Sarah Katz, his youngest daughter and only child residing in the US, attended with Vicki. We adjourned to the hotel bar, and most of us shared a lovely dinner—all in Michael's memory.

The papers were published in a special section of *Social Science History* ("Michael B. Katz 2015 SSHA memorial session," 2017).

In 2015 I was a keynote speaker at the Big Ten's Committee on Institutional Cooperation's (CIC) Conference on Graduate Education in the Humanities at Penn State University.

Related scholarly activities during this time included *Looking Backward and Looking Forward: Perspectives on Social Science History*, co-edited with Leslie Page Moch and Philip McMichael (2005), selected presentations and discussions from special retrospective and prospective sessions at the 25th annual meeting of the SSHA in 2001, and "History's War of the Wor(l)ds. An Afterword" in Sigurdur Gylfi Magnusson's *The History War: Essays and Narratives on Ideology* (2007, pp. 475–481).

I also continued my active national and international professional engagement with the history of children and youth, urban history, interdisciplinarity, and literacy studies until retirement in 2017. Not only were they my regular areas of instruction, but I attended, organized sessions, and spoke at SSHA meetings on these topics and themes through 2015.

A career-crowning, lifetime tribute came as I retired with a special session on "Harvey J. Graff, Literacy Studies, and Composition," at the annual meeting of the Conference on College Composition and Communication in 2017. Mike Rose (UCLA), John Duffy (Notre Dame), Patrick Berry (Syracuse), my former doctoral student Michael Harker (Georgia State), Amy Wan (Queens College, CUNY), and Peter Mortensen (University of Illinois) all presented papers honoring my contributions (a selection of these papers along with a response from me were later published in *Across the Disciplines*; see Duffy et al., 2024)

~~~

Seventh, as in Dallas and San Antonio, colleagues, friends, and some neighbors in Columbus inextricably intertwined. They are inseparable from place, academics, and often the political domain. Their routes to professional relationships and then friendships vary but almost all share some of these threads. Among them are our neighbors, all of whom have or have had OSU connections: Chris Zacher (now deceased) and Kay Bea Jones, Ed and Dianne Efsic, Jep and Joyce Hostetler (now living in a progressive, Mennonite retirement community in Goshen, Indiana), Emily Foster and Lee Brown (now deceased), and more recently Nalani Stolz, Claire Verschraegen, and Ram Murthy.

There are also a great many OSU connections, from English, History, and Education colleagues and friends to people met through LiteracyStudies@OSU, university reform activities, and others. They include Ellen Manovich, Nick Sincere, Elizabeth Renker, Alan Farmer and Sarah Neville, Brian McHale and Esther Gottlieb, Steve and Janet Rissing, Randy Roth and Allison Sweeney, Brian Joseph and Mary Clark, Peter Shane and Martha Chamalla, Jake Risinger and Memory Blake, Kevin Cox, Ruth Friedman, Bob (deceased) and Sabine Holub, Marcia Farr and Mike Maltz (now retired), Ruth Colker, Beverly Moss, Brenda Brueggeman, Louis and Pat Ulman, Mollie Blackburn, Jared Gardner and Beth Hewitt, Amy Shuman, Alice Conklin and Geoffrey Parker, Mary Cayton, Kevin Boyle and Vicky Getis, Cynthia Brokaw, Elaine (Dr. E.) Richardson, Leslie Moore and Mark Moritz, Mike and Teresa Bevis, Sabra Weber (now retired), Ed Adelson,

Steve Acker, Ann Hamilton, Phil and Mary Lynn Binkley, Tom and Carol Mauger, Susan and Scott Fisher, Molly Blackburn, Patricia Enciso, Louie Ulman, Chris Highley, and Frank Donoghue.

Continuing non-Columbus friends, some dating from high school, graduate school, and Dallas include Gail and Bob Rudenstein, Ava and Art Doppelt, Chad and Pam Gaffield, Mike and Natalie Doucet, Natalie Zemon Davis (deceased in 2023), Ian and Gunilla (deceased in 2022) Winchester, Steve Weissman, Marvin and Janie Cohen, Bob Bradley and Carolyn Herrington, Paul Peretz and Jean Shroedel, Dan and Barbara Orlovsky, Tony Fracchia and Pearl Garza, Patty and Carl Hill, Soledad Jasin, Cathy Civello and Gary Worsham, Cindy Maciel-Reyes and George Reyes, Johanna Drucker, Michael Wilson, Erik Austin, M. J. Maynes and Ron Aminzade, Leslie Moch, Kathy Underwood and Gary Stark, Renate Bridenthal, Harriet Lightman and George Huppert, Barbara Hanawalt, Ellen Dwyer, Jim and Julie Turner, Shirley Brice Heath, Deborah Brandt, John and Kathy Duffy, Patrick and Sho Berry, Grey Osterud, Kathleen Doria and Ruben Silva, Bradley Kayser and Gemma Kennedy, Jerry Jacobs, and Jeff Pooley.

~~~

In this chapter thus far, I have written less about Vicki and me. That is not intentional. It follows from the calmer domestic currents of the Columbus years.

McDonald remained a happy member of the family until the early 2010s when he developed a series of ailments, ranging from his skin to his eyes, his kidneys, and his heart. His vet referred him to the excellent OSU Veterinary Hospital where he received extraordinary care and love. With the assistance of an implanted heart pacemaker (donated by the manufacturer to the teaching hospital), he lived until age 15, which he reached in 2013.

Knowing that he was irreplaceable—and after pondering that for six months—we began to collect a new family of robot pets, introduced in Chapter One. Our current four generations are beloved by our "surrogate grandchildren" and some of our adult, even senior friends. Those older than the age of three operate varying levels of artificial intelligence creations better than I do.

Despite Ohio State's explicit commitment to assist Vicki to quickly obtain suitable employment, more than a year passed after our arrival with no results. As chance had it, the direct link to her position for nine years at OSU's Nisonger Center, a federally-funded University Center for Excellence in Developmental Disabilities, was a LiteracyStudies@OSU public forum on literacy in medicine and health. The center's director was among the speakers. Vicki attended, found his comments stimulating, and contacted him. An interview and job offer came soon after.

For most of those years, she coordinated and promoted the center's exemplary Next Chapter Book Club program. Each club consisted of a group of adults with intellectual and developmental disabilities. They met in semi-public places like the cafés of bookstores, large stores, or coffee houses, with two trained volunteer leaders. Each member took their turn reading a book page aloud; some were experts, while others could barely sound out a few words. Vicki developed literacy curricula, wrote grant proposals, and conducted and analyzed research interviews. She and other staff co-authored a how-to book that explained the program and provided guidelines to others (Fish & Rabidoux, with Ober & Graff, 2009). As with her work with the American Heart Association, her "life with literacy" paralleled and intersected with mine.

When the Nisonger Center's director asked her to initiate a newsletter, Vicki created, designed, co-wrote, edited, and expanded the *NisongerNews* from a four-page, quarterly, PDF file with 130 readers to a semi-annual, hyperlinked webpage with more than 1,100 listserv members. As program manager of communications and dissemination, she wrote and/or edited many online curricula and teachers' guides, brochures, and webpages. Budget cuts ended her position in 2014, after which she retired. She concluded that over her working lifetime, each time one career ended, a new, more fulfilling, and better-paid one followed. That is, until the final one.

At home Vicki devoted time to the Indianola Forest (Homeowners) Association as active member and treasurer and was a once-removed advisor to LiteracyStudies@OSU. When not tending to her plants and flowers, she does photography (now with her phone), Hatha yoga, Yamuna body rolling, other exercises, and receives regular massage therapy. She also manages our finances, investments, taxes, and technology. In 2023, she began to publish her poems written in the late 1970s.

Our exciting travel continued. We spent lovely holidays in the Canadian Maritime provinces of Nova Scotia and New Brunswick in 2006 and Newfoundland in 2008. The latter venture entailed a cruise on a small, newly refitted sailing ship from Halifax along the coast of Newfoundland.

During one of the Maritime trips, my doctoral student Kelly Bradbury moved into our home to care for McDonald (only to deal with the dining room ceiling falling down). On one of the Swedish jaunts, our dear friend and fellow dog lover, Ruth Friedman, moved into our house to stay with McDonald. It takes a village, as they say.

We had a sensational visit to Greece in 2011. Beginning in Athens, we explored the sites of Greek antiquity and Christianity, including Nafplio, Olympia, Delphi, and the mountaintop monastery at Meteora. We also sampled the lovely islands of Santorini and Crete, which were full of archeological and architectural wonders. We will never forget dining at the end of the trip on an outdoor balcony watching the sunset over the Acropolis. This trip also allowed me to follow literacy's historical paths.

Summer 2012 took us to Ireland, first enjoying the streets and sights in Dublin, then renting a car and driving more than 2,000 kilometers around the island to Dingle, Galway City, Achill Island, Donegal, and back to Dublin via Drogheda.

We returned to the UK in 2013 and stayed in the same Crescent Hotel on Cartwright Gardens as on our first trip to London in 1974. It aged less well than we had. In Scotland we revisited the Isle of Skye as well as other Highland spots and enjoyed one of our best meals at the Castle Terrace Restaurant in Edinburgh with colleague Rab Houston and his wife.

In 2015 we returned to South America, another "trip of a lifetime." We toured the Galápagos Islands aboard a three-masted, ecologically friendly, tall ship called the Mary Anne with an excellent Ecuadorian guide and a finely self-selected group of fellow naturalists and environmentalists.

It's difficult to describe the wildlife that is unique to these islands, made famous by Charles Darwin's voyage on the Beagle in 1835. On many hikes and excursions, we saw sea turtles, sea lions, marine and land iguanas, Sally Lightfoot crabs, giant tortoises, pelicans, finches, blue- and red-footed boobies, Nasca boobies, great frigatebirds, tropicbirds, flamingoes, penguins, and wave albatrosses (our favorite), doing their amazing mating dance. Our base before and after the cruise was the delightful Hotel La Casona de la Ronda in historic Quito, almost at the Equator.

*Figure 10.5. Harvey and Vicki at the Equator in Ecuador, 2015.*

We also explored the cities of Ohio, getting to know and appreciating Cleveland and Cincinnati, their museums, green spaces, and restaurants. And we continued to travel across the country, including a visit with several UTSA friends in San Antonio in spring 2016 and, along with UTD friend Paul Monaco, a trip to Yellowstone and Glacier National Parks in Montana that summer.

I suffered and recovered from several health incidents. My right eye required five cornea transplants and my left eye one. Under the expert and humane care of ophthalmologists Tom Mauger, followed by Andrea Sawchyn and Rebecca Kuennen, I read and write without complications. They made me a "tenured patient" and presented me with a physician's jacket embossed with my name.

In 2010 a lifetime of lower back pain, treated in San Antonio, led to spinal surgery on several vertebrae. My OSU Wexner Medical Center internist highly recommended a surgeon at Riverside Hospital who expertly performed that procedure. After the addition of two titanium rods and six titanium screws holding me together, a week's recuperation, a brief period of wearing a back brace, and physical therapy, I fully recovered. Over time, I began to acknowledge the contributions of my excellent physicians to my lifetime of activity and achievements. I thank them explicitly in my books, as all writers should.

~~~

Eighth, and finally, there is place—in particular, the city of Columbus and within it *The* Ohio State University. Until my retirement, I had been less involved in the place that I call home for 20 years than at any previous time. My (over)commitments to OSU, LiteracyStudies@OSU, my students, and my research partly but do not fully explain it.

Columbus is not only the smallest city that I have lived in, relative to the time time that I lived in it, but also the most lacking in a clear identity, written history, or sense of itself. Although it is now the 14th largest city in the United States and the Ohio state capital, it is identified more with a college football team (the Ohio State Buckeyes) than anything else. (See my essays under Columbus Past and Present in the Appendix.)

Ironically—no, contradictorily—newspaper columnists, amateur historians, and radio and TV shows (*Curious Cbus* of WOSU Public Media or *Columbus on the Record* of WOSU Public Broadcasting Service, for example) grasp at straws to fabricate earlier identities to put behind the falsely forward-looking metropolis—in other words, from which it has moved on. These include, laughably, calling Columbus "Cowtown" (confused by the *Columbus Dispatch*'s editorial board with "Crop Town") or "Arch City." There is no ongoing, critical attempt to construct a contemporary identity. Developers' and city boosters' marketing are not serious efforts. They are distractions at best. At worst, they are fabrications.

Fantastic dreams of fictitious futures fail to substitute for a factual, shared past. Recently, several self-described "planners" imagined Columbus as a city on the water—the Amsterdam or Venice of central Ohio. Dredging connections between small lakes and other bodies of water was somehow meant to evoke the grand canals. None of these false images represents accurately any part of the city's history or a plausible future. Unlike Dallas, which often proclaims that it has no history to hold back its advancement or any geo-historical reason to exist, Columbus plods on, hoping that its Major League Soccer or National Hockey League professional teams will compensate for the absence of a Major League Baseball, National Football League, or National Basketball Association team.

In contrast, San Antonio, Toronto, Chicago, and Pittsburgh, the other cities where I have lived, have significant, documented, and published histories and, to a greater extent, representative city government and both public *and* private institutions with distinctive, public presences—and an array of major professional sports teams as well.

Even Dallas has more serious research about it in print than Columbus. The lack of documented histories is both cause and effect of this series of contradictions. On one hand, Columbus has few if any defining events, landmarks, or personalities. Its geographic location is quite ordinary. On the other hand, the necessary and inextricably interconnected linkage of institutions and historiographical constructions is largely absent.

Ohio State's History Department long disdained local and state history as demeaning to its grand but unfulfilled self-conceptions and rhetorical self-promotion. Thus, its students do not regularly excavate the region's past. My colleague, geographer Kevin Cox's documented study of the city, *Boomtown Columbus* (2021), is a rare scholarly statement. Contrastingly, there is no such false pride and local and regional disdain among scholars at Harvard, Columbia, the University of Chicago, Penn, or UC Berkeley, for example.

Institutional and historiographical failures underlie the weakness of local historical, archival, landmark, even folklore traditions. An entity called the Ohio History Connection passes inadequately for a state historical society. Hosting the Ohio State Fair and printing old photographs in *The Columbus Dispatch* do not make a city. *The Columbus Dispatch* and *Columbus Monthly* print either fake history or insignificant anecdotes with no context or interpretation. Little state or local history is studied or taught at any level.

Paralleling the weakness of institutions and also helping to explain the lack of identity is the weakness of Columbus' media. I discussed this in "Columbus' Identity Crisis and Its Media," in which I argued,

> Columbus is a city in search of itself. "Cap City" lacks an identifying and unifying identity. Neither site of the state capital nor home of Ohio State football carries that weight. Nor does ranking in the top 20–25 largest US cities. A sign of its insecurity comes in the habit of its institutions claiming to be the "best" in the state or nation, and failing to admit whether this comes from popularity contests or expert evaluations. Typically, the

ranking is a more nebulous "one of the best." The mayor's promotion of the city's "equity agenda" remains largely rhetorical. At best, only COSI [Center of Science and Industry] and the corruption-ridden Columbus Zoo have legitimate claims.

A "great city" requires excellent local media. Its newspapers and television and radio stations must be committed to more than boosterism or cheerleading. They must develop and practice excellence in terms of constructive, reflective, and responsible criticism of the city's institutions, significant groups, and leaders. In this, Columbus' media fail.

None of the city's major media maintains a consistent focus on the city and its needs. While occasionally ground-breaking, their investigative reporting is limited and inconsistent. No one has established a tradition of constructive social, political, or cultural criticism. Especially at the present challenging moment, Columbus urgently cries out for this….

Together, Columbus' leading media do not provide the active, responsible reporting and criticism that a city in search of itself, seeking to advance, and working to meet its challenges requires. By all accounts and both direct and indirect indicators, they all fear backlash if they move in these directions and directly confront the city's most pressing issues. Columbus' political and institutional leaders too often share these hesitations. I call on them to rise to the challenges now. (Graff, 2021a)

That essay stimulated general assent other than one ridiculous attack, not on me but on the news site that published me, Columbus Underground (Downing & Oliphint, 2021). I replied forcefully in "Response to Columbus Alive" (2021m).

~~~

Unlike Dallas or San Antonio, Columbus offered me few ongoing opportunities for participating in the city's discovery and interpretation of itself. Neither active historical society, city landmarks commission, public library activities, nor other formal and informal associations that I found in all my other cities exist to any serious or rigorous extent in Columbus. This is central to Columbus' exceptionality, what I named "The Columbus Way." That phrase is catching on more widely.

As a result, until my transition to public education in retirement, my major relationships lay in assisting a handful of news reporters at *The Columbus Dispatch*, now owned by Gannett. With a focus on higher education and the University District abutting OSU, I also advised some city, neighborhood, state, and political reporters. That has largely stopped.

~~~

So, an overwhelmingly successful culmination of my professional career came to a more or less predictable end in 2017. As described earlier, I left my Ohio Eminent Scholar chair and concluded LiteracyStudies@OSU as a direct result of the English Department's, the College of Arts and Sciences', and the provost's self-admitted failure to honor their commitments. Many of the broken promises were made in writing.

In the end, neither that nor the unpredicted achievements of my institutional and academic programs mattered. The then English department chair fumbled my emeritus status for more than six months, neither of my departments ever announced my retirement, and I was not invited to join the Emeritus Academy for several years.

My accomplishments from 2004–2017 live on in the minds and careers of many faculty members, staff members, and now former students, a muffled institutional memory. They also live on well beyond Columbus and Ohio State and in my own memory. So be it.

# Epilogue. Intersecting Endings and Beginnings

This historian's life with literacy and continuing education go on, without formal institutional classrooms, gradebook, faculty meetings, peer or student reviews, or monthly salary. As Chapter One explains, the intersections of the personal, the political, the academic, and place continue to entangle in productive and satisfying ways. It is a story of actions, reactions, activism, and reform intermixing with transitory goals, successes, failures, and limits.

There are many lessons, for active careers and for retirement. I hope that this book makes them clear. In one of many possible summations, I have lived a full, successful, and impactful life in academia and found a life beyond it by developing ways to build upon those foundations and their many lessons. In other words, there are new beginnings in the endings.

For me, it is a lifelong—and continuing—expedition of self- and other learning, helping, supporting, connecting, correcting, and interrelating. These activities are not unique to a life involved with universities but have a vital role and responsibility within them—both with and without institutional cooperation.

And for me, the journeys—plural—intertwine with the intellectual, especially the new histories; literacy; education; children, youth, and families; cities; and the striving to work *inter*disciplinarily. It led from a mix of progressive and traditional curricula and instruction in grade and high schools to the electives I selected at Northwestern, great good fortune and innovative knowledge and tutelage at Toronto, and opportunities inseparable from obstacles at public universities in two states and three cities. It spanned older and new campuses. These contradictions are central and inescapable. They cannot be ignored or wished away.

As I have tried to make clear in this book, these experiences are inseparable from the complicated, often contradictory currents of the 1950s and 1960s, the rest of the 20th century, and the first decades of the 21st century. Without a road map or plan, they took me from Pittsburgh to Evanston-Chicago, Toronto, Dallas, San Antonio, and Columbus.

The values of my family created a life committed to equality at all levels, especially for racial, gender, and minority rights and equity. That intersected at all points with the personal, the political, the academic, and place, as it should.

~~~

This past year underscores how clearly my circles repeatedly complete. My close friends and family tease me about now operating "Harvey U": no tuition or debt for "students"; very small classes of all ages; every participant both teaches and learns from the others, including the "old prof"; all topics have historical foundations (for more on "Harvey U," see Graff, 2022aa). One continuing "class" consists of six to eight college seniors across disciplines at several universities. My connections with each of them, often accidental or indirect, allow me to continue as a professor without walls, grading, or Rate My Professors. I have almost but not quite learned what technical systems engineering is.

I have brought the Ohio State section together in my dining room sometimes for takeout meals and potluck dinners. The interactions are enormously satisfying to all.

One member is now in law school; another is taking a gap year and filing applications. A third is beginning an entry level job in publishing and serving as an intern in a student mental health nonprofit. High school participants are beginning college.

The two newest undergraduate members meet with us over takeout from Winston's Coffee and Waffles and discuss Marx, Heidegger, Wittgenstein, classic and contemporary fiction, and current cultural politics. The 2023–2024 and continuing OSU group comprises six students—first-year students, juniors, and seniors.

A second "class" was the Columbus Reform group that met regularly in my living room. My local essays lead progressive residents to contact me. This results in acquaintances and often friendships across ages, occupations, backgrounds, and opinions. I connect the participants in this growing group with each other. We began to develop collective efforts directed at educating Columbus' publics, supporting city charter reform, and advocating for affordable housing. Multiple-year efforts to cooperate with both the City of Columbus and Ohio State off-campus representatives showed promise but then stopped. On the one hand, neither has interest in genuine collaboration or in changing tried but failing ways. On the other hand, serving neighbors and taxpaying residents works against both Columbus' and OSU's profit motives. (See my relevant essays, listed in the Appendix.)

*Figure Epilogue.1. The Seniors at "Harvey U": Matthew Snyder, Justin Kim, Vicki, Harvey with Trossie, Tara Johnson, and Jeanelle Wu, October 2022.*

As they did during my active professorial years, my writings continue to make an impact and my concepts join popular vocabulary: from "the literacy myth" to "conflicting paths," "the Dallas myth," "undisciplining knowledge," the "Second Big Lie," "white fright and flight," "the New Illiterates," "Moms *Against* Liberty," and "The Columbus Way." I hear my recent concept—describing current book banning as "the new illiteracy" (Pérez & Graff, 2022)—on CNN, NPR, and MSNBC. It also appears in print, along with the critical race theory "nondebate" (Graff, 2022d).

~~~

Finally, Vicki and I completed a 50-year-old "circle" by visiting Toronto, our home from 1970 to 1975, in September 2022 and Chicago-Evanston a year later. Although I had returned several times over the half century since we moved to Dallas, time commitments for lectures, seminars, and conferences prevented my walking the city streets and personally observing changes.

When our former professor in the early 1970s and friend since then, 94-year-old Natalie Zemon Davis, told me in August 2022 that she was experiencing health problems, we decided to make another journey to Toronto. It was fulfilling and in many ways life-confirming and life-completing. We spent entire days pounding the pavement, discovering that most of the older city we loved remained amid the new towers of 40 to 60 stories. Despite enormous growth in all dimensions, Toronto remains a welcoming, truly diverse, public-oriented, world city.

With friends from graduate school, we celebrated the city past and present by seeing it; sharing in its historical, visual, and culinary highlights; and engaging in impromptu conversations with strangers, especially with young people in the university area. We had a wonderful catch-up conversation with Natalie, who passed away a year later. Returning to Columbus, we stopped for a few days in Detroit to see my brother Gary—still a hardworking, quite successful rock music journalist—and meet his partner, Stacey.

One year later, we completed another Midwestern driving trip: to Cincinnati to see a former graduate student who is now a professor there, a cousin, and the city; Indianapolis, especially for the best-in-world Children's Museum of Indianapolis; Goshen, Indiana, to see former next-door neighbors in a progressive Mennonite retirement community; Notre Dame, Indiana, to see longtime literacy studies colleague and friend John Duffy and his wife; and especially Chicago and Evanston.

Staying in the Lincoln Park neighborhood of Chicago, where we will relocate in fall 2024, we had a lovely meal with another former graduate student and her family. She is a historian of early printed food recipes. After more walking, wonderful eating, and seeing other sites, we returned to Northwestern University. The university archivist Kevin Leonard conducted an oral history interview with me about student activism and student life at the university in the late 1960s when I was an undergraduate activist. We walked the campus, remembering the old and taking stock of the new. It was a "trip" in more than one sense.

We dined with old friends, starting with former UT-Dallas faculty colleague Marvin Cohen and wife Janey. He left academia after his UTD introduction for a successful career in social philanthropy in Chicago.

The next evening, we had a gourmet vegetarian dinner with Harriet Lightman, a close friend from the Newberry in 1979–1981. She recently ended her career as associate director of Northwestern University Library after beginning as a doctoral graduate in early modern French history. We had a fine breakfast with the new vice president of research and education of the Newberry Library, our old stomping grounds. This trip ended with a voyage on the high-speed ferry across Lake Michigan to visit my brother in Detroit and our friend, retired historian Mary Cayton in nearby Canton.

~~~

May 17–19, 2024, represents another point of culmination and celebration, the Expanding Literacy Studies/HJG Reunion. Approximately 40 former graduate students from three universities along with a handful of former undergraduates, close friends, and colleagues met at Ohio State for a reunion and celebration of at least four anniversaries. Conversations with former doctoral students—all currently teaching—Kelly Bradbury, Shawn Casey, Michael Harker, Nora McCook, Caitlin Ryan, and Julia Voss early in 2023 led to the mutual discovery that the upcoming year marked the following:

- 15 years since the landmark 2009 Expanding Literacy Studies International Interdisciplinary Conference for Graduate Students
- 20 years since the 2004 founding of LiteracyStudies@OSU
- 45th anniversary of The Literacy Myth (1979c, with its revised reissue 1991/2023b)
- 75th birthday celebration of HJG, Juneteenth 2024

And here I pause the paths of my 75 years, with time to get resoled and resouled. I hope that they provide at least a set of signposts for others.

# Afterword. Near Final Reflections on Literacy and Literacy Studies, 2022: Excerpts From *Searching for Literacy: The Social and Intellectual Origins of Literacy Studies*

**Abstract.** In the popular and political imaginary, literacy is synonymous with culture and progress. It exists in dizzying varieties; there are hundreds of proclaimed literacies. But literacy also resists universal transmission. Literacy's place in popular culture is ambiguous. Corporate capitalism celebrates reading and writing in consumer terms. Inclusive and useful definitions of literacy must be anchored in reading and writing across languages, symbol or sign systems, media, and domains of communication. They may be spoken, written, printed or pictorially formed, electronically produced and distributed. Literacies are interactive, dialectically related, and require translation and negotiation.

## Chapter 1. Back to Basics

In the popular and political imaginary, literacy is a *sine qua non of culture and progress, for individuals, societies, nations*.[1] It exists in dizzying varieties; there are hundreds of proclaimed literacies. But literacy also seems to resist universal transmission. The reasons commonly given are as many as they are contradictory. They range from individual to institutional and political failings (Graff and Duffy, 2007; Hamilton, 2012).

Literacy's place in popular culture is one tellingly ambiguous sign. Corporate capitalism celebrates reading and writing in normative, consumer, and durable terms—for its own benefit.

These proclamations are revealingly, though poorly, expressed. Other voices are more mixed.

In their prime time and website videos promoting a line of "Kids" pens, BIC Pens declares awkwardly and apparently without irony, "Fight for your WRITE." Tritely playing with the concept of "right," the company announces unequivocally: "Writing helps children become more confident, creative and awesome!

---

1. This material originally appeared as the first chapter in *Searching for Literacy: The Social and Intellectual Origins of Literacy Studies*, by Harvey J. Graff, 2022e, pp. 3–27, Palgrave Macmillan, (https://doi.org/10.1007/978-3-030-96981-3). It has been reproduced exactly as it appeared in its original publication without further editing. Reprinted with permission.

Writing is an important learning tool that gives children the power to share their thoughts and ideas with the world in a meaningful way. That's why BIC wants parents, teachers and caregivers to join us and Fight For Your Write!"

> Why Fight For Your Write with BIC?
>
> Join BIC on our mission to save handwriting and Fight For Your Write. Writing is an important vehicle for communication because it distinguishes us and promotes individuality. Did you know that writing is also a critical learning tool for children? Writing helps kids become better readers, boosts their confidence and sparks their creativity. Together we want to show children just how great writing can be and how great they can be![1]

But write what? Communicate what? How does writing do this? Are we even meant to take this seriously? These promotions are so badly written that they seem to parody the very arguments they make.

The bottom line is "PRODUCTS. Transform Boring Into Fun with These Amazing BIC® Products—Colorful and Bold Pens and Pencils with Personality." With no evidence, we are to believe that

> The perfect BIC® pen, pencil or marker can make a child feel inspired to write. At BIC, we understand how our products can reflect a child's personality, express what they want to become one day, or just let the world know, "Purple is my signature color." We offer so much variety and style; kids and adults will be amazed by what they find.

"Fight For Your Write," indeed.

In an age with an expert to cite on any subject, BIC's efforts to back up its claims are laughable at best.[2] The vague and unfocused nature makes these claims almost impossible to support. That provides an important clue to exaggerated estimates of the value of literacy when taken out of meaningful contexts. It is also a powerful clue to the uses and abuses of literacy—reading and writing across modes of communication and comprehension—as an object of commodification and consumption.

Is it noteworthy that BIC's claims for writing with its Kids pens are virtually the same as those of the promoters of laptops, tablets, and other electronic devices—their marketplace competitors?

Does this translate into anything more than a high-tech effort to sell low-tech pens under the thin cover of "Join us. Support our mission to save handwriting"?[3]

Without a word about the relationship to its own profitability, Scholastic, the large publisher of school-age and school-related print and digital materials, promotes "A Child's Right to Read" and an effort to "Encourage a child to Read Every Day."[4] Not surprisingly, with false personalization, it informs consumers that "Your Purchase Puts Books into the Hands of Kids."

Selling "five books that shaped your life," it asks "What's Your Bookprint?"

Even more emphatically, its deterministic formula for a better world—"Read Every Day. Lead a Better Life"—embellishes "The Reading Bill of Rights." Adopting and all but parodying the discourse of human rights used in governmental and NGO national and local literacy campaigns, this declaration is part of "Scholastic's global literacy campaign" to sell books. Breathlessly, Scholastic begins a mixed metaphorical roster of "beliefs" with this prelude:

> Today we live in a world full of digital information. Yet reading has never been more important, for we know that for young people the ability to read is the door opener to the 21st century to hold a job, to understand their world, and to know themselves. That is why we are asking you to join our Global Literacy Call to Action. We call this campaign "Read Every Day. Lead a Better Life." We are asking parents, teachers, school- and business-leaders, and the general public to support their children's right to read for a better life in the digital world of the 21st century.

Literacy is "the birthright of every child in the world as well as the pathway to succeed in school and to realize a complete life." Every child has a right to a "'textual lineage'—a reading and writing autobiography which shows that who you are is in part developed through the stories and information you've experienced." "We believe that in the 21st century, the ability to read is necessary not only to succeed but to survive—for the ability to understand information and the power of stories is the key to a life of purpose and meaning." But, apparently, not to write particularly well or to appreciate literacy in the context of actual lives.

Meanwhile, Swedish furniture and housewares giant IKEA addresses parents, pushing the power of its "bookbook" (aka product catalogue) to sell its products, including books, pens, desks, and bookcases. Its paean to the catalogue in the form of a traditional printed and bound book is meant to be poetic and amusing. The video is clever. A sweet Swedish voice announces, "Once in a while something comes along that changes the way we live, a device so simple and intuitive, using it seems almost familiar. . . . It's a bookbook."[5]

Under the heading "Books & games," IKEA also sells print: "Home improvement *books* for you, coffee table *books* for a rainy day and bedtime *books* for your favorite little bookworms . . . ." But the ad can do no better than play obviously with the terms and elements of so-called smartbooks and ebooks.

## From Sales to Performance

On other hand, a very different viewpoint emerges in rap artist Kanye West's breakthrough album. Celebrating "The College Dropout," West memorably describes poor African American young people, lacking BICs and IKEA:

> You know the kids gon' act a fool
> When you stop the programs for after-school
> And they DCFS, some of 'em dyslexic
> They favorite 50-Cent song "12 Questions"
> We scream: "rocks, blow, weed, park", see, now we smart
> We ain't retards, the way teachers thought
> Hold up, hold fast, we make more cash
> Now tell my momma I belong in that slow class
> Sad enough we on welfare
> They tryna put me on the school bus with the space for the wheelchair

As a result:

> Drug dealin' just to get by
> Stack ya' money 'til it get sky high
> (Kids, sing! Kids, sing!)
> We wasn't s'posed to make it past 25
> Joke's on you, we still alive
> Throw your hands up in the sky and say:
> "We don't care what people say."[6]

West evokes a more practical and gritty everyday reality than BIC and IKEA for a different population whose use of reading and writing connects much more closely to survival than to consumption. His world's "uses of literacy" constitute a different set of spaces (Hoggart, 1961).

No less memorably, and likely in response to West, comic and video artist Weird Al Yankovic defends good grammar and criticizes "Word Crimes." He directs us to another putative dimension of literacy. To the critics of prescriptive and inflexible grammar, who hold one reflexive definition of literacy, Weird Al was instantly anathema. But it is quite likely that he raised his voice and his fancy video technology in parody, satirizing such censures.[7] Not surprisingly, scholars missed this move. Listen:

> If you can't write in the proper way
> If you don't know how to conjugate
> Maybe you flunked that class
> And maybe now you find
> That people mock you online
> [Bridge:]
> Okay, now here's the deal
> I'll try to educate ya
> Gonna familiarize
> You with the nomenclature

You'll learn the definitions
Of nouns and prepositions
Literacy's your mission
And that's why I think it's a
[Chorus:]
Good time
To learn some grammar
Now, did I stammer
Work on that grammar
You should know when
It's "less" or it's "fewer"
Like people who were
Never raised in a sewer
I hate these word crimes
Like I could care less
That means you do care
At least a little
Don't be a moron
You'd better slow down
And use the right pronoun
Show the world you're no clown
Everybody wise up![8]

Consider the contradictions. Superficially, the clash between West and Weird Al is cavernous. The one celebrates success—of a sort—but to which reading, writing, and arithmetic may contribute in noncanonical, unschooled ways. The other promotes proper grammar and condemns orthographic and stylistic gaffes. Both are long traditions, albeit differently valued and certified as proper or not. Is it odd to ask if Yankovic might lean toward a strict literacy with some levity? By smiling at the new word games, as well as word crimes of text speak and much more, does he in effect point us in new directions?

These examples also suggest that inclusive and useful definitions of literacy must be anchored in reading *and* writing across languages, symbol or sign systems, media, and domains of communication. By *reading*, I refer to the means and modes of understanding or comprehending—that is, making meaning. And by *writing*, I refer to the means and modes of expressing or communicating meaning. Those symbols and media include but are not limited to traditional alphabetic, numeric, and visual systems; some are embodied in humanity, the physical and the constructed environment. They may be spoken, written, printed or pictorially formed, electronically produced and distributed. None exists in isolation from the others. In performance, each practice shapes the others. Literacies are interactive, dialectically related, and require translation and negotiation, as I will explain in this book.[9]

## Literacy Now

Today few subjects attract the attention or spark responses as powerful as literacy does. Claims of literacy's and illiteracy's presumed consequences surround us. Few pressing issues—whether individual and collective well-being, social welfare and security, and the state of the nation, domestic or foreign—escape association with literacy. Divisive issues of politics, and of race, class, nationality, gender, or geography constantly run up against it (Graff, 2011b).

Despite literacy's acknowledged importance, its powers on the one hand, and the dangers of its diminution, on the other hand, are taken out of context and consequently exaggerated. Literacy is seldom defined. This adds to the illusion of its efficacy and the underlying confusion (Graff, 1979, 1981a, 1981b, 1987, 1991, 1995, 2010, 2011a).

We live at an awkward and challenging moment in the history of literacy and the study of literacy. It is also a critical time for literacy as we now understand and practice it. At once, we are told relentlessly by press, pundits, and policy wonks that *literacy is declining* and the threats to civilization are dire. The indicators of decline are mixed and often far from measures of reading and writing: from school completion rates, grade levels, and diverse test scores, local, national, or international, and all but unimaginable anecdotal examples often from social media. Individual wellbeing, economic competitiveness, and national security are all at stake. The problem, it sometimes seems, is worst in the advanced societies. But to other commentators, it lies in the underdeveloping areas. We are not forced to choose among them, of course. Any such competition harms all.

At the same time, we thrive in a new era of a seemingly endless flowering of many or multiple literacies. They range from the "'new' literacies" of "new media" of visuality, screens, moving and animated images, numbers and symbols, to assertions of literacies, of some kind or other, of every imaginable subject, from aural to emotional, food, sex, culture, and countless others. And we are also told, even less clearly and coherently, that literacy, as we have known it, is irrelevant in the age of post-everything. I have compiled a list of almost five hundred "literacies" that I have seen mentioned *in print* (Graff, 2011b).

No wonder confusion is rife. In this context, it is not surprising that a newly proclaimed field of literacy studies—home for almost three or four decades of an avowedly revisionist "new literacy studies"—seems to lack direction (Graff, 1979; Street, 1984; Barton, 2006). Is it ironic that a field of inquiry rooted in fundamental dichotomies—literacy versus illiteracy and literacy versus orality; autonomous conceptions of literacy as universal versus ideologically driven approaches to literacy; global versus local manifestations of literacy—veers back and forth between them?

Literacy studies never quite breaks free of dominant presumptions or stakes out fundamentally new grounds for understanding. Despite repeated recognitions of the ideological nature of the subject (sometimes termed "the bias of literacy,") prominently by my own book *The Literacy Myth* in 1979 and Brian Street's *Literacy in Theory and Practice* in 1984, the study and understanding of literacy remains riddled with unacknowledged ideological assumptions. The most pervasive and persistent pivots around a "great divide," as Goody and Watt (1968) conceived it in "The Consequences of Literacy" (originally published in 1963).

It remains unfortunate that Street's important argument that different views of literacy tend to understand it as "autonomous" as opposed to "ideological" obscured the fact that both the "autonomous" or universal, ahistorical, and uncontextual *and* the "ideological" approaches are themselves riddled with ideological assumptions. The reigning assumptions and their confusions are displayed, for example, from UNESCO to the *Cambridge Handbook of Literacy* (Olson and Torrance, 2009), and the United States National Center for Family Literacy, which despite its name is a private charitable foundation. Given the importance of literacy and its complicated dimensions, the power of assumptions is inescapable. But they need to be taken into account consistently for honest and useful scholarship and subsequent policy and practice.

As an academic, and also a public interest, literacy studies obsessively proclaims its novelty. But as this book shows, *it is not new*. Interest in, studying, speculating, and worrying about literacy has a long and formative history. To an unappreciated extent, recent literacy studies are also rooted fundamentally in its own disciplinary and multidisciplinary past. It campaigns relentlessly for recognition, identification, institutional location, and funding. It also has striking applied and commercial elements. It is tied, at least in part, to quests for national economic and cultural superiority. And it promotes its commitment to making a better world. And yet, it ignores and neglects to build on its own heritage and genealogy.

At the same time, literacy studies neglects disciplinary and interdisciplinary relationships of its recent founding and to which it seeks to contribute—and their conflicts and divides. This derives from and simultaneously results in *neglect of its own history*, long and short term. Major divisions, and with them, missed opportunities, often persist powerfully. These include problems of parts and wholes, and definitions, discourse, and relationships. Promotion and exaggeration, and gross comparisons or distinction making, resulting in what I have defined as a *literacy myth* (a well-known misconception), are rampant. In repeating claims for its importance, literacy's students and proponents too often either or both implicitly or explicitly undercut their own efforts. This is one among many contradictions (Graff and Duffy, 2007; Graff, 1979, 2010, 2012, 2014, 2015).

## Searching for Literacy

*Searching for Literacy: The Social and Intellectual Origins of Literacy Studies* explores these issues from an original critical, historical, and comparative perspective. Informed by and following from my series of studies in the history of literacy and my latest book, *Undisciplining Knowledge: Interdisciplinarity in the*

*Twentieth Century*, it asks how the study and understanding of literacy and literacies have developed (Graff, 2015). But it also inquires more broadly into what we might call the social and historical understanding of the production and organization of knowledge with literacy as its focus.

In this book, I argue that the condition of literacy studies is more expected than ironic or paradoxical. That does not lessen its consequences. It is one result of the failure of a fragmented field of study to learn from its own history, on one hand, and to seek out critical relationships between and among approaches to literacy and different modes of reading and writing, on the other hand. It also speaks to the fundamental power of what I termed "the literacy myth," the exaggerated expectations of the power of literacy—that is, the ability to read and write—by itself (Graff, 1979; see also Graff, 2010, 2011a).

These problems matter. Why they matter should, I hope, be obvious. Literacy, I assert, is too important to be left to its proponents alone, from compositionists and digital specialists to pedagogues, on one hand, and to policy pundits, development economists and sociologists, and purveyors of books and other accoutrements of literacy and schooling, on the other. The evidence, however masked and muddled, is clear: literacy *alone* does not lead to development, health, and progress, either for individuals or for society. If literacy is to be viewed as a human right, a recent call to arms, then it must follow, or at least be inseparable from, the rights to life, shelter, safety, nourishment, and basic well-being. In other words, literacy must always be viewed as *one among other* fundamentals and *always* in interaction with other key factors.

Too often that is not the case, and the costly failures surround us. Many axiomatic formulas or prescriptions simply do not take this basic understanding and its overwhelming logical and empirical support into account. It has proven too easy (and on occasion too profitable) to do so. With some sympathy, I point to the pronouncements and programs of UNESCO, especially Education for All and Literacy for Life (see Arnove and Graff, 2008). With less sympathy, I point to BIC or IKEA or those who compete to supply textbooks and laptops to the world. When the focus shifts to conceptualizing relationships, much changes. That is a necessary but very tardy step.

What is to be done? This book is not a guide to policy. Rather it is a critique and a series of (admittedly incomplete) steps on the road to revisioning literacy *and* the study of literacy in relationship to each other. Some would call my concerns epistemological, how we understand, how we know. My concern lies principally with literacy and what has come to be called literacy studies, a very loose cluster of diverse interests in literacy and literacies of all kinds within universities, government agencies, and nongovernment organizations, a disorganized set of topics and researchers across disciplines and departments with aspirations to both disciplinarity and interdisciplinarity, recognition, and organization. In significant part, I am interested in the historical sociology, organization, and production of knowledge (Graff, 2001, 2011a, 2015).

My method in *Searching for Literacy* combines criticism and historical understanding. In inquiring into the roots and webs of interests in literacy over time and across fields of study, I probe understandings and rediscover leads, openings, and understandings that have been lost, for example, from linguistic anthropology; psychology; literature and composition; science, numeracy, and graphics; and movement and performance to history, in chapters that focus on these fundamental subjects. Despite a rhetoric and some genuine efforts at interdisciplinarity and integration, more than a century of disciplinarization and departmentalization has led to substantial separation and its deleterious consequences. Among the questions asked in this book is how we may learn from the past to fashion new understandings of the present and new paths to the future.

## Literacy Studies Past and Future

Literacy studies' overarching *and underlying discourse and assumptions link it inseparably to the presumption of change, progress, and advancement, whether of individuals or larger collectivities. Dominant thinking about literacy is governed by an image—an epistemology, if you will—of change. Theories, expectations, metaphors, and analogies almost always have this set of associations at their core. The linkage dates at least from the Greek classical era. The modern heritage or legacy is overwhelmingly positive. That set of presumed "consequences," following Jack Goody and Ian Watt, or "implications," as Goody imprecisely revised his formula, has long dominated approaches and interpretations, obscuring more complicated or differing relationships (Goody and Watt,* 1968; Goody, 1968). Both progressive and conservative proponents agree on this, even when their versions of the "proper" acquisition, practices, and uses of literacy differ sharply.[10]

Closer, critical examination and shifts in emphasis reveal a different set of relationships and promote other understandings. The image is not wrong but *partial*, incomplete, distorting *when taken by itself*. Literacy's uses and impacts are also aligned with continuities and control. The three dominating millennial thrusts across literacy's long history are government, religion, and trade or exchange, and their developing needs. These forces contradict or, often, reshape literacy's linkages with progressive change. In a few words, literacy's impacts are dialectical and contradictory, seldom simple or unmediated.

Similarly, literacy has at least as often been associated with the life of groups as with the individualistic legacy that dominates our powerful inherited images. On the one hand, we must focus on the *collective* as well as individual uses of literacy, as people throughout the ages have done in their everyday and more exceptional practices. On the other hand, both the collective and the individual dimensions influence how the other acquires, uses, and is affected by reading and writing. Neither exists alone. Consider schooling or religious or governmental practices, or popular reading culture, or the collective aspects of artistic and scientific endeavors. How the interrelationships and their balances shift is a matter for questions and study at any point in time or place. Simple images quickly give way.

Dominant images emphasize literacy for liberation (which can be quite restrictive) and individual advancement, and less often for collective progress (or conservative reaction). The hugely simplified temporal association of classical Athenian democracy with the incomplete literacy of male citizens (and the distortions of the search for confirming evidence) is an epochal case in point (Harris, 1989). However incomplete an association, it stimulated a powerful, indeed determinative influence and set of expectations over the past two millennia. The approximate temporal relationships and seminal (but perhaps unrepresentative) individual examples of legendary Greek and Roman thinkers and (sometimes) writers prompted a parallel association between the emergence of Greek philosophy, drama, and science following (by centuries) the development of the Greek alphabet (Goody and Watt, 1968; Ong, 1958). Eric Havelock, (1963) and his uncritical followers see the remaking of the human mind by the invention and spread of a Greek alphabet. Similar patterns echo in the images of the impact of print and now electronic media.

Although scholars of India and China point to the breakthroughs in science and other intellectual domains with nonwestern alphabets and probably lower levels of general literacy, the linkages with literacy in the establishment and operation of the Greek and Roman empires suggest greater ambiguities (Gough, 1968; Harris, 1989). Control and restriction are as much a part of the legacies and uses of literacy as liberation and progress, as Paulo Freire powerfully reminds us in his seminal work. That confusion goes hand in hand with those who conflate the impacts of restricted or limited and mass literacy, for example, on intellectual or scientific-technological advances or even the circulation of information (Clanchy, 1993; Eisenstein, 1979; Grafton, 1980; Grafton et al., 2002; Harris, 1989; Houston, 2002; Vincent, 2000).

Recognizing the ongoing relationships among the media, especially but not only the oral, on one side, and the written, printed, and electronic, on the other side, adds to a transformed understanding. Instead of the ahistorical and anti-human notion of world-redefining (and formulaic) shifts *from* one dominant medium (or communicative-cognitive regime) *to* another—quintessentially the oral to the written and onward—the oral *never* loses its importance and life-shaping impact. Nor does writing in whatever form of performance, reproduction, distribution, or transmission totally replace it. Too often understandings of literacy's development and impact take the formula of a transition or transformation from X to Y, often if not always in the form of a dichotomy. The following chapters explore these complications.

Despite more than a millennium of constructs of a dichotomous remaking of the known world, speech across diverse media and writing across other domains continue to interact, shaping and reshaping each other. It is no accident that ethnographers never cease to rediscover that people still talk . . . and then pat themselves on the back for their perspicacity and powers of observation. Multiple, multimodal, and "new" literacies call out for comparative study; that is, in relationship and interaction with each other, as they are actually used.

Remaking literacy studies requires an adjustable, multi-focal historical lens. Often longer term, it moves between the wide angle and the close focus, the larger and the local. It refuses to dichotomize apparent oppositions that turn out to be critical relationships when examined directly. Similarly, it requires the study and assimilation of historical and contemporary investigations to replace the appropriation and repetition of images, illusions, and icons. Seemingly powerful and formulaic short-hands—from "oral to literate," "the domestication of the savage mind," or "the world on paper," with scant regard for source criticism, contextualization, or representativeness can stand no longer. The deeply rooted faith in the power of literacy itself must be understood as itself a historical development. The power and impact, along with the quantity and quality of literacy—among the media—need to be demonstrated, and not simply presumed and equated with expected outcomes. Powerful but incomplete and misleading dichotomies must be replaced with complicated narratives.

Literacy and literacy studies are best understood with more attention to a longer chronological span of intellectual and socio-cultural development. It demands a broader, more dynamic focus on literacy's place and play among a wide array of disciplines and institutional locations. Subfields in disciplines or interdisciplines that deal with literacy include reading, writing, anthropology, child and human development, cognitive studies, formal and sociolinguistics, comparative and development studies, communication and media studies including popular culture studies, science and mathematics, and the visual and performing arts. How seldom they address one another. Cross-, multi-, and interdisciplinarity are among the grounds for comparative studies of literacy.

Literacy studies also suffers from an "internalist" bias. How easily literacy is conceptualized as an "independent variable" in the tradition of Brian Street's autonomous model. Once there is literacy, all else follows—more or less. The need for study dramatically declines.

"External" factors and developments—sometimes listed as affecting levels of literacy, most famously by Lawrence Stone (1969) in a roster of seven elements—demand more systematic (and less random or superficial) attention.[11] Social, cultural, demographic, and political economic forces—such as wartime demands or anticipated economic or civic needs, consequences of global cross-cultural contacts and colonialism, the cycles of the "discovery" of new social problem—all combine in fact and perceptions, often with contradictions, and with shifting currents within and across disciplines. Sometimes they stimulate changing views. Yet, studies of highly localized, limited populations, times, and places, and ecological macrocorrelations of highly aggregated, often ambiguous quantitative data are seldom compared or contrasted. Causes and consequences are seldom identified or clarified. In the context of universities and their organization of knowledge, those shifts in interest and approach should lead to criticism and comparison, different assertions, and sometimes institutional articulations both within and outside the boundaries of departments or divisions that take the name of interdisciplinarity. Literacy's relationships, for example, with demographic behavior, economic performance, or political participation are among the telling cases in point.

## Historicizing Literacy Studies

A more complete and useful approach to literacy studies begins no later than the 1920s and 1930s, not the 1970s and 1980s. It looks back carefully to the period spanning the modernizing currents of mid-eighteenth century through the early twentieth century. It embraces a longer glance back to the Renaissance and also classical antiquity. It locates in historical context the dynamic building blocks for our expectations, understandings (including theories and policies), institutions, and expectations that culminate in modern literacies and their complications, and literacy studies, the principal disciplines and where and when they cross.

Modern arrangements and judgments, typically institutionalized in distinct fields of study, grew from the foundational currents of Renaissance rediscoveries of scholarship and knowledge and Enlightenment emphases on human malleability, perfectionism, learning capabilities, environmentalism, and institutionalism. They were partly reinterpreted by Romanticism's deeply divided recognition of the power and significance of the "other," the alien or primitive within ourselves and in "strangers," both within the modernizing West and in "newly discovered" regions. Questions about language—and its media and forms—and social order lay at the core of both.

The beginnings and foundations of literacy studies also lay in "civilization's" encountering many "Wild Children" (*enfants sauvages*), noble or savage, and South Sea islanders and other indigenous peoples whom explorers confronted around the world. The reading and writing of the "primitives"—across media and modes of understanding—was sometimes recognized. Inseparable were missionaries (whose work in creating alphabets and written languages initially to "translate" the Bible in aid of their proselytizing is fundamentally a part of literacy studies and linguistics); and conquerors, colonizers, and colonists. They all deployed early (and later) modern notions of Western literacy and its expected influences in their efforts at expansion, "conquest," and domesticating and elevating the primitive and different. Herein lay often missed points of contact between psychology and anthropology, among other fields.

Then and later, at home and abroad the poor, "minorities," immigrants, and others became more threatening than those farther afield. In anthropology and the arts, the primitive and the oral were grounds for celebration at times, complicating positive associations of literacy and negative associations of illiteracy. Strong currents from the Enlightenment and Romanticism intertwined, sometimes contradicting but sometimes supporting expectations about progress and modern development—and their connections with literacy (written culture). Herein lay, in part, the origins of modern social science, the arts, and literature.

From earlier eras, including the Renaissance and classical antiquity, came, haltingly at first, the conviction that writing, and the reading of it, were, at least in some significant circumstances, superior to other means of communication, especially the oral. On one hand, this was a functional development, but, on the other hand, personal and eventually collective cognitive change might follow, some persons of influence thought. So commenced early literacy studies, its theories and institutions.

The first general uses of reading and writing derived from the needs of religion, government, and commerce. Slowly there developed a faith in the powers of formal instruction in places called schools, initially for the relatively few, primarily boys but with informal tutelage for others including girls. Some agendas stressed socialization for citizenship and its correlates. Other agendas emphasized literacy in terms of useful or necessary practices or abilities, from clerks to clerics, rhetors to rulers.

Over time, places for instruction expanded to include many more and to focus especially on the young. This was an epochal conjuncture, with a powerful influence on future generations, and the realms of learning. In these formulations, literacy stood at the center of training that embraced social attitudes and control, and civic morality, along with at least rudimentary intellectual practices, and training in skills for productive contributions to economy, polity, and society. The tools began with simplified alphabets that helped to link signs and sounds to words and sentences, and expanded to include paper, pens, and various means of reproducing and circulating texts that were first handwritten and later printed. The superiority of technology and the inferiority of the "unlettered" stood as certainties, framing constructions of literacy. Literacy's story, right and wrong, came to occupy the center (though often implicitly) of the rise of civilization and progress in the West and over time the rest of the world.

These elements became inseparable as they joined capitalism's efforts to remake the world—and the word, written, printed, and reproduced—in the image of the marketplace and its institutions (with other images and sounds). Equally inseparable was the quest to remake the young, in particular, for the strange new world. These efforts mark, and also serve as representations of, literacy in the traditions that emerged to study and understand literacy from the Renaissance (or earlier) forward. They also stimulated uses of literacy, in conjunction with other media and collective action, for resistance and reform.

Not surprisingly, the development and institutionalization of disciplines in the nineteenth- and twentieth-century Western university incorporated the understandings of literacy to which they were the heirs, especially but not only in the social sciences—anthropology, linguistics, psychology, sociology, economics, politics—and the humanities—classics, history, literature, philosophy. Early relationships resisted efforts at change. The resulting disciplinary fragmentation not only contributed to efforts to build interdisciplinary literacy studies, but also limits them. They underwrite the many contradictions—what I call "the literacy myth," for one—in the place of literacy in Western cultures, and the lives of many persons yesterday and today.

## Disciplining and Undisciplining Literacy Studies

Possibilities and limits on opportunities for novel understanding stem from the interplay within and across what I call "disciplinary clusters." (The humanities, arts, social sciences, and basic sciences constitute major disciplinary clusters.) No less important is the sometimes very dynamic interplay—critical and complementary—between disciplines. Of this, the key disciplines of anthropology, linguistics, and psychology provide powerful examples. Among them, orality and oral literature, everyday and privileged writing practices, the ubiquity of "reading" across multiple media, and the search for cognitive and noncognitive "implications" of literacy are telling. So, too, is literacy's active presence as values, ideology, and cultural, economics, and political capital. Destabilizing times can become opportunities to advance or to fall from favor for disciplinary approaches, and moments for interdisciplinary movements—and, importantly, literacy and literacies. These are the focus of this book, and the stimuli for writing it.

For literacy studies, across the past two centuries at least, one of the most powerful forces has been the fear, and often the certainty, that literacy is declining (or not rising), and that with it, families, morality, social order, progress, and socioeconomic development are also declining. This accompanied one of the most momentous transformations in the history of literacy and its study: from a premodern order in which literacy was feared and (partly) restricted, to a more modern order in which illiteracy (or literacy gained and practiced outside of formal institutional controls) constitutes a great threat.

When taken comparatively, and further heightened by international conflict or competition, social disorder and division, international migration of "aliens," rising fertility and mortality, failure of "human capital" to grow, and similar circumstances, literacy levels all become flashpoints for study and action to reverse the dreaded tide. Schools and popular culture attract attention which has in turn the potential to propel disciplinary action and conflict, and, sometimes, interdisciplinary efforts.

The apparently endless "crisis" of literacy in the mid- to late twentieth and early twenty-first centuries is inseparable from Cold War and more recent international anxieties, global economic restructuring and collateral social and cultural change, communicative and media transformation, and both new and persisting inequalities. Seemingly unprecedented "social problems" become calls for and stimulants of interdisciplinary "solutions." Literacy campaigns stir passions in the underdeveloping and developed worlds. Literacy's roles as either or both causes or consequences are very tricky to unravel, a complication in literacy studies' development.

For literacy studies, these complications often impinge on one or another of the "great divides" prominent among approaches that see literacy—almost by its very nature—as universal, unmediated, and transformative in its impact (the autonomous model). Often cited are reading or writing as the "technology of the intellect," the power of the Greek alphabet, the impact of print, cognitive shifts from alphabets, writing, or reading, and the like. Constructing this tradition of study and understanding—comparatively—was relatively uncomplicated. In recent decades, however, others have emphasized increasingly the socio-cultural influences and contextual effects from literacy as acquisition, practice, and use. Among the elements stressed are psychological theories, schools and other environments, families and communities, cultures of practice, and practice and use of reading and writing among media old and new. The reorientation remains incomplete.

Literacy studies' paths are revealing. In the second half of the twentieth century, in conjunction with other disciplines and interdisciplines, literacy studies has taken social, contextual, cognitive, linguistic, and historical, among other "turns." With the turns came the adoption of signifying French theorist "godfathers" from Lucien Lévy-Bruhl and Claude Lévi-Strauss to Pierre Bourdieu and Bruno Latour. These developments at times interact with and deepen conflicts among disciplines and promote interest in interdisciplinary resolution. The turns, with inadequate testing and criticism, become dead ends.

Recent years witness an emphasis on the everyday and the practical, including the concept of practice itself. This has led to an incomplete and halting but revealing effort to overturn the dominance of grand theories that stressed the universal importance of the written over the oral, the printed over the written, the literate over the unlettered and untutored—consequences and implications of literacy. Practice and context, explored in a variety of circumstances and traditions, partly supplanted presumptions of the unmediated powers and advantages of literacy.

In part, recent literacy studies' emergence stemmed from perceptions of the inadequacy of earlier conceptualizations and presumptions, the search for new methods and sources on which to base a major revision, and reactions to it.

Literacy studies continues to struggle with foundational dichotomies—the making of myths and images—between oral and literate, writing and print, print and electronic, and literacy as transformative. They continue to guide and divide opinion and orient studies. Consequently, the long-standing neglect of rich research on orality and oral literature to which this book returns is almost as much a mark of the limits of many interdisciplinary endeavors as of the power of disciplines. The proponents of the New Literacy Studies have not reclaimed Albert Lord, Milman Parry, or Lev Vygotsky, among others. The persistence and importance of orality is regularly rediscovered across disciplines, as are the newly fashionable "multiple literacies," new emphasis on multilinguality or translation, and curiosity about visuality. None is new. Nor are the collective foundations of reading, writing, and "written culture." The heterogeneity of constructions of the cognitive domain also plagues literacy studies, another instructive matter of connections.

Among the most important—and least appreciated—critical elements are the absolutely crucial connections among myths and images—historical and contemporary—*and* expectations, and the ways that they are embedded in and come to undergird attitudes, policies, institutions, and judgments. To deal with this set of world-shaping conjunctures, we must cast our nets widely. We need to study literacy and literacies in new ways in their widest living circumstances and relationships, lived and written, experienced and recorded.

It is seemingly easy to study writing and "print." But it has been so hard to study reading and writing as practiced across media and modes of understanding and expression, especially in their formative and fundamental relationships to conceptions, ideologies, policies, institutions, and expectations.

~~~

Striving for recognition, literacy studies occupies ambiguous ground, both disciplinarily and interdisciplinarily. In part, this is a question of location. But it is also a question of status. The "rise" of literacy studies, part of its emergence and development, contributes to its presence in many academic departments and disciplines. This holds for education, the social sciences, and the humanities, but also (to a lesser extent) the sciences, medicine, public health, the law, and business. This pattern is problematic in some critical respects. It is dis- and unorganized. In the pantheon of disciplines, centers of interest in literacy studies usually do not rank highly. That the study of literacy, for reasons good and bad, is often seen as basic or elementary does not boost its standing. By reputation, it is often viewed as inseparable from schools or colleges of education.

Proclaimed interdisciplinary literacy studies at times become promotional labels: new, relevant, sexy—in academic terms—and appealing for applied and practical reasons to citizens, governments, and corporations, from "how to" to publishing texts and other aids. Perceptions of crises or at least serious problems with popular literacy abilities add to this mix. Such promotion, which is less problematic in professional schools than other institutions, aims to benefit programs and their home departments, colleges, or universities. It also can provoke negative reactions (Graff, 2015).

In addition to education, the social sciences of anthropology, linguistics, and psychology are often the homes of literacy studies and the New Literacy Studies. At one time or another, each of these disciplines has claimed the status of a science, applied if not always "pure" or "basic." Psychology, followed by linguistics, exhibits the greatest ambitions, with strong interests in reading, writing, development, and cognition. All three are divided between scientific and cultural, quantitative and qualitative, cognitive and material, hard and soft orientations. All three stress contemporary and sometimes comparative relevance, usually reserving the strongest claims for the perspectives, methods, and theories of their own discipline, even when also proclaiming their interdisciplinarity. Practitioners in these fields often occupy central places in interdisciplinary literacy centers, programs, or concentrations in Education. Claiming attention, they remain divided and disconnected from historical perspectives. Each is the subject of a chapter in this book.

*Searching for Literacy: The Origins of Literacy Studies* begins an applied intellectual, cultural, and institutional history, taking literacy studies back to its pre-disciplinary and disciplinary foundations: identifying and probing its roots. Relationships are sought, and with them, clarifications and revisions, new beginnings and steps toward a different future for literacy studies and fundamental literacies. It is an experiment in the social history of knowledge.

Toward that end, in the following chapters, I explore literacy and literacy studies in the disciplinary and interdisciplinary domains of linguistics, psychology, anthropology, literature-reading-writing, arts and sciences, and history. Education is highlighted throughout. I probe both achievements and limits within a historical context of the history of literacy and the history of literacy in the disciplines. In searching for the origins of literacy studies critically, historically, and comparatively, my goal lies in the intellectual and practical reconstruction of the field of literacy studies.

## Notes

1. See http://bicfightforyourwrite.com.
2. See the thin "report" from Hanover Research entitled "The Importance of Teaching Handwriting in the 21st Century," with footnotes mainly to newspaper articles, on the BIC website. No specific documentation is provided.
3. On the history of handwriting and its ideologies, see Thornton, *Handwriting in America* (1996).
4. See http://www.scholastic.com/readeveryday.
5. See www.youtube.com/watch?v=MOXQ07nURs0.
6. See http://genius.com/albums/Kanye-west/The-college-dropout.
7. See http://www.youtube.com/watch?v=8GvoH-vP0Dc.
8. See http://www.azlyrics.com/lyrics/weirdalyankovic/wordcrimes.html.
9. Graff and Duffy (2007) elaborate: "We define literacy here not in terms of values, mentalities, generalized knowledge, or decontextualized quantitative measures. Rather, literacy is defined as basic or primary levels of reading and writing and their analogies across different media, activities make possible by a technology or a set of techniques for decoding and reproducing printed materials, such as alphabets, syllabaries, pictographs, and other systems, which themselves are created and used in specific historical and material contexts. Only by grounding definitions of literacy in specific, qualified, and historical particulars can we avoid conferring upon it the status of myth" (Graff, 2011a, 37).

10. Full references to Goody's subsequent writing and the debates over the "Goody thesis" appear in Chap. 3.
11. Compare Stone, "Literacy and Education in England" (1969) with Schofield, "Measurement of Literacy in Pre-industrial England" (1968). Schofield criticized the very general nature of Stone's factors, which ranged from religion to stratification, but was more concerned about primary sources and literacy's role in economic development.

## References

Arnove, Robert F., and Harvey J. Graff, eds. (2008) *National Literacy Campaigns and Movements: Historical and Comparative Perspectives.* New Brunswick, N.J.: Transaction.

Barton, David. (2006) *Literacy: An Introduction to the Ecology of Written Language.* Oxford: Blackwell.

Clanchy, Michael T. (1993) *From Memory to Written Record: England, 1066–1307.* 2d ed. Oxford: Blackwell.

Eisenstein, Elizabeth. (1979) *The Printing Press as An Agent of Change: Communications and Cultural Transformations in Early Modern Europe.* 2 vols. Cambridge: Cambridge University Press.

Goody, Jack. (1968) "Introduction: The Implications of Literacy," *Literacy in Traditional Societies*, ed. Jack Goody. Cambridge: Cambridge University Press, 1–26.

Goody, Jack, and Ian Watt. (1968) "The Consequences of Literacy," in Jack Goody, ed., *Literacy in Traditional Societies*, ed. Goody. Cambridge: Cambridge University Press, 27–68.

Gough, Kathleen. (1968) "Implications of literacy in traditional China and India," in *Literacy in Traditional Societies*, ed. Goody. Cambridge: Cambridge University Press, 69–84.

Graff, Harvey J. (1979) *The Literacy Myth: Literacy and Social Structure in the Nineteenth-Century City.* New York and London: Academic Press.

———. (1981a) *Literacy in history: An Interdisciplinary Research Bibliography.* New York: Garland.

———, ed. (1981b) *Literacy and Social Development in the West.* Cambridge: Cambridge University Press.

———. (1987) *The Legacies of Literacy: Continuities and Contradictions in Western Society and Culture.* Bloomington: Indiana University Press.

———. (1991) *The Literacy Myth*, with new introduction. New Brunswick, N.J.: Transaction.

———. (1995) *The Labyrinths of Literacy: Reflections on Literacy Past and Present*, rev. and exp. ed. Pittsburgh: University of Pittsburgh Press.

———. (2001) "The Shock of the 'New Histories': Social Science Histories and historical literacies. Presidential Address, Social Science History Association, 2000," *Social Science History*, 25: 483–533.

———. (2010) "*The Literacy Myth* at Thirty," *Journal of Social History*, 43: 635–661.

———. (2011a) *Literacy Myths, Legacies, and Lessons: New Studies on Literacy.* New Brunswick, N.J.: Transaction.

———. (2011b) "Many Literacies: Reading Signs of the Times," in *Literacy Myths, Legacies, and Lessons: New Studies on Literacy*, ed. Graff. New Brunswick, N.J.: Transaction, 15–33.
———. (2012) "Literacy Studies and Interdisciplinary Studies: Reflections on History and Theory," in *Valences of interdisciplinarity: Theory, practice, pedagogy*, ed. Ralph Foshay. Cultural Dialectics Series. Edmonton, Alberta: AU/Athabasca University Press, 273–307
———. (2014) "Epilogue: Literacy Studies and Interdisciplinary studies with Notes on the Place of Deborah Brandt" in *Literacy, Economy, and Power: Writing and Research after Literacy in American Lives*, ed. Julie Nelson Christoph, John Duffy, Eli Goldblatt, Nelson Graff, Rebecca Nowacek, and Bryan Trabold. Carbondale: Southern Illinois University Press, 202–226.
———. (2015) *Undisciplining Knowledge: Interdisciplinarity in the Twentieth century*. Baltimore: Johns Hopkins University Press.
———., and John Duffy. (2007) "The Literacy Myth," *Encyclopedia of Language and Education*, vol. 2, *Literacy*, ed. Brian Street; Nancy Hornberger, general editor. Berlin and New York: Springer, 41–52.
Grafton, Anthony T. (1980) "The Importance of Being Printed," *Journal of Interdisciplinary History*, 11: 265–286.
———, Elizabeth L. Eisenstein, and Adrian Johns. (2002) "How Revolutionary Was the Print Revolution?" *American Historical Review*, 107: 84–128.
Hamilton, Mary. (2012). *Literacy and the politics of representation*. London: Routledge.
Harris, William V. (1989) *Ancient Literacy*. Cambridge, Mass.: Harvard University Press.
Havelock, Eric A. (1963) *Preface to Plato*. Cambridge, Mass.: Belknap Press.
Hoggart, Richard. (1961) *The Uses of Literacy: Changing Patterns in English Mass Culture*. Boston: Beacon.
Houston, R. A. (2002) *Literacy in Early Modern Europe: Culture and Education, 1500–1800*. 2d ed. London: Longman.
Olson, David R., and Nancy Torrance, eds. (2009) *The Cambridge Handbook of Literacy*. Cambridge: Cambridge University Press.
Ong, Walter. (1958) *Ramus, Method, and the Decay of Dialogue*. Cambridge, Mass.: Harvard University Press.
Schofield, Roger S. (1968) "The Measurement of Literacy in Pre-industrial England," in Jack Goody, ed., *Literacy in Traditional Societies*, ed. Jack Goody. Cambridge: Cambridge University Press, 311–325.
Stone, Lawrence. (1969) "Literacy and Education in England, 1640–1900," *Past & Present* 42: 69–139.
Street, Brian. (1984) *Literacy in Theory and Practice*. Cambridge: Cambridge University Press.
Thornton, Tamara Plakins. (1996) *Handwriting in America: A Cultural History*. New Haven: Yale University Press.
Vincent, David. (2000) *The Rise of Mass Literacy: Reading and Writing in Modern Europe* Cambridge: Polity Press.

# Epilogue. Many Paths, Many Futures

**Abstract.** To advance constructively, theoretically, empirically, and humanely, literacy studies needs to be framed as historical, comparative, and critical. Literacy studies scholars should stop congratulating themselves and end their sometimes reckless pursuit and celebration of the "new." In many ways, literacy studies should learn from, though not return to, its roots. I propose five paths to revised, renewed literacy studies.

## Literacy and Literacies Are Relational and Dialectical

The conceptualization and investigation of interrelationships must replace the presumption of dichotomies and divides.[1] The explosion of many, multi-, and multiple literacies without an explicit search for their relationships, connections, and associations, including their dialectical shaping and reshaping of one another, jeopardizes both the original breakthroughs and risks the loss of recognizable forms of literacy in theory and practice. We must trace relationships among literacies and languages across media and modes of comprehension and expression, from the alphabetic to other symbolic, visual, spatial, embodied, and performative.

## Historical Awareness Is Fundamental

Conceptions and practices of literacies are historically constructed, established, institutionalized, revised, and transmitted. This awareness of the direct and indirect, explicit and implicit, persistence of theories and expectations should inform scholars' analysis of what is new and what is, instead, the familiar presented in a new guise. Similarly, it moderates the usual overemphasis on change and underestimation of the power of continuities.

## Context Gives Meaning to Literacy and Creates the Ground for Its Study and Practice

The most effective path to avoid the conundrums and contradictions that result from formulaic notions of progress and decline in the historical study of literacy lies in the specification of context. Fundamentally, literacy has no meaning outside of distinct temporal and spatial locations, which are neither local nor global but are defined by their connections to and differences from other settings.

---

1. This material originally appeared as the epilogue in *Searching for Literacy: The Social and Intellectual Origins of Literacy Studies*, by Harvey J. Graff, 2022e, pp. 271–275, Palgrave Macmillan, (https://doi.org/10.1007/978-3-030-96981-3). It has been reproduced as it appeared in its original publication. Reprinted with permission.

## Translation Is Inseparably Intertwined with Matters of Literacy

Literacy involves making and communicating meaning across media and modes of understanding and expression from one person or set of persons to others via the symbol and sign systems that constitute languages. Acts of reading and writing that cross time and space and link disparate groups are usefully viewed in terms of the theory and practice of translation. This recognition facilitates placing literacy in its proper comparative communicative contexts. No less importantly, it reduces the need to invent redundant neologisms such as transliterate, translingual, and transnational, which proliferate the varieties of literacies and segregate rather than interrelate them. This path also promotes learning from the wide range of theories and practices of translation and the critical distinctions they offer.

## Negotiation Provides an Especially Human Approach to the Study and Practice of Literacy and Literacies

In recent years, literacy studies scholars have sought new concepts and metaphors for reading, writing, and beyond. In a critical discussion of hybrid literacies, Elizabeth Moje mentions the transcendence of either/or binaries via third-space or "thirdness" as one articulation with respect to identities and locations. After reviewing alternative terms, Moje favors navigation as a "term of distinction." "The concept of navigating thus acknowledges the roles of space, time, and context in how people engage in literate practice or enact identities in a new way that hybridity or hybrid literacies cannot" (Moje et al., 2008, 366). Moje's primary focus falls on teaching and learning in a relatively formal and normative sense.[1]

My focus is broader; it aims to include but go beyond schooling. For that reason, I find the concept, theory, practice, metaphor, and notion of negotiation more fitting, flexible, relational, and deeply human than notions of navigation or hybridity. It parallels translation. Negotiation is not deterministic, essentialist, limited, or oriented toward a finite goal; it is more adaptive and can be individual or group-centered. If a person can navigate as part the process of negotiation, the term recognizes the agency as well as the constraints and contradictions, of leaders and learners, their choices and options, experiential learning by doing amidst the give and take of the widest variety of contexts or environments. It embraces both individual and collective, formal and informal activities. I believe it is more amenable to exploring and practicing a dialectical interrelational approach to multiple literacies across different media and modes of understanding and communication.

Anne Haas Dyson (1989, 2003) offers the fullest demonstration of negotiation in the development of literacy in her study of elementary school learners in Oakland, California. Dyson's pioneering use of the concept of negotiation is richly suggestive. Although I developed and adopted the term developed independently, this concurrence shows its potential. We learn from Dyson's example and her description of how young people recontextualize across media and modes of understanding and expression.

Following her interest in how youngsters "tinker with drawn and written worlds" (1989, 76), Dyson shows how they negotiate social compromises among themselves and the styles and genres they use to move between their media sources. She portrays an elementary school student "negotiating among his imaginary, social, and experiential worlds" (182) and "negotiating between symbolic media: visual and verbal magic" (186) as they developed and changed. In the process, these first and second graders "renegotiated the relationship between drawing and writing." Manuel, a first grader, learned "to coordinate his pictures and his texts more closely, not by making art notes but by finding words for visual images without abandoning narrative action." He "worked to bring his drawn and written art closer together, capturing the physical beauty of his pictures in his texts" (186). "In his search, Manuel also kept in mind the language of the story he was developing. He was creating visual art, but he was working within the tension between language, on the one hand, and line, color, and shape, on the other" (197). "Discovering a way to bring his own visual sense and his reflective style into his dramatic texts would contribute to Manuel's emergence as an acknowledged artist—a social star—in the second grade" (183).

Negotiation claims a central place in new studies of literacy, I suggest.

Following these and other paths, literacy studies, old and new, may change for the better.

Why does it matter?

That is a question I ask each of us to ponder and to answer for ourselves and together. I quote the Norwegian scholar Johan Galtung:

> What would happen if the whole world became literate? Answer: not so very much, for the world is by and large structured in such a way that it is capable of absorbing the impact. But if the whole world consisted of literate, autonomous, critical, constructive people, capable of translating ideas into action, individually or collectively—the world would change. (1976, 93)

## Note

The words "negotiation" and "navigation" appear fairly often in writings about children's and adolescents' reading, but a thorough bibliographic search turned up no work that developed or reflected on these concepts.

## References

Dyson, Anne Haas. (1989). *Multiple Worlds of Child Writers: Friends Learning to Write*. New York: Teachers College Press.

———. (2003). "'Welcome to the Jam': Popular Culture, School Literacy, and the Making of Childhood," *Harvard Educational Review* 79: 328–361.

Galtung, Johan. (1976). "Literacy, Education and Schooling for What?" in ed., *A Turning Point for Literacy: Adult Education for Development. The Spirit and Declaration of Persepolis*, ed. Léon Bataille. Oxford: Pergamon Press, 93–105.

Moje, Elizabeth Birr, Melanie Overby, Nicole Tysvaer, and Karen Morris. (2008). "The Complex World of Adolescent Literacy: Myths, Motivations, and Mysteries," *Harvard Educational Review* 78:107–154.

# References

Alves, Steven. (Producer). (2001). *A history of American teenagers* [Film]. Hometown Productions.

Ariès, Philippe. (1962). *Centuries of childhood: A social history of family life* (Robert Baldick, Trans.). Jonathan Cape.

Arnove, Robert F. & Graff, Harvey J. (Eds.). (2008). *National literacy campaigns: Historical and comparative perspectives*. Transaction Publishers. (Original work published 1987 by Plenum Press)

Aurell, Jaume. (2015). Making history by contextualizing oneself: Autobiography as historiographical intervention," *History and Theory, 54*(2), 244–268. https://doi.org/10.1111/hith.10756.

Bailyn, Bernard. (1960). *Education in the forming of American society: Needs and opportunities for study*. University of North Carolina Press.

Bailyn, Bernard. (1967). *The ideological origins of the American revolution*. Harvard University Press.

Barr, Jeremy. (2021, October 6). Critical race theory was the hot topic on Fox News this summer. Not so much anymore. *The Washington Post*. https://www.washingtonpost.com/media/2021/10/06/fox-news-critical-race-theory/.

Berry, Patrick W. (2018). *Doing time, writing lives: Refiguring literacy and higher education in prison*. Southern Illinois University Press.

Bhavani, Kum-Kum, Kent, Kathryn R. & Twine, France Widdance. (Eds.). (1998). Feminsms and youth cultures [Special issue]. *Signs: Journal of Women in Culture and Society, 23*(3). https://www.journals.uchicago.edu/toc/signs/1998/23/.

Bivens, Joy L. & Graff, Harvey J. (2004). Coming of age in Chicago. *Chicago History, 33*(2), 12–31. https://tinyurl.com/ysvxenda.

Bloch, Marc. (with Strayer, Joseph R.). (1963). *The historian's craft* (Peter Putnam, Trans.). Alfred A. Knopf.

Booker, Chris. (2018, December 5). *Buckeye Nation Rewards loyalty program connects fans, university*. Ohio State News. https://news.osu.edu/buckeye-nation-rewards-loyalty-program-connects-fans-university/.

Boyle, Kevin. (2021). *The shattering: America in the 1960s*. W. W. Norton and Company.

Bradbury, Kelly Susan. (2016). *Reimagining popular notions of American intellectualism: Literacy, education, and class*. Southern Illinois University Press.

Braudel, Fernand. (1992). *Civilization and capitalism*, 15th-18th century (Vols. 1–3; Siân Reynolds, Trans.). University of California Press.

Brint, Steven. (2018). *Two cheers for higher education: Why American universities are stronger than ever—and how to meet the challenges they face*. Princeton University Press. https://doi.org/10.1515/9780691184890.

Cipolla, Carlo M. (1969). *Literacy and development in the west*. Penguin Books.

Civello, Catherine A. (1997). *Patterns of ambivalence: The fiction and poetry of Stevie Smith*. Camden House.

Clement, Victoria. (2018). *Learning to become Turkmen: Literacy, language, and power, 1914–2014*. University of Pittsburgh Press. https://doi.org/10.2307/j.ctv11wjs0.

Coleman, James S. (with Johnstone, John W. C. & Jonassohn, Kurt). (1961). *The adolescent society: The social life of the teenager and it impact on education*. Free Press of Glencoe.

Coleman, James S., Bremner, Robert H., Clark, Burton R., Davis, John B., Eichorn, Dorothy H., Grilliches, Zvi, Kett, Joseph F., Ryder, Norman B., Doering, Zahava Blum & Mays, John M. (1974). *Youth: Transition to adulthood. Report of the Panel on Youth of the President's Advisory Committee*. University of Chicago Press.

Cox, Kevin R. (2021). *Boomtown Columbus: Ohio's sunbelt city and how developers got their way*. Ohio State University Press.

Davis, Natalie Zemon. (1975). *Society and culture in early modern France: Eight essays*. Stanford University Press.

Demos, John. (1970). *A little commonwealth: Family life in Plymouth Colony*. Oxford University Press.

Doucet, Brian & Doucet, Michael. (2022). *Streetcars and the shifting geographies of Toronto*. University of Toronto Press.

Downing, Andy & Oliphint, Joel. (2021, July 26). The list: Reasons that Columbus Underground opinion piece is trash. *Columbus Monthly*. https://www.columbusmonthly.com/story/entertainment/human-interest/2021/07/26/list-reasons-columbus-underground-opinion-piece-trash/5376123001/.

Drucker, Johanna. (2014). *Graphesis: Visual Forms of Knowledge Production*. Harvard University Press.

Drucker, Johanna & Graff, Harvey J. (1991). Crises in expression and representation. *Intellectual History Newsletter*, 13, 74–82.

Duffy, John M. (2007). *Writing from these roots: Literacy in a Hmong-American community*. University of Hawaiʻi Press. https://www.jstor.org/stable/j.ctt6wr3sd.

Duffy, John, Rose, Mike, Harker, Michael, Berry, Patrick W., Mortenson, Peter & Graff, Harvey J.. (2024). Harvey J. Graff: A tribute. *Across the Disciplines*, 21(1/2), 60–74. https://doi.org/10.37514/ATD-J.2024.21.1.05.

Duguid, Stephen. (1998). *British Columbia prison education research project: Final report*. Simon Fraser University Institute for the Humanities. https://www.sfu.ca/humanities-old/ifeps/report.htm.

Eisenstein, Elizabeth L. (1980). *The printing press as an agent of change: Communications and cultural transformations in early-modern Europe, volumes I and II*. Cambridge University Press. https://doi.org/10.1017/CBO9781107049963 (Original work published 1979).

Elder, Glen H., Jr. (1999). *Children of the Great Depression* (25th anniversary ed.. Routledge. https://doi.org/10.4324/9780429501739 (Original work published 1974).

Elder, Glen H., Jr., Johnson, Monica Kirkpatrick & Crosnoe, Robert. (2003). The emergence and development of life course theory. In J. T. Mortimer & M. J. Shanahan (Eds.), *Handbook of the life course* (pp. 3–19). Springer. https://doi.org/10.1007/978-0-306-48247-2_1.

Elkind, David. (1981). *The hurried child: Growing up too fast too soon.* Addison-Wesley Publishing.
Elkind, David. (1984). *All grown up and no place to go: Teenagers in crisis.* Addison-Wesley Publishing.
Elkind, David. (1987). *Miseducation: Preschoolers at risk.* Alfred A. Knopf.
Elkins, Stanley M. (1959). *Slavery: A problem in American institutional and intellectual life.* University of Chicago Press.
Erikson, Erik H. (1950). *Childhood and society.* W. W. Norton & Company.
Erikson, Erik H. (1968). *Identity: Youth and crisis.* W. W. Norton & Company.
Fabricant, Michael & Brier, Stephen. (2016). *Austerity blues: Fighting for the soul of public higher education.* Johns Hopkins University Press. https://doi.org/10.1353/book.47913.
Fairbanks, Robert B. (1998). *For the city as a whole: Planning, politics, and public interest in Dallas, Texas, 1900–1965.* Ohio State University Press.
Fish, Tom & Rabidoux, Paula. (with Ober, Jillian & Graff, Vicki L. W.). (2009). *Next Chapter Book Club: A model community literacy program for people with intellectual disabilities.* Woodbine House.
Flacks, Mickey & Flacks, Dick. (2018). *Making history/making blintzes: How two red diaper babies found each other and discovered America.* Rutgers University Press. https://doi.org/10.36019/9780813589251.
Freire, Paulo. (1970a). The adult literacy practice as cultural action for freedom. *Harvard Educational Review, 40*(2), 205–225. https://doi.org/10.17763/haer.40.2.q7n227021n148p26.
Freire, Paulo. (1970b). Cultural action and conscientization. *Harvard Educational Review, 40*(3), 452–477. https://doi.org/10.17763/haer.40.3.h76250x720j43175.
Freire, Paulo. (1970c). *Pedagogy of the oppressed* (Myra Bergman Ramos, Trans.). Herder and Herder.
Freire, Paulo. (1973). *Education for critical consciousness.* Seabury Press.
Frickel, Scott, Albert, Mathieu & Prainsack, Barbara. (Eds.). (2016). *Investigating interdisciplinary collaboration: Theory and practice across disciplines.* Rutgers University Press.
Frisch, Michael H. (1972). *Town into city: Springfield, Massachusetts, and the meaning of community, 1840–1880.* Harvard University Press.
Funk and Wagnalls. (1983). Literacy. In *Funk and Wagnalls new encyclopedia* (pp. 156–157).
Gaffield, Chad. (2020) Clio and computers in Canada and beyond: Contested past, promising present, uncertain future. *The Canadian Historical Review, 101*(4), 559–584. https://doi.org/10.3138/chr-2020-0020.
Galerstein, Carolyn L. & Graff, Harvey J. (1978). *Women and public policy: A report.* Women and Public Policy Conference, 1976 (Box 1, Folder 8), The University of Texas at Dallas Women's Studies Archive Collection (UA008-20), The University Archives, Special Collections and Archives Division, Richardson, TX, United States.
Galvão, Ana Maria de Oliveira, de Gouvêa, Maria Cristina Soares & Gomes, Ana Maria Rabelo. (2016). Interview with H. Graff & B. Street. *Educação em Revista, 32*(2), 267–282. https://doi.org/10.1590/0102-4698156010.

Genovese, Eugene D. (1961). *The political economy of slavery: Studies in the economy and the society of the slave South*. Pantheon Books.
Genovese, Eugene D. (1969). *The world the slaveholders made: Two essays in interpretation*. Pantheon Books.
Genovese, Eugene D. (1974). *Roll, Jordan, roll: The world the slaves made*. Pantheon Books.
Goodman, Paul. (1960). *Growing up absurd: Problems of youth in the organized society*. Vintage Books.
Goodman, Paul. (1964). *Compulsory miseducation*. Horizon Press.
Goody, Jack. (Ed.). (1968). *Literacy in traditional societies*. Cambridge University Press.
Graff, Harvey J. (n.d.). *Union Station* [Brochure]. Dallas Historic Landmark Preservation Committee. https://dallascityhall.com/departments/sustainable development/historicpreservation/HP%20Documents/Landmark%20Structures/Union%20Station%20Historic%20Landmark%20Brochure%20Pg%202.png.
Graff, Harvey J. (1971a). Notes on methods for studying literacy from the manuscript census. *Historical Methods Newsletter*, 5(1), 11–16. https://doi.org/10.1080/00182494.1971.10593955.
Graff, Harvey J. (1971b). *Towards a meaning of literacy: Literacy and social structure in Hamilton, Ontario, 1861* [Master's thesis, University of Toronto]. OISE/University of Toronto Library Theses Collection.
Graff, Harvey J. (1972a). Approaches in the historical study of literacy. *Urban History Review/Revue d'histoire urbaine*, 1(3), 6–11. https://doi.org/10.7202/1020604ar.
Graff, Harvey J. (1972b). Towards a meaning of literacy: Literacy and social structure in Hamilton, Ontario, 1861. *History of Education Quarterly*, 12(3), 411–431. https://doi.org/10.2307/367520.
Graff, Harvey J. (1973a). Literacy and social structure in Elgin County, Canada West: 1861. *Histoire sociale/Social History*, 6(11), 25–48. https://hssh.journals.yorku.ca/index.php/hssh/article/view/40700.
Graff, Harvey J. (1973b). Patterns of dependency and child development in the mid-nineteenth century city: A sample from Boston 1860. *History of Education Quarterly*, 13(2), 129–143. https://doi.org/10.2307/367396.
Graff, Harvey J. (1974). Introduction to "Literacy studies in Sweden: Some examples." In Ian Winchester (Ed.), *The Canadian social history project: Report number 5, 1973–74* (pp. 85–88). Ontario Institute for Studies in Education.
Graff, Harvey J. (1975a). Literacy in history [Review of the books *Popular education in eighteenth century England*, by Victor E. Neuberg, *Literacy in society*, edited by Victor E. Neuberg & *Literacy in colonial New England: An enquiry into the social context of literacy in the early modern west*, by Kenneth A. Lockgridge]. *History of Education Quarterly*, 15(4), 467–474. https://doi.org/10.2307/368031.
Graff, Harvey J. (1975b). *Literacy and social structure in the nineteenth-century city* (Document ID 302781148) [Doctoral dissertation, University of Toronto]. ProQuest Dissertations & Theses Global. https://www.proquest.com/docview/302781148/fulltextPDF.

Graff, Harvey J. (1975c). What the 1861 Census can tell us about literacy: A reply. *Histoire sociale/Social History*, *8*(16), 337–349. https://hssh.journals.yorku.ca/index.php/hssh/article/view/40825.

Graff, Harvey J. (1976a). Counting on the past: Quantification in history. *Acadiensis: Journal of the History of the Atlantic Region/Revue d'histoire de la région Atlantique*, *6*(1), 115–129. https://journals.lib.unb.ca/index.php/Acadiensis/article/view/11426.

Graff, Harvey J. (1976b). Respected and profitable labour: Literacy, jobs and the working class in the nineteenth century. In Gregory S. Kealey & Peter Warrian (Eds.), *Essays in Canadian working class history* (pp. 58–82). McClelland and Stewart.

Graff, Harvey J. (1976c). Selected bibliography: Urban, social, sociological, demographic, and quantitative history. In Ian Winchester (Ed.), *Canadian social history project: Report number 6, 1975–76* (pp. 1–16). Ontario Institute for Studies in Education.

Graff, Harvey J. (1977a). Crime and punishment in the nineteenth century: A new look at the criminal. *Journal of Interdisciplinary History*, *7*(3), 477–491. https://doi.org/10.2307/202576.

Graff, Harvey J. (1977b). "The new math": Quantification, the "new" history, and the history of education. *Urban Education*, *11*(4), 403–440. https://doi.org/10.1177/0042085977114005.

Graff, Harvey J. (1977c). "Pauperism, misery, and vice": Illiteracy and criminality in the nineteenth century. *Journal of Social History*, *11*(2), 245–268. https://doi.org/10.1353/jsh/11.2.245.

Graff, Harvey J. (1978a). Basic education. In Dallas Public Library (Ed.), *Issues and alternatives: A guide for the policy maker* [Microfiche]. Main Reading Room (MC 2253), National Library of Australia, Canberra, ACT, Australia.

Graff, Harvey J. (1978b). Literacy and history. In *Literacy Bibliographies* (Vol. 11). International Institute for Adult Literacy Methods.

Graff, Harvey J. (1978c). Literacy: How many views? *Interchange*, *9*(2), 26–29. https://doi.org/10.1007/BF01816513.

Graff, Harvey J. (1978d). Literacy past and present: Critical approaches in the literacy/society relationship. *Interchange*, *9*(2), 1–21. https://doi.org/10.1007/BF01816511.

Graff, Harvey J. (1978e). The "new" social history and the Southwest: The Dallas Social History Project. *East Texas Historical Journal*, *16*(2), Article 10. https://scholarworks.sfasu.edu/ethj/vol16/iss2/10/.

Graff, Harvey J. (1978f). The reality behind the rhetoric: The social and economic meanings of literacy in the mid-nineteenth century: The example of literacy and criminality. In Neil McDonald & Alf Chaiton (Eds.), *Egerton Ryerson and his times* (pp. 187–220). Macmillan Company of Canada.

Graff, Harvey J. (1978g). Youth: A humanistic perspective. In Dallas Public Library (Ed.), *Issues and alternatives: A guide for the policy maker* [Microfiche]. Main Reading Room (MC 2253), National Library of Australia, Canberra, ACT, Australia.

Graff, Harvey J. (1979a). Interpreting historical literacy: The pattern of literacy in Quebec—A comment. *Histoire sociale/Social History*, 12(24), 444–455. https://hssh.journals.yorku.ca/index.php/hssh/article/view/39018.

Graff, Harvey J. (1979b). Literacy, education, and fertility, past and present: A critical review. *Population and Development Review*, 5(1), 105–140. https://doi.org/10.2307/1972320.

Graff, Harvey J. (1979c). *The literacy myth: Literacy and social structure in the nineteenth-century city*. Academic Press.

Graff, Harvey J. (1980a). [Review of the book *Historical studies of changing fertility*, edited by Charles Tilly]. *Labour/La Travailleur*, 5, 242–245. https://www.lltjournal.ca/index.php/llt/article/view/2528/2931.

Graff, Harvey J. (1980b). [Review of the book *Theoretical methods in social history*, by Arthur L. Stinchcombe]. *American Journal of Sociology*, 85(6), 1442–1446. https://www.journals.uchicago.edu/doi/10.1086/227177.

Graff, Harvey J. (1980c). Scrivendo un libro sulla storia dell'alfabetismo occidentale: riflessioni di merito e di metodo [Writing a book on the history of western literacy: Reflections on merit and method]. In *Notizie, alfabetismo e cultura scritta* (pp. 3–14). University of Perugia.

Graff, Harvey J. (1981a). *Literacy in history: An interdisciplinary research bibliography*. Garland Publishing.

Graff, Harvey J. (1981b). Literacy, jobs, and industrialization: The nineteenth century. In Harvey J. Graff (Ed.), *Literacy and social development in the west: A reader* (pp. 232–260). Cambridge University Press.

Graff, Harvey J. (Ed.). (1981c). *Literacy and social development in the west: A reader*. Cambridge University Press.

Graff, Harvey J. (1981d). Reflections on the history of literacy: Overview, critique, and proposals. *Humanities in Society*, 4, 303–333.

Graff, Harvey J. (1982a). Ambassador Park celebrates city landmark designation. *Historic Dallas*, 3(4), 3. https://texashistory.unt.edu/ark:/67531/metapth887916/m1/3/.

Graff, Harvey J. (1982b). Community pride keeps unique district preserved. *Historic Dallas*, 3(3), 8. https://texashistory.unt.edu/ark:/67531/metapth888107/m1/12/.

Graff, Harvey J. (1983). The city, crisis, and change in American culture: Perceptions and perspectives. In Donald A. Hicks & Norman J. Glickman (Eds.), *Transition to the 21st century: Prospect and policies for economic and urban-regional transformation* (pp. 113–152). JAI Press.

Graff, Harvey J. (1986a). *Alfabetizzazione e sviluppo sociale in occidente* [*Literacy and social development in the west*] (D. Camporesi, Trans.) il Mulino.

Graff, Harvey J. (1986b). Crisis, crisis, where is the crisis? Recent popular sociologies of education [Review of the books *The world crisis in education: The view from the eighties*, by Philip H. Coombs, *Illiterate America*, by Jonathan Kozol & *The schools we deserve: Reflections on the educational crises of our times*, by Diane Ravitch]. *Contemporary Sociology*, 15(1), 17–20. https://doi.org/10.2307/2070886.

Graff, Harvey J. (1986c). Doctoral seminar in the history of ideas. *Intellectual History Newsletter*, 8, 27–31.

Graff, Harvey J. (1986d). [Review of the book *The needs of strangers: An essay on privacy, solidarity, and the politics of being human*, by Michael Ignatieff]. *Criminal Justice History*, 7, 212–215.

Graff, Harvey J. (Ed.). (1987a). *Growing up in America: Historical experiences*. Wayne State University Press.

Graff, Harvey J. (1987b). *The legacies of literacy: Continuities and contradictions in western culture and society*. Indiana University Press.

Graff, Harvey J. (1987c). [Review of the book *Beyond the Gutenberg galaxy: Microcomputers and the emergence of post-typographic culture*, by Eugene F. Provenzo, Jr.]. *History of Education Quarterly*, 27(1), 155–156. https://doi.org/10.2307/368599.

Graff, Harvey J. (1987d). [Review of the book *The closing of the American mind*, by Allan Bloom]. *Society*, 25(1), 98–101. https://doi.org/10.1007/BF02695403.

Graff, Harvey J. (1987e). [Review of the books *The origins of public high schools: A reexamination of the Beverly High School controversy*, by Maris A. Vinovskis & *The last little citadel: American high schools since 1940*, by Robert Hempel]. *Journal of Social History*, 20(4), 803–807. https://doi.org/10.1353/jsh/20.4.803.

Graff, Harvey J. (1989). *Storia dell'alfabetizzazione occidentale* [*History of western literacy*] (Vols. 1–3; B. Forino, Trans.). il Mulino.

Graff, Harvey J. (1990). O mito do alfabetismo [The literacy myth] (Tomaz Tadeu da Silva, Trans.). *Teoria & Educação*, 2, 30–64.

Graff, Harvey J. (1991a). *Literacy, myths, and lessons: Keynote address*. New Hampshire Humanities Council Conference.

Graff, Harvey J. (1991b). Towards 2000: Poverty and progress in the history of education. *Historical Studies in Education/Revue d'histoire de l'éducation*, 3(2), 191–210. https://doi.org/10.32316/hse/rhe.v3i2.1266.

Graff, Harvey J. (1993a). Literacy, myths, and legacies: Lessons from the past/thoughts for the future. *Interchange*, 24(3), 271–286. https://doi.org/10.1007/BF01434777.

Graff, Harvey J. (1993b). *Literacy's myths and legacies: From lessons from the history of literacy, to the question of critical literacy* [Plenary address]. Conference on Literacy and Power, Griffith University, Brisbane, QNS, Australia.

Graff, Harvey J. (1994a). *The culture of cities*. H-Urban. https://networks.h-net.org/node/22277/pages/40886/graff-culture-cities-1994.

Graff, Harvey J. (1994b), Literacy, myths, and legacies: Lessons from the history of literacy. In Ludo Verhoeven (Ed.), *Functional literacy: Theoretical issues and educational implications* (pp. 37–60). John Benjamins Publishing.

Graff, Harvey J. (1994c). Literacy, myths, and lessons: Keynote address. In *Adult literacy: An international urban perspective* (pp. 15–39). UNESCO.

Graff, Harvey J. (1994d). Teaching the history of literacy at the University of Texas. *SHARP News*, 3(2), 3–4. https://hdl.handle.net/20.500.14394/43438.

Graff, Harvey J. (1994e). Using first-person sources in social and cultural history: A working bibliography. *Historical Methods*, 27(2), 87–93. https://doi.org/10.1080/01615440.1994.1059422.6

Graff, Harvey J. (1995a). *Conflicting paths: Growing up in America*. Harvard University Press.

Graff, Harvey J. (1995b). *Dallas: The course*. H-Urban. https://networks.h-net.org/node/22277/pages/40888/graff-dallas-course-1995.
Graff, Harvey J. (1995c). *The labyrinths of literacy: Reflections on literacy past and present*. University of Pittsburgh Press. (Original work published 1987 by Falmer Press)
Graff, Harvey J. (1995d). *Reading and writing the city*. H-Urban. https://networks.h-net.org/node/22277/pages/40895/graff-reading-and-writing-city-1995.
Graff, Harvey J. (1996a). *Dallas: The course [revised]*. H-Urban. https://networks.h-net.org/node/22277/pages/40890/graff-dallas-course-revised-1996.
Graff, Harvey J. (1996b). *The development of American urban society*. H-Urban. https://tinyurl.com/yumv9akk.
Graff, Harvey J. (1996c). Reading and writing the city. *Intellectual History Newsletter*, *18*, 103–108.
Graff, Harvey J. (1997a). *The development of American urban society*. H-Urban. https://networks.h-net.org/node/22277/pages/40894/graff-development-american-urban-society-1997.
Graff, Harvey J. (1997b). The persisting power and costs of the literacy myth: A comment on *Literacy, economy and society: Results of the first International Adult Literacy Survey (IALS)*. In *Working papers on literacy* (ED410468, pp. 3–6). ERIC. http://files.eric.ed.gov/fulltext/ED410468.pdf (Reprinted from "The persisting power and costs of the literacy myth: A comment on *Literacy, economy and society: Results of the first International Adult Literacy Survey (IALS)*", 1996, Literacy Across the Curriculum, 12(2), 4–5.)
Graff, Harvey J. (1997c, December 31). Comment: Race between San Antonio, Dallas like fabled tortoise and the hare. *San Antonio Express-News*.
Graff, Harvey J. (1998). Comment: City must create own mold for public universities. *San Antonio Express-News*.
Graff, Harvey J. (1999a). Interdisciplinary explorations in the history of children, adolescents, and youth—for the past, present, and future. *Journal of American History*, *85*(4), 1538–1547. https://doi.org/10.2307/2568273.
Graff, Harvey J. (1999b). Teaching and historical understanding: Disciplining historical imagination with historical context. In Bernice A. Pescosolido & Ronald Aminzade (Eds.), *The social worlds of higher education: Handbook for teaching in a new century* (pp. 280–294). Pine Forge Press.
Graff, Harvey J. (1999c). Teaching [and] historical understanding: Disciplining historical imagination with historical context. *Interchange*, *30*(2), 143–169. https://doi.org/10.1023/A:1007669001861.
Graff, Harvey J. (2000). *The culture of cities*. H-Urban. https://networks.h-net.org/node/22277/pages/40884/graff-culture-cities-2000.
Graff, Harvey J. (2001a). Growing up in America [Lesson plan]. *OAH Magazine of History*, *15*(4), 55–59. https://www.jstor.org/stable/25163467.
Graff, Harvey J. (2001b). Literacy. In Paul S. Boyer (Ed.), *The Oxford companion to United States history* (pp. 450–451). Oxford University Press. https://tinyurl.com/e258aen7.
Graff, Harvey J. (2001c). Literacy's myths and legacies: From lessons from the history of literacy, to the question of critical literacy. In Ian Angus (Ed.),

*Anarcho-modernism: Toward a new critical theory. In honour of Jery Zaslove* (pp. 169–184). Talonbooks.

Graff, Harvey J. (2001d). Literacy's myths and legacies: From lessons from the history of literacy, to the question of critical literacy. In Peter Freebody, Sandy Muspratt & Bronwyn Dwyer (Eds.), *Difference, silence, and textual practice: Studies in critical literacy* (pp. 1–29). Hampton Press.

Graff, Harvey J. (2001e). The nineteenth-century origins of our times. In Ellen Cushman, Eugene R. Kintgen, Barry M. Kroll, and Mike Rose (Eds.), *Literacy: A critical sourcebook* (pp. 211–233). Bedford/St. Martin's.

Graff, Harvey J. (2001f, June 24). Alamo city's different futures: "Fast Forward" left important points muddled. *San Antonio Express-News*.

Graff, Harvey J. (2001g, October 10). *Cities: Communities, spaces, and places*. H-Urban. https://networks.h-net.org/node/22277/pages/40882/graff-cities-communities-spaces-and-places-2001.

Graff, Harvey J. (with Petrucci, Armando). (2002a). *Alfabetismo di massa: mito storia realtà* [Literacy of the masses: Myth, history, reality] (L. Sosio, Trans.). Sylvestre Bonnard.

Graff, Harvey J. (2002b, February 16). *The city in history: The culture of cities*. H-Urban. https://networks.h-net.org/node/22277/pages/40883/graff-city-history-culture-cities-2002.

Graff, Harvey J. (2002c, February 16). *Searching for cities past and future*. H-Urban. https://networks.h-net.org/node/22277/pages/40896/graff-searching-cities-past-and-future-2002.

Graff, Harvey J. (2003). Introduction to historical studies of literacy. *Interchange*, 34(2–3), 123–131. https://doi.org/10.1023/B:INCH.0000015893.54858.f1.

Graff, Harvey J. (2004). Literacy. In Adam Kuper & Jessica Kuper (Eds.), *The social science encyclopedia* (3rd. ed., pp. 587–598). Routledge. https://doi.org/10.4324/9780203496169 (Original work published 1985).

Graff, Harvey J. (2005). Presidential address 2000: The shock of the "'new' (histories)": Social science histories and historical legacies. In Harvey J. Graff, Leslie Page Moch, Philip McMichael & Julia Woesthoff (Eds.), *Looking backward and looking forward: Perspectives on social science history* (pp. 13–56). University of Wisconsin Press. (Reprinted from "The shock of the '"new" [histories]': Social science histories and historical legacies" [President's address], 2001, *Social Science History*, 25[4], 483–533, https://doi.org/10.1017/S0145553200012207).

Graff, Harvey J. (2007a). Bibliography of the history of literacy in Western Europe and North America. In Harvey J. Graff (Ed.), *Literacy and historical development: A reader* (pp. 417–440). Southern Illinois University Press.

Graff, Harvey J. (2007b). *Literacy and historical development: A reader*. Southern Illinois University Press.

Graff, Harvey J. (2007c). Literacy, myths, and legacies: Lessons from the history of literacy. In Harvey J. Graff (Ed.), *Literacy and historical development: A reader* (pp. 12–37). Southern Illinois University Press. (Reprinted from *The labyrinths of literacy: Reflections on literacy past and present*, pp. 318–349, by Harvey J. Graff, 1995, University of Pittsburgh Press)

Graff, Harvey J. (2008a). *The Dallas myth: The making and unmaking of an American city*. University of Minnesota Press.

Graff, Harvey J. (2008b). Teaching the history of growing up. *Newsletter: Society for the History of Children and Youth, 11*.

Graff, Harvey J. (2009a). Assessing the history of literacy: Themes and questions. In Harvey J. Graff, Alison Mackinnon, Bengt Sandin & Ian Winchester (Eds.), *Understanding literacy in its historical contexts: Socio-cultural history and the legacy of Egil Johansson* (pp. 243–264). Nordic Academic Press. https://doi.org/10.2307/j.ctt9qdhp8.18 (Reprinted from *Escribir y leer en Occidente*, pp. 5–46, edited by Armando Petrucci & Francisco M. Gimeno Blay, 1995, Universitat de Valencia)

Graff, Harvey J. (2009b). "The Critical Historiography of Childhood": Introduction. *Society for the History of Children and Youth Bulletin*, (14), 8–11. https://web.archive.org/web/20100626150006/http://www.history.vt.edu/Jones/SHCY/Newsletter14/Issue14.pdf.

Graff, Harvey J. (2010a). *The literacy myth* at thirty. *Journal of Social History, 43*(3), 635–661. https://doi.org/10.1353/jsh.0.0316.

Graff, Harvey J. (2010b). The literacy myth: Literacy, education and demography. *Vienna Yearbook of Population Research, 8*, 17–24. https://doi.org/10.1553/populationyearbook2010s17.

Graff, Harvey J. (2010c, January 31). The troubled discourse of interdisciplinarity [Letter to the editor]. *The Chronicle of Higher Education*. https://www.chronicle.com/article/the-troubled-discourse-of-interdisciplinarity/.

Graff, Harvey J. (2012). Literacy studies and interdisciplinary studies: Reflections on history and theory. In Raphael Foshay (Ed.), *Valences of interdisciplinarity: Theory, practice, pedagogy* (pp. 273–307). Athabasca University Press.

Graff, Harvey J. (2013). The legacies of literacy studies. *Literacy in Composition Studies, 1*(1), 15–17. https://doi.org/10.21623/1.1.1.4.

Graff, Harvey J. (2014a). Epilogue: Literacy studies and interdisciplinary studies with notes on the place of Deborah Brandt. In John Duffy, Julie Nelson Christoph, Eli Goldblatt, Nelson Graff, Rebecca S. Nowacek & Bryan Trabold (Eds.), *Literacy, economy, and power: Writing and research after "Literacy in American Lives"* (pp. 203–226). Southern Illinois University Press.

Graff, Harvey J. (2014b, May 5). *Harvey Graff explains why interdisciplinary history is often treated with disrespect (interview)*. History News Network. https://www.historynewsnetwork.org/article/harvey-graff-explains-why-interdisciplinary-histor.

Graff, Harvey J. (2014c, June 12). Throwing the baby out with the interdisciplinary bath water [Letter to the editor]. *The Chronicle of Higher Education*. https://www.chronicle.com/blogs/letters/throwing-the-baby-out-with-the-interdisciplinary-bath-water/.

Graff, Harvey J. (2015a). *Undisciplining knowledge: Interdisciplinarity in the twentieth century*. Johns Hopkins University Press. https://doi.org/10.1353/book.40922.

Graff, Harvey J. (2015b, September 30). An education in sloganeering. *The Wall Street Journal*. https://www.wsj.com/articles/an-education-in-sloganeering-1443655643.

Graff, Harvey J. (2015c, December 17). *Not a popularity contest*. Inside Higher Ed. https://www.insidehighered.com/views/2015/12/18/how-misguided-university-policies-are-harming-humanities-arts-and-sciences-essay.

Graff, Harvey J. (2016a). Em busca do letramento: as origens sociais e intelectuais des estudos sobre letramento [Searching for Literacy: The Social and Intellectual Origins of Literacy Studies]. *Revista Brasileira de História da Educação*, 16(1), 215–231. https://periodicos.uem.br/ojs/index.php/rbhe/article/view/40773.

Graff, Harvey J. (2016b). The "problem" of interdisciplinarity in theory, practice, and history. *Social Science History*, 40(4), 775–803. https://doi.org/10.1017/ssh.2016.31.

Graff, Harvey. (2016c, May 17). Interdisciplinarity as ideology and practice. *Items: Insights from the Social Sciences*. https://items.ssrc.org/interdisciplinarity/interdisciplinarity-as-ideology-and-practice/.

Graff, Harvey J. (2021a, July 23). *Columbus' identity crisis and its media*. Columbus Underground. https://columbusunderground.com/opinion-columbus-identity-crisis-and-its-media/.

Graff, Harvey J. (2021b, August 17). Guest post: Remembering Mike Rose in person and in print. *Just Visiting*. https://www.insidehighered.com/blogs/just-visiting/guest-post-remembering-mike-rose-person-and-print.

Graff, Harvey. (2021c, August 18). Ohio State's VAX-A-NICKEL giveaway [Letter to the editor]. *The Lantern*. https://www.thelantern.com/2021/08/letter-to-the-editor-ohio-states-vax-a-nickel-giveaway/.

Graff, Harvey J. (2021d, September 7). Interdisciplinarity is not about the humanities aping the sciences. *Times Higher Education*. https://www.timeshighereducation.com/blog/interdisciplinarity-not-about-humanities-aping-sciences.

Graff, Harvey J. (2021e, September 12). *Colleges must learn from sports figures about mental health*. Inside Higher Ed. https://www.insidehighered.com/views/2021/09/13/colleges-can-learn-sports-figures-about-mental-health-opinion.

Graff, Harvey J. (2021f, September 14). The decline of a once vital neighborhood: Columbus' University District. *Columbus Free Press*. https://columbusfreepress.com/article/decline-once-vital-neighborhood-columbus%E2%80%99-university-district.

Graff, Harvey J. (2021g, September 16). For Ohio State, bigger is not better. *Columbus Free Press*. https://columbusfreepress.com/article/ohio-state-bigger-not-better.

Graff, Harvey J. (2021h, September 18). A post-retirement career as a public academic meets the moment's need. *Times Higher Education*. https://www.timeshighereducation.com/blog/post-retirement-career-public-academic-meets-moments-need.

Graff, Harvey J. (2021i, October 8). Columbus' University District: Students and the institutions that fail them. *Columbus Free Press*. https://columbusfreepress.com/article/columbus%E2%80%99-university-district-students-and-institutions-fail-them.

Graff, Harvey J. (2021j, October 20). *Testing can save democracy*. Inside Higher Ed. https://www.insidehighered.com/views/2021/10/21/civics-test-should-be-required-hold-public-office-opinion.

Graff, Harvey J. (2021k, October 30). History lessons can help disciplines to survive. *Times Higher Education*. https://www.timeshighereducation.com/opinion/history-lessons-can-help-disciplines-survive.

Graff, Harvey J. (2021l, November 6). Ohio State isn't having a crime crisis; it's having a leadership crisis. *Columbus Free Press*. https://columbusfreepress.com/article/ohio-state-isn%E2%80%99t-having-crime-crisis-it%E2%80%99s-having-leadership-crisis-0.

Graff, Harvey J. (2021m, November 7). Response to Columbus Alive, "The list: Reasons that Columbus Underground opinion piece is trash," by Andy Downing and Joel Oliphint, Columbus Alive, July 26: A visit to journalism fantasy land. *Columbus Free Press*. https://columbusfreepress.com/article/response-columbus-alive-%E2%80%9C-list-reasons-columbus-underground-opinion-piece-trash%E2%80%9D-andy.

Graff, Harvey J. (2021n, November 25). My young heroes. *Columbus Free Press*. https://columbusfreepress.com/article/my-young-heroes.

Graff, Harvey J. (2021o, December 6). Busting myths: The Ohio State University promotes public health crises. *Columbus Free Press*. https://columbusfreepress.com/article/busting-myths-ohio-state-university-promotes-public-health-crises-0.

Graff, Harvey J. (2021p, December 31). The history of book banning. *Publishers Weekly*. https://www.publishersweekly.com/pw/by-topic/columns-and-blogs/soapbox/article/88195-harvey-j-graff-examines-the-history-of-book-banning.html.

Graff, Harvey J. (2022a) Book banning past and present. *Against the Current*, (218). https://againstthecurrent.org/atc218/book-banning-past-and-present/.

Graff, Harvey J. (2022b). The inseparability of "historical myths" and "permanent crises" in the humanities. *Journal of Liberal Arts and Humanities*, 3(9), 16–26. https://jlahnet.com/wp-content/uploads/2022/09/2.pdf.

Graff, Harvey J. (2022c). The new literacy studies and the resurgent literacy myth. *Literacy in Composition Studies*, 9(1), 47–53. https://doi.org/10.21623/1.9.1.4.

Graff, Harvey J. (2022d). The nondebate about critical race theory and our American moment. *Journal of Academic Freedom*, 13. https://www.aaup.org/JAF13/nondebate-critical-race-theory-our-american-moment.

Graff, Harvey J. (2022e). *Searching for literacy: The social and intellectual origins of literacy studies*. Palgrave Macmillan. https://doi.org/10.1007/978-3-030-96981-3.

Graff, Harvey J. (2022f, January 10). The banality of university slogans. *Washington Monthly*. https://washingtonmonthly.com/2022/01/10/the-banality-of-university-slogans/.

Graff, Harvey J. (2022g, January 12). *The dilemmas of disciplines going public*. Inside Higher Ed. https://www.insidehighered.com/views/2022/01/13/academic-disciplines-changing-roles-public-domain-opinion.

Graff, Harvey J. (2022h, January 17). Slogans are no substitute for concrete university policies and programmes. *Times Higher Education*. https://www.timeshighereducation.com/blog/slogans-are-no-substitute-concrete-university-policies-and-programmes.

Graff, Harvey J. (2022i, January 19). Sloganeering and the limits of leadership. *Academe Blog*. https://academeblog.org/2022/01/19/sloganeering-and-the-limits-of-leadership/.
Graff, Harvey J. (2022j, January 23). Busting myths: The Misrepresentation and marketing of 'financial literacy'—the fallacies and dangers of FL4ALL. *Columbus Free Press*. https://columbusfreepress.com/article/busting-myths-misrepresentation-and-marketing-%E2%80%9Cfinancial-literacy%E2%80%9D-fallacies-and-dangers.
Graff, Harvey J. (2022k, January 30). Busting myths: The disappearance of journalistic standards as opinion essays replace the news. *Columbus Free Press*. https://columbusfreepress.com/article/busting-myths-disappearance-journalistic-standards-opinion-essays-replace-news.
Graff, Harvey J. (2022l, February 10). Academic collegiality is a contradictory, self-serving myth. *Times Higher Education*. https://www.timeshighereducation.com/blog/academic-collegiality-contradictory-self-serving-myth.
Graff, Harvey J. (2022m, February 16). Busting Myths: How many "projects" does it take to obstruct a truly American history? *Columbus Free Press*. https://columbusfreepress.com/article/busting-myths-how-many-%E2%80%9Cprojects%E2%80%9D-does-it-take-obstruct-truly-american-history.
Graff, Harvey J. (2022n, February 16). *A call to colleagues: Speak out and support children, teachers, librarians, and free speech—and the present and future of your own institutions, too* [Online forum post]. American Historical Association Member Forum.
Graff, Harvey J. (2022o, March 7). Collegiality needs a reboot. *Times Higher Education*. https://www.timeshighereducation.com/blog/collegiality-needs-reboot.
Graff, Harvey J. (2022p, March 14). Busting myths: Ohio State University versus "campus safety." *Columbus Free Press*. https://columbusfreepress.com/article/busting-myths-ohio-state-university-versus-%E2%80%9Ccampus-safety%E2%80%9D.
Graff, Harvey J. (2022q, March 25). *Teaching outside the box*. Inside Higher Ed. https://www.insidehighered.com/advice/2022/03/25/retired-professor-teaches-and-learns-beyond-classroom-opinion.
Graff, Harvey J. (2022r, April 2). Ignore the books: There is no single big problem with higher education. *Times Higher Education*. https://www.timeshighereducation.com/blog/ignore-books-there-no-single-big-problem-higher-education.
Graff, Harvey J. (2022s, May 5). *Myths shape the continuing "crisis of the humanities."* Inside Higher Ed. https://www.insidehighered.com/views/2022/05/06/myths-underlie-humanities-crisis-discourse-opinion.
Graff, Harvey J. (2022t, May 17). Universities are not giving students the classes or support they need. *Times Higher Education*. https://www.timeshighereducation.com/blog/universities-are-not-giving-students-classes-or-support-they-need.
Graff, Harvey J. (2022u, July 26). The best scholarship is political but with no ideological stamp. *Times Higher Education*. https://www.timeshighereducation.com/blog/best-scholarship-political-no-ideological-stamp.

Graff, Harvey J. (2022v, August 7). Busting myths: Recreating universities for the 21st century without repeating the errors and myths of the 20th century. *Columbus Free Press*. https://columbusfreepress.com/article/busting-myths-recreating-universities-21st-century-without-repeating-errors-and-myths-20th.

Graff, Harvey J. (2022w, August 28). Busting myths: The United States' worst managed large public university? Ohio State's 5½ "D's": Disorganization, dysfunction, disengagement, depression, dishonesty, and undisciplined [Part I]. *Columbus Free Press*. https://columbusfreepress.com/article/busting-myths-united-states%E2%80%99-worst-managed-large-public-university-ohio-state%E2%80%99s-5%C2%BD-%E2%80%9Cd%E2%80%99s%E2%80%9D.

Graff, Harvey J. (2022x, August 31). Busting myths: The United States' worst managed large public university? Ohio State's 5½ "D's": Disorganization, dysfunction, disengagement, depression, dishonesty, and undisciplined [Part II]. *Columbus Free Press*. https://columbusfreepress.com/article/busting-myths-united-states%E2%80%99-worst-managed-large-public-university-ohio-state%E2%80%99s-5%C2%BD-%E2%80%9Cd%E2%80%99s%E2%80%9D-0.

Graff, Harvey J. (2022y, November 10). Busting myths: How universities fail their students: The president may be "born to be a Buckeye," but the students are not. *Columbus Free Press*. https://columbusfreepress.com/article/busting-myths-how-universities-fail-their-students-president-may-be-%E2%80%9Cborn-be-buckeye%E2%80%9D.

Graff, Harvey J. (2022z, November 22). *Learning through teaching*. Inside Higher Ed. https://www.insidehighered.com/advice/2022/11/23/professors-should-both-teach-and-learn-their-students-opinion.

Graff, Harvey J. (2022aa, December 21). I'm retired but I'm still running my own unofficial university. *Times Higher Education*. https://www.timeshighereducation.com/opinion/im-retired-im-still-running-my-own-unofficial-university.

Graff, Harvey J. (2023a). Lessons from the 1960s: Paths to rediscovering universities. *Against the Current*, (223). https://againstthecurrent.org/lessons-from-the-1960s-paths-to-rediscovering-universities/.

Graff, Harvey J. (2023b). *The literacy myth: Cultural integration and social structure in the nineteenth century*. The WAC Clearinghouse. https://wac.colostate.edu/books/landmarks/literacy-myth/ (Original work published 1991 by Transaction Publishers).

Graff, Harvey J. (with Heath, Shirley Brice). (2023c). *Literacy myths, legacies, and lessons: New studies on literacy*. The WAC Clearinghouse. https://wac.colostate.edu/books/landmarks/literacy-legacies/ (Original work published 2011 by Transaction Publishers).

Graff, Harvey J. (2023d). Opinion: The persistent "reading myth" and the "crisis of the humanities." *College Composition and Communication*, 74(3), 575–580. https://doi.org/10.58680/ccc202332367.

Graff, Harvey J. (2023e). The power of models and examples in education and higher education. *Journal of Educational Thought/Revue de la Pensée Educative*, 56(2). https://doi.org/10.55016/ojs/jet.v56i2.78058.

Graff, Harvey J. (2023f, March 22). Finding a permanent job in the humanities has never been easy. *Times Higher Education*. https://www.timeshighereducation.com/blog/finding-permanent-job-humanities-has-never-been-easy.

Graff, Harvey J. (2023g, April 18). Humanities could change the world—if only they could change themselves. *Times Higher Education*. https://www.timeshighereducation.com/blog/humanities-could-change-world-if-only-they-could-change-themselves.

Graff, Harvey J. (2023h, April 28). *Lessons for becoming a public scholar*. Inside Higher Ed. https://www.insidehighered.com/opinion/career-advice/2023/04/28/lessons-becoming-public-scholar.

Graff, Harvey J. (2023i, June 16). The young heroes of the writing world. *Publishers Weekly*. https://www.publishersweekly.com/pw/by-topic/columns-and-blogs/soapbox/article/92567-the-young-heroes-of-the-writing-world.html.

Graff, Harvey J. (2023j, November 29). Speaking out on the Israel-Hamas conflict doesn't mean taking sides. *Times Higher Education*. https://www.timeshighereducation.com/blog/speaking-out-israel-hamas-conflict-doesnt-mean-taking-sides.

Graff, Harvey J. (2023k, December 14). *Scholar activism doesn't require taking sides* [Letter to the editor]. Inside Higher Ed. https://www.insidehighered.com/opinion/letters/2023/12/14/scholar-activism-doesnt-require-taking-sides-letter.

Graff, Harvey J. & Abdul, Ameer. (2022, February 3). Busting myths: The other immigrants and diverse American dreams. *Columbus Free Press*. https://columbusfreepress.com/article/harvey-j-graff-ameer-abdul-busting-myths-columbus-free-press-other-immigr.

Graff, Harvey J., Barton, Charles & Baron, Alan R. (1979). *Dallas, Texas: A bibliographical guide to the sources of its social history to 1930*. University of Texas at Dallas.

Graff, Harvey J. & Duffy, John. (2008). Literacy myths. In Nancy H. Hornberger (Ed.), *Encyclopedia of language and education* (Vol. 2, 2nd ed., pp. 457–468). Springer. https://doi.org/10.1007/978-0-387-30424-3_34.

Graff, Harvey J. & Hanson, Susan. (2008). Not your mother's literacy, but perhaps your daughter's. *English@OSU*, 2(1).

Graff, Harvey J., Jacobs, Jerry A., Maynes, Mary Jo & Sewell, William H., Jr. (n.d.). *A forum on interdisciplinarity*. Scholarly Commons, University of Pennsylvania, Philadelphia, PA, USA. https://repository.upenn.edu/exhibits/orgunit/interdisciplinarity_forum.

Graff, Harvey J., Mackinnon, Alison, Sandin, Bengt & Winchester, Ian. (Eds.). (2003a). [Special issue]. *Interchange*, 34(2–3). https://link.springer.com/journal/10780/volumes-and-issues/34-2.

Graff, Harvey J. Mackinnon, Alison, Sandin, Bengt & Winchester, Ian. (2003b). Literacy, religion, gender, and social history: A socio-cultural history for the 21st century. *Interchange*, 34(2–3), 117–122. https://doi.org/10.1023/B:INCH.0000015892.39199.81.

Graff, Harvey J., Mackinnon, Alison, Sandin, Bengt & Winchester, Ian. (Eds.). (2009). *Understanding literacy in its historical contexts: Socio-cultural history and the legacy of Egil Johansson*. Nordic Academic Press. https://doi.org/10.2307/jj.919489.

Graff, Harvey J., Moch, Leslie Page & McMichael, Phillip. (with Woesthoff, Julia). (2005). *Looking backward and looking forward: Perspectives on social science history*. University of Wisconsin Press.

Graff, Harvey J. & Monaco, Paul. (1980). *Quantification and psychology: Toward a "new" history*. University Press of America.

Graff, Harvey J. & Prentice, Alison. (1979). *Children and schools in nineteenth-century Canada* [Booklet]. Robert B. Haas Family Arts Library Special Collections Repository (Canada's Visual History Slide Collection, Box 3, "Mixed Materials," Call number VRC 80), Arts Library, Yale University, New Haven, CT, United States.

Graff, Harvey J., Stern, Mark, Chowkwanyun, Merlin, O'Mara, Margaret, Hacsi, Timothy, Gordon, Leah & Amerstam, Daniel. (2015, November 12–15). *Michael B. Katz: His contribution and legacy to social science history and beyond: A round table discussion* [Conference presentation]. Pluralism and community: Social science history perspectives, 40th annual meeting of the Social Science History Association, Baltimore, MD, United States.

Graff, Vicki L. W. (2023). We do these things. *Journal of Expressive Writing*, (September 4). https://www.journalofexpressivewriting.com/post/we-do-these-things.

Grafton, Anthony T. (1980). The importance of being printed [Review of the book *The printing press as an agent of change: Communications and cultural transformations in early-modern Europe*, by Elizabeth L. Eisenstein]. *Journal of Interdisciplinary History*, 11(2), 265–286. https://doi.org/10.2307/203783.

Greven, Phillip J., Jr. (1970). *Four generations: Population, land, and family in colonial Andover, Massachusetts*. Cornell University Press.

Gutman, Herbert G. (1977a). *The black family in slavery and freedom, 1750–1925*. Vintage Books.

Gutman, Herbert G. (1977b). *Work, culture, and society in industrializing America: Essays in American working-class and social history*. Vintage Books.

Halperin, Eric. (2021, September 1). *Columbus police, Ohio State team up to fight crime in University District*. NBC4i. https://www.nbc4i.com/news/local-news/ohio-state-university/columbus-police-ohio-state-team-up-to-fight-crime-in-university-district/.

Handlin, Oscar. (1941). *Boston's immigrants, 1790–1880: A study in acculturation*. Harvard University Press.

Handlin, Oscar. (1951). *The uprooted: The epic story of the great migrations that made the American people*. Little, Brown and Company.

Hannah-Jones, Nikole & Watson, Renée. (2021). *The 1619 Project: Born on the water* (Nikkolas Smith, Illus.). Kokila.

Harker, Michael. (2015). *The lure of literacy: A critical reception of the compulsory composition debate*. SUNY Press.

Havelock, Eric A. (1963). *Preface to Plato*. Belknap Press.

Heath, Shirley Brice. (1983). *Ways with words: Language, life, and work in communities and classrooms*. Cambridge University Press.

Hendrix, Sheridan. (2021, September 2). Columbus, Ohio State police departments step up safety measures in University District. *The Columbus Dispatch*. https://tinyurl.com/22unw7tx.

Hershberg, Theodore. (Ed.). (1981). *Philadelphia: Work, space, family, and group experience in the 19th century*. Oxford University Press.
Hill, Christopher. (1961). *The century of revolution, 1603–1714*. Thomas Nelson and Sons.
Hill, Christopher. (1972). *The world turned upside down: Radical ideas during the English revolution*. Temple Smith.
Hill, Patricia Evridge. (1996). *Dallas: The making of a modern city*. University of Texas Press. https://doi.org/10.7560/731035.Hobsbawm, Eric (1962). *The age of revolution: 1789–1848*. Weidenfeld & Nicolson.
Hobsbawm, Eric. (1964). *Labouring men: Studies in the history of labour*. Weidenfeld & Nicolson.
Hoggart, Richard. (1957). *The uses of literacy: Aspects of working-class life with special reference to publications and entertainments*. Chatto & Windus.
Holt, John. (with Fromme, Allan). (1964). *How children fail*. Delta.
Holt, John. (1967). *How children learn*. Pitman Publishing.
Innis, Harold A. (1951). *The bias of communication*. University of Toronto Press.
Jacobs, Jerry A. (2014). *In defense of disciplines: Interdisciplinarity and specialization in the research university*. University of Chicago Press. https://doi.org/10.7208/chicago/9780226069463.001.0001.
Jaschik, Scott. (2015, September 9). "Undisciplining Knowledge." Inside Higher Ed. https://www.insidehighered.com/news/2015/09/10/author-discusses-new-book-interdisciplinarity.
Katz, Michael B. (1968). *The irony of early school reform: Educational innovation in mid-nineteenth century Massachusetts*. Harvard University Press.
Katz, Michael B. (1975). *The people of Hamilton, Canada West: Family and class in a mid-nineteenth-century city*. Harvard University Press.
Katz, Michael B. (1979). An apology for American educational history [Review of the book *The revisionists revised: A critique of the radical attack on the schools*, by Diane Ravitch]. *Harvard Educational Review*, 49(2), 256–275. https://doi.org/10.17763/haer.49.2.45468761687720k4.
Katz, Michael B. (1987). *Reconstructing American education*. Harvard University Press.
Keniston, Kenneth. (1965). *The uncommitted: Alienated youth in American society*. Harcourt, Brace & World.
Keniston, Kenneth. (1968). *Young radicals: Notes on committed youth*. Harcourt, Brace & World.
Keniston, Kenneth. (1971). *Youth and dissent: The rise of a new opposition*. Harcourt Brace Jovanovich.
Kett, Joseph F. (1977), *Rites of passage: Adolescence in America, 1790–present*. Basic Books.
Kiniry, Malcolm & Rose, Mike. (1990). *Critical strategies for academic writing*. Bedford Books.
Kiniry, Malcolm & Rose, Mike. (1993). *Critical strategies for academic writing* (2nd ed.). Bedford Books.
Kiniry, Malcolm & Rose, Mike. (1997). *Critical strategies for academic writing* (3rd ed.). Bedford Books.

Knox, Tom. (2021, February 17). *Innovation District to spearhead economic growth, research and expanded talent*. Ohio State News. https://news.osu.edu/innovation-district-to-spearhead-economic-growth-research-and-expanded-talent/.

Koughan, Frank. (Writer & Producer). (2012, September 25). Dropout nation (Season 2012, Episode 20) [Documentary film]. In Kevin Vargas & Lisa Kalikow (Producers), *Frontline*. Frontline; Left/Right Docs. https://www.pbs.org/wgbh/frontline/documentary/dropout-nation/.

Kozol, Jonathan. (1967). *Death at an early age: The destruction of the hearts and minds of negro children in the Boston public schools*. Houghton Mifflin.

Lasch, Christopher. (1965). *The new radicalism in America, 1889–1963: The intellectual as a social type*. Alfred A. Knopf.

Lasch, Christopher. (1969). *The agony of the American left*. Alfred A. Knopf.

Laslett, Peter. (1984). *The world we have lost: England before the Industrial Age* (3rd ed.). Charles Scribners' Sons. (Original work published 1965)

Lauter, Paul. (2020). *Our sixties: An activist's history*. University of Rochester Press. https://doi.org/10.1515/9781787449183.

Lefebvre, Henri. (1971). *Everyday life in the modern world* (Sacha Rabinovitch, Trans.). Allen Lane Penguin Press.

Le Roy Ladurie, Emmanuel. (1978). *Montaillou: Promised land of error* (Barbara Bray, Trans.). Vintage Books.

Leslie, Warren. (with Graff, Harvey J. & Hill, Patricia Everidge). (1998). *Dallas public and private: Aspects of an American city*. Southern Methodist University Press. (Original work published 1964 by Grossman Publishers)

LiteracyStudies@OSU. (n.d.). *LiteracyStudies@OSU* [Brochure]. https://tinyurl.com/bk8y4mhy.

Lockridge, Kenneth A. (1970). *A New England town the first one hundred years: Dedham, Massachusetts, 1636–1736*. W. W. Norton & Company.

Lockridge, Kenneth A. (1974). *Literacy in colonial New England: An enquiry into the social context of literacy in the early modern west*. W. W. Norton & Company.

Lord, Alfred B. (2000). *The Singer of Tales*. 2nd ed., ed. Stephen Mitchell and Gregory Nagy. Harvard University Press.

Luo, Di. (2022). *Beyond citizenship: Literary and personhood in everyday China, 1900–1945*. Brill. https://doi.org/10.1163/9789004524743.

Magnusson, Sigurdur Gylfi. (2007). *Sögustríð: Greinar og frásagnir um hugmyndafræði* [*The history war: Essays and narratives on ideology*]. Icelandic University Press.

Magnusson, Sigurdur Gylfi. (2021). *Archive, slow ideology and egodocuments as microhistorical autobiography*. Routledge. https://doi.org/10.4324/9781003177661.

Manovich, Ellen L. (2018). "Time and change will surely show": Contested urban development in Ohio State's University District, 1920–2015, *Journal of Social History*, 51(4), 1069–1099. https://doi.org/10.1093/jsh/shx040.

Martin, David. (2013). *The education of David Martin: The making of an unlikely sociologist*. Regent College Publishing.

Martin, Ginny. (Director). (1985). *Legacies of the land: A tale of Texas*. KERA; American Archive of Public Broadcasting. https://americanarchive.org/catalog/cpb-aacip-526-445h990b9z.

Mattingly, Paul H. (2017). *American academic cultures: A history of higher education*. University of Chicago Press.
Maynes, Mary Jo, Pierce, Jennifer L. & Laslett, Barbara. (2008). *Telling stories: The use of personal narratives in the social sciences and history*. Cornell University Press.
McLuhan, Marshall. (1962). *The Gutenberg galaxy: The making of typographic man*. University of Toronto Press.
McLuhan, Marshall. (1964). *Understanding media: The extensions of man*. McGraw-Hill Book Company.
Mercadante, Linda. (2006). *Bloomfield Avenue: A Jewish-Catholic Jersey girl's spiritual journey*. Cowley Publications.
Michael B. Katz 2015 SSHA memorial session [Special section]. (2017). *Social Science History*, 41(4), 757–776. https://www.cambridge.org/core/journals/social-science-history/issue/8AB6B166DAA2AE13CCE378DCA1A43124.
Microsoft. (1998). Literacy. In *Encarta* [CD Rom].
Millgram, Elijah. (2015). *The great endarkenment: Philosopohy for an age of hyperspecialization*. Oxford University Press.
Mohamed, Feisal G. (2021, July 28). I love the public humanities, but. . . . *Chronicle of Higher Education*. https://www.chronicle.com/article/i-love-the-public-humanities-but.
Mondell, Allen & Mondell, Cynthia. (1983). *West of Hester Street* [Film]. Media Projects.
Moore, Barrington, Jr. (1966). *Social origins of dictatorship and democracy: Lord and peasant in the making of the modern world*. Beacon Press.
National Archives. (1954, May 17). *Opinion, Brown v. Board of Education*. U.S. National Archives and Records Administration. https://catalog.archives.gov/id/1656510.
Newfield, Christopher. (2016). *The great mistake: How we wrecked public universities and how we can fix them*. Johns Hopkins University Press. https://doi.org/10.56021/9781421421629.
Northwestern University Libraries. (n.d.). *They demanded courageously: The 1968 Northwestern bursar's office takeover*. https://sites.northwestern.edu/bursars1968/history/why-students-made-demands/.
Office of Student Life. (2024). *Residential experience*. The Ohio State University. https://studentlife.osu.edu/campus-living.
The Ohio State University. (n.d.). *Scarlet & Gray Advantage*. https://advantage.osu.edu/.
The Ohio State University Foundation. (2013). *The Ohio State University advancement strategic plan 2013–2018*. The Ohio State University. https://advancement.osu.edu/sites/default/files/migrated/assets/files/ADV_StrategicPlan_2013.pdf.
Olson, David R. (1994). *The world on paper: The conceptual and cognitive implications of writing and reading*. Cambridge University Press.
Ong, Walter J. (1958). *Ramus, method, and the decay of dialogue*. Harvard University Press.
Pauley, Bruce F. (2016). *Pioneering history on two continents: An autobiography*. University of Nebraska Press. https://muse.jhu.edu/book/36127.
Payne, Darwin. (1994). *Big D: Triumphs and troubles of an American supercity in the 20th century*. Three Forks Press.

Pérez, Ashley Hope. (2015). *Out of darkness*. Carolrhoda Lab.
Pérez, Ashley Hope & Graff, Harvey J. (2022, January 28). Book ban in Washington County is an example of the "new illiteracy." *The Salt Lake Tribune*. https://www.sltrib.com/opinion/commentary/2022/01/28/ashley-hope-prez-harvey-j/.
Ravitch, Diane. (1978). *The revisionists revised: A critique of the radical attack on the schools*. Basic Books.
Reichman, Hank. (2022, January 10). Per aspera ad astra. *Academe Blog*. https://academeblog.org/2022/01/10/per-aspera-ad-astra/.
Riesman, David & Jencks, Christopher. (1968). *The academic revolution*. Doubleday & Company.
Rissing, Steve. (with Graff, Harvey J.) (2015, June 5). Early-college programs lack many benefits of the real thing. *The Columbus Dispatch*. https://tinyurl.com/263p6uvk.
Rivers, Corinne. (2021, August 27). Ohio State increasing security, patrolling due to "frequency and severity of crime." Fox 19 Now. https://www.fox19.com/2021/08/27/ohio-state-increasing-security-patrolling-due-frequency-severity-crime/.
Schofield, Roger. (1968). The measurement of literacy in pre-industrial England. In Jack Goody (Ed.), *Literacy in traditional societies* (pp. 311–325). Cambridge University Press.
Schumm, Jeanne Shay & Radenich, Marguerite C. (1984). Readers'/writers' workshop: An antidote for term paper terror. *Journal of Reading*, 28(1), 13–19. https://www.jstor.org/stable/40007583.
Schweder, Richard A. (2009). *The child: An encyclopedic companion*. University of Chicago Press. https://press.uchicago.edu/books/TheChild/index.html.
Scribner, Sylvia & Cole, Michael. (1981). *The psychology of literacy*. Harvard University Press.
Shorter, Edward. (1971). *The historian and the computer: A practical guide*. W. W. Norton & Company.
Shorter, Edward. (1975). *The making of the modern family*. Basic Books.
Siegelbaum, Lewis H. (2019). *Stuck on communism: Memoir of a Russian historian*. Northern Illinois University Press. https://www.jstor.org/stable/10.7591/j.ctvpwhh3c.
Solomon, Don. (Ed.). (2014). Harvey Graff on interdisciplinarity. *News of the National Humanities Center*, (Spring/Summer), 8–9, 18. https://tinyurl.com/mhwr2twf.
Stampp, Kenneth M. (1956). *The peculiar institution: Slavery in the ante-bellum South*. Vintage Books.
Steedman, Carolyn. (1992). *Past tenses: Essays on writing, autobiography, and history*. Rivers Oram Press.
Stone, Lawrence. (1965). *The crisis of the aristocracy, 1558–1641*. Clarendon Press.
Stone, Lawrence. (1969). "Literacy and education in England, 1640–1900," *Past & Present*, 42(1), 69–139. https://doi.org/10.1093/past/42.1.69.
Stone, Lawrence. (1977). *The family, sex and marriage in England, 1500–1800*. Weidenfeld & Nicolson.
Street, Brian V. (1984). *Literacy in theory and practice*. Cambridge University Press.
The struggle for literacy [Special section]. (1986). *The Wilson Quarterly*, 10(2), 94–133. https://www.jstor.org/stable/i40009990.

Szilagy, Sarah. (2023, August 24). *Ohio State president's salary will be among the highest in the Big Ten.* NBC4. https://tinyurl.com/w5y65rnp.

Thernstrom, Stephan. (1964). *Poverty and progress: Social mobility in a nineteenth century city.* Harvard University Press.

Thernstrom, Stephan & Sennett, Richard. (Eds.). (1969). *Nineteenth-century cities: Essays in the new urban history.* Yale University Press.

Thompson, E. P. (1964). *The making of the English working class.* Pantheon Books.

Thompson, E. P.. (1967). Time, work-discipline, and industrial capitalism. *Past & Present, 38*(1), 56–97. https://doi.org/10.1093/past/38.1.56.

Tilly, Charles. (1964). *The Vendée: A sociological analysis of the counter-revolution of 1793.* Harvard University Press.

Tilly, Charles. (1981). *As history meets sociology.* Academic Press.

Tilly, Charles & Landes, David. (Eds.). (1971). *History as social science.* Prentice Hall.

Tranchin, Rob. (Director & Producer). (1992). *First steps* [TV documentary]. KERA.

Tranchin, Rob (Writer) & Voight, Tom (Director). (1991). A better childhood (ABC) quiz [TV series episode]. In Rob Tranchin (Producer), *Family project.* KERA; American Archive of Public Broadcasting. https://americanarchive.org/catalog/cpb-aacip-445c25c223c.

The University of Texas at Dallas. (n.d.-a). *About us.* https://www.utdallas.edu/about-us/.

The University of Texas at Dallas. (n.d.-b). *Academics.* https://www.utdallas.edu/academics/.

The University of Texas at Dallas. (n.d.-c) *History & traditions.* https://www.utdallas.edu/about-us/history-traditions/.

The University of Texas at Dallas. (n.d.-d). *Interactive timeline.* https://www.utdallas.edu/about-us/history-traditions/interactive-timeline/.

Van Noorden, Richard. (2015, September 16). The undisciplinarian. *A View From the Bridge:* Nature's Books and Arts Blog. https://blogs.nature.com/aviewfromthebridge/2015/09/16/the-undisciplinarian/.

Williams, Raymond. (1958). *Culture and society, 1780–1950.* Columbia University Press.

Williamson, Harold F. & Wild, Payson S. (1975). *Northwestern University: A history, 1850–1975.* Northwestern University.

Winegarten, Ruthe & Schechter, Cathy. (1990). *Deep in the heart: The lives and legends of Texas Jews: A photographic history.* Eakin Press.

Wiseman, Frederick. (Director). (1968). *High school* [Film]. Zipporah Films.

World Book. (1993). Illiteracy. In *The world book encyclopedia* (Vol. 18, pp. 78–79).

World Book. (1995). Literacy. In *The world book encyclopedia.*

Wrigley, E. A. (1969). *Population and history.* Weidenfeld and Nicholson.

Wrigley, E. A. (Ed.). (1972). *Nineteenth-century society: Essays in the use of quantitative methods for the study of social data.* Cambridge University Press.

# Appendix. Harvey J. Graff Curriculum Vitae

Professor Emeritus of English and History,
Ohio Eminent Scholar in Literacy Studies, and
Academy Professor,
The Ohio State University

## Personal

*Citizenship: United States*  *Birthplace: Pittsburgh, Pennsylvania*

## Education

| | |
|---|---|
| 1970 | Northwestern University, Bachelor of Arts, Honors in History (History and Sociology) |
| 1971 | University of Toronto, Master of Arts (History and History of Education) |
| 1973 | Newberry Library Institute in Social, Demographic, and Family History, Certificate |
| 1975 | University of Toronto, Doctor of Philosophy (History and History of Education) |

## Honors and Awards

| | |
|---|---|
| 1970 | Phi Beta Kappa |
| 1970–1971 | Woodrow Wilson Fellowship |
| 1971–1973 | University of Toronto and Ontario Institute for Studies in Education Fellowships and Assistantships |
| 1972–1974 | Ontario Institute for Studies in Education Research Grants |
| 1973 | Newberry Library Institute Fellowship, Spencer and Mellon Foundations |
| 1973–1975 | Central Mortgage and Housing Corporation (Canada) Fellowship in Urban Studies |
| 1976 | National Endowment for the Humanities Summer Fellowship |
| 1976–1977 | University of Texas at Dallas Research Grants |
| 1976 | Texas Committee for the Humanities Program Grant |
| 1976–1977 | Mathematics Social Science Board and National Science Foundation Grant with Paul Monaco |
| 1977 | The Swedish Institute, Guest Scholarship |
| 1977 | Umeå University, Sweden, Guest Scholar |
| 1978 | American Council of Learned Societies, Grant-in-Aid |

| | |
|---|---|
| 1978 | Texas Committee for the Humanities Publication Grant |
| 1979–1980 | National Endowment for the Humanities Fellowship, The Newberry Library |
| 1979–1982 | Spencer Fellowship, National Academy of Education |
| 1980–1981 | Research Associate, The Newberry Library |
| 1983–1985 | University of Texas at Dallas, Research Grants (Doctoral Students) |
| 1984 | American Antiquarian Society Peterson Fellowship (declined) |
| 1985–1986 | Newberry Library, Short-term Fellowship |
| 1987–1989 | University of Texas at Dallas, Research Grants (Doctoral Students) |
| 1987 | American Educational Studies Association Critics Choice Award |
| 1988–1989 | American Antiquarian Society/National Endowment for the Humanities Fellowship |
| 1991, 1992 | Spencer Foundation Research Grants |
| 1991 | Katherine Ripley Award for Electronic Media, Planned Parenthood of Dallas and Northeast Texas; Matrix Award, Dallas Professional Chapter of Women in Media; Silver Award for Local Programs, Corporation for Public Broadcasting to KERA, Channel 13 (PBS), Family Project, "A Better Childhood (ABC) Quiz," 1991, chief advisor and commentator |
| 1995 | Nominated for the Grawemeyer Award in Education |
| 1997–1998 | University of Texas at Dallas Special Faculty Development Assignment for Research |
| 1999–2004 | University of Texas at San Antonio Faculty Awards for Research and Travel |
| 1999–2000 | Social Science History Association, President; Vice President, 1998–1999 |
| 2001 | Doctor of Philosophy honoris causa, University of Linköping, Sweden, for contributions to scholarship |
| 2001 | Swedish Bicentennial Research Fund, International Conference Grant (to University of Linköping) |
| 2001 | Social Science History Association grant to prepare book from 25th anniversary meeting |
| 2002 | University of Texas at San Antonio Faculty Development Research Leave |
| 2004- | Ohio Eminent Scholar in Literacy Studies |
| 2004–2015 | LiteracyStudies@OSU Initiative programming grants, College of Humanities |
| 2004–2010 | Ohio State University, Institute for Collaborative Research and Public Humanities Award to found and develop the Literacy Studies Working Group |

| | |
|---|---|
| 2005–2006 | Ohio State University, Arts and Sciences Colleges Interdisciplinary Curricular Enhancement Award (declined in favor of alternative funding) |
| 2006 | Distinguished Lecturer, Mary Lou Fulton Endowed Symposium Series, Arizona State University |
| 2006–2008 | Grant to Develop Graduate Interdisciplinary Specialization in Literacy Studies, Graduate School, Ohio State University |
| 2007 | Special Research Assignment, Ohio State University |
| 2007–2016 | Major funding to support LiteracyStudies@OSU: An Initiative, College of Humanities, with additional funds from Colleges of the Arts and Sciences, College of Art, College of Biological Sciences, College of Dentistry, Department of English, Department of Entomology, and University Libraries, The Ohio State University, to support an annual lecture |
| 2008–2010 | Grant for Research and Creativity in the Arts and Humanities, OSU |
| 2010 | Gartner Lecturer, Honors Program, Southern Methodist University |
| 2010 | Distinguished Undergraduate Research Mentor Award, OSU |
| 2011 | Nominated for the Grawemeyer Award in Education |
| 2011 | Masters of City and Regional Planning, CRP OneBook Program, and SPA Student Association Invitee, University of Texas at Arlington |
| 2011–2012 | Faculty Professional Leave, The Ohio State University |
| 2013 | Social Science History Association Award for Unmatched Record of Participation in the Annual Meeting, 1976–2013 and Counting |
| 2013–2014 | Birkelund Fellow, National Humanities Center Fellow |
| 2013–2014 | Center for Advanced Study in the Behavioral Sciences, Stanford University (declined) |
| 2014 | Visiting Professor, Federal University of Minas Gerais and State University of Rio de Janeiro, on Brazil federal grant (UERJ) (CNPq) |
| 2015–2016 | Center for Real Estate, Fisher College of Business, Ohio State University, Research Grant |
| 2016 | Nominated for the Grawemeyer Award in Education |
| 2016 | Visiting Scholar, Dedman College Interdisciplinary Institute, Southern Methodist University (canceled due to illness) |
| 2017 | Harvey J. Graff, Literacy Studies, and Composition, Tribute Session at the Conference on College Composition and Communication, 2017 |
| 2017 | Professor Emeritus of English & History and Ohio Eminent Scholar in Literacy Studies, The Ohio State University |
| 2020 | Most Influential Historians in the World |

| 2022 | Academy Professor in Emeritus Academy, The Ohio State University |
| --- | --- |
| 2023 | American Antiquarian Society elected to full membership |
| 2023 | Nominated to American Academy of Arts and Sciences, American Philosophical Society, National Academy of Education |
| 2024 | Expanding Literacy Studies/HJG Reunion, The Blackwell Inn, Columbus, Ohio, May 17–19, 2024 |

## Professional Employment

| 1973 | Northwestern University, Summer School, Instructor |
| --- | --- |
| 1974–1975 | Ontario Institute for Studies in Education, Extramural Lecturer |
| 1975–1998 | University of Texas at Dallas, Assistant to Associate (with tenure) to Professor of History and Humanities |
| 1980 | Loyola University, Chicago, Visiting Adjunct Professor, History |
| 1981, 1982 | Simon Fraser University, Summer School, Visiting Professor, English and Education, English and History |
| 1998–2004 | University of Texas at San Antonio, Professor of History; doctoral faculty in Culture, Literacy, and Language, and English, graduate faculty in Public Administration; Director, Division of Behavioral and Cultural Sciences, 1998–1999 |
| 2004–2017 | Ohio State University, Ohio Eminent Scholar in Literacy Studies and Professor of English and History |

## Publications

### Scholarly

#### Books

*Dallas, Texas: A Bibliographic Guide to the Sources of its Social History*, with Alan R. Baron and Charles Barton (Austin, Texas: University of Texas Press, 1979) [First published: University of Texas at Dallas, Southwest Center for Economic and Community Development, *Papers*, 1977]

*Children and Schools in Nineteenth-Century Canada/L'école canadienne et l'enfant au dix-neuvième siècle*, with Alison Prentice (Ottawa: National Museum of Civilization, Canada's Visual History Series, 1979; revised ed., CD-ROM, 1994)

*The Literacy Myth: Literacy and Social Structure in the Nineteenth-Century City* (New York and London: Academic Press, Studies in Social Discontinuity Series, 1979); [*Society magazine Book-of-the-Month; nominated for a number of professional book awards discussed at a session of the Social Science History Association, 1981*; excerpted in *Journal of Reading*; Malcolm Kiniry and Mike Rose, *Critical Strategies for Academic Thinking and Writing* (New York: Bedford Books-St. Martins Press, 1st ed.,1990; 2nd ed., 1995; 3rd ed., 1998); *plenary session to mark 30th*

*anniversary of publication,* Expanding Literacy Studies International Interdisciplinary Studies Conference for Graduate Students, *Ohio State University, April 2009]*
Quantification and Psychology: Toward a New History, co-editor and contributor, with Paul Monaco (Washington, DC: University Press of America, 1980) [Papers from the MSSB-NSF Quantification and Psychohistory Conference, April, 1977]
Literacy in History: An Interdisciplinary Research Bibliography (New York: Garland Publishing, Inc., 1981) [Previously published (in part): Chicago: The Newberry Library, Family and Community History Center, 1976; addendum, 1979]
Literacy and Social Development in the West, editor and contributor (Cambridge: Cambridge University Press, Studies in Oral and Literate Culture, 1981); Italian edition: *Alfabetizzazione e sviluppo sociale in Occidentale. Problemi e prospecttive* (Bologna: Il Mulino, 1986); Chinese in preparation
The Legacies of Literacy: Continuities and Contradictions in Western Society and Culture (Bloomington: Indiana University Press, 1987; paper, 1991) [Discussed at a session of the Social Science History Association, 1987; American Educational Studies Association Critics Choice Award, 1987; Society magazine book-of-the-month; nominated for a number of book awards] Italian edition: *Storia dell'Alfabetizzazione Occidentale*, 3 vols. (Bologna: Il Mulino, 1989); excerpted in David Crowley and Paul Heyer, eds., *Communication in History* 2nd, 3rd, 4th, 5th ed. (White Plains, NY: Longman, 1995–2006; 6th ed. Routledge, 2010) and Spanish translation; Ellen Cushman, Eugene Kintgen, Barry Kroll, and Mike Rose, eds., *Literacy: A Critical Sourcebook* (New York: Bedford/St. Martins Press, 2001; Chapter Five reprinted in *Communication in History: Stone Age Symbols to Social Media* (Routledge, 2023)]
National Literacy Campaigns: Historical and Comparative Perspectives, co-editor with Robert F. Arnove (New York: Plenum Publications, 1987) [Introduction reprinted in Ellen Cushman, Eugene Kintgen, Barry Kroll, and Mike Rose, eds., *Literacy: A Critical Sourcebook* (New York: Bedford/St. Martins Press, 2001), 591–615]
The Labyrinths of Literacy: Reflections on Literacy Past and Present (Sussex: Falmer Press, 1987) [Collection of my essays] Portuguese edition (Brazil: Artes Medicas, 1994); Chinese in preparation; extracts reprinted in Gitta Stagl, *Literatur, Lekture, Litterariat* (Vienna: Buro Medienberbund Osterreichischer Bundesverlag)
Growing Up in America: Historical Experiences, editor (Detroit: Wayne State University Press, 1987)
The Literacy Myth: Cultural Integration and Social Structure in the Nineteenth Century (New Brunswick, NJ: Transaction Publishers, 1991) [New edition with new introduction] (Republished by Routledge, 2017)
Conflicting Paths: Growing Up in America (Cambridge, MA: Harvard University Press, 1995) [Choice Magazine Outstanding Academic Book Award, 1995; discussed at a session of the Social Science History Association; excerpted in Paula S. Fass and Mary Ann Mason, eds., *Childhood in America* (New York: New York University Press, 2000); Project Gutenberg Internet Text Archive]
The Labyrinths of Literacy (Pittsburgh: University of Pittsburgh Press, Composition, Literacy, and Culture Series, 1995) [Revised and expanded collection of my essays]
Dallas Public and Private by Warren Leslie (1964), co-editor with Patricia E. Hill (Dallas: Southern Methodist University Press, 1998) [New edition with new introduction]

*Alfabetismo di massa: mito storia realtà*, in the series "Il Sapere Del Libro" (Milan: Edizioni Sylvestre Bonnard, 2002), [Essays on the history of literacy, in Italian translation; series includes Roger Chartier, Robert Darnton, Anthony Grafton, Donald McKenzie]

"Understanding Literacy in its Historical Contexts: Past Approaches and Work in Progress," special double issue, *Interchange*, 34, 2–3 (2003), co-editor with Alison Mackinnon, Bengt Sandin, and Ian Winchester [Papers from an international conference, Vadstena, Sweden, May 2002, "Egil Johansson, the Demographic Database, and Socio-Cultural History for the 21st Century: Literacy, Religion, Gender, and Social History"]

"Teen Chicago," special issue *Chicago History*, 33, 2 (2004), consulting editor and advisor

*Looking Backward and Looking Forward: Perspectives on Social Science History*, co-editor with Leslie Page Moch and Philip McMichael (Madison: University of Wisconsin Press, 2005) (BIS *History and Theory*, 2006) [Presentations and discussion from special retrospective and prospective sessions at the 25th annual meeting of the Social Science History Association, 2000]

*Literacy and Historical Development*, editor and contributor (Carbondale: Southern Illinois University Press, 2007)

*The Dallas Myth: The Making and Unmaking of an American City* (Minneapolis: University of Minnesota Press, 2008) [Discussed at a session at the Social Science History Association, Miami, 2008; Gartner Lecture, Honors Program, Southern Methodist University, 2010; Masters of City and Regional Planning, CRP OneBook Program, and SPA Student Association Invitee, University of Texas at Arlington, 2011]

*National Literacy Campaigns and Movements: Historical and Comparative Perspectives*, co-editor with Robert F. Arnove, new edition with new introduction (New Brunswick, NJ: Transaction Publishers, 2008)

*Understanding Literacy in its Historical Contexts: Socio-Cultural History and the Legacy of Egil Johansson*, co-editor with Alison Mackinnon, Bengt Sandin, and Ian Winchester (Lund, Sweden: Nordic Academic Press, 2009) [Expanded version of *Interchange* special issue, 33, 2 (2003) with support from the Swedish Bicentennial Fund/Stiftelsen Riksbankens Jubileunsfond, Linköping University, and Ohio State University]

*Literacy Myths, Legacies, and Lessons: New Studies of Literacy* (New Brunswick, NJ: Transaction Publishers, 2011; republished by Routledge, 2017)

*Undisciplining Knowledge: Interdisciplinarity in the Twentieth Century* (Baltimore: Johns Hopkins University Press, 2015) [Discussed at a session of the Social Science History Association, Baltimore, 2015; honored at a Book Celebration, Rochester Institute of Technology, 2016; featured in *Inside Higher Education*; *Nature*, Social Science Research Council, *Items*; History News Network, Scholarly Commons-University of Pennsylvania]

*Searching for Literacy: The Social and Intellectual Origins of Literacy Studies* (London: Palgrave Macmillan, 2022)

*The Literacy Myth: Cultural Integration and Social Structure in the Nineteenth Century*, Fourth edition (Fort Collins, Colo.: Landmarks Series, The WAC Clearinghouse, 2023) [https://wac.colostate.edu/books/landmarks/literacy-myth/] [Republication with new chapters]

*Literacy Myths, Legacies, and Lessons: New Studies of Literacy,* Third edition (Fort Collins, Colo.: Landmarks Series, The WAC Clearinghouse, 2023) [https://wac.colostate.edu/books/landmarks/literacy-legacies/ ] [Republication with new chapters]

*My Life with Literacy: The Continuing Education of a Historian. Intersections of the Personal, the Political, the Academic, and Place* (Fort Collins, Colo.: The WAC Clearinghouse, and Boulder: University Press of Colorado, 2024)

*Reconstructing the "Uni-versity" from the Ashes of the "Multi- and Mega-versity": Past Present, and Future of Higher Education* (Lanham, MD: Lexington Books, in progress) (ed.)

*Changing Paths of Academic Lives: Revising How We Understand Higher Education, 1960s to 2020s and Beyond,* collection of original essays (Fort Collins, Colo.: Practices and Possibilities Series, The WAC Clearinghouse and Boulder: University Press of Colorado, , in progress)

*Universities Caught Between the Past and the Future: Knowledge, Literacy, and Politics. Essays by Harvey J. Graff,* collection of essays in progress

*The Columbus Way: The Biggest U.S. City Without an Identity and a History,* collection of essays in progress

## Articles

"Notes on Methods for Studying Literacy from the Manuscript Census," *Historical Methods Newsletter,* 5 (1971), 11–16

"Towards a Meaning of Literacy: Literacy and Social Structure in Hamilton, Ontario," *History of Education Quarterly,* 12 (1972), 411–431

"Patterns of Dependency and Child Development in the-Mid-Nineteenth Century City: A Sample from Boston 1860," *History of Education Quarterly,* 13 (1973), 129–143

"Literacy and Social Structure in Elgin County, Canada West," *Histoire sociale/Social History,* 6 (1973), 25–48

"Crime and Punishment in the Nineteenth Century," Canadian Social History Project, *Report,* 5 (1973–1974), 124–162 [Reprinted in *Records of the Past: New Sources in Social History,* ed. Edward Jackson and Ian Winchester (Toronto: Ontario Institute for Studies in Education, 1979), 171–203]

"Introduction" to "Literacy Studies in Sweden," by Egil Johansson, in *ibid.*, 85–88 [Reprinted in *Records of the Past,* ed. Jackson and Winchester, 207–210]

"What the 1861 Census Can Tell Us About Literacy," *Histoire sociale/Social History,* 8 (1975), 337–347

"Literacy and History: Review Essay," *History of Education Quarterly,* 15 (1975), 467–474

"Towards a Meaning of Literacy: Literacy and Social Structure in Hamilton, Ontario," in *Education and Social Change: Themes from Ontario's Past,* ed. Michael B. Katz and Paul Mattingly (New York: New York University Press, 1975), 246–270

"Selected Bibliography: Urban, Social, Sociological, Demographic, and Quantitative History," Canadian Social History Project, *Report,* 6 (1975–1976), 1–16 [Reprinted in *Orillia, the Computer, and Social History,* ed. Ian Winchester (Toronto: Ontario Institute for Studies in Education)]

"Counting on the Past: Quantification in History—an essay review," *Acadiensis: Journal of the History of the Atlantic Region,* 5 (1976), 115–129

"Respected and Profitable Labour: Literacy, Jobs and the Working Class," in *Essays in Canadian Working Class History*, ed. Gregory S. Kealey and Peter Warrian (Toronto: McClelland and Stewart, 1976), 58–82, 202–207

"Crime and Punishment in the Nineteenth Century: A New Look at the Criminal," *Journal of Interdisciplinary History*, 7 (1976–1977), 477–491 [Reprinted in *Crime and Justice in American History. 11. Theory and Methods in Criminal Justice History, Part 1*, ed. Eric Monkkonen (Munich: K.G. Saur, 1992), 152–166]

"The 'New Math': Quantification, the 'New' History, and the History of Education," *Urban Education*, 11 (1977), 403–440

"The Conference on Quantitative History and Psychohistory," with Paul Monaco, *Psychohistory*, 1 (1977–1978), 7–10

"'Pauperism, Misery, and Vice': Illiteracy and Criminality in the Nineteenth Century," *Journal of Social History*, 11 (1977–1978), 245–268

"Reply to Daniel and Lauren Resnick, 'The Nature of Literacy,'" *Harvard Educational Review*, 48 (1978), 301–303

"Literacy: How Many Views?" *Interchange*, 9 (1978), 25–29

"Literacy Past and Present: Critical Approaches in the Literacy-Society Relationship," *Interchange: A Journal of Educational Studies*, 9 (1978), 1–21

"Literacy and History," International Institute for Adult Literacy Methods, Tehran, *Literacy Bibliographies*, 11 (February, 1978)

"The 'New' Social History and the Southwest: The Dallas Social History Project," *East Texas Historical Journal*, 16 (1978), 52–62 [Previously published: Southwest Center for Economic and Community Development, *Papers*, 1976–1977]

"The Reality Behind the Rhetoric: The Social and Economic Meanings of Literacy in the Mid-Nineteenth Century—the Example of Literacy and Criminality," in *Egerton Ryerson and His Times: Essays on the History of Education*, ed. Neil McDonald (Toronto: Macmillan, 1978), 187–220

"Literacy, Work, and Industrial Development in the Nineteenth Century," *Societas: A Review of Social History*, 9 (1979)

"Interpreting Historical Literacy: The Pattern of Quebec. A Comment," *Histoire sociale/Social History*, 12 (1979), 444–454

"Literacy, Education, and Fertility, Past and Present: A Critical Review," *Population and Development Review*, 5 (1979), 105–140

"Reply to Eric Monkkonen on the Social Historical Study of Criminality," *Journal of Interdisciplinary History*, 9 (1979), 465–471

"Scrivendo un libro sulla storia dell'alfabetismo occidentale: riflessioni di merito e di metodo," *Notizie, Alfabetismo e cultura scritta* (University of Perugia, Italy) (December, 1980), 3–14

"Introduction," with Paul Monaco, *Quantification and Psychology*, 1–70

"Theoretical Methods in Social History: Review," *American Journal of Sociology*, 85 (1980), 1442–1446

"Fertility, Demography, and History: Essay Review," *Labour/Le Travailleur*, 5 (1980), 242–245

"Reflections on the History of Literacy: Overview, Critique, and Proposals," *Humanities in Society*, 4 (1981), 303–333. [Portuguese translation: "O mito do alfatetismo,"

*Teoria & Educacao* (Brazil), no. 2 (1990), 30–64, special issue on literacy]
"Introduction," *Literacy and Social Development in the West*, 1–13
"Literacy, Jobs, and Industrialization: The Nineteenth Century," *ibid.*, 232–260
"The Legacies of Literacy," *Journal of Communication*, 32 (1982), 12–26. [Reprinted in Eugene R. Kintgen, Barry M. Kroll, and Mike Rose, eds., *Perspectives on Literacy* (Carbondale: Southern Illinois University Press, 1988), 82–91; Open University, DT200. *Introduction to Communication Technology*, Open University Reader, E825; Janet Maybin, ed., *Language and Literacy in Social Practice* (Clevedon, Philadelphia, and Adelaide: Multilingual Matters, 1994), 151–167; Greek translation, Hellenic Open University, 1999; Mastin Prinsloo and Mike Baynham, eds., *Literacy Studies. Volume 1. Great Divides and Situated Literacies* (Los Angeles: Sage, 2013), 145–160]
"Literacy, in Literature as in Life: An Early Twentieth-Century Example," *History of Education Quarterly*, 23 (1983), 279–296
"I lasciti dell'alfabetismo," *La critica sociologica*, 67 (1983), 6–21
"Literacy and Social Development in North America: On Ideology and History," in *Aspects of Literacy in the Eighteenth and Nineteenth Centuries*, ed. W.B. Stephens (Leeds: Museum of the History of Education, University of Leeds, 1983), 82–97, 103–106
"*On Literacy*: Essay Review," *Language and Society*, 12 (1983), 559–563
"On Literacy in the Renaissance: Overview and Reflections," *History of Education*, 12 (1983), 69–85 [Reprinted in Gary McCulloch, ed., *The Routledge/Falmer Reader in History of Education* (London: Routledge, 2005). 51–67]
"The City, Crisis, and Change in American Culture: Perceptions and Perspectives," in *Transition to the* 21st *Century: Prospects and Policies for Economic and Urban-Regional Transformation*, ed. Donald Hicks and Norman Glickman (Greenwich, CT: JAI Press, 1983), 113–152 [Revised consultant's paper for the President's Commission for a National Agenda for the Eighties, Panel on Metropolitan America, 1980]
"(Breaking) The Bounds of Literacy: A Comment," *Interchange*, 15 (1984), 53–57
"Early Adolescence in Antebellum America: The Remaking of Growing Up," special historical issue, *Journal of Early Adolescence*, 5 (Winter, 1985), 411–427
"Literacy," *The Social Science Encyclopaedia*, ed. Adam Kuper and Jessica Kuper (London: Routledge and Kegan Paul, 1985), 469–471; 2nd revised edition, 1994; 3rd revised edition, 2004, 2:587–589
"The History of Literacy," *Historical Social Research/Historische Sozialforschung* (Germany), 34 (1985), 37–43 [Papers from the Bellagio Conference on the Transformation of Europe, 1984]
"The Needs of Strangers," *Criminal Justice History*, 7(1986), 212–215
"The History of Literacy: Toward the Third Generation," *Interchange*, Special Anniversary Issue, Illuminating Education: The Uses of Science, History, and Philosophy in Educational Thought, 17, 2 (1986), 122–134 [Italian translation, "Gli studi di storia dell'alfabetizzazione: Verso la terza generzione," *Quaderni Storici*, no. 64 (1987), 203–222] [Reprinted in *Illuminating Education: The Uses of Science, History and Philosophy in Educational Thought* (Toronto: OISE Press, 1986)]
"Discussion: Educational Relevance of the Study of Expertise," *ibid.*, 19–24

"Discussion: Mining the Human Sciences," *ibid.*, 172–177 (editor and introduction)

"W.B. Hodgson, 'Exaggerated Estimates of Reading and Writing as Means of Education,'" *History of Education Quarterly*, 26 (1986), 377–393

"Crisis, Crisis, Where is the Crisis? Recent Popular Sociologies of Education," *Contemporary Sociology*, 15 (1986), 17–20

"The History of Childhood and Youth: Beyond Infancy?" *History of Education Quarterly*, 26 (1986), 95–109

"The Legacies of Literacy," in *Literacy, Society, and Schooling: A Reader*, ed. Suzanne de Castell, Allan Luke, and Kieran Egan (Cambridge: Cambridge University Press, 1986), 61–86 [Spanish translation: "El Legado de la Alfabetizacion: Constantes y Contradicciones de la Sociedad y la Cultura Occidentales," *Revista de Educacion*, 288 (1989), 7–34]

"Doctoral Seminar in the History of Ideas," *Intellectual History Newsletter*, 8 (April, 1986), 27–31

"National Literacy Campaigns: Historical and Comparative Lessons," with Robert F. Arnove, *Phi Delta Kappan*, 69 (1987), 202–206 [Reprinted in *Adult Literacies: Intersections with Elementary and Secondary Education*, ed. Caroline Beverstock and Anabel P. Newman (ERIC, 1991), 51–55]

"Introduction," *Growing Up in America: Historical Perspectives*, xi-xix, et seq.

"Introduction," with Robert F. Arnove, *National Literacy Campaigns*, 1–28; new ed., *National Literacy Campaigns and Movement* (New Brunswick, N.J: Transaction Publishers, 2008 [Reprinted in Ellen Cushman, Eugene Kintgen, Barry Kroll, and Mike Rose, eds., *Literacy: A Critical Sourcebook* (New York: Bedford/St. Martins Press, 2001), 591–615]

"Provenzo's Galaxy: Post-McLuhan Culture?," *History of Education Quarterly*, 27 (1987), 155–156

"High School History," *Journal of Social History*, 20 (1987), 803–807

"The Closing of the American Mind," *Transaction/SOCIETY*, 25 (Nov.-Dec., 1987), 25th Anniversary Issue, 98–101

"Families and Politics: Beyond Public/Private Dichotomies and Empty Theories. Essay Review," *Journal of Family History*, 13 (1988), 433–439

"Whither the History of Literacy? The Future of the Past," *Communication*, special issue on the history of literacy, 11 (1988), 5–22

"National Literacy Campaigns," with Robert F. Arnove, *Alberta Journal of Educational Research*, 34 (1988), 215–223

"Critical Literacy versus Cultural Literacy: Reading Signs of the Times? A Review of E.D. Hirsch, Jr., *Cultural Literacy*," *Interchange*, 20 (1989), 46–52, with "Response" by Hirsch, 61–64

"Towards 2000: Progress and Poverty in the History of Education," *Historical Studies in Education*, 3 (1991), 191–210 [Distinguished Lecture, Canadian History of Education Association, Annual Meeting, 1990]

"Introduction to the 1991 Edition," *The Literacy Myth*, xiii-xxxiii

"Remaking Growing Up: Nineteenth-Century America," *Histoire sociale/Social History*, 24 (1991), 35–59 [United States Working Group, International Commission for the History of Social Movements and Social Structures and International Congress on Historical Sciences, 1990]

"Literacy, Libraries, Lives: New Cultural and Social Histories," *Libraries & Culture*, 26, (1991), 24–45 [Reprinted in *Reading and Libraries: Proceedings of Library History Seminar VIII* (1990), ed. Donald G. Davies, Jr. (Austin: Graduate School of Library and Information Science, University of Texas at Austin, 1991), 24–45] [Distinguished Plenary Address, Library History Seminar, 1990]

"Crisis in Expression and Representation: Syllabus," *Intellectual History Newsletter*, 13 (1991), 74–82

"National Literacy Campaigns in Historical and Comparative Perspective: Legacies, Lessons, and Issues" with Robert F. Arnove, in *Emergent Issues in Education: Comparative Perspectives*, ed. Philip G. Altbach, Gail P. Kelly, and Arnove (Albany: SUNY Press, 1992), 283–294

"Literacy, Myths and Legacies: Lessons from the Past/Reflections for the Future," *Interchange*, 24 (1993), 271–286 [Invited Address, Bard College Conference on Education for Complexity in the 21st Century, 1991]

"Literacy Patterns in Historical Perspective," in *Reading Across the Life Span*, ed. Steven R. Yussen and M. Cecil Smith. Recent Research in Psychology (Berlin and New York: Springer Verlag, 1993), 73–91

"Literacy, Myths, and Lessons: Keynote Address," in *Adult Literacy: An International Urban Perspective*. Proceedings of a Conference, August, 1992, The United Nations, New York, co-sponsored by City University of New York, Literacy Assistance Center of New York City, and UNESCO (New York, 1994), 15–39

"A Response to Abraham Stahl's 'Cultural Literacy: A Positive View,'" *Interchange*, 25 (1994), 227–228

"Using First-Person Sources in Social and Cultural History: A Working Bibliography," *Historical Methods*, 27 (1994), 87–92

"Literacy, Myths, and Legacies: Lessons from the History of Literacy," in *Functional Literacy: Theoretical Issues and Educational Implications*, ed. Ludo Verhoeven (Amsterdam: John Benjamins Pub. Co., 1994), 37–60 [Proceedings of the International Conference on Attaining Functional Literacy, The Netherlands, 1991] [Keynote Address]

"Teaching the History of Literacy," *SHARP News* [Society for the History of Authorship, Reading, and Publishing], 3 (Spring, 1994), 3–4

"National Literacy Campaigns: Historical and Comparative Lessons," special issue on literacy, *Texas Journal of Ideas, History, and Culture*, 16 (Spring/Summer, 1994), 12–17, 68

"Literacy, Myths, and Legacies: Lessons from the History of Literacy," in *The Labyrinths of Literacy* (Pittsburgh: University of Pittsburgh Press, Composition, Literacy, and Culture Series, 1995), 318–349 [Reprinted in *Literacy and Historical Development*, ed. Harvey J. Graff (Carbondale: Southern Illinois University Press, 2007)]

"Assessing the History of Literacy in the 1990s: Themes and Questions," in *Escribir y leer en Occidente*, Armando Petrucci and M. Gimeno Blay (Valencia, Spain: Universitat de Valencia, 1995), 5–46 [Plenary Address, Conference on Writing and Reading in Western Europe, Valencia, Spain, 1993] [Reprinted in *Understanding Literacy in its Historical Contexts*, co-editor with Alison Mackinnon, Bengt Sandin, and Ian Winchester (Lund, Sweden: Nordic Academic Press, 2009), 243–264]

"Early Modern Literacies," in *Communication in History*, ed. David Crowley and Paul Heyer, 2nd, 3rd, 5th ed. (White Plains, NY: Longman, 1995–2006) [Spanish translation, Barcelona: Bosch Casa Editorial, 1997]

"The Persisting Power and Costs of the Literacy Myth. A Comment on *Literacy, Economy and Society: Results of the First International Adult Literacy Survey (IALS)*, Organisation for Economic Co-Operation and Development and Statistics Canada (1995)," *Literacy Across the Curriculum*, Centre for Literacy, Montreal, 12 (1996), 4–5 [Reprinted in *Working Papers on Literacy*, Centre for Literacy, No. 1, 1997] [First in a series of invited comments]

"Reading and Writing the City," *Intellectual History Newsletter*, 18 (1996), 103–108

"A Response to Stan Jones, 'Ending the Myth of the "Literacy Myth": A Response to Critiques . . .'" with Brian V. Street, *Literacy Across the Curriculum*, Centre for Literacy, Montreal, 13, 1 (1997), 4–6

"Introduction" to *Dallas Public and Private* by Warren Leslie (1964) with Patricia E. Hill (Dallas: Southern Methodist University Press, 1998), xi-xxv

"Teaching [and] Historical Understanding: Disciplining Historical Imagination with Historical Context," *Interchange*, 30 (1999), 143–169

"Interdisciplinary Explorations in the History of Children, Adolescents, and Youth—for the Past, Present, and Future," *Journal of American History*, 85 (1999), 1538–1547 [Reprinted in *Newsletter, Society for the History of Children and Youth*, 11 (Winter 2008)]

"Teaching Historical Understanding: Disciplining Historical Imagination with Historical Context," in *The Social Worlds of Higher Education: Handbook for Teaching in a New Century*, ed. Bernice A. Pescosolido and Ronald Aminzade (Thousand Oaks, CA: Pine Forge Press/Sage Publications for the American Sociological Association, 1999), 280–294

"Interdisciplinary Explorations in the History of Children, Adolescents, and Youth—for the Past, Present, and Future," *Journal of American History*, 85 (1999), 1538–1547

"President's Report," *Social Science History Association Newsletter*, Winter 2000 and Summer 2000

"The Shock of the '"New" Histories': Social Science Histories and Historical Literacies," Presidential Address, Social Science History Association, 2000, *Social Science History*, 25, 4 (Winter 2001), 483–533 [Reprinted in *Looking Backward and Looking Forward: Perspectives in Social Science History*, ed. Harvey J. Graff, Leslie Page Moch, and Philip McMichael (Madison: University of Wisconsin Press, 2005), 13–56]

"Literacy's Myths and Legacies," in *Anarcho-Modernism: Toward A New Critical Theory. In Honour of Jery Zaslove*, ed. Ian Angus (Vancouver: Talonbooks, 2001), 169–184

"Literacy," in *The Oxford Companion to United States History*, ed. Paul Boyer (New York: Oxford University Press, 2001), 450–451

"Literacy's Myths and Legacies: From Lessons from the History of Literacy, to the Question of Critical Literacy," *in Difference, Silence and Textual Practice: Studies in Critical Literacy*, ed. Peter Freebody, Sandy Muspratt, and Bronwyn Dwyer (Cresskill, NJ: Hampton Press, 2001), 1–29 [Plenary Address, Conference on Literacy and Power, Griffith University, Australia, 1993]

"The Nineteenth-Century Origins of Our Times," in *Literacy: A Critical Sourcebook*, ed. Ellen Cushman, Eugene R. Kintgen, Barry M. Kroll, and Mike Rose (New York: Bedford/St. Martins Press, 2001), 211–233

"Growing Up in America," *Magazine of History* (Organization of American Historians), 15, 4 (Summer, 2001), 55–59 [Family History issue, ed. Linda Gordon and Steven Mintz]

"General Introduction" and "Introduction to Historical Studies of Literacy," special double issue, *Interchange*, 34, 2–3 (2003), "Understanding Literacy in its Historical Contexts: Past Approaches and Work in Progress," co-editor with Alison Mackinnon, Bengt Sandin, and Ian Winchester, 117–122, 123–131 [Papers from an international conference, Vadstena, Sweden, May 2002, "Egil Johansson, the Demographic Database, and Socio-Cultural History for the 21st Century: Literacy, Religion, Gender, and Social History"]

"Coming of Age in Chicago," *Chicago History*, 33, 2 (2004), 12–31, with Joy L. Bivens, special issue on Teen Chicago

"Introduction" to the book, 3–10, and to sections on "Twenty-Five Years Later: SSHA in the Eyes of its Founding Spirits," 57–58; "Looking Backward, Looking Forward: Social Science History at 2000. Critical Perspectives," 69; and "Literacy as Social Science History: Its Past and Future," 153–154; in *Looking Backward and Looking Forward: Perspectives in Social Science History*, ed. Harvey J. Graff, Leslie Page Moch, and Philip McMichael (Madison: University of Wisconsin Press, 2005)

"Introduction," in *Literacy and Historical Development: A Reader* (Carbondale: Southern Illinois U P, 2007), 1–11

"History's War of the Wor(l)ds. An Afterword," in Sigurdur Gylfi Magnusson, *The History War: Essays and Narratives on Ideology/Sögustríð: Greinar og frásagnir um hugmyndafræði* (Reykjavík: Háskólaútgáfan, published by the Icelandic University Press and The Center for Microhistorical Research at the Reykjavik Academy, 2007), 475–481

"Teaching the History of Growing Up," *Newsletter, Society for the History of Children and Youth*, 11 (Winter 2008)

"Literacy Myths," with John Duffy, *Encyclopedia of Language and Education*, 2nd ed., Vol. 2 Literacy, ed. Brian V. Street and Nancy Hornberger (Berlin and New York: Springer, 2007), 41–52, and subsequent editions

"Bibliography of the History of Literacy in Western Europe and North America," in *Literacy and Historical Development: A Reader* (Carbondale: Southern Illinois U P, 2007), 417–439 [Reprinted in *Understanding Literacy in its Historical Contexts*, co-editor with Alison Mackinnon, Bengt Sandin, and Ian Winchester (Lund, Sweden: Nordic Academic Press, 2009), 265–300]

"New Introduction" to *National Literacy Campaigns and Movements: Historical and Comparative Perspectives*, co-editor with Robert F. Arnove, new edition (New Brunswick, NJ: Transaction Publishers, 2008), xi–xvi

"The Critical Historiography of Childhood: A Session from the Society for the History of Children and Youth biennial conference, 2009," with James Block, Rebecca de Schweinitz, Colin Heywood, Jennifer Ritterhouse, and Michael

Zuckerman, *Society for the History of Children and Youth Bulletin*, No. 14 (Fall, 2009). [http://www.history.vt.edu/Jones/SHCY/Newsletter14/Issue14.pdf]

"Introduction," with Alison Mackinnon, Bengt Sandin, and Ian Winchester, *Understanding Literacy in its Historical Contexts: Socio-Cultural History and the Legacy of Egil Johansson*, co-editor with Alison Mackinnon, Bengt Sandin, and Ian Winchester (Lund, Sweden: Nordic Academic Press, 2009), 7–13

"Introduction to Historical Studies of Literacy," *Understanding Literacy in its Historical Contexts*, co-editor with Alison Mackinnon, Bengt Sandin, and Ian Winchester (Lund, Sweden: Nordic Academic Press, 2009), 14–22

"The Literacy Myth: Literacy, Education, and Demography," *Vienna Yearbook of Population Research*, 8 (2010), 17–23 [reprinted in *The Literacy Myth*, The WAC Clearinghouse 2023 ed.]

"*The Literacy Myth* at Thirty," *Journal of Social History*, 43 (Spring, 2010), 635–661 [reprinted in *The Literacy Myth*, The WAC Clearinghouse 2023 edition]

"Literacy Studies and Interdisciplinary Studies: Reflections on History and Theory," in *Valences of Interdisciplinarity: Theory, Practice, Pedagogy*, ed. Raphael Foshay, Cultural Dialectics Series (Edmonton, Alberta: AU/Athabasca University Press, 2012), 273–307

"The Legacies of Literacy Studies," inaugural symposium, *Literacy in Composition Studies Journal*, 1, 1 (2013), 15–17 (adapted from the Session on Legacies, Gateways, and the Future of Literacy Studies, Conference on College Composition and Communication, 2012) [reprinted in *The Literacy Myth*, The WAC Clearinghouse 2023 edition]

"Harvey Graff on Interdisciplinarity," an interview, *News of the National Humanities Center*, (Spring/Summer, 2014), 8–9, 18; excerpted in *History News Network*, May 5, 2014

"Epilogue: Literacy Studies and Interdisciplinary Studies with Notes on the Place of Deborah Brandt," in *Literacy, Economy, and Power: Writing and Research after Literacy in American Lives*, ed. Julie Nelson Christoph, John Duffy, Eli Goldblatt, Nelson Graff, Rebecca Nowacek, and Bryan Trabold (Carbondale, Ill.: Southern Illinois University Press, 2014), 202–226

Undisciplining Knowledge [http://jhupressblog.com/2015/09/09/undisciplining-knowledge/]

"*Undisciplining Knowledge: Interdisciplinarity in the Twentieth Century*: Q&A," *Inside Higher Education*, September, 10, 2015

"The Undisciplinarian: Three Questions," *Nature*, September 16, 2015. *Nature*'s Books and the Arts Blog [https://tinyurl.com/yckbj2vb]

"How misguided university policies are harming the humanities, arts and sciences," *Inside Higher Education*, December, 18, 2015

"Interdisciplinarity as ideology and practice," Social Science Research Council, *Items* (reintroduced), May, 2016 [https://tinyurl.com/25s4p3e8]

Joint interview with Brian Street on the Development of Literacy Studies, by Ana Maria de Oliveira Galvao, Maria Cristina Soares de Gouvea, and Ana Maria Rebelo Gomes, *Educação em Revista* (Federal University of Minas Gerais, Brazil) 32 (Summer 2016), 267–282. Reprinted as "Em busca do letramento: as origens sociais e intelectuais des estudos sobre letramento (Searching for Literacy: The Social and Intellectual Origins of Literacy Studies)," *Revista Brasileira de História da Educação* 16 (2016), 215–231, 232–252 (Portuguese and English). Reprinted in English, "An Interview with Harvey J. Graff & Brian Street," *Literacy in Composition Studies*, 5 (March, 2017), 49–66 [reprinted in *The Literacy Myth,* The WAC Clearinghouse 2023 edition]

"The 'problem' of interdisciplinarity in theory, practice, an history," *Social Science History*, special 40*th* anniversary issue, 40, 4 (Dec., 2016), 775–803

"A Forum on Interdisciplinarity," co-author with Jerry A. Jacobs, Mary Jo Maynes, and William H. Sewell, Jr., *Penn Scholarly Commons* 2017 [http://repository.upenn.edu/interdisciplinarity_forum/]

"Literacy Myths," with John Duffy, in *Literacies and Language Education*, ed. Brian Street, *Encyclopedia of Language and Education*, 3rd ed. (Berlin and New York: Springer International, 2017)

"Michael B. Katz 2015 SSHA Memorial Session," organizer and introduction, with Leah N. Gordon, Margaret O'Mara, Mark J. Stern, and Merlin Chowkwanyun, "*Social Science History*, 41 (2017), 757–776

"The new literacy studies and the resurgent literacy myth," *Literacy in Composition Studies*, 9, 1 (2022), 47–53 [reprinted in *The Literacy Myth,* The WAC Clearinghouse 2023 edition and in *Literacy Myths, Legacies, and Lessons,* The WAC Clearinghouse 2023 edition]

"The inseparability of 'historical myths' and 'permanent crises' in the humanities," *Journal of Liberal Arts and Humanities*, 3, 9 (Sept. 2022), 16–26

"The nondebate about critical race theory and our American moment: The interaction of past, present, and alternative futures," special issue on Memory Laws or Gag Laws? Disinformation Meets Academic Freedom, *Journal of Academic Freedom*, 13 (Fall, 2022)

"The persistent 'reading myth' and the 'crisis of the humanities,'" *CCC/College Composition and Communication*, 74, 3 (Feb. 2023), 575–580 [reprinted in *The Literacy Myth,* The WAC Clearinghouse 2023 edition]

"Scholarly book authors' bill of rights," *Journal of Intellectual Freedom and Privacy*, 7, 4 (2022). 5–8 [August, 2023]

"The power of models and examples in education and higher education," *Journal of Educational Thought*, 56, 2 (2023), 117–124

"Pay to Play —Publish for a Price: The Myths and Manipulation of the New Corporate Open-Access Journals," *Journal of Educational Thought*, 56, 3 (2023), 267–274

"Pay to Play —Publish for a Price: The Myths and Manipulation of the New Corporate Open-Access Journals," *Journal of Intellectual Freedom and Privacy*, 8, 4 (2023) [2024]

"Literacy Studies and Composition through the work of Harvey J. Graff, Tribute Session, Conference on College Composition and Communication 2017 including Response by Graff," *Across the Disciplines*, 21, Spring, 2024

"Choosing college wisely: Comparative earning data as a key factor in selecting colleges and majors," with David Levy, *Change*, June, 2024

"Writing and reading: The missing elements in historical and contemporary studies of English writing," Special issue on "Confluences of Writing Studies and the History of the English Language," *Across the Disciplines*, Fall, 2024

"The causes and consequences of poverty and impoverishment—broadly construed/constructed—in academia, past and present," Special issue on Academic Poverty, *Academic Labor: Research and Artistry,* Fall, 2024

"From Multi-versity and Mega-versity, back to Uni-versity: The impossible dream of changing 'incentive structures' and 'business models,'" *Journal of Educational Thought,* forthcoming

"Why professors—led by the humanities—are our own worst enemies, and what we can do about it," *Journal of Educational Thought, forthcoming*

"Disconnecting Gown and Town: Campus Partners for Urban Community Development, Ohio State University," under review

## Journalism and Local Articles to 2015

"Who Decides? Who Controls? A Perspective on Our Urban Past," Southern Resources Center, *The Housing and Community Development Act of 1974: Promise and Practice. A Handbook on Public Policy* (Dallas: Southern Resources Center, 1976)

"History, Philosophy, and Philosophy of History," *Texas Books in Review*, 1 (1977)

"Reviews in Southwestern History," *Texas Books in Review*, 2 (1978)

City of Dallas Historic Landmarks Publications: "Swiss Avenue Historic District," 1978; "Old Fair Park Fire Station," 1978; "Union Station," 1979; "Oak Lawn Fire Station," 1980; "Federal Reserve Bank," 1980; "Trinity Methodist Church," 1980; "Miller Shingle Style House," 1981 [Reprinted in *Historic Dallas*, 3 (Spring, 1982)]; "South Boulevard/Park Row," 1982 [Reprinted in *Historic Dallas*, 3 (Summer, 1982)]; "Saint Paul United Methodist Church," 1982; "Ambassador Hotel," 1982 [Reprinted in *Historic Dallas*, 3 (Fall, 1982)]; "Melrose Hotel," 1983; "Majestic Theatre," 1983; "Cedar Crest," 1984; "Magnolia Building," 1984; "Fair Park," 1985

"Basic Education" and "Youth," *Issues and Alternatives: A Guide to the Policy Maker* (Dallas: Dallas Public Library, Public Interest Information Network, 1979)

"How Can You Celebrate a Sesquicentennial If You Have No History? Reflections on Historical Consciousness in Dallas," essay commissioned by the *Dallas Morning News* for Texas State Sesquicentennial, 1986

"Race between San Antonio, Dallas like fabled tortoise and the hare: Commentary," *San Antonio Express-News,* Dec. 31, 1997

"City must create own mold for public universities," *San Antonio Express-News,* Aug. 23, 1998

"Alamo City's Different Futures," Insight, *San Antonio Express-News,* June 24, 2001

Letters to the Editor, *Columbus Dispatch,* 2004–2015

"Not Your Mother's Literacy, But Perhaps Your Daughter's" with Susan Hanson, *English @ OSU,* 2, 1 (Spring 2008)

"The Troubled Discourse of Interdisciplinarity," Letter to the Editor, *Chronicle of Higher Education,* Feb. 5, 2010

"Booktalk," Ohio State University, *On Campus,* October, 2012

"Throwing the Baby Out With the Interdisciplinary Bath Water," Letter to the Editor, *Chronicle of Higher Education,* June 12, 2014

"Early-college programs lack many benefits of the real thing," Commentary, with Steve Rissing, *Columbus Dispatch*, June 7, 2015

"An Education in Sloganeering," *Wall Street Journal*, Oct. 1, 2015

## Education and Curriculum

Contributor, H-Education Electronic Network, graduate syllabuses, 2003–2016

Contributor, SHARP, Electronic Network, graduate syllabuses, 2003, 2005

Contributor, H-Child Electronic Network, graduate and undergraduate course syllabuses, 1998–2016

Contributor, H-Urban Electronic Network, urban graduate and undergraduate course syllabuses,1994–2016

Contributor, Urban History Association, *Syllabus Exchange*, 1990 and *Syllabus Exchange II and Sampler*, 1993

## General and Public

### Books

*Women and Public Policy: Conference Proceedings*, with Carolyn L. Galerstein (Richardson: University of Texas at Dallas, 1977)

*Women and Public Policy: A Report*, with Carolyn L. Galerstein (Richardson: University of Texas at Dallas, 1978)

### Encyclopedia Entries

"Literacy," *Funk and Wagnalls New Encyclopedia*, 1983, 156–157

"Illiteracy," *The World Book Encyclopedia*, 1993 ed., Vol. 18, 78–79

"Literacy," in *Microsoft Encarta*

"Literacy," *The World Book Encyclopedia*, 1995 and future eds.

"Literacy" in *Microsoft Encarta*, 1998, new entry

"Literacy Myths," with John Duffy, in *Literacies and Language Education*, ed. Brian Street, *Encyclopedia of Language and Education*, 2nd ed. 2007; 3rd ed. 2017 (Berlin and New York: Springer International)

### Book Reviews

*History of Education Quarterly* (3); *Acadiensis; Texas Books in Review* (4); *American Journal of Sociology* (2); *Labour/Le Travail; American Historical Review* (4); *Journal of American History* (4); *Language in Society; Journal of Interdisciplinary History* (4); *Journal of Social History* (3); *Canadian Historical Review; Criminal Justice History; Contemporary Sociology* (2); *Transaction/SOCIETY; American Anthropologist* (2); *Journal of Family History; Interchange; Comparative Studies in Society and History*

## Research and Teaching Interests

Historical and Contemporary Studies of Literacy; Modern North American and Western European (comparative) Social History; United States and Canadian History;

History of the Family and Women; Urban History; History of Social Policy; History of Social Institutions; History of Population and Social Structure; Nineteenth-Century Society and Culture; History of Literacy; History of Children, Adolescents, and Youth; History of Education; Public and Applied History; Local and Community History; Approaches/Methods in History; Theory and Method in the Humanities and the Social Sciences

## Additional Professional Experience
### Academic

- Canadian Social History Project, Ontario Institute for Studies in Education and University of Toronto, consultant, 1973–1975
- Conference on Quantitative History and Psychohistory (sponsored by the Mathematics Social Science Board, National Science Foundation), coordinator (with Paul Monaco), 1977
- *Journal of Family History*, Bibliographic Project, consultant, 1977–1979
- National Endowment for the Humanities, reviewer and panelist, 1977-; consultant, 1978-
- Workshop on Women in Higher Education, Texas A&M University, College Station, Texas, university representative, 1978
- *Historical Atlas of Canada*, consultant, 1979–1982
- Newberry Library: Fellow; Research Associate; Fellowship Committee; Family and Community History Center Associate, 1979–1981; fellowship reviewer, 1979–
- Newberry Library Renaissance Conference, Advisory Committee, 1981–1982
- President's Commission for a National Agenda for the Eighties, consultant, 1980
- National Institute of Education, consultant, 1980-
- Fertility Determinants Project, Indiana University, consultant, 1983
- Annenberg School of Communications, University of Southern California, Annenberg Scholars Program, 1983
- NEH Implementation Grant, University of Texas at Dallas, "The Art of Translation in an Interdisciplinary Curriculum: Re-Creative Dynamics in the Humanities", consultant/instructor, 1983–87
- American Antiquarian Society, Program on the History of the Book in American Culture, Advisory Board, 1985–1988, 1988–1991
- Humanities Institute, Simon Fraser University, consultant "The Story of Literacy," television series project (proposed), conference planning, and other projects, 1985–2016
- United States Working Group, International Commission for the History of Social Movements and Social Structures, and International Congress on Historical Sciences, member, 1990
- Everyday Literacy Practices In and Out of Schools in Low Socioeconomic Urban Communities Project, Griffith University, Australia, consultant, 1993–

- A Study of Effectiveness in Prison Education, Simon Fraser University, Graduate Liberal Studies Program, consultant, l993
- Resource member, UNESCO Institute of Education Literacy Exchange Network, 1994-
- H-Urban (H-Net Humanities and Social Sciences Online), Board of Advisors, 1995–
- Great Cities Program, Electronic Network, University of Illinois at Chicago and H-Net, Advisory Board, 1995–2002
- Great Cities Project, University of Illinois at Chicago and H-Urban, "The History of Community Organizing and Community-Based Housing and Economic Development in an International Context," on-line seminar, International Advisory Board, 1995–1999
- Stanton Sharp Symposium on the History of the Family, Southern Methodist University, advisor, 1996–2016
- William P. Clements Center for Southwest Studies, Department of History, Southern Methodist University, Fellow, 1996–2016
- *Signs: Journal of Women in Culture and Society*, special issue on "Feminisms and Youth Culture," advisor and manuscript reviewer, 1996
- H-Childhood (H-Net Humanities and Social Sciences Online), Board of Advisors, 1998–2016
- Chicago Historical Society, "Teen Chicago," principal academic advisor, 2001–2004, a multi-year project in the history of teens, oral history, public programming, publications, and transformation of the roles of people in museums and historical societies [see below]
- *The Child: An Encyclopedic Companion* (University of Chicago Press, 2009), Advisory Board, 2001–2009
- Urban History Association, Board of Directors, 2002–2004
- "Literacy, Religion, Gender, and Social History: A Socio-Cultural History for the 21st Century. An International Conference for Egil Johansson," Vadstena, Sweden, May, 2002, co-organizer, coordinator, and speaker, with scholars in Sweden, Australia, and Canada, with support from the Swedish Bicentennial Research Fund to University of Linköping (Bengt Sandin)
- University of California, Berkeley, Center for Children and Youth Policy and Department of History, Conference on Rethinking Child Development, October, 2005, one of a series of small conferences to bring together historians and social scientists on the subject of childhood, 2005–2006
- McGill University, Arts Faculty Humanities Program and Interdisciplinary Studies Review, External Expert, 2007
- Communications and Society Program of the Aspen Institute for the Knight Commission on the Information Needs of Communities in a Democracy, Advisory Board, 2008–2010
- Carnegie Mellon University, Department of History, President's Advisory Board, 2008–2009
- Bedford Bibliography for Teachers of Writing, consultant, 2010
- National Public Radio, Radiolab program, interview on the origins of cities, 2010

- Scientific Committee of I SIHELE 2010, International Seminar on the History of Teaching Reading and Writing, theme: "The constitution of the field of history of literacy in Brazil." promoted by Gphellb–Research Group "History of Teaching Language and Literature in Brazil", Faculty of Philosophy and Sciences, Post-Graduate Program in Education at Universidade Estadual Paulista—Campus Marilia, Brazil, member, 2010
- Advisory Board, Museum of Writing, online collaborative project, Institute of English Studies, University of London, and Faculty of Information Studies and University Library, University of California, Los Angeles, 2010-
- Scientific Committee, ABAlf-Brazilian Congress on Literacy, "The meanings of literacy in Brazil: what we know, what we do and what we want?" and I SIHELE, International Seminar on the History of Teaching Reading and Writing, "Methods and teaching materials in the history of the initial teaching of reading and writing in Brazil," 2013
- Scientific Committee, I CONBAlf (Brazilian Congress on Literacy)—Associacao Brasileira de Alfabetizacao (Brazilian Association of Literacy), 2015
- External reviewer: National Endowment for the Humanities; Newberry Library; Center for Advanced Studies in the Behavioral Sciences; National Institute of Education; Social Sciences and Humanities Research Council of Canada; American Council of Learned Societies; Center for English Language Achievement (CELA), SUNY at Albany; Montana State University; Spencer Foundation, Major Grants

## Editorial

- *Interchange: A Quarterly Review of Education*, Editorial Board, 1974–1975; Corresponding Editor, 1975–1976; Consulting Editor, 1985-
- *History of Education Quarterly*, Editorial Board, 1979–1983
- *Historical Methods*, Editorial Board, 1987–1989
- *Interdisciplinary Perspectives in Social History Series*, State University of New York Press, General Editor, 1979–85 [3 books published]
- *Interdisciplinary Studies in History Series*, Indiana University Press, General Editor, 1982- [19 books contracted; 11 published]
- State University of New York Press, consultant, 1979–1985
- Garland Publishing, Inc., consultant, 1979–1981
- Indiana University Press, consultant, 1982-
- Wayne State University Press, consultant, 1985–1989
- *Wilson Quarterly*, special issue on literacy, advisor, Spring, 1986
- *Studies in Written Language and Literacy*, John Benjamins Publishing Company, Amsterdam, Editorial Board, 1992-
- *Social Science History*, Editorial Board, 1994–1997
- *Historical Social Research/Historische Sozialforchung* (Germany), Consulting Editor, 1998-
- *Literacy and Numeracy Studies: An International Journal* (Australia), International Editorial Board, 1998–2020

- *Journal of Language, Identity, and Education*, Editorial Board, 2000–2007
- *American Periodicals*, Editorial Advisory Board, 2005-
- Computers & Composition Digital Press (CCDP), International Editorial Board, 2007-
- *Literacy in Composition Studies*, Founding Editorial Board, 2012-
- Book and Manuscript Reviewer: *History of Education Quarterly; Journal of American History; Histoire sociale/Social History; American Historical Review; Southwestern Historical Quarterly; American Journal of Sociology; Texas Books in Review; Journal of Family History; Social Science History; William and Mary Quarterly; Historical Methods; Journal of Social History; Journal of Library History/Libraries and Culture; Educational Studies; Journal of Interdisciplinary History; Canadian Historical Review; Curriculum Inquiry; Acadiensis; Contemporary Sociology; Labour/Le Travailleur; Language in Society; Criminal Justice History; Society; American Anthropologist; American Ethnologist; Interchange; Journal of Modern History; Historical Studies in Education; Proceedings, American Antiquarian Society; American Literature; Journal of Higher Education; Journal of the History of the Behavioral Sciences; Journal of Urban History; Urban History; Victorian Studies; Signs; Library Quarterly; Journal of Educational Thought; Journal of Language, Identity, and Education; College Composition and Communications*; Cornell University Press; University of Chicago Press; University of Wisconsin Press; State University of New York Press; Indiana University Press; Cambridge University Press; Academic Press; Oxford University Press; University of Tennessee Press; Plenum Publications; Sage Publications; Southern Methodist University Press; Northern Illinois University Press; Wayne State University Press; Houghton Mifflin; University of Pennsylvania Press; University of Massachusetts Press; Rutgers University Press; Columbia University Press; Greenwood Publishing; University of Pittsburgh Press; Bloomsbury Press

## University

### *University of Toronto and Ontario Institute for Studies in Education, 1970–1975*

- Department of History and Philosophy of Education: Research Assistant; Member: General Assembly, departmental committees (admissions, searches, orientation, evaluation, research and development, programmes and graduate studies, nominating, library, admissions policy)

### *University of Texas at Dallas, 1975–1998*

- Member: School and College of Arts and Humanities; Faculty associate: School of Social Science and School of General Studies (years vary); Graduate faculties in Arts and Humanities, Education, Interdisciplinary Studies
- University-wide: Council on Teacher Education; Teacher Certification Review Team in History and English; Task Force on Role and Scope of Teacher Education; Faculty Senate Election Committee; Search Committees;

Women's Studies Committee; Committee on Women's Archive and Research Collections; Committee on Student Fellowships and Scholarships (Chair, 1983–84); Committee on Research; Urban Studies Group; Dallas Research Group; Association of Women Faculty (Member and Speakers Committee); Faculty Review Committees; Accreditation Self-Study, Graduate Studies Committee; Committee on Parking and Security; Library Committee; J. Erik Jonsson Papers, advisor
- School of Arts and Humanities: Committee on Teacher Education; Faculty Agenda Committee and Parliamentarian; Search Committees (and chair); Target-of-Opportunity Search Committees (and chair); College Steering and Interdisciplinary Studies Committees; Community College Liaison; Graduate Advisory Board and Planning Committee; Committee on Urban History; Graduate Studies Committee; Advisory Committee on Law and Human Values Program; Faculty Ad Hoc Review Committees (and chair); Faculty Personnel Review Committee; Committee on Grants and Development; Committee on Graduate Student Assistantships; Course and Curriculum Committee; Task Force on Undergraduate Studies; Cecil Green Lectures Committee; Core Curriculum Committees (and chair); Planning and Budget Committee; Library Development Committee; Nominating Committee; Grant Proposal Committees

## *Simon Fraser University, 1981–2021*

- Consultant, Humanities Institute conferences and programs, external studies programs; Special Arrangements Doctoral Committee member

## *University of Texas at San Antonio, 1998–2004*

- Director, Division of Behavioral and Cultural Sciences, 1998–1999
- Member: Department of History; Doctoral faculty and Doctoral Studies Committee, Ph.D. Program in Culture, Literacy, and Language, Division of Bilingual and Bicultural Studies; Doctoral Faculty, Ph.D. Program in English; Graduate Faculty, Department of Public Administration (Urban Studies); Learning Community and Freshman Seminars for Undergraduate Studies faculty
- Division Faculty Review Advisory Committee; Division Periodic Performance Evaluation (Post-Tenure Review) Committee and Chair; Division Scholarship Committees
- History Faculty Search Committees; Department Restructuring Committee; Department By-Laws Committee; Department Faculty Review Advisory Committee and Chair; Department Periodic Performance Evaluation (Post-Tenure Review) Committee; Graduate Program Admissions Committee; Library Liaison for History; Graduate Studies Advisory Committee; MA Comprehensive Examination Committees and Chair; MA Thesis Committees and Chair
- Department of Public Administration Search Committee
- Ph.D. in Public Policy Program Committee

- Doctoral Program in Culture, Literacy, and Language Doctoral Studies Committee; Qualifying Exam Committees; Dissertation Committees
- College of Education and Human Development, Faculty Review Advisory Committee
- University Faculty Review Advisory Committee

## The Ohio State University, 2004–2017

- Ohio Eminent Scholar in Literacy Studies, Professor of English and History; Faculty Associate, Department of Comparative Studies
- Faculty affiliate: Diversity and Identity Studies Collaborative; Humanities Institute; International Poverty Solutions Collaborative, A University Center for Innovation; Mershon Center for International Security Studies; Center for Medieval and Renaissance Studies; Kirwan Institute for the Study of Race and Ethnicity; Project Narrative
- Department of English; Rhetoric, Composition, and Literacy section; American Literature before 1900 section; Politics and Culture section; Senior Faculty Selective Investment Search Committee; Associate Professor reviews; Nominated for Professor of the Year, Graduate and Undergraduate, 2005, Graduate, 2006, Graduate, 2007; Promotion and Tenure Committee; Graduate Studies Programs and Policies Committee; Presidential Fellowships Subcommittee; Estrich Award Subcommittee; Diversity Committee; MA Exams Revision Committee; Awards and Nominations Committee
- Department of History; American and European History; Curriculum Constellations; Modern America Initiative, 2008–
- Advisory Committee, Center for Historical Research (CHR), Family, Kinship and Households: New Perspectives
- Popular culture faculty
- Doctoral Student Advisor and Supervisor, Examination Committee Chair and Member; Doctoral Dissertation Director and Committee Member, Doctoral Dissertation Defense Committees; MA Examination Committees, Dance, English, History, Education
- Director, LiteracyStudies@OSU and Literacy Studies Working Group, Institute for Collaborative Research and Public Humanities and College of Humanities, campus-wide interdisciplinary literacy initiative: working groups, public programs and visiting speakers series, Graduate Interdisciplinary Specialization/minor, university-wide graduate students interdisciplinary seminar, History of the Book group, international interdisciplinary graduate student conference Expanding Literacy Studies (2009), registered student society, and related activities, 2004–
- Member, Advisory Board, Building Public Space Initiative, Institute for Collaborative Research and Public Humanities
- Director and advisor, Graduate Interdisciplinary Specialization (minor) in Literacy Studies (final approval, 2007)
- Faculty Advisor and Coordinator, International, Interdisciplinary Graduate Students Conference, Expanding Literacy Studies, for and by graduate

students, The Ohio State University, April 3–5, 2009
- Faculty Advisor, Graduate Students Interdisciplinary Literacy Studies Organization; Appalachian Literacy GradGroup; History of the Book GradGroup
- Organizer and member, History of the Book Group; History of Reading, Writing, and Book Arts Working Group, sponsored jointly by the Institute for Collaborative Research and Public Humanities and LiteracyStudies@OSU
- Working Group on Public Humanities, Institute for Collaborative Research and Public Humanities
- The Neighborhood Institute, working group of the Institute for Collaborative Research and Public Humanities, Advisory Board
- Working Group on the Future of the University
- Civic Engagement Committee, College of the Arts and Sciences

**University-wide:**
- President's and Provost's Advisory Council
- Ohio State Teaching Enhancement Program (OSTEP) Steering Committee
- Committee to Select Distinguished University Lecturers, 2005–07, chair
- University Council on Literacy Studies, founding member
- Working Group on Revising Undergraduate Education
- Doctoral Dissertation Defense Committees, 2005–2017

## External Reviewer and Evaluator, Tenure and Promotion

Simon Fraser University; University of Minnesota; Stockton State College; Indiana University (6); Ohio University (2); Wellesley College; University of Michigan (2); Stanford University; Georgia State University; Royal Melbourne Institute of Technology; University of California at Los Angeles (2); Bowling Green State University; University of Wisconsin-Milwaukee; University of Toledo; Ohio State University Library; Arizona State University; University of Notre Dame, University of Michigan, University of Illinois

## External Evaluator, Theses and Dissertations

Southern Methodist University; Simon Fraser University, Canada; University of New South Wales (Aust.); James Cook University (Aust.); University of Technology Sydney (Aust.)

## Public History: General

- Potomac Educational Resources, Inc.: A Research and Consulting Group for Educational Policy and Public History, Advisory Board of Scholars, 1979–1987
- New Hampshire Humanities Council, "Literacy: Myths and Legacies" Conference, advising humanist, 1989–91; Keynote Speaker and panelist, 1991

- Conference on Humanistic Perspectives on Public Policy, Texas Committee for the Humanities (TCH), San Antonio, university representative, 1976
- Texas Committee for the Humanities (NEH), consultant, 1976-
- Conference on Women and Public Policy, Dallas (sponsored by TCH), coordinator, 1976
- Texas Coalition for Juvenile Justice Reform, Program on Status Offenders (sponsored by TCH), consultant, Advisory Board, discussant, 1977
- Dallas Public Library, Humanities Resources Information System Project (sponsored by NEH, NSF, TCH), Advisory Board; Humanities Involvement Group; consultant, 1977–1979; Dallas and Texas History Division, Advisor, 1984–89
- "It Made a Difference": Women in Texas History Project, consultant, 1979–1982
- Chicago Metro History Fair, final fair judge, 1980
- Illinois Humanities Council, consultant, 1980–1981
- *Handbook on Texas Women*, advisor, 1983-
- *Handbook of Texas History*, advisor, 1984–1985
- Folklore Media Center, Dallas, Advisory Board, 1984–1989
- Italian National Radio, "America Coast to Coast," commentator, 1984, 1987
- Pictorial History of Texas Jews, Advisory Board, 1988–1990
- Louisiana State University at Shreveport, Master of Arts in Public History program, advisor, 1992–1998
- Fort Worth Museum of Science and History, Texas History Gallery, Advisory Board, 1992–1998
- University of Adelaide, Australia, Radio, 1993
- San Antonio History Fair, judge, 2000–2004
- *Dallas Times Herald*; *Dallas Morning News*; *San Antonio Express-News*; [London] *Times Educational Supplement*; KERA-Channel 13, Dallas; National Public Radio, *The Nation*, *HuffingtonPost*, *HuffingtonPostLive* resource and contributor
- KERA-90.1 FM (NPR Dallas), advisor
- San Antonio History Website Development Project (NEH grant to UTSA), Advisory Group, 2001–2004
- Chicago Historical Society, "Teen Chicago," principal academic advisor, 2001–2004, a multi-year project in the history of teens, oral history, public programming, publications, and transformation of the roles of young people in museums and historical societies, with funding from the Joyce Foundation, Elizabeth Morse Charitable Trust, Chicago Community Trust, Nathan Cummings Foundation, Field Foundation of Illinois; James S. Kemper Foundation, Illinois Humanities Council, and National Endowment for the Humanities; American Association of Museums Excellence in Education Award and Muse Award (Media & Technology) Honorable Mention, 2005
- LifeTimes/Everyday Life in America: A New Way of Doing History, Scholarly Advisory Board, 2002-
- NPR Chicago, Series on Children and Adolescents, advisor, 2003–
- Radio and television talk shows, interviews, moderator

## Community and Local

- Dallas Social History Project, director, 1975–1979
- Texas local and regional historical societies and groups, consultant and advisor, 1976–2004
- Southern Resource Center, Dallas, Project on the Community Development Act of 1974 and the East Dallas Community, sponsored by the Texas Committee for the Humanities (TCH), consultant and humanist, 1976
- Fuerza de los Barrios, Fort Worth, Trinity River Project (sponsored by TCH), consultant and humanist presenter, 1976
- Research Group on School Desegregation, White Flight and Busing, Dallas, 1976–1978
- Kaplan, Gans, and Kahn, Consultants, 1976–1978
- Dallas Historical Society: Consulting Historian, 1976–1989; "A Return to the Neighborhoods" Project, Advisory Board, 1977–1979; Seminar on Community History, historian and speaker, 1982
- Collaborative Approach to Services for the Elderly, University of Texas Council of Presidents, resource person, 1977–1998
- City of Dallas, Historic Landmark and Preservation Committee, Historic Marker Taskforce, 1977–1981; Publicity Taskforce, 1981–1985; author, landmark brochures, 1977–1985; Archives Committee, 1983–1988
- Dallas (area) Social History Group, founder and coordinator, 1981–1988
- *Historic Dallas* (Historic Preservation League), correspondent, 1981–1983
- Historic Preservation League, Dallas, advisor; Neighborhoods Book Committee, 1983–1986
- North Texas Phi Beta Kappa Association, Committee on Awards, Special Projects Committee, 1981–1984; Vice President, 1982–1984; President, 1984–1986
- Phi Beta Kappa—Dallas Public Library, Annual Lecture on Culture and the City, Founder and Chair, Advisory Committee, 1983–1987
- "Folk Life in Dallas," (TCH), humanities advisor and speaker, 1983
- Dallas Sesquicentennial Commission, Historical Publications Committee, 1984–1986
- Dallas Historical Society and Alpha Xi Omega, HRA, Inc. of Alpha Kappa Alpha Sorority, "Black Dallas Remembered" Oral History Project, consultant; presenter, public forums, 1985–1987
- Dallas Public Library, Symposium on Dallas Past and Present, advisor, coordinator and participant, 1986
- Dallas Jewish Historical Society, Advisory Board, 1987–1998
- Concepts International, Dallas, consultant, 1989

## Media, Film, and Education

- Knowledge Network (British Columbia, Educational Television), presenter/interviewee, 1981

- "West of Hester Street" (Cinema docudrama on the Galveston Movement, 1907–1910), featured extra, 1982
- KERA-90.1 FM (NPR), advisor on news programs
- KERA, Channel 13 (PBS), Dallas, "News Edition," commentator, 1983–1986
- KERA Television, "Legacies of the Land: A Documentary on the Myths, Legends, and Traditions of Texas" (TCH), Advisory Board, 1983–1985
- Dallas County Community College District and Harper and Row, Telecourse: "The American Adventure," consultant and participant/interviewee, 1985–1986 (26 half-hour programs for 600 colleges in 45 states and PBS Adult Learning Network)
- KERA, Channel 13 (PBS), Family Project, Advisory Board, 1991–1992; "A Better Childhood (ABC) Quiz," 1991, chief advisor and commentator (Katherine Ripley Award for Electronic Media, Planned Parenthood of Dallas and Northeast Texas; Matrix Award, Dallas Professional Chapter of Women in Media; Silver Award for Local Programs, Corporation for Public Broadcasting); "First Steps," 1992, principal advisor, radio commentator
- "A History of American Teenagers in the Twentieth Century," Steven Alves, Hometown Productions, producer, documentary series in development, Board of Advisors and Project Scholar, 1996–2000 (funded by NEH)
- "Rewriting Literacy," documentary film series, Board of Advisors and Project Scholar, 1998–2000 (proposed to NEH and others)
- National Public Radio, "The Changing Face of America" national initiative, New Media Division, Talk of the Nation, All Things Considered, Morning Edition, 2000–2001, advisor, consultant, and electronic discussion moderator
- NPR Chicago, Series on Children and Adolescents, advisor, 2003–2004
- Exhibiting Adolescence/Adolescents—experimental graduate seminar, University of Texas at San Antonio, 2004, exploring different approaches to "exhibiting" adolescents and adolescence, with the assistance of the Witte Museum, San Antonio, and the Chicago Historical Society
- "Drop Out Nation: The Death of the American Dream," documentary film, Public Broadcasting Council of Central New York," Syracuse, reviewer, 2010

## Other Educational

- Women for Change, Inc., Dallas, Seminar on Education, humanist panelist, 1975
- Eastfield College, Division of Humanities, Dallas County Community College District, consultant, 1978
- Conference on Quality Education for Black Students in Texas, Austin (sponsored by TCH), consultant and humanist panelist, 1976

## Professional Society Activities

- Canadian Association for American Studies, Executive Committee, student member, 1972–1975; Program Committee, 1974

- American Educational Research Association, Program Committee, Division F (Historiography), 1973
- Canadian Population Studies Group, Steering and Program Committees, 1974–1976
- History of Education Society, Nominating Committee, 1976, 1979
- Southwest Coordinating Committee on Women in the Historical Profession, coordinator, 1977–1979
- Social Science History Association, Regional Network Coordinator, 1976–1984; Program Committee, 1980; Allan Sharlin Memorial Award Committee, founding chair, 1984–1985, member, 1984–1986; Executive Committee, 1987–1989; Vice President and President-Elect, 1998–1999; President, 1999–2000; member Executive Committee, 2000–2003; ex-officio member, Search Committee for New Editor of *Social Science History*; ex-officio member, Committee on the Future of SSHA [As SSHA President in 1999–2000, I presided over the 25th anniversary of the organization. Entitled "Looking Backward and Looking Forward: Perspectives on Social Science History," the program featured both a celebration and a critical stock-taking. A number of special activities marked the occasion which was also reflected in my Presidential Address. I also established the Committee on the Future of SSHA which reported in 2001]
- Urban History Association, Board of Directors, 2002–2004
- Society for the History of Children and Youth, Executive Committee, 2003–2007

## Conference Session Chairing

- Little Community Conference, Brandeis University, 1972
- History of Education Society, Chicago, 1973; Cambridge, Mass., 1976; Toronto, 1977; Chicago, 1978; Vancouver, 1983; Chicago, 1984
- Canadian Association for American Studies, Ottawa, 1974
- Canadian Historical Association, Edmonton, 1975
- Southwestern Social Science Association, Houston, 1978
- Social Science History Association, Cambridge, Mass., 1979; Rochester, 1980; Bloomington, Ind., 1982; Washington, DC, 1983; Toronto, 1984; St. Louis, 1986; New Orleans, 1987; Chicago, 1988; Washington, DC, 1989; Minneapolis, 1990; New Orleans, 1991; Chicago, 1992; Baltimore, 1993; Atlanta, 1994; Chicago, 1995; New Orleans, 1996; Washington, DC, 1997; Chicago, 1998; Fort Worth, 1999; Pittsburgh, 2000; St. Louis, 2002; Baltimore, 2003; Chicago, 2004; Portland, 2005; Minneapolis, 2006; Chicago, 2007; Long Beach, 2009; Chicago, 2010; Boston, 2011; Vancouver, 2012; Chicago, 2013; Toronto, 2014; Baltimore, 2015
- American Studies Association, Kansas City, 1996
- Society for the History of Children and Youth, University of Maryland, Baltimore County, 2003; Marquette University, Milwaukee, 2005; Linköping University, Norrköping, Sweden, 2007; University of California, Berkeley, 2009; Columbia University, New York, 2011

- American Studies Association of Texas, San Antonio, 2003 [Students in my Fall 2003 doctoral seminar English 7063 presented their work on a panel entitled "Reading Critically the Sources of Children and Childhood: Literary and Historical Perspectives." I chaired the session. At the conference's end, *this was designated an "outstanding session"*]
- Urban History Association, Tempe, Arizona, 2006

## Lectures and Papers
### Conference Participation

- The Little Community Conference, Brandeis University, 1972
- History of Education Society, Chicago, 1973
- Canadian Association for American Studies, Ottawa, 1974
- Canadian Historical Association, Edmonton, 1975
- Women for Change, Seminar on Education, Dallas, 1975
- Time, Space, and Man: Interdisciplinary Symposium on Microdemography in Historical Perspective, Umeå, Sweden, 1977
- Fort Worth Committee for the Humanities and Texas Coalition for Juvenile Justice, Juvenile Justice and the Community, Fort Worth, 1978
- Social Science History Association, Cambridge, Mass., 1979
- Conference on Literacy in Post-Reformation Europe, University of Leicester, England, 1980
- Library of Congress Center for the Book-National Institute of Education, History of Literacy Conference, Washington, DC, 1980
- American Antiquarian Society, Conference on Printing and Society in Early American, Worcester, Mass., 1980
- Social Science History Association, Rochester, 1980
- Bard College Conference on Crisis in Literacy: Cultural Hard Times, invited speaker, 1981
- Simon Fraser University, SITE Program on Literacy, 1981
- History of Education Society, Pittsburgh, 1981
- Social Science History Association, Nashville, 1981
- Tenth World Congress of Sociology, Mexico City, 1982
- Wellcome Institute for the History of Medicine, Conference on Medicine, Printing, and Literacy in the European Renaissance, London, 1982
- Social Science History Association, Bloomington, Ind., 1982
- Dallas Public Library, Folklife in Dallas, 1983
- Annenberg School of Communications, University of Southern California, Creating Meanings: The Literacies of Our Times, 1984
- International Commission for the Application of Quantitative Methods to History, The Transformation of European Society, Rockefeller Conference Center, Bellagio, Italy, 1984
- Social Science History Association, Chicago, 1985

- Ontario Institute for Studies in Education, University of Toronto, 20th Anniversary Cutting Edge of Educational Research Conference, 1985
- International and Comparative Education Society, Toronto, 1986
- Dallas Public Library, Symposium on Dallas Past and Present, 1986
- Social Science History Association, St. Louis, 1986
- Social Science History Association, New Orleans, 1987
- Simon Fraser University, Institute for Humanities, Conference on The Legacy of J. S. Woodsworth and the Welfare State in Canada, 1988
- Social Science History Association, Chicago, 1988
- Library History Seminar VIII, Bloomington, IN, Distinguished Plenary Address, 1990
- Canadian History of Education Association, Biennial Meeting, Ottawa, Distinguished Speaker, 1990
- Social Science History Association, Minneapolis, 1990
- Conference on American Urban History, Chicago Historical Society, 1990
- Bard College Conference on Education for Complexity in the 21st Century, invited speaker, 1991
- International Conference on Attaining Functional Literacy: A Cross-Cultural Perspective, Tilburg University and The Netherlands National Commission for UNESCO, Keynote Speaker, 1991
- Social Science History Association, New Orleans, 1991
- New Hampshire Humanities Council Conference on Literacy, Myths, and Lessons, Keynote Speaker, 1991
- Seminar on Children and the History of Childhood, Department of Child Studies, Tema, Linköping University, Sweden, 1992
- Conference on Adult Literacy: An International Urban Perspective, The United Nations [UNESCO, CUNY, and New York City]: Keynote Speaker, 1992
- Social Science History Association, Chicago, 1992
- American Educational Research Association, Special Interest Group on Basic Research on Reading and Literacy, Atlanta, Invited Address, 1993
- Conference on Writing and Reading in Western Europe: Its Nature, Functions, and Conflicts, Universidad Internacional Menendez Pelayo, Valencia, Spain, opening lecture, 1993
- Conference on Literacy and Power: Difference, Silence and Textual Practice, Griffith University, Brisbane, Australia, Plenary Address, 1993
- Institute on Literacies, Language and Social Justice, Melbourne, Plenary Address, 1993
- Australian Reading Association, First International Meeting, Literacy for the New Millennium, Melbourne, Keynote Speaker, 1993
- Social Science History Association, Baltimore, 1993
- Social Science History Association, Atlanta, 1994
- Emory University Graduate Institute for the Liberal Arts and Dana Foundation Workshop for Teachers on Narrative and Education, 1994
- Social Science History Association, Chicago, 1995

- Stanton Sharp Symposium on the History of the Family, Southern Methodist University, 1996
- Social Science History Association, New Orleans, 1996
- American Studies Association, Kansas City, 1996
- Association of Graduate English Students, Kent State University, Fourth Annual National Graduate Student Conference, Intersections in English Studies, keynote speaker, 1997
- Social Science History Association, Washington, DC, 1997
- Social Science History Association, Chicago, 1998
- The University and the City: Urban Education and the Liberal Arts, Wayne State University, 1999
- Social Science History Association, Fort Worth, 1999
- Conference on College Composition and Communication (CCCC), Annual Meeting, Educating the Imagination and Reimagining Education, Minneapolis, featured speaker, 2000
- Institute for Literary History and National Conference, Prospero's Plots and Caliban's Critique: Literacies, Texts, and Nationalisms in the New World, Miami University (Ohio), featured speaker and discussant, 2000
- Social Science History Association, Looking Backward and Looking Forward: Perspectives on Social Science History, Presidential Address and Presidential Sessions, Pittsburgh, 2000
- Social Science History Association, Chicago, 2001
- "Literacy, Religion, Gender, and Social History: A Socio-Cultural History for the 21st Century. An International Conference for Egil Johansson," Vadstena, Sweden, May, 2002, co-organizer and coordinator, speaker and session chair
- Social Science History Association, St. Louis, 2002
- Society for the History of Children and Youth, Baltimore, 2003
- Social Science History Association, Baltimore, 2003
- Conference on College Composition and Communication (CCCC), Annual Meeting, Educating the Imagination and Reimagining Education, San Antonio, featured speaker with Deborah Brandt, 2004
- Western States Rhetoric and Literacy Conference, "Big Rhetorics, Big Literacies: The Discourses of Power," Arizona State University, keynote address, 2004
- Conference on "From Woodblocks to the Internet: Chinese Publishing and Print Culture in Transition," Ohio State University, keynote address, 2004
- Social Science History Association, Chicago, 2004
- National Council of Teachers of English Assembly for Research Conference, "Literacies Across Time, Space, and Place: New Directions in Literacy Research for Political Action," Keynote Address with Deborah Brandt, Ohio State University, 2005
- Conference of the Society for the History of Children and Youth, Milwaukee, 2005
- University of California, Berkeley, Conference on Rethinking Child Development, 2005

- Social Science History Association, Portland, 2005
- Urban History Association, Tempe, Arizona, 2006
- Social Science History Association, Minneapolis, 2006
- Society for the History of Children and Youth, Linköping University, Norrköping, Sweden, 2007
- Social Science History Association, Chicago, 2007
- Conference on College Composition and Communication (CCCC), Annual Meeting, Writing Realities, Changing Realities, New Orleans, 2008
- Conference on Politics, Activism and the History of America's Public Schools: Marking the 40th Anniversary of Michael B, Katz's *The Irony of Early School Reform*, University of Pennsylvania, 2008
- Social Science History Association, Miami, 2008
- Scope of Interdisciplinarity Conference, Athabasca University, Edmonton Alberta, Canada, 2008
- Expanding Literacy Studies International Interdisciplinary Conference for Graduate Studies, Columbus, 2009: plenary session in recognition of the 30th anniversary of the publication of *The Literacy Myth*
- Twentieth Anniversary Seminar on Child Studies at the Department of Child Studies, Linköping University, Sweden, 2009
- Society for the History of Children and Youth, University of California, Berkeley, 2009
- Social Science History Association, Long Beach, California, 2009
- Gartner Honors Lecture, Southern Methodist University, 2010
- "The Literacy Myth Now Thirty Years Old Revisited," a forum on Graff's *The Literacy Myth*, Humanities Institute, Simon Fraser University, Vancouver, Canada, 2010
- A Symposium on Critical Perspectives on Understanding Literacy in a Technological Age, British Columbia Institute of Technology, Vancouver, 2010, keynote address
- Social Science History Association, Chicago, 2010
- Society for the History of Children and Youth, Columbia University, New York, 2011
- Social Science History Association, Boston, 2011
- Masters of City and Regional Planning, CRP OneBook Program, and SPA Student Association Invitee and Lecturer, University of Texas at Arlington, 2011
- Conference on College Composition and Communication (CCCC), Annual Meeting, featured speaker, Writing Gateways, St. Louis, 2012
- Social Science History Association, Vancouver, 2012
- Social Science History Association, Chicago, 2013
- Social Science History Association, Toronto, 2014
- IV Colóquio Internacional Letramento e Cultura Escrita (4th International Conference of Literacy and Written Culture), Minas Gerais, Brazil, 2014, keynote
- CIC Conference on Graduate Education in the Humanities, Keynote Speaker, Penn State University, 2015

- Social Science History Association, Baltimore, 2015
- Michael B. Katz, His Contribution and Legacy to Social Science History and Beyond, special session, Social Science History Association, Baltimore, 2015
- Conference on College Composition and Communication (CCCC), Annual Meeting, Session on Harvey J. Graff, Literacy Studies, and Composition, Portland, 2017
- Literacy Studies/HJG Reunion, "The Graffaganza or ExGraffaganza": At least four major anniversaries, reunion and meeting of at least four generations, and celebration of all of us, Blackwell Inn, Columbus, Ohio, May 17–19, 2024

## Invited Lectures and Seminars

University of Western Ontario, 1973, 1977; Dallas organizations, 1975–; Southern Methodist University, 1977; University of Texas at Dallas, 1978–1996; University of Chicago, 1979, 1980; The Newberry Library, Chicago, 1979, 1980; University of Toronto and the Ontario Institute for Studies in Education, 1980; University of Delaware, 1980; University of Pennsylvania, 1980; Northeastern Illinois University, 1980; Fairleigh Dickinson University, 1981; Indiana University, 1981; Simon Fraser University, Canada, 1981, 1982; University of British Columbia, 1981, 1982; Dallas Historical Society, 1982; Wellcome Institute for the History of Medicine, London, 1982; Rice University, 1983; Stanford University, 1986; Southern Methodist University, 1988; American Antiquarian Society, 1989; Florida State University, 1990; Indiana University, 1992; Linköping University, Sweden, 1992; Stockholm University, Sweden, 1992; Umeå University, Sweden, 1992; Centre for Literacy, Montreal, 1993; National Literacy Secretariat, Multiculturalism and Citizenship Canada, 1993; Australian universities (Griffth, LaTrobe, Adelaide, South Australia, Macquarie, Wollongong, University of Technology-Sydney, Queensland Institute of Technology, Central Queensland), 1993; Simon Fraser University, 1993; Washington University, 1994; Georgia State University, 1994; Carleton University, Canada, 1995; Teachers College, Columbia University, 1996; Kent State University, 1997; University of California at Los Angeles: Forum for Print and Electronic Culture, California Center for the Book, and Department of Library and Information Studies Seminar, 2000; University of Linköping, Sweden, 2001, 2002; University of Notre Dame, 2001; The Ohio State University, 2004; Division of Late Medieval and Reformation Studies, University of Arizona, 2004; Center for Writing Studies, University of Illinois, 2005; Arizona State University, 2006, Miami University, Ohio, 2006; Kent State University, 2009; University of Texas at Arlington, 2009; Southern Methodist University, 2010; Simon Fraser University, 2010; British Columbia Institute of Technology, Vancouver, 2010; University of Texas at Arlington, 2011, University of California at Los Angeles, 2013; Federal University of Minas Gerais, Brazil, 2014; State University of Rio de Janeiro, Brazil, 2014; University of Calgary, 2014; Rochester Institute of Technology, 2016; Southern Methodist University, 2016; Kirwan Institute for the Study of Race and Ethnicity, Ohio State University, 2021; Zayed University, United Arab Emirates, 2022; Centre for Interdisciplinary Studies, Coimbra University, Portugal, 2023–2024

## Biographical References

Directory of Psychosocial Investigators; Directory of American Scholars, History; Who's Who in America; Who's Who in the South and Southwest; International Who's Who in Education; Who's Who in the Midwest; Current Authors; International Authors and Writers Who's Who; Men of Achievement; Dictionary of International Biography; Who's Who in American Education; Who's Who in Education; Contemporary Authors; Outstanding Scholars of the 20th and the 21st Century; Outstanding Intellectuals of the 20th and 21st Century; Outstanding People of the 21st Century; Who's Who in Humanities Higher Education; Academic Keys; Who's Who; Wikipedia; World's Most Influential Historians

## Retirement Activities, 2021-

### Collaborative Relationships and Advising

- American Historical Association, 2021–23, invited to rejoin, active on Forum
- American Association of University Professors, 2021–23, invited to join, active on Academe Blog and journals
- Scholars Strategy Network (SSN) [https://scholars.org/scholar/harvey-graff], 2022–
- *Journal of Intellectual Freedom and Privacy*, Editorial Board, 2022-
- Proposal and manuscript reviewer: Cambridge University Press, Bloomsbury Press, Palgrave Macmillan
- Invited to write endorsements for new books, many publishers
- Public office holders and City staff in Columbus, State of Ohio government, and U.S, federal government, advisor
- Invited advisor to reporters: *Columbus Dispatch, Cleveland Plain Dealer, New York Times, Washington Post, Columbus Free Press,* PBS News Hour, WAMU Washington, DC, other NPR stations, BBC, and others
- NPR Interviews and consulting: WCPN Cleveland, NH-Pacifica, KJZZ Phoenix; KERA Dallas
- Busting Myths column, *Columbus Free Press,* 2021-
- Faculty, administrators, and students at Ohio State University including Student Life, Provost, Colleges of Arts and Sciences, Humanities Collaboratory, Architecture, Engineering, Education, Departments of English, Geography, History. 2000–
- Students, high school to graduate school in Columbus and across the U.S., advisor and interviewee for research projects, 2021-
- Kirwan Institute for the Study of Race and Ethnicity, Ohio State University, Forum on Fiction and Fact about Critical Race Theory, 2021
- Zayed University, United Arab Emirates, public lecture, Jan. 5, 2022, and advisor on interdisciplinarity, 2021-
- International historical researchers, advisor, 2021-
- Morgan Harper for Ohio U.S. Senate campaign, advisor, 2021–2022
- Public Education Partners. Advisor, 2021-

- Honesty in Ohio Education, advisor, 2021-2022; From the Desk of Harvey Graff on website and bulletins, 2021-
- RedWine.Blue—Banned Book Busters, advisor, 2021-22
- BannedBookBox, advisor, 2021-
- Moms Demand Action, advisor, 2021-22
- Battle of Homestead Pennsylvania. 2021-2022
- ACLU Missouri, Ohio, Texas, advisor, 2021-
- Protect Our Youth from Steroids (POYS), advisor, 2022-
- The Seniors at Harvey U., 2022-
- Friends of the Public Library, Llano County, Texas, 2022-
- Freedom to Read Foundation, 2021-
- PEN America, 2022-
- Teen Chicago, 20th anniversary planning, 2004-2024
- "The Students at Harvey U," informal group of undergraduate students with the Graffs, 2022-
- Northwestern University journalism student video interview project, subject, 2022
- Joe Motil for Mayor of Columbus Campaign, 2022-23
- Columbus Reform, Affordable Housing, and Charter Reform Ad Hoc Coalition, convener, 2022-2023
- Muhlenberg College, Dana Scholars program, advisor on senior honors thesis, 2023
- Notre Dame University, advisor on senior honors thesis, 2023
- Ohio State University, advisor on senior honors theses, 2023, 2024
- Bloomfield State College, NJ, advisor to humanities faculty on programs, 2023
- DegreeChoices.com, advisor and contributor, 2023-2024
- Monocle Daily Radio News, London, interviews, 2023
- PEN America, Spotlight on PEN Members, June 28, 2023
- American Antiquarian Society and Newberry Library, advisor on public humanities, 2023-
- "People without history. The public use of subordinate writings in the early modern and modern periods," Universidad de Alcala, Spain and University of Genoa, Scientific Committee, 2023-2024
- Northwestern University Archives and Library, oral history interviewee on student activism in late 1960s, Sept. 18, 2023. https://f.io/DxheuVQQ
- Ireland's Classic Hits Radio, Nighttime Talk with Niall Boylan interview "Book Banning with Professor Harvey J. Graff," Sept. 27, 2023 [https://open.spotify.com/episode/7EW7DlU3fVkCJuZrkTF5e9?si=dabd7d351239406e]
- North Carolina Campus Engagement and Ohio Campus Compact, "[The Value of] Teaching Public [and] Scholarship: Lessons from Two Practitioners," Keynote speaker, Sept. 28, 2023 [https://www.youtube.com/watch?v=EL-y6sEFWPE]
- *New York Times*, interview on reading instruction and Reading Recovery. 2023

- Chris Banks documentary filmmaker on the ongoing bills and policies in Florida that censor and/or restrict education, including banning and restricting books, advisor and interviewee, 2023
- Centre for Interdisciplinary Studies (CEIS20), University of Coimbra, Portugal, advisor, 2023-
- *Washington Post*, advisor on reporting on U.S. Postal Service and Amazon delivery. 2023
- *MassLive*, advisor on Congressional hearing with women elite university presidents, 2023
- Literacy Studies/HJG Reunion, "The Graffaganza or ExGraffaganza": At least four major anniversaries, reunion and meeting of at least four generations, and celebration of all of us, Blackwell Inn, Columbus, Ohio, May 17–19, 2024

## Essays and Letters to Editors Post-Retirement

(Scholarly publications listed with Books and Articles above)

### Retirement as "Public Education"

"A post-retirement career as a public academic meets the moment's need," *Times Higher Education*, Sept 18, 2021

"A call to colleagues: Speak out and support children, teachers, librarians, and free speech—and the present and future of your own institutions, too," American Historical Association Member Forum, Feb. 16, 2022

"Teaching outside the box: A retired professor's continuing education," *Inside Higher Education*, Mar.25, 2022

"I'm retired but I'm still running my own unofficial university," *Times Higher Education*, Dec. 21, 2022

"Giving away 30,000 books is harder but more rewarding than I imagined," *Times Higher Education,* Mar. 13, 2024

### Universities

"How misguided university policies are harming the humanities, arts and sciences," *Inside Higher Education*, December, 18, 2015

"Colleges can learn from sports figures about mental health," *Inside Higher Education*, Sept. 13, 2021

"Ross Douthat wouldn't know a new college from old," *Academe Blog*, Nov 17, 2021

"The Banality of University Slogans: Whether its ad campaigns for football season, gauzy reports from the provost, or rhetoric from the school's president, higher education abounds with empty rhetoric," *Washington Monthly*, Jan. 10, 2022

"Essay critical of Louis Menand's book review is disappointing," Letter to the Editor, *Chronicle of Higher Education*, Jan. 12, 2022

"Slogans are no substitute for concrete university policies and programmes," *Times Higher Education*, Jan. 17, 2022

"Sloganeering and the Limits of Leadership," *Academe Blog*, Jan. 19, 2022

"The latest caricature and attack on legitimate academic freedom: Amna Khalid and Jeffrey Aaron Snyder, 'The purpose of a university isn't truth. It's inquiry: Defenders of academic freedom forget this at their own peril,'" Letter to the Editor, *Chronicle of Higher Education*, Feb. 10, 2022

"Academic collegiality is a contradictory self-serving myth," *Times Higher Education*, Feb. 10, 2022

"Collegiality needs a reboot," *Times Higher Education*, Mar. 7, 2022

"Should colleges make anti-racism part of their mission?" Letter to the Editor, *Chronicle of Higher Education*, Mar. 22, 2022

"Ignore the books: there is no single Big Problem with higher education," *Times Higher Education*, Apr. 2, 2022

"Myths Shape the Continuing 'Crisis of the Humanities,'" *Inside Higher Education*, May 6, 2022

"Universities are not giving students the classes or support they need," *Times Higher Education*, May 17, 2022

"When 'Heterodoxy' is Orthodoxy," Letter to the Editor, *Inside Higher Education*, June 3, 2022

"The Fallacies of 'the Shadow Curriculum,'" *Academe Blog*, July 1, 2022

"The best scholarship is political but with no ideological stamp," *Times Higher Education*, July 26, 2022

*Searching for Literacy: The Social and Intellectual Origins of Literacy Studies*, Social Science Matters #SocSciMatters [https://www.palgrave.com/gp/blogs/social-sciences/graff]

"How Young People Have Changed," Letter to the Editor, *Inside Higher Education*, Aug. 4, 2022

"Recreating universities for the 21st century without repeating the errors and myths of the 20th century?" Busting Myths, *Columbus Free Press*, Aug. 7, 2022

"Universities Must Help the New 'Lost Generation,'" *Academe Blog*, Sept. 16, 2022

"The inseparability of 'historical myths' and 'permanent crises' in the humanities," *Journal of Liberal Arts and Humanities*, 3, 9 (Sept., 2022), 16–26

"Flawed Survey on the 'Liberal Arts,'" Letter to the Editor, *Inside Higher Education*, Sept. 20, 2022

"Growing up was always hard to do. It's getting harder, and universities are doing little to help," Busting Myths, *Columbus Free Press*, Sept. 26, 2022

"The enterprise of scientific misconduct: Malpractice at Ohio State University," Busting Myths, *Columbus Free Press*, Oct. 26, 2022

"How universities fail their students: The president may be "born to be a Buckeye," but the students are not. A call to eliminate Offices of Student Life and invest directly in students' lives," Busting Myths, *Columbus Free Press*, Nov. 10, 2022

"Wikipedia, Once Shunned, Now Embraced in the Classroom," Nov. 9, 2022, Letter to the Editor, *Inside Higher Education*, Nov. 14, 2022

"The US' new open access mandate must not line the pockets of grifters," *Times Higher Education,* Nov. 17, 2022

"Learning Through Teaching," *Inside Higher Education*, Nov. 23, 2022

"Demythifying: An author and retired professor challenges some long-held university press assumptions," *Publishers Weekly*, Dec. 19, 2022/"Demythifying the University Press, *Publishers* Weekly (online), Dec. 16, 2022

"I'm retired but I'll still running my own unofficial university," *Times Higher Education*, Dec. 21, 2022

"Lessons from the 1960s: Paths to Rediscovering Universities," *Against the Current*, 223 (Mar.-Apr., 2023; online Dec. 24, 2022)

"An Ahistorical Argument About Asian-American Bias," Letter to the Editor, *Inside Higher Education*, Jan. 1, 2023

"Universities and cities often fail both homeowners and students," *Times Higher Education*, Jan. 22, 2023

"Lessons from the 1960s: Paths to Rediscovering Universities," *Against the Current*, 223 (Mar.-Apr., 2023, 12–14, corrected)

"Scholarly book authors' Bill of Rights," American Historical Association Forum, Mar. 6, 2023 (short)

"Finding a permanent job in the humanities has never been easy. The lost golden age of hiring and wider social appreciation of the disciplines never existed," *Times Higher Education*, Mar. 22, 2023

"*Conflicting Paths: Growing Up in America* discussed in Steven Mintz, "How to Ease the Path to Adulthood," *Inside Higher Education*, Mar. 30, 2023

"The *New York Times*, Universities, and the Humanities: History and Clarity," New York Times," Busting Myths, *Columbus Free Press*, Apr. 6, 2023

"Humanities could change the world—if only they could change themselves," *Times Higher Education*, Apr. 18, 2023

"Lawmakers rush to cancel public higher education in Ohio," *Cincinnati Enquirer*, Apr. 19, 2023

"Lessons for Becoming a Public Scholar," *Inside Higher Education*, April 28, 2023

"US universities' engineering colleges are anything but collegiate," *Times Higher Education*, May 17, 2023

"Trivializing Teaching and Oversimplifying Economics: A flawed and foolish effort to quantify the cost of minutes of teaching," *Inside Higher Education*, June 14, 2023

"Why all college rankings suck, at their best," with David Levy, *DegreeChoices*, June 19, 2023

"US universities should teach a genuinely common core of knowledge," *Times Higher Education*, June 28, 2023

"The Rise, Dilution, and Death of Affirmative Action, 1970–2023," *Inside Higher Education*, July 13, 2023

"Supporters must bear some blame for affirmative action's tragic reversal," *Times Higher Education*, July 16, 2023

"Can educational return on investment be meaningfully measured?" with David Levy, *Times Higher Education*, July 30, 2023

"Scholarly book authors' bill of rights," *Journal of Intellectual Freedom and Privacy*, 7, 4 (2022). 5–8 [August, 2023]

"Offices of student and academic affairs must call off the turf war: The mutual suspicion of autonomous bureaucracies ignores the multifarious needs of living, learning, maturing young people," *Times Higher Education*, Aug. 12, 2023

"Historical Inaccuracy on Selective Admissions: Essay on the Supreme Court's decision misconstrues issues," *Inside Higher Education*. Aug. 16, 2023

"The power of models and examples in education and higher education," *Journal of Educational Thought*, 56, 2 (2023), 117–124

"Out of control fraternities and sororities control the 21st century university on and off campus, Part One," Busting Myths, *Columbus Free Press*, Oct. 10, 2023

"Universities must embrace, not hinder, student journalism: Nurturing investigative skills will make for a better democracy—even if it embarrasses campus administrators in the process," *Times Higher Education*, October, 16, 2023

"A major huge university versus its students, neighbors, and their city: The Ohio State University," Busting Myths, *Columbus Free Press*, Nov. 2, 2023

"Slogan University Revisited. When did Offices of Compliance and Integrity [sic]. Student Life, Student Conduct, Campus Safety become just the opposite? The example of one of the largest U.S. universities, Part One," *Columbus Free Press*, Nov. 14, 2023

"When universities speak about controversial issues," Letter to the Editor, *Washington Post*, Nov. 17, 2023

"Slogan University Revisited. When did Offices of Compliance and Integrity [sic]. Student Life, Student Conduct, Campus Safety become just the opposite? The example of one of the largest U.S. universities, Part Two," Busting Myths, *Columbus Free Press*, Nov. 19, 2023

"Former university presidents: stop blaming faculty for your mistakes," *Times Higher Education*, Nov. 20, 2023

"Speaking out on the Israel-Hamas conflict doesn't mean taking sides," *Times Higher Education*, Nov. 29, 2023

"Why the House Targeted Those 3 Presidents," Letter to the Editor, *Inside Higher Education*, Dec. 7, 2023

"Scholar Activism Doesn't Require Taking Sides," Letter to the Editor, *Inside Higher Education*, Dec. 14, 2023

"Poor-quality presidential searches lead to poor quality appointments," *Times Higher Education*, Jan. 13, 2024

"Do not blame college professors for decades of failures of administrators, trustees, and legislators, especially your own," Busting Myths, *Columbus Free Press*, Jan. 24, 2024

"Context is as important to plagiarism as to antisemitism accusations," *Times Higher Education*, Jan. 25, 2024

"How *not* to conduct presidential searches, over and over? The example of one major public university: The Ohio State University," Busting Myths, *Columbus Free Press*, Jan. 31, 2024

"Scholarly book authors' bill of rights," Busting Myths, *Columbus Free Press*, Feb. 8, 2024

"Giving away 30,000 books is harder but more rewarding than I imagined," *Times Higher Education*, Mar. 13, 2024

"Your students won't read any more? Are you sure you're paying attention?" *Times Higher Education*, Apr. 18, 2024

"Choosing college wisely: Comparative earning data as a key factor in selecting colleges and majors," with David Levy, *Change* June, 2024

"From Multi-versity and Mega-versity, back to Uni-versity: The impossible dream of changing 'incentive structures' and 'business models,'" *Journal of Educational Thought*, forthcoming

"Why professors—led by the humanities—are our own worst enemies, and what we can do about it," *Journal of Educational Thought*, forthcoming

"The causes and consequences of poverty and impoverishment—broadly construed/constructed—in academia, past and present," Special issue on Academic Poverty, *Academic Labor: Research and Artistry,* Fall, 2024

"University sexual harassment, abuse, assault, and the myths of collegiality," co-authored, in preparation

### Disciplines and Interdisciplines

"Interdisciplinarity is not about the humanities aping the sciences," *Times Higher Education*, Sept. 7. 2021

"History lessons can help disciplines to survive," *Times Higher Education*, Oct. 30, 2021

"The dilemmas of disciplines going public," *Inside Higher Education*, Jan. 13, 2022

"How many 'projects' does it take to obstruct a truly American history?" Busting Myths, *Columbus Free Press*, Feb. 16, 2022

"Shouldn't Ivy League graduates know better than to remake American history?" Busting Myths, *Columbus Free Press*, Feb. 24, 2022

"Battle of the books: A professor examines the 1619, 1620, 1776, and 1836 projects," *Publishers Weekly*, Feb. 28, 2022; "Battle of the Books: When Historical Reassessments Collide: A professor examines the 1619, 1620, 1776, and 1836 projects," online Feb. 25, 2022

"The inseparability of 'historical myths' and 'permanent crises' in the humanities," *Journal of Liberal Arts and Humanities*, 3, 9 (Sept., 2022), 16–26

"Flawed Survey on the 'Liberal Arts,'" *Inside Higher Education*, Sept. 20, 2022

"Doubling down on Nathan Heller's flawed essay: English professors shouldn't repeat romanticized myths about the state of their field," *Inside Higher Education*, Mar. 24, 2023

"The persistent 'reading myth' and the 'crisis of the humanities,'" *CCC/College Composition and Communication*, 74, 2 (Feb. 2023). 575–580 [reprinted in *The Literacy Myth,* The WAC Clearinghouse 2023 edition]

"The *New York Times*, Universities, and the Humanities: History and Clarity," New York Times," Busting Myths, *Columbus Free Press,* Apr. 6, 2023

"Humanities could change the world—if only they could change themselves," *Times Higher Education,* Apr. 18, 2023

"Lessons for Becoming a Public Scholar," *Inside Higher Education*, April 28, 2023

"US universities' engineering colleges are anything but collegiate," *Times Higher Education,* May 17, 2023

"Is engineering a good major? A reality check for prospective students," with Olga Knezevic, *DegreeChoices*, May 24, 2023 [https://tinyurl.com/4brdaj4w]

"Undisciplining Knowledge: Interdisciplinarity as an ideology and as practices," *Journal of Educational Thought*, 56, 1 (2023), 5–12

"US universities should teach a genuinely common core of knowledge," *Times Higher Education,* June 28, 2023

"The Ohio Humanities Council v. the Humanities and Humanity," Busting Myths, *Columbus Free Press,* Aug. 16, 2023

"An Anachronistic View of the Nature of Thinking: Arguing for a permeable, evolving definition," Letter to the Editor, *Inside Higher Education,* Oct. 24, 2023

## Literacy and Communications

"Civics tests should be required to hold public office," *Inside Higher Education,* Oct. 21, 2021

"The new literacy studies and the resurgent literacy myth," *Literacy in Composition Studies,* 9, 1 (2022), 47–53 [reprinted in *The Literacy Myth,* The WAC Clearinghouse 2023 edition; *Literacy Myths, Legacies, and Lessons,* The WAC Clearinghouse 2023 edition]

"Essay critical of Louis Menand's book review is disappointing," Letter to the Editor, *Chronicle of Higher Education,* Jan. 12, 2022

"The Misrepresentation and Marketing of 'Financial Literacy': The Fallacies and Dangers of FL4ALL," Busting Myths, *Columbus Free Press,* Jan. 23, 2022 [reprinted in *The Literacy Myth,* The WAC Clearinghouse 2023 edition]

*Searching for Literacy: The Social and Intellectual Origins of Literacy Studies,* Social Science Matters #SocSciMatters [https://tinyurl.com/4n5b4knm]

New Books Network (NBN) podcast, From *The Literacy Myth* to *Searching for Literacy,* August 5, 2022 [https://newbooksnetwork.com/the-literacy-myth]

"Relocating literacy in higher education," *Academe Blog,* Aug. 18, 2022 [reprinted in *Literacy Myths, Legacies, and Lessons,* The WAC Clearinghouse 2023 edition]

"Searching for Literacy," *Cleveland Plain Dealer/Cleveland.com,* Sept. 2, 2022

"*Searching for Literacy: The Social and Intellectual Origins of Literacy Studies,*" *Columbus Free Press,* Sept. 5, 2022

"The ridiculous proliferation of subject 'literacies' is harming education," *Times Higher Education,* Oct. 3, 2022 [reprinted in *Literacy Myths, Legacies, and Lessons,* The WAC Clearinghouse 2023 edition]

"Wikipedia, Once Shunned, Now Embraced in the Classroom," Nov. 9, 2022, Letter to the Editor, Inside Higher Education, Nov. 14, 2022

"*Searching for Literacy* by Harvey J. Graff," *Littsburgh,* Jan. 14, 2023

"'The evidence is NOT clear; The jury is NOT in': Why politicians can never dictate educational programs & policies," Busting Myths, *Columbus Free Press,* Feb. 28, 2023

"Scholarly book authors' Bill of Rights," American Historical Association Forum, Mar. 6, 2023 (translated into Spanish)

"The persistent 'reading myth' and the 'crisis of the humanities,'" *CCC/College Composition and Communication,* 74, 2 (Feb. 2023). 575–580 [reprinted in *Literacy Myths, Legacies, and Lessons,* The WAC Clearinghouse 2023 edition]

"The Young Heroes of the Writing World: A new wave of very young authors is trying to change the world," *Publishers Weekly,* June 16 online, June 19, 2023 in print [reprinted in *Literacy Myths, Legacies, and Lessons,* The WAC Clearinghouse 2023 edition]

Mike DeWine, ignorant slogans, and the non-'science of reading': The Ohio Way," Busting Myths, *Columbus Free Press*, June 30, 2023

"How can you recover reading when there was none? A revealing case study of academic dishonesty, capitalizing education, institutional and collegial collusion, and damage to children: The Ohio State University and Heinemann Publishing's Fountas and Pinnell aka Reading Recovery, Part One," Busting Myths, *Columbus Free Press*, July 12, 2023 [reprinted in *Literacy Myths, Legacies, and Lessons*, The WAC Clearinghouse 2023 edition]

"The Ohio State University and Heinemann Publishing's Fountas and Pinnell aka Reading Recovery, Part Two," Busting Myths, *Columbus Free Press*, July 17, 2023 [reprinted in *Literacy Myths, Legacies, and Lessons*, The WAC Clearinghouse 2023 edition]

"How can you recover reading when there was none? A revealing case study of academic dishonesty, capitalizing education, institutional and collegial collusion, and damage to children: The Ohio State University and Heinemann Publishing's Fountas and Pinnell aka Reading Recovery, Part Three," Busting Myths, *Columbus Free Press*, July 21, 2023 [reprinted in *Literacy Myths, Legacies, and Lessons*, The WAC Clearinghouse 2023 edition]

"The Misrepresentation and Marketing of 'Financial Literacy': The Fallacies and Dangers of FL4ALL: Reprinted with new introduction for the elementary education of the Ohio State Legislature, February, 2024," Busting Myths, *Columbus Free Press*, Feb. 11, 2024

"Scholarly Book Authors' Bill of Rights," *Journal of Intellectual Freedom and Privacy*, 7, 4 (2022), 5–8 [August, 2023]

"Your students won't read any more? Are you sure you're paying attention?" *Times Higher Education*, Apr. 18, 2024

"Literacy Studies and Composition through the work of Harvey J. Graff, Tribute Session, Conference on College Composition and Communication 2017 including Response by Graff," *Across the Disciplines*, 21, Spring, 2024

"AI or AU? Artificial Intelligence or Artificial UnIntelligence: One Damn Thing After Another. Contradictions without Dialectics," with Sean Kamperman, *Against the Current*, forthcoming

"Writing and reading: The missing elements in historical and contemporary studies of English writing," Special issue on "Confluences of Writing Studies and the History of the English Language," *Across the Disciplines*, Summer, 2024

## Media and Communications

"Columbus' identity crisis and its media," *Columbus Underground*, July 23, 2021

"Response to *Columbus Alive*, 'The list: Reasons that *Columbus Underground* opinion piece is trash,' by Andy Downing and Joel Oliphint, *Columbus Alive*, July 26: A visit to journalism fantasy land," Busting Myths, *Columbus Free Press*, Nov. 7, 2021

"America First: An Excavation of Trumpism and the Trump Agenda," *Columbus Free Press*, Oct. 24, 2021 [Reprinted with new introduction May 7, 2022]

"The triumph of the new 'fake news' in the legitimate press," Busting Myths, *Columbus Free Press*, Dec. 19, 2021

"How conservative opinion writers fail their readers," Busting Myths, *Columbus Free Press*, Dec. 25, 2021

"Media misconceptions and the ten minute historical memory," Busting Myths, *Columbus Free Press*, Dec. 29, 2021

"Can we resurrect our 'founding' faith in the American 'People'?" Busting Myths, *Columbus Free Press*, Jan. 15, 2022

"The *Columbus Dispatch*: The decline of a metropolitan daily newspaper," Busting Myths, *Columbus Free Press*, Jan. 20, 2022

"The disappearance of journalistic standards in opinion essays as they replace the news," Busting Myths, *Columbus Free Press*, Jan. 30, 2022

"The media mangle the Big Lie and the nondebate over critical race theory," Busting Myths, *Columbus Free Press*, Feb. 7, 2022

"Columbus' major 'news media' against democratic politics and the public," Busting Myths, *Columbus Free Press*, Mar. 10, 2022

"WOSU, the nation's worst NPR affiliate? The challenge of criticizing a self-parody of a 'news and information' station," Busting Myths, *Columbus Free Press*, Mar. 20, 2022

"A citizen vs. Postmaster Louis DeJoy and his crippling of the U.S. Postal service," Busting Myths, *Columbus Free Press*, Mar. 24, 2022

"Peer reviewing is becoming more cavalier, self-serving and ignorant," *Times Higher Education*, June 2, 2022

"Academics' publishing options are an ever wilder west. Beware!" *Times Higher Education*, June 24, 2022

"Editors have become so wayward that academic authors need a bill of rights," *Times Higher Education*, August 18, 2022

"I call on the *Columbus Dispatch*, aka *Dishpan* or *Dishrag,* to do the city a public service and close up shop," Busting Myths, *Columbus Free Press*, Nov. 5, 2022

"The US' new open access mandate must not line the pockets of grifters," *Times Higher Education,* Nov. 17, 2022

"Demythifying: An author and retired professor challenges some long-held university press assumptions," *Publishers Weekly*, Dec. 19, 2022 / "Demythifying the University Press," *Publishers Weekly* (online), Dec. 16, 2022

"Mis-advice on Academic Journal Submissions: An essay provides outdated advice that could hurt scholars, especially younger ones," *Inside Higher Education*, Feb. 12, 2022

"Book Publishers," American Historical Association Members Forum, Feb.-Mar. 2023

"Scholarly book authors' bill of rights, (short version)." American Historical Association Members Forum, Mar. 6, 2023

"Scholarly Book Authors' Bill of Rights," *Journal of Intellectual Freedom and Privacy*, 7, 4 (2022), 5–9 [August 2023]

"Universities must embrace, not hinder, student journalism: Nurturing investigative skills will make for a better democracy—even if it embarrasses campus administrators in the process," *Times Higher Education,* October, 16, 2023

"There is no *Columbus Dispatch;* Columbus does not have a daily news-paper: Yet they continue to demand advance payment and bill regularly, Busting Myths, *Columbus Free Press,* Dec. 28, 2023

"Pay to Play —Publish for a Price: The Myths and Manipulation of the New Corporate Open-Access Journals," *Journal of Educational Thought*, 56, 3 (2023), 267–274

"Scholarly book authors' bill of rights," Busting Myths, *Columbus Free Press,* Feb. 8, 2024

"Pay to Play —Publish for a Price: The Myths and Manipulation of the New Corporate Open-Access Journals," *Journal of Intellectual Freedom and Privacy*, 8, 4 (2023)[2024]

## Book Banning

"Know Nothings: A scholar and author examines the banning of books, past and present," *Publishers Weekly*, Jan. 3, 2022; "Harvey J. Graff Examines the History of Book Banning," online Dec. 31, 2021

"Book ban in Washington County is an example of the 'new illiteracy,'" with Ashley Perez, *Salt Lake Tribune*, Jan. 28, 2022

"I wrote 'Out of Darkness' for my high school students. Now high schools are removing it," by Ashley Hope Perez. Harvey J. Graff contributor, *Dallas Morning News*, Feb. 11, 2022

"A call to colleagues: Speak out and support children, teachers, librarians, and free speech—and the present and future of your own institutions, too," American Historical Association Member Forum, Feb. 16, 2022

"Book banning isn't about content; it's a fight for supremacy in culture wars," by Ashley Hope Pérez and Harvey J. Graff, *The Herald Times* (Bloomington, Indiana), Mar. 10, 2022

"The right-wing truck convoys arrive in Ohio: The unconstitutionality and inhumanity of Book Banners," Busting Myths, *Columbus Free Press*, Apr. 14, 2022

"Book banning past and present and the rights of young readers," *Academe Blog*, Apr. 22, 2022"Dark money fuels Kansas and Missouri school book banners. Don't let the minority rule," *Kansas City Star*, Apr. 28, 2022

"Book Banning Past and Present," *Against the Current*, 218 (May-June, 2022), 6–7 [reprinted in *Literacy Myths, Legacies, and Lessons,* The WAC Clearinghouse 2023 edition]

"The Book Business Ecosystem Is Under Attack," *Publishers Weekly* online, June 17, 2022; "An Ecosystem Under Attack," *Publishers Weekly*, June 20, 2022

"The rights to read and write and to organize: Local roots of democracy and our historical moment," Busting Myths, *Columbus Free Press*, July 24, 2022

"The Libraries of Llano County, Texas: The End of Civility, Legality, the Rights of the Young to Learn and Mature, and the Public Itself," *Journal of Intellectual Freedom & Privacy*, 7, 3 (Fall, 2022), 10–11

"Book Banning and Education Restrictions: Our Moment of Rising Resistance," *Against the Current*, 225 (July-August, 2023), 8–10 [reprinted in *Literacy Myths, Legacies, and Lessons,* The WAC Clearinghouse 2023 edition]

Graff interviewed on censorship and book banning on Monocle Daily international news from London, July 12, 2023 (story begins at 21 minutes, Graff at 27 minutes) [https://monocle.com/radio/shows/the-monocle-daily/2507/]

Ireland's Classic Hits Radio, Nighttime Talk with Niall Boylan interview "Book Banning with Professor Harvey J. Graff," Sept. 27, 2023 [https://tinyurl.com/a5a2wnt4]

"I'm with the Banned: The Unseen History of Reading Banned Books," forthcoming

### Critical Race Theory and Education

"Republicans assault fact-based American history and promote popular ignorance," *Columbus Dispatch*, May 28, 2021

"The attack on critical race theory threatens our democracy," *Inside Higher Education*, Aug. 2, 2021

"There Is No Debate About Critical Race Theory: How a network of GOP politicians and conservative activists are trying to create controversy where there is none," *Washington Monthly*, Sept. 4, 2021

"The New White Fright and Flight and the Critical Race Theory Nondebate," *Academe Blog*, Sept. 29, 2021

"Ohio Education Promotes Racism and Restricting Equity, Again," *Columbus Free Press*, Oct. 27, 202

"DeWine whines about critical race theory," Busting Myths, *Columbus Free Press*, Dec. 11, 2021

"Marketing the second biggest lie: The Faith & Freedom Caucus vs. American history & Christianity," Busting Myths, *Columbus Free Press*, Dec. 14, 2021

"The media mangle the Big Lie and the nondebate over critical race theory," Busting Myths, *Columbus Free Press*, Feb. 7, 2022

"The U.S. and Canada: Confronting the past in the present," Busting Myths, *Columbus Free Press*, Feb. 14, 2022

"How many 'projects' does it take to obstruct a truly American history?" Busting Myths, *Columbus Free Press*, Feb. 16, 2022

"Shouldn't Ivy League graduates know better than to remake American history?" Busting Myths, *Columbus Free Press*, Feb. 24, 2022

"Battle of the books: A professor examines the 1619, 1620, 1776, and 1836 projects," *Publishers Weekly*, Feb. 28, 2022; "Battle of the Books: When Historical Reassessments Collide: A professor examines the 1619, 1620, 1776, and 1836 projects," online Feb. 25, 2022

"The State of Ohio assaults its own children: The war on the public and especially those least able to defend themselves," Busting Myths, *Columbus Free Press*, Mar. 6, 2022

"The Nondebate about Critical Race Theory and Our American Moment," special issue on Memory Laws or Gag Laws? Disinformation Meets Academic Freedom, *Journal of Academic Freedom*, Vol. 13, Fall, 2022

"The Second Big Lie and the Battle for the Past," *Academe Blog*, Nov. 29, 2022

"Ohio must act to stop Nazi indoctrination masquerading as homeschooling curriculum," Letter to the Editor, *Cleveland Plain Dealer*, Feb. 2, 2023

"Against Book Banning and Education Restrictions: Our Moment of Rising Resistance," *Against the Current*, 225 (July-August, 2023), 8–10

## Ohio State University

**Pre-2021**

"Throwing the Baby Out with the Interdisciplinary Bath Water," Letter to the Editor, *Chronicle of Higher Education*, June 12, 2014

"Early-college programs lack many benefits of the real thing," Commentary, with Steve Rissing, *Columbus Dispatch*, June 7, 2015

"An Education in Sloganeering," *Wall Street Journal*, Oct. 1, 2015

**2021-**

"The decline of a once vital neighborhood: Columbus' University District," *Columbus Free Press*, Sept 14, 2021

"For Ohio State, bigger is not better," *Columbus Free Press*, Sept. 16, 2021

"Columbus' University District: Students and the institutions that fail them," *Columbus Free Press*, Oct. 8, 2021

"OSU isn't having a crime crisis; it's having a leadership crisis," Busting Myths, *Columbus Free Press*, Nov 2, 2021

"'Update' to Ohio State isn't having a crime crisis," Busting Myths, *Columbus Free Press*, Nov. 13, 2021

"The Ohio State University promotes public health crises," Busting Myths, *Columbus Free Press*, Dec. 6, 2021

"OSU Falters Once Again, a continuing tragedy," Busting Myths, *Columbus Free Press*, Feb. 28, 2022

"Ohio State versus 'campus safety,'" Busting Myths, *Columbus Free Press*, Mar. 13, 2022

"How Columbus, Ohio State University, and major developers destroyed a historic neighborhood," Busting Myths, *Columbus Free Press*, Part One, Apr. 26, 2022

"How Columbus, Ohio State University, and major developers destroyed a historic neighborhood," Busting Myths, *Columbus Free Press*, Part Two, Apr. 29, 2022

"How Columbus, Ohio State University, and major developers destroyed a historic neighborhood—a continuing saga," Busting Myths, *Columbus Free Press*, May 2, 2022

"Universities are not giving students the classes or support they need," *Times Higher Education*, May 17, 2022

"The United States' most disorganized university? Ohio State's '5½ D's': Disorganization, dysfunction, disengagement, depression, dishonest, and undisciplined, Part One," Busting Myths, *Columbus Free Press*, Aug. 28, 2022

"The United States' most disorganized university? Ohio State's '5½ D's': Disorganization, dysfunction, disengagement, depression, dishonest, and undisciplined, Part Two," Busting Myths, *Columbus Free Press*, Aug. 31, 2022

"The City of Columbus and The Ohio State University: Two peas in a pod, one bigger than the other, relatively speaking, but so much the same. Part One," Busting Myths, *Columbus Free Press*, Oct. 8, 2022

"The City of Columbus and The Ohio State University: Two peas in a pod, one bigger than the other, relatively speaking, but so much the same. Part Two," Busting Myths, *Columbus Free Press*, Oct. 14, 2022

"The enterprise of scientific misconduct: Malpractice at Ohio State University," Busting Myths, *Columbus Free Press*, Oct. 26, 2022

"The OSU Way: Slogans over Truth and Honesty in Graduation Rates and Student Well-Being," Busting Myths, *Columbus Free Press*, Oct. 27, 2022

"How universities fail their students: The president may be 'born to be a Buckeye,' but the students are not. A call to eliminate Offices of Student Life and invest directly in students' lives," Busting Myths, *Columbus Free Press*, Nov. 10, 2022

"University bragging rights: OSU whimpers but doesn't bite or swallow," Busting Myths, *Columbus Free Press*, Nov. 27, 2022

"Columbus' home grown illegal landlords in a destroyed historic district," Busting Myths, *Columbus Free Press*, Dec. 11, 2022

"I'm retired but I'll still running my own unofficial university," *Times Higher Education*, Dec. 21, 2022

"*The* Ohio State University: Not 'a failed presidency,' by itself, but a *failing university*, Part One," Busting Myths, *Columbus Free Press*, Jan. 7, 2023

"*The* Ohio State University: Not 'a failed presidency,' by itself, but a *failing university*, Part Two," Busting Myths, *Columbus Free Press*, Jan. 11, 2023

"Universities and cities often fail both homeowners and students," *Times Higher Education*, Jan. 22, 2023

"Kristina Johnson breaks her two-and-a-half months of silence and begins an anti-factual, myth-making campaign for rehabilitation," Busting Myths, *Columbus Free Press*, Feb. 22, 2023

"*The* Ohio Student University vs. *The* Students, *The* Law, and *The* Truth. The Victims of Dr. Richard Strass and of OSU," Busting Myths, *Columbus Free Press*, Mar. 14, 2023

"A call for reparations from the City of Columbus, the large corporate landlords, and *The* Ohio State University for the destruction of neighborhoods with a focus on the University District," Busting Myths, *Columbus Free Press*, Apr. 1, 2023

"Lawmakers rush to cancel public higher education in Ohio," *Cincinnati Enquirer*, Apr. 19, 2023

"Lawless, Unsafe, and Dirty: The Dying University District." Busting Myths, *Columbus Free Press*, May 2, 2023

"Ohio State University and its Dying University District: The Oval and the Campus Beyond," Busting Myths, *Columbus Free Press*, May 5, 2023

"US universities' engineering colleges are anything but collegiate," *Times Higher Education,* May 17, 2023

"Is engineering a good major? A reality check for prospective students," with Olga Knezevic, *DegreeChoices*, May 24, 2023 https://www.degreechoices.com/blog/is-engineering-a-good-major/

"After more than 150 years, *The* Ohio State University administration abandons campus and the landmark Oval, and secretly goes into hiding off-campus," Busting Myths, *Columbus Free Press,* June 21, 2023

"Mike DeWine's right wing Republican Party and the destruction of public higher education in Ohio," Busting Myths, *Columbus Free Press*, June 14, 2023

"How can you recover reading when there was none? A revealing case study of academic dishonesty, capitalizing education, institutional and collegial collusion, and damage to children: The Ohio State University and Heinemann Publishing's Fountas and Pinnell aka Reading Recovery, Part One," Busting Myths, *Columbus Free Press*, July 12, 2023

"The Ohio State University and Heinemann Publishing's Fountas and Pinnell aka Reading Recovery, Part Two," Busting Myths, *Columbus Free Press*, July 17, 2023

"How can you recover reading when there was none? A revealing case study of academic dishonesty, capitalizing education, institutional and collegial collusion, and damage to children: The Ohio State University and Heinemann Publishing's Fountas and Pinnell aka Reading Recovery, Part Three," Busting Myths, *Columbus Free Press*, July 21, 2023

"August 2, 2023 Weekly Headline Notes," *Columbus Free Press,* Aug. 2, 2023

"Emergency Bulletin: The City of Columbus, OSU, and landlords against student tenants and homeowners—dramatic case in point," *Columbus Free Press,* Aug. 21, 2023

"The 150-year-old, 90,000 student-staff-and faculty university that won't grow up: *The* Ohio State University Buckeyes led by Brutus Buckeye, Part One," Busting Myths, *Columbus Free Press,* Aug. 23, 2023

"Sen. Cirino versus students' right to learn," Letter to the Editor, *Cleveland Plain Dealer*, Aug. 24, 2024

"*The* Ohio State University Fumbles Again: The Board of Trustees who have no understanding of higher education selects the most unqualified campus president in modern American university history," *Columbus Free Press*. Aug. 26, 2023

"The 150-year-old, 90,000 student-staff-and faculty university that won't grow up: *The* Ohio State University Buckeyes led by Brutus Buckeye, Part Two," Busting Myths, *Columbus Free Press,* Aug. 30, 2023

"State Senator Jerry Cirino versus the State of Ohio, Public Higher Education, Free Speech and Academic Freedom, and Students' Right to Learn," Busting Myths, *Columbus Free Press,* Sept. 5, 2023

"Out of control fraternities and sororities control the 21st century university on and off campus, Part One," Busting Myths, *Columbus Free Press,* Oct. 10, 2023

"Universities must embrace, not hinder, student journalism: Nurturing investigative skills will make for a better democracy—even if it embarrasses campus administrators in the process," *Times Higher Education,* October, 16, 2023

"A major huge university versus its students, neighbors, and their city: *The* Ohio State University," Busting Myths, *Columbus Free Press,* Nov. 2, 2023

"Slogan University Revisited. When did Offices of Compliance and Integrity [sic]. Student Life, Student Conduct, Campus Safety become just the opposite? The example of one of the largest U.S. universities, Part One," *Columbus Free Press,* Nov. 14, 2023

"Slogan University Revisited. When did Offices of Compliance and Integrity [sic]. Student Life, Student Conduct, Campus Safety become just the opposite? The example of one of the largest U.S. universities," Part Two, Busting Myths, *Columbus Free Press,* Nov. 19, 2023

"How can you have an 'intellectual diversity center' [sic] when the center has no intellectual diversity? *The* Ohio State University turns harder right at the orders of the anti-democratic Ohio State Legislature and anti-intellectual Board of Trustees," Busting Myths, *Columbus Free Press*, Dec. 3, 2023

"The national right-wing ideologues target right-wing Columbus and Ohio: The National Association of Scholars [sic] and *Wall Street Journal* Opinion Page vs. *The* Ohio State University," Busting Myths, *Columbus Free Press*, Dec. 11, 2023

"Poor-quality presidential searches lead to poor quality appointments," *Times Higher Education,* Jan. 13, 2024

"How *not* to conduct presidential searches, over and over? The example of one major public university: *The* Ohio State University," Busting Myths, *Columbus Free Press*, Jan. 31, 2024

"Living in a University District: How universities and their cities fail both homeowners and student renters," forthcoming

"Disconnecting Gown and Town: Campus Partners for Urban Community Development, Ohio State University," under review

### Columbus Past and Present

"Columbus' identity crisis and its media," *Columbus Underground*, July 23, 2021

"Response to *Columbus Alive*, 'The list: Reasons that *Columbus Underground* opinion piece is trash,' by Andy Downing and Joel Oliphint, *Columbus Alive*, July 26: A visit to journalism fantasy land," Busting Myths, *Columbus Free Press*, Nov. 7, 2021

"Notes on current politics in Columbus and Ohio: Thoughts in response to questions from my editor," *Columbus Free Press*, Oct. 21, 2021

"Columbus City Government is Undemocratic and Disorganized: It's 2021 and we need a revolution in this city," Busting Myths, *Columbus Free Press*, Nov. 20, 2021

"Columbus searches for its Downtown with historical, urbanist, and developers' blinders," Busting Myths, *Columbus Free Press*, Dec. 22, 2021

"Columbus, *Ohio*, searches to be a city: The myth of the Columbus Way," Busting Myths, *Columbus Free Press*, Jan. 9, 2022

"Intel and the Ohio Way: Secrecy, deals, public neglect, myth making, and re-election campaigning," Busting Myths, *Columbus Free Press*, Jan. 27, 2022

"Columbus' major 'news media' against democratic politics and the public," Busting Myths, *Columbus Free Press*, Mar. 10, 2022

"Is Columbus really a City?" Busting Myths, *Columbus Free Press*, Apr. 7, 2022

"Columbus isn't Cowtown or Silicon Valley Heartland; It's the lawless wild-wild-Midwest," Busting Myths, *Columbus Free Press*, April 20, 2022

"How Columbus, Ohio State University, and major developers destroyed a historic neighborhood," Busting Myths, *Columbus Free Press*, Part One, Apr. 26, 2022

"How Columbus, Ohio State University, and major developers destroyed a historic neighborhood," Busting Myths, *Columbus Free Press*, Part Two, Apr. 29, 2022

"How Columbus, Ohio State University, and major developers destroyed a historic neighborhood—A continuing legacy," Busting Myths, *Columbus Free Press*, May 2, 2022

"My short life as a 'civic leader' in the directionless maze called the City of Columbus, Part One, Busting Myths, *Columbus Free Press*, May 11, 2022

"My short life as a 'civic leader' in the directionless maze called the City of Columbus, Part Two," Busting Myths, *Columbus Free Press*, May 14, 2022

"Franklinton, 1797–2022 and Columbus' Contradictions, Part 1," *Columbus Free Press*, June 5, 2022

"Franklinton, 1797–2022 and Columbus' Contradictions, Part 2," *Columbus Free Press*, June 9, 2022

"How the Harvard Business School and the Columbus Way attempt to enrich each other: Lessons in the promiscuous relationships between Columbus' private interests and an elite university's profiteering," with Bob Eckhart, Busting Myths, *Columbus Free Press*, June 12, 2022

"An open letter to Kenny McDonald, new head of the 'Columbus Partnership,'" Busting Myths, *Columbus Free Press*, June 16, 2022

"The Columbus Way versus the rights of residents, Part One," Busting Myths, *Columbus Free Press*, June 21, 2022

"The Columbus Way versus the rights of residents, Part Two, Busting Myths, *Columbus Free Press*, June 24, 2022

"The Columbus Way versus the rights of residents, Part Three," Busting Myths, *Columbus Free Press*, June 27, 2022

"The Columbus Way versus the rights of residents, Part Four," Busting Myths, *Columbus Free Press*, June 30, 2022

"Remaking the City of Columbus for the 21st or is it the 20th century?" Busting Myths, *Columbus Free Press*, July 5, 2022

"My ongoing struggles for responsibility from the City of Columbus," Busting Myths, *Columbus Free Press*, July 12, 2022

"Is Columbus the corruption capital of a corrupt state? Mismanagement, no management, and corruption in the 2020s," Busting Myths, *Columbus Free Press*, July 17, 2022

"Mr. Mayor and City Council: May I introduce you to the city of Columbus? Beyond the Short North and the Scioto River Bank, there is a diverse complicated city," Busting Myths, *Columbus Free Press*, July 31, 2022

"Still searching for Downtown: 'Ideas considered for Downtown plan,'" Busting Myths, *Columbus Free Press*, Aug. 14, 2022

"Frederic Bertley, Salesperson, Meet Science and English Expression," Busting Myths, *Columbus Free Press*, Aug. 17, 2022

"You can't sue City Hall, can you? But we should educate the public and use the ballot box: That's the American Way, not the Columbus Way," Busting Myths, *Columbus Free Press*, Aug. 21, 2022

"Columbus continues as franchise and fast-food chain leader: Columbus Classical Academies," Busting Myths, *Columbus Free Press*, Aug. 24, 2022

"Why I remain in Columbus despite Columbus. . . ." Busting Myths, *Columbus Free Press*, Sept. 16, 2022

"Columbus, meet a 'real' city: Toronto," Busting Myths, *Columbus Free Press*, Oct. 1, 2022

"The City of Columbus and The Ohio State University: Two peas in a pod, one bigger than the other, relatively speaking, but so much the same. Part One," Busting Myths, *Columbus Free Press*, Oct. 8, 2022

"The City of Columbus and The Ohio State University: Two peas in a pod, one bigger than the other, relatively speaking, but so much the same. Part Two," Busting Myths, *Columbus Free Press*, Oct. 14, 2022

"Why won't Columbus, *Ohio,* grow up?" Busting Myths, *Columbus Free Press*, Oct. 22, 2022

"Abandoned by my elected and unelected officials (unless I pay to play): The Columbus Way, Part One," Busting Myths, *Columbus Free Press*, Oct. 30, 2022

"Abandoned by my elected and unelected officials (unless I pay to play): The Columbus Way, Part Two," Busting Myths, *Columbus Free Press*, Nov. 2, 2022

"I call on the *Columbus Dispatch,* aka *Dishpan* or *Dishrag,* to do the city a public service and close up shop," Busting Myths, *Columbus Free Press,* Nov. 5, 2022

"How universities fail their students: The president may be "born to be a Buckeye," but the students are not. A call to eliminate Offices of Student Life and invest directly in students' lives," Busting Myths, *Columbus Free Press*, Nov. 10, 2022

"The City that breaks its laws has a police force that refuses to enforce the city's laws: The Columbus Way, Part One," Busting Myths, *Columbus Free Press*, Nov. 13, 2022

"The City that breaks its laws has a police force that refuses to enforce the city's laws: The Columbus Way, Part Two," Busting Myths, *Columbus Free Press*, Nov. 16. 2022

"Andy Ginther as Columbus, *Ohio's* very own shabby 21st century limitation of New York City's 1860–1870s Boss Tweed," Busting Myths, *Columbus Free Press*, Nov. 19, 2022

"Columbus meet another 'real' city, nearby, smaller, but . . . Pittsburgh," Busting Myths, *Columbus Free Press*, Nov. 30, 2022

"Columbus' anachronistic, private interest-dominated 'area commissions' and 'neighborhood organizations' must go," Busting Myths, *Columbus Free Press*, Dec. 3, 2022

"Columbus City Council muddies, no —defaces art in public: $250,000 in uninformed boosterism for the 'little city that can't,'" Busting Myths, *Columbus Free Press*, Dec. 8, 2022

"Columbus' home-grown illegal landlords in a destroyed historic district," Busting Myths, *Columbus Free* Press, Dec. 11, 2022

"The plague city: Daily life in Columbus, Ohio," Busting Myths, *Columbus Free Press*, Dec. 17, 2022

"Columbus mayor election campaign, 2023," Busting Myths, *Columbus Free Press*, Jan. 1, 2023

"Columbus, *Ohio:* Rude and Crude: The little big city that refuses to represent. serve, or respect its publics, Part One," Busting Myths, *Columbus Free Press*, Jan. 15, 2022

"Columbus, *Ohio:* Rude and Crude: The little big city that refuses to represent. serve, or respect its publics, Part Two," Busting Myths, *Columbus Free Press*, Jan. 19, 2023

"A city versus its neighborhoods: Columbus, *Ohio,"* Busting Myths, *Columbus Free Press*, Jan. 25, 2023

"Appreciating—so to speak—Columbus and Ohio humor, such as they are . . .," Busting Myths, *Columbus Free Press,* 1, 2023

"Unsafe at any speed: The unsafe city—from mayor to city council to CPD," Busting Myths, *Columbus Free Press,* Feb. 16, 2023

"*J'accuse:* The City of Columbus Division of Public (aka Private) Service," Busting Myths, *Columbus Free Press,* Mar. 3, 2023

"Columbus' right wing Democrats vs. the city's publics," Busting Myths, *Columbus Free Press,* Mar. 8, 2023

"The Columbus City Council and City Attorney's Office the First Amendment on March 6, 2023," Busting Myths, *Columbus Free Press*, Mar. 10, 2023

"How can a city with no history destroy its history? The Columbus Way," Busting Myths, *Columbus Free Press*, Mar. 18, 2023

"'A community for all-ages mixer': Community, History, Jazz, and Food in Columbus," *Columbus Free Press,* Mar. 20, 2023

"Career politician and candidate for re-election: Andy Ginther's Anti-State of the City Address, March 2023," Busting Myths, *Columbus Free Press,* Mar. 25, 2023

"A call for reparations from the City of Columbus, the large corporate landlords, and *The* Ohio State University for the destruction of neighborhoods with a focus on the University District," Busting Myths, *Columbus Free Press,* Apr. 1, 2023

"Rob Dorans and the real Columbus 'crew' vs. the city of Columbus, again," Busting Myths, *Columbus Free Press,* Apr. 8, 2023

"The plague of Columbus' streets and sidewalks: Electric scooters illegally fueled by the City's Division of Public (aka Private) Services," Busting Myths, *Columbus Free Press,* Apr. 14, 2023

"Why does Columbus have no legitimate media" Busting Myths, *Columbus Free Press*, Apr. 2023

"Lawless, Unsafe, and Dirty: The Dying University District." Busting Myths, *Columbus Free Press,* May 2, 2023

"Ohio State University and its Dying University District: The Oval and the Campus Beyond," Busting Myths, *Columbus Free Press,* May 5, 2023

Columbus' identity failure: The mad scramble to fabricate a 'brand' for the biggest little city in the US," Busting Myths, *Columbus Free Press,* May 11, 2023

"The private city and the secret city: Columbus is dying and no one in Colemanville knows or cares. Part One," Busting Myths, *Columbus Free Press,* May 20, 2023

"The private city and the secret city: Columbus is dying and no one in Colemanville knows or cares. Part Two," Busting Myths, *Columbus Free Press,* May 25, 2023

"The private city and the secret city: Columbus is dying and no one in Colemanville knows or cares. Part Three," Busting Myths, *Columbus Free Press,* June 2, 2023

"Andy Ginther, Guns, and Unsafe Columbus," Busting Myths, *Columbus Free Press*, June 7, 2023

"Andy Ginther doesn't live in Columbus. Does he live in the United States? On planet Earth?" Busting Myths, Columbus, Free Press, June 26, 2023

"The Columbus US Postal Service fails well beyond the national USPS. It lies about its illegal lack of service and private profiteering in advertisements paid for by my taxes, and lies to my face. Under major investor Louis DeJoy, only Amazon counts," Busting Myths, *Columbus Free Press*, July 6, 2023

"A week in the life of the failing City of Columbus: One weekend's low lights," Busting Myths, Columbus Free Press, July8, 2023

"August 2, 2023 Weekly Headline Notes," *Columbus Free Press,* Aug. 2, 2023

"The broken, no—the evil—triangle of the City of Columbus vs. its residents. Destroying the physical city and the semblance of neighborhoods: Zoning

(Un)enforcement, Public (Private) Service, and 311, with the assistance of OSU, the City Attorney, CPD, City Council, and Mayor, Part One," Busting Myths, *Columbus Free Press,* Aug. 4, 2023

"The broken, no—the evil—triangle of the City of Columbus vs. its residents. Destroying the physical city and the semblance of neighborhoods: Zoning (Un) enforcement, Public (Private) Service, and 311, with the assistance of OSU, the City Attorney, CPD, City Council, and Mayor, Part Two," Busting Myths, *Columbus Free Press,* Aug. 8, 2023

"Emergency Bulletin: The City of Columbus, OSU, and landlords against student tenants and homeowners—dramatic case in point," *Columbus Free Press,* Aug. 21, 2023

"Columbus is lost among midwestern metropolises. Can it learn from others and finally begin to find itself? Or is it too late?" Busting Myths, *Columbus Free Press,* Oct. 4, 2023

"A City versus its people. The unjust city: The Columbus Way. Part One," Busting Myths, *Columbus Free Press,* Oct. 22, 2023

"A City versus its people. The unjust city: The Columbus Way. Part Two," Busting Myths, *Columbus Free Press,* Oct. 27, 2023

"Columbus 2023 Mayor's and City Council Elections: If you can't do your job and be re-elected fairly, then lie, cheat, and steal the election. The Anti-democratic Columbus Way," Busting Myths, *Columbus Free Press,* Nov. 8, 2023

"Nov. 7, 2023 confirms the continuing reign of anti-democratic Columbus," Busting Myths, *Columbus Free Press,* Nov. 10 , 2023

"The City of Columbus continues to prove itself incapable of learning: The contradiction and corruption of ever-expanding public subsidies for private development 'tax abatements,'" Busting Myths, *Columbus Free Press,* Nov. 26, 2023

"Andy Ginther and his crowd can't even lie with straight prose: 'Plan will help city meet housing demand,' Guest Essay, Dec. 3, 2023," Busting Myths, *Columbus Free Press,* Dec. 6, 2023

"Exposing the Obvious: Columbus City Council Commits Fraud with its Fake District Representative Deceptive Marketing Scheme," Busting Myths, *Columbus Free Press,* Dec. 17, 2023

"There is no *Columbus Dispatch;* Columbus does not have a daily news-paper: Yet they continue to demand advance payment and bill regularly, Busting Myths, *Columbus Free Press,* Dec. 28, 2023

"What happens to a 'neighborhood church' when the neighborhood and the church turn to absentee profit-taking and against the residents? The contradictions of the Indianola Presbyterian Church in the 21st century," Busting Myths, *Columbus Free Press,* Jan. 8, 2024

"Columbus City Attorney, Mayor, and Council vs. the Law and the People," Busting Myths, *Columbus Free Press,* Jan. 22, 2024

"Columbus, *Ohio:* Lost and Forgotten, Even at Home?" Busting Myths, *Columbus Free Press,* Feb. 20, 2024

"The City and the developers who control it versus the physical city and its peoples," circulated Apr. 13, 2024

"'Quasi-public local development head made millions even after leaving': The *Columbus Dispatch* does not understand The Columbus Way," circulated Apr. 13, 2024

"Disconnecting Gown and Town: Campus Partners for Urban Community Development, Ohio State University," under review

## Ohio Issues

"Ohio Republicans," Letter to the Editor, *Columbus Dispatch*, Mar. 9, 2021

"Dave Yost, Ohio AG," Letter to the Editor, *Cleveland Plain Dealer*, April 1, 2021

"Voter ID laws," Letter to the Editor, *Columbus Dispatch*, April 16, 2021

"Ohio Covid response," Letter to the Editor, *Cleveland Plain Dealer*, Apr. 19, 2021

"Ohio policy failures," Letter to the Editor, *Columbus Dispatch*, May 14, 2021

"Republicans imitate other states," *Cleveland Plain Dealer*, May 16, 2021

"Troy Balderson, US Representative," Letter to the Editor, *Columbus Dispatch*, May 22, 2021

"Dave Yost v. American history," Letter to the Editor, *Cincinnati Enquirer*, May 30, 2021

"DeWine's blundered coronavirus response. Vax-A-Million didn't help," *Columbus Dispatch*, June 25, 2021

"State legislators and critical race theory," Letter to the Editor," *Cleveland Plain Dealer*, June 27, 2021

"Vaxx-A-Million," Letter to the Editor, *Columbus Dispatch*, July 12, 2021

"VAX-A-NICKEL," Letter to the Editor, *The Lantern*, Aug. 18, 2021

"Why aren't Ohio's GOP officials taking action to address AAPI hate?" Letter to the Editor, *Cleveland Plain Dealer*, Aug. 25, 2021

"Where is the Ohio Democratic Party?" Letter to the Editor, *Toledo Blade*, Aug. 29, 2021

"Ohio's elected Republicans fail their public," *Columbus Free Press*, Oct. 2, 2021

"Governor Mike DeWine's Continuing Covid Failures: The Ohio Tragedy," *Columbus Free Press*, Oct. 13, 2021

"Notes on current politics in Columbus and Ohio: Thoughts in response to questions from my editor," *Columbus Free Press*, Oct. 21, 2021

"Ohio Education Promotes Racism and Restricting Equity, Again," *Columbus Free Press*, Oct. 27, 2021

"Ohio State Republicans continue to imitate increasingly recklessly," Letter to the Editor, *Cleveland Plain Dealer*, Nov. 17, 2021

"An Open Letter to the Ohio Democratic Party: Where are you and why have you lost touch with D/democracy?" Busting Myths, *Columbus Free Press*, Nov. 17, 2021

"Gov. DeWine abandons science and the public," Busting Myths, *Columbus Free Press*, Dec. 1, 2021

"DeWine whines about critical race theory," Busting Myths, *Columbus Free Press*, Dec. 11, 2021

"Mike DeWine Seemed Like One of the Few Republicans Serious About Fighting COVID. He's Not," *Washington Monthly*, Dec. 31, 2021

"Texas and Florida secede from reality; Ohio imitates," Busting Myths, *Columbus Free Press*, Jan. 4, 2022

"Intel and the Ohio Way: Secrecy, deals, public neglect, myth making, and re-election campaigning," Busting Myths, *Columbus Free Press*, Jan. 27, 2022

"An Open Letter to the Ohio undemocratic Party," Busting Myths, *Columbus Free Press*, Feb. 20, 2022

"The State of Ohio assaults its own children: The war on those least able to defend themselves," Busting Myths, *Columbus Free Press*, Mar. 6, 2022

"The Ohio Attorney General vs. Science, Ethics, and Law," Busting Myths, *Columbus Free Press*, Mar. 27, 2022

"Is Mike DeWine actually a governor?" Busting Myths, *Columbus Free Press*, Apr. 3, 2022

"2022's most successful voting suppression campaign: Ohio's State Redistricting Commission and Anti-democracy in action," *Columbus Free Press*, May 24, 2022

"Ohio's campaign of unconstitutional voter suppression continues," Letter to the Editor, *Cleveland Plain Dealer*, Dec. 7, 2022

"DeWine, AG Yost, State Department of Education all fail Ohio, Young, old, and in between," Busting Myths, *Columbus Free Press*. Feb. 8, 2023

"Lawmakers rush to cancel public higher education in Ohio," *Cincinnati Enquirer*, Apr. 19, 2023

"Mike DeWine's right wing Republican Party and the destruction of public higher education in Ohio," Busting Myths, *Columbus Free Press*, June 14, 2023

"Mike DeWine, ignorant slogans, and the non-'science of reading': The Ohio Way," Busting Myths, *Columbus Free Press*, June 30, 2023

"August 2, 2023 Weekly Headline Notes," *Columbus Free Press*, Aug. 2, 2023

"The Ohio Humanities Council v. the Humanities and Humanity," Busting Myths, *Columbus Free Press,* Aug. 16, 2023

"Senator Cirino versus Students' Right to Learn," Letter to the Editor, *Cleveland Plain Dealer*, Aug. 24, 2023

"State Senator Jerry Cirino versus the State of Ohio, Public Higher Education, Free Speech and Academic Freedom, and Students' Right to Learn," Busting Myths, *Columbus Free Press*, Sept. 5, 2023

"The Misrepresentation and Marketing of 'Financial Literacy': The Fallacies and Dangers of FL4ALL: Reprinted with new introduction for the elementary education of the Ohio State Legislature, February, 2024," Busting Myths, *Columbus Free Press,* Feb. 11, 2024

"The failure of education—public and private—in Ohio: State Senator Brenner and the Buckeye Institute fail to respond to State Senator DeMora via USA Today/Gannett *Columbus Dispatch* unchecked "opinion page." In other words, buckeye nuts to all!" circulated Apr. 20, 2024

"The failure of education—public and private—in Ohio: State Senator Brenner and the Buckeye Institute fail to respond to State Senator DeMora," (brief), circulated Apr. 20, 2024

### National Issues

"Covid policy making," with Vicki L. W. Graff, Letter to the Editor, *New York Times*, May 18, 2021

"America First: An Excavation of Trumpism and the Trump Agenda," *Columbus Free Press*, Oct. 24, 2021 [Reprinted with new introduction May 7, 2022]

"Texas and Florida secede from reality; Ohio imitates," Busting Myths, *Columbus Free Press*, Jan. 4, 2022

"My New Year's wish list: Beyond media misconceptions and our ten-minute historical memory," Busting Myths, *Columbus Free Press*, Dec. 29, 2021

"The CDC stumbles again," Letter to the Editor, *Washington Post*, Jan. 3, 2022

"The other immigrants and diverse American dreams," with Ameer Abdul, Busting Myths, *Columbus Free Press*, Feb. 3, 2022

"The U.S. and Canada: Confronting the past in the present," Busting Myths, *Columbus Free Press*, Feb. 14, 2022

"A citizen vs. Postmaster Louis DeJoy and his crippling of the U.S. Postal service," Busting Myths, *Columbus Free Press*, Mar. 24, 2022

"The Columbus US Postal Service fails well beyond the national USPS. It lies about its illegal lack of service and private profiteering in advertisements paid for by my taxes, and lies to my face. Under major investor Louis DeJoy, only Amazon counts," Busting Myths, *Columbus Free Press*, July 6, 2023

"Natural powers and the lessons of contradictions: Changing lives and environments," *Columbus Free Press*, July 26, 2023

"How the *New York Times* got it so wrong: The politicization of scientific misconduct," *Columbus Free Press,* Aug. 11, 2023

"We live in unprecedented times, but not for the reasons that the media or politicians tell us," Busting Myths, *Columbus Free Press,* Sept. 21, 2023

"Why the House Targeted Those 3 Presidents," Letter to the Editor, *Inside Higher Education*, Dec. 7, 2023

"Unprecedented Times, or Media Narrative; Looking Toward 2024," *Against the Current*, 228 (Jan.-Feb., 2024), 28–30

## Personal

"Celebrating Jan Reiff," UCLA History Dept. Tribute page, May 24 2021

"Remembering Mike Rose in person and in print," *Inside Higher Education*, Aug. 18, 2021, UCLA Graduate School of Education and Information Sciences Tribute

"My young heroes: For Thanksgiving," *Columbus Free Press*, Nov. 25, 2021

"My New Year's wish list: Beyond media misconceptions and our ten-minute historical memory," Busting Myths, *Columbus Free Press*, Dec. 29, 2021

"Remembering Jack Hartman, Media Insider, retired professor, and committed citizen (1945–2023)," *Columbus Free Press,* Mar. 29, 2023

"Bob Holub, "colleague and friend remembered," Ohio State University Germanic Studies Dept. Tribute page, Aug. 29, 2023

www.ingramcontent.com/pod-product-compliance
Lightning Source LLC
Chambersburg PA
CBHW052131070526
44585CB00017B/1785